Becoming an Automotive Sales Professional

A real world, step-by-step tutorial on achieving success in the Profession of Automotive Sales

M.I. Seka

2014 Edition

Providential Press
Phoenix, Arizona

ISBN-13:978-0615820354 (Providential Press)

ISBN-10:0615820352

Acknowledgments:

Thank you to all the people who have helped make this book happen. I especially want to thank my pride for not letting me give up, my greed for keeping me motivated, my envy for wanting better things out of life, my sense of duty to leave this world better than I found it and my sense of time for adding an element of urgency in to everything I do.

I especially want to thank and acknowledge my parents for being there when I needed them the most. They are beautiful people. I have nothing but love and respect.

Foreword:

Although the job of a used car sales-man is often portrayed as distrustful, sleazy and crooked by most people and the media, this book is not about a job and it's not about being a sales-man.

This book is about building a career and becoming a successful sales professional: The profession of an automotive sales advisor.

You can't make over $100K a year, enjoy extremely high job security and be highly sought after in a job or in a role as a salesman. There are jobs and then there are professions. Jobs are short term and don't require commitment or expertise. A profession requires commitment and a continuing education to become the best at what you do. You'll also need to master your craft by developing a professional **attitude**, **product knowledge** and **enthusiasm**. For this, you will be rewarded with a very high income, extremely high job security and very few expense.

A real commitment is required to become a professional. Get out of the job mindset. Just by reading this book and taking the lessons presented to heart, you're already taking your fist steps to becoming a true professional and working toward a goal where you'll be paid exactly what you are worth.

I have been in the automotive business for over 10 years, and this book is the culmination of my extensive knowledge and experience. Over the course of my career, I've made my share of both major and minor mistakes—as do most people—but the important thing is that I've learned from my mistakes and can now share the lessons I've learned in order to help you in your career as a professional automotive sales advisor.

I've written this book with more information and insight into the profession of automotive sales as well as general sales than perhaps 15 of the top books on the subject. All presented in an easy-to-digest format with plenty of real world scenarios to help you cut through the clutter, reduce your learning curve and get you to wrap your head around the reasons behind the concepts.

In any profession there are concepts, jargon, strategies and insight that a green pea/newbie/freshy will be unfamiliar with until they get a few years of experience under their belt. I've outlined these concepts with easy-to-understand scenarios to help you better understand the reasoning behind them. By applying the lessons outlined in this book you're helping advance your knowledge and experience by several years, giving you a distinct advantage over the average sales advisors. This will enable you to hasten your success and immediately start earning the kind of high six-figure income available in the profession of automotive sales.

I've also presented some advanced selling techniques, and those that are simple, that most advanced sales professionals have forgotten. These are the foundation for a successful career in automotive sales.

Included throughout the book are numerous scenarios and stories from my past experiences that will help you better grasp the concepts, courses of action to take and expected results to help you succeed.

Although, it's impossible for me to include every possible scenario that can happen on a lot, during a deal or client visit, I've tried to include the most common types of things that happen on a lot and how to deal with them and the results you should expect.

Just as you, the sales advisor, need a commitment from a buyer to show they're serious about purchasing a vehicle *today*, I ask that you give *yourself* a commitment to achieve your goals in life with a career in sales by applying these techniques. I can give you the road map, the tools, the information, the directions and the action plan, but ultimately it's up to you to act upon those pieces of information.

The money is out there. The opportunity is out there. The only thing left is you and your ambition. I have outlined not just *what* you should do, but *how* and <u>why</u> you should do them. Other books or training material will only tell you to do certain things without fully explaining *why* you should do them or how.

If you're already selling vehicles for a living and aren't making the money you want, then you need to incorporate some of the lessons I've outlined for you into your everyday selling process. Especially the simple ones like rapport building.

If you're new to the business of selling vehicles, then you definitely need to read, reread and follow what I've outlined for you in this book. Being green or new to the business will be difficult for you for about three months until you get your head around the whole concept of how a dealership works. Reading this book will enhance what you learn at the dealership. The information in this book will help in telling you what you need to become a better sales advisor. A six-figure income of $100,000 or higher is easy if you know what to look for and what to prepare for in a career being an Automotive Sales Advisor.

It will be up to you as to how you use that information. Will you read it today and forget it tomorrow? Will you apply the lessons I've outlined here to your everyday career or life? The choice is ultimately yours. Only you can act on that information to achieve your goals.

Like the saying goes, "Good things come to those that wait, only after the hustlers have gotten what they've wanted."

In any occupation there are a majority of mediocre workers whose only goal is to earn a livable wage and then there are a small number of exceptional professionals who hustle by looking at the bigger picture, continuously learning, trying new things, innovating and investing in their careers. It is those professionals who have the attitude and enthusiasm that propels them to make well over $1 million a year. By reading this book, you're laying the foundation to achieving much more than you've thought possible. $1 million a year won't come easy, but only in time with the proper attitude, commitment, and enthusiasm.

No matter what path your life takes you, sales permeate every aspect that involves social interactions. Even if you don't start or continue your career in automotive sales, the lessons presented here can be invaluable in your daily interactions with other people as well as in your life.

I've taken this journey and have not regretted it. Being in the sales profession has expanded my outlook on life beyond my wildest imaginations. Whether you sell cars or do something else with your life, the lesson learned in the profession of automotive sales can help prepare you for any career that involves personal interactions with people.

Introduction: What it Takes to be a Professional Sales Advisor.

A Solid Reputation for Repeat & Referral

Like I said previously, when most people think of car sales they think of a sleazy business: the image of the plaid wearing, lying through their teeth, manipulating car salesmen. The fact is that there are shady characters in every industry. There are doctors that over-charge the insurance companies without doing the work, lawyers that pad their bills without representing to the best of their abilities, construction companies that use shoddy materials to save on costs and financial planners that talk clients into shady investments just so they can make high commissions. The stories are many and across all industries and professions.

One of the reasons the car business has gotten such a bad rap is because just about anybody can work as a car salesman. The barrier to entry is very low so the dealerships hire anybody who can talk. There isn't much in the way of training so the green salesmen will try to compensate for this with false promises, lies and deception. The lure of a high income attracts anybody who thinks he can be endearing to clients, without integrity, ethics or long-term goals.

There is a big difference between a salesman or a sales person and a professional sales advisor. Salesmen want to sell you a vehicle today, but a professional wants to sell you, and your sphere of influence, a vehicle for the rest of your life. A salesman only thinks about how much he can get away with today. A professional develops long-term relationships and works toward long-term goals and plans accordingly. A professional develops a solid reputation. A professional works toward their future.

The idea of the profession of automotive sales as being a sleazy is now a myth. In this modern internet era, people have access to the same, if not more, information than the sales people. Gone are the days that salesmen could lie and cheat a client out of their money. The client has access to all the costs, fees, financing rates, resale prices, options and reliability ratings associated with a vehicle.

The fact is that, car makers closely track client complaints as it can potentially hurt their brands. If a dealership receives too many complaints, the maker can fine the dealership and if it continues, they can pull their license agreement with them. Dealerships these days are very careful in how they treat their clients.

Ethics are very important in life and in business. Unethical businesses, business people or individuals quickly lose their core support. People who trade the future for the present are doomed to only live in the present. A Sales Advisor who doesn't cultivate clients for the future works extra hard to sell in the present. A solid, trustworthy reputation is the basis of all long-term relationships. Only with repeat and referrals business can you truly be called a professional and graduate to your highest income potential. Repeat business and referrals are the foundation to success in any career, no matter what line of work you're in. No business can survive for too long with a bad reputation or without repeat and referral business.

To be truly successful in any business, you need to be a true professional and treat everyone with respect, dignity and honesty. Unethical salesmen who lie, cheat, steal, over-promise and under-deliver have a very short career path in any business. To really reach your true potential in this business and in your life, you have to be a professional. This means you have to work hard toward your long-term goals and you need an attitude that you're in business for the long run. You don't just want to sell a vehicle to this one individual; you want to sell a vehicle to each one of this person's family and friends and acquaintances.

The profession of automotive sales gives anyone who has desire and is driven a lucrative career. Note that I said career and not a job. You can't make a six-figure salary at a job.

A Professional Sales Advisor as an Entrepreneur

Being a professional sales advisor is the same as being in business for yourself except you don't have to invest in a building, rent, inventory, employees, equipment or advertising. The dealership does all that for you.

To be a successful entrepreneur you must know the buyer and the seller. You already know the seller: the dealership. They have all the inventory as well as service and products to help you succeed. You know the buyer because they walk onto the lot every day, contact you on the internet or call giving you opportunities to do business with them. Exploiting those opportunities rests solely with you.

Let me tell you from my experience of being in business for many years, the best business is when you act as a mediator between the buyer and the seller without ever touching or investing in the product. At the dealership the buyers come to you, ready to do business. Your job is getting them to do business with you and you alone.

Selling vehicles is different than any other sales job in that the clients come to you to purchase the second most expensive item of their lives. Everyone who comes on a car lot is looking to buy a vehicle. You must convince them to buy from you and not somewhere else. That doesn't mean you can't or shouldn't go and prospect for business. Everyone needs a vehicle. It's a big ocean out there and your job as a professional is to know where the fish are and how to get the fish to bite.

Take advantage of everything a dealership has to offer. The only thing the dealership requires of you is your commitment, professionalism and time.

When I was a junior in High School, my two best friends and I pooled what little money we had and started buying and selling cars that we bought from the salvage auction.

When a vehicle is involved in an accident where the repair costs exceed the value of the vehicle or a vehicle has been stolen and hasn't been recovered for over a month, the insurance company will deem it salvaged when recovered. They will then send it to an auction specializing in damaged vehicles. By law the title will also state that the vehicle is salvaged in most states.

Yeah... most of the time the cars were damaged but not un-repairable. Once we found people to fix the cars at a reasonable price, we went to work on finding the right cars.

We slowly found our way regarding which cars to buy, where to fix them, where to sell them, how to price them and how to market them.

We were making an average of $1,000 profit per unit for about a year selling three or five cars per month. It was decent money, but we all had school and jobs so we all couldn't put in equal amount of time in the business.

This was my first taste of the car business and I quickly figured out:

- Cars are a necessity for people. It means freedom. The pools of clients are enormous
- Most people loved their cars more than they do themselves. They are willing to spend a lot on their vehicles
    - They take better care of their cars than they do themselves
- Almost everyone has about $2,000 to spend on a car. Vehicles are a big expense and people know this
- You never know peoples' tastes. Something you'd think will never sell, sells the next day at full asking

price. Vehicles are an extension of the clients' personality

I continued selling a car here and there while I was in college and after I graduated. Even with a full time job, I continued to sell vehicles at dealerships and on my own.

I've always had a strong entrepreneurial streak, but the timing was never right for me to fully pursue it. After working in the private sector for a few years as an accountant, I saved up some money and borrowed even more to open my own used car dealership.

Times were good and times were great before times became very rough.

Now you can't make millions of dollars from selling cars unless you have your own successful dealership, but you can make a descent six-figure salary selling cars for a dealership. Either way, this book will show you how to sell vehicles so you can make enough money to open up your options.

Until you get to the point where you have enough resources to go into business for yourself, I'll give you a detailed breakdown on what it takes to get to those six figures in no time.

There are tricks, techniques and jargon to any career. This book discusses what you need to succeed in becoming a professional automotive sales advisor. To be successful in this profession, you don't need a college degree, money or connections.

All you need is drive.

The drive to have a career not just a job. The drive to be a professional and not just an average mediocre individual that gets in the way. The career of a professional sales advisor can be more lucrative than the average lawyer, doctor, politician or CEO.

Being in sales is especially rewarding as nothing happens in a company until the sales person sells something. At one point in their lives, everyone should be in sales.

Although I mainly discuss new car dealerships, almost everything transfers over to the independent used car dealer. The process, the service, the concepts and the steps.

I can only present you with ways of making your career successful; it's up to you to act upon that information.

While this book is extensive and touches on things that you'll find unfamiliar at first, after <u>applying</u> what you've learned here, you can make your success so much easier.

I've set up a website called www.<u>**autosalesadvisor.com**</u> where you can download applications that can help you stay motivated, marketing material to help you set yourself apart from other sales people and industry insight to help you stay ahead of the curve. Please visit the site and make full use of what it has to offer.

Being a successful Automotive Sales Professional takes time, energy, patience, attitude, product knowledge and enthusiasm. <u>Continuous learning</u> assures you of those attributes and qualities.

Contents

1.   A Brief History of the Car Business

Karl Benz was granted a patent in 1879 in Mannheim, Germany for the internal combustible engine. He was also granted a patent for the first motorcar or Motorwagen in 1886. This was a 3 wheeled carriage with an internal combustion engine attached to it.

The motorcar had a 2 horsepower engine and a top speed of 10 M.P.H. The first long distant road trip consisted of 121 miles by Karl's wife, Bertha.

Karl Benz's motor-wagen

Although he wasn't the first to come up with the concept of the car or the internal combustion engine, he was however the first to get it right and patent it. Like most inventions that get patents, they're built on the ideas and hard work of many inventors, dreamers and risk takers.

Benz began selling his motorcar starting in 1888.

It wasn't until Henry Ford and his expansion of the assembly line, which was based on Ransom Old's assembly line in his Oldsmobile factory and modeled after the assembly line techniques pioneered by Marc Brunel in England, that allowed motorcars to be affordable for the average man on the street.

Henry Ford's assembly line reduced the time it took to build a car from 12.5 hours to 1.5 hours, reducing costs significantly. This allowed the average assembly line worker to purchase a vehicle with only a four month's salary.

Competition became fierce.

By 1920 there were more than 200 car makers in the U.S. By the 1930's there were only forty three, and after the Great Depression, there stood only 17. Innovations like standard parts, interchangeable parts and one maker having various sub makes similar to G.M. having Chevy, Pontiac and Cadillac, became the standard.

There was not any production of vehicles in the first part of the 1940's because of World War II. All manufacturing was geared toward military equipment. All oil, tire and gas were rationed and diverted to the military.

WWII ended in 1945 and a wave of returning GIs came home with money to burn. The economic boom had begun. The dealerships couldn't keep vehicles on their lot long enough. With the economic boom, people started moving out to the suburbs and a vehicle became a necessity. Not only did people want a car, but also they needed a car.

After WWII, the U.S. was the only game in the world as they were producing a majority of the world's goods. Europe and Japan were in shambles and destroyed. The rest of the world still remained undeveloped. The U.S. was the only industrial power left. As a result, there was little demand for oil/gas from the rest of the world but it was plentiful and cheap in the U.S. As a result, Americans wanted big cars: cars with fins, chrome and big proportions.

Manufacturers made huge productions of new models being rolled out with celebrities and parties and much fanfare. New models kept coming out with very little change in options or features. The only major change was the new styling and pricing.

During these times the only advertising manufacturers had were T.V., radio and print. The situation remains the same today, except the internet has replaced much of radio and print. Financing was just starting to take off, increasing the market of buyers that could now afford a vehicle.

During the 1950's, some of the less efficient car makers began to go out of business as price became an increasing pressure on the car makers. Since most of the vehicles had pretty much the same mechanical features, price and style were the only things left for the manufacturers to compete on.

Word of mouth was the only research available. Sure, there were car magazines, but magazines won't give bad reviews about car makers knowing that doing so will alienate that maker from ever advertising with them again.

Since there were so many cars sold from 1945 to the 1950's, a used car market started to develop. This coupled with the loosening of credit terms increased the pool of potential buyers even further.

In the 60's, while the husband was at work, women needed a vehicle to taxi around the kids. Now most households had to have two vehicles, increasing the demand for vehicles even further.

Gas was still cheap in the 60's and people had plenty of disposable income, which gave rise to the muscle cars because by then, Baby Boomers were coming of age to drive and wanted something different than their parents.

1965 was a huge year for car sales since most Baby Boomers were turning twenty.

Toyota introduced their first car in 1966.

With increasing fuel prices, insurance rates and emission laws increased, the era of the muscle car came to a close in the 1970's. The Baby Boomers needed more family-oriented vehicles. The small-engine imports were in a perfect position to take advantage of the changing times.

In the 1980's the Japanese cars, especially Toyota, took off due to incredible reliability ratings and gas mileage. Chrysler came out with the minivan. The electronic industry was booming and fuel injection was introduced, increasing gas mileage and reducing emissions.

Up until the 1990's, the only advertising outlet for dealerships was television, newspapers and radio. Not much information was available for consumers to do research on. Consumers were usually limited to dealerships within their vicinity when looking for used vehicles. Ill-informed and with limited options, consumers were left with little bargaining power. Dealerships took advantage of this weakness to make record profits, especially on used vehicles. It was during this time that the car salesman was associated with a thief. This continued well into the 1980's.

With the introduction to the internet in the 90's, consumers began to have increased access to information on various makes and models, dealership reputation, choices of vehicles and payment options. Armed with better information and better educated, consumers began demanding more and more from dealerships. Increased competition as well as better-informed consumers began taking a toll on car dealer's bottom line.

In response, many dealerships have started to experiment with a one-price policy where they don't negotiate on the price of the vehicle. Saturn was one of the first to try this approach which was very well received by consumers. Unfortunately, GM shut down Saturn as part of their restructuring plans.

This outline is neither complete nor detailed in regard to the history of the car business. This is just an overview of how we came to where we are today. I want to give you the big picture of what came before and a general idea of what's to come. A professional needs to know the history of their profession or industry to make sense of it today. As you can see from history, outside influences impact the choices consumers make in regard to purchases. Gas prices, emission laws, safety, individuality and changing lifestyles all affect the consumer's buying decisions. You, as a professional, need to learn to pick up on this, to effectively tailor your message to the consumer.

The Evolution of the Industry

The internet has completely changed the car industry. Consumers have access to huge amounts of information at their fingertips and on demand. As a result, consumers are becoming more savvy and demanding, which puts a lot of pressure on a dealer's bottom line.

I've had instances where I was negotiating with the wife on the price of a vehicle while the husband was searching on his phone for comparable vehicles in the area and using that information in the negotiations.

Car makers are not as complacent as they once were and are working to get their act together, especially the U.S. automakers. Reliability has become a major factor, which means that it's only noticed if it's missing. Once the consumer deems your product unreliable, it can take years if not decades to repair. It is a hard lesson that the U.S. automakers have had to learn, and are still learning.

With global warming becoming a bigger issue coupled with dwindling world oil reserves, most future vehicles will use primarily electric or some sort of hybrid energy source, but not necessarily oil.

Most car deals will take place in cyber space rather than at the dealership. Dealerships will still exist as a place for the client to try out the vehicles as well as a place for the sales advisor to build value in their vehicles, themselves as an advisor and their dealership, but the negotiations will mainly take place on the internet. Already, dealerships are not negotiating on their internet prices.

Most reputable car makers will go to a one-price policy where games used by dealerships to entice clients will be eliminated. Dealers will compete on service, availability of inventory, features of vehicles and reputation. This will give rise to the super dealerships where they will have hundreds of vehicles available for sale. Sales advisors will need to be especially skilled at building value in their vehicles and matching the clients' wants and needs to those vehicles.

What this means for the future sales advisor is that they need to be well versed in selling over the phone and on the internet. Sales advisors will also need to be well educated as to new technological features, their benefits and their applications.

2.   The Business of Automotive Sales

You're a Sales Advisor, Consultant or Agent, Never a salesman/sales Person!

Traditionally, people who sold anything were referred to as salesmen or saleswomen. There is nothing wrong with that except in the field of auto sales, the term *used car salesman* or *car salesman* is associated with a negative image. It is an extremely negative stereotype to overcome when you are trying to convince a client to trust you with the second largest purchase in their lives. Most of this stereotype is fabricated from the media and some is deserved, as there are some very unscrupulous used car dealerships out there that will do and say anything for a sale.

From here on you will either refer to yourself as a <u>sales advisor/adviser</u> or a <u>sales consultant/agent</u>. Never a salesman or a sales person. After all, you're not selling shoes. You're selling a vehicle that costs tens of thousands of dollars.   Being an advisor/consultant/agent is the correct term because you're not just selling, you're advising based on the needs, wants and capabilities of the client. You're advising them, consulting them or acting as their agent. For the rest of the book I will refer to anyone in auto sales as a professional <u>advisor</u>. You should do the same. To be a true professional, you want to project an image of professionalism, expertise and ethics.

A Career in Sales

Remember that this is a career in sales. To be successful in sales, a few things must be done:

- Find the decision Maker

- Build <u>trust</u> in yourself, your company and your brand with that person

- Show/Build <u>value</u> in your product by gearing it toward the clients' wants and needs

It's no different if you're a sales advisor talking to a client or a large corporation marketing your product. A corporation first markets or sells to the target audience (decision makers), then through various channels (shows, commercials, magazines, sponsorships), builds trust with the target audience and displays the value of their product by convincing them that their product will improve their lives on a number of different levels.

What it takes to Succeed in Auto Sales

The only requirements needed to be a successful automotive sale professional are a **drive to succeed and a professional attitude**.   The drive to succeed encompasses willingness to learn (continuous learning), honesty, ethics, integrity, product knowledge and enthusiasm for a lucrative career. Attitude means that you're focused on becoming a professional and having a career, not just a job.

Notice that I didn't mention money. There is a lot of money to be made in the car business and money is a direct result of your drive and attitude. You must have the drive and attitude first and the money will easily come.

Because you don't need a higher degree of education to become a successful auto sales advisor, the barrier to entry is very low. Anybody who wants a job with a dealership who displays a small amount of confidence and a willingness to learn can work as a sales advisor at a dealership. Turnover is very high. The reason for that is because the vast amount of people who enter this industry only have a job mentality and not a career mentality. If you visit a dealership, you will clearly see that there are only a few sales professionals and a bunch of salesmen who are earning a meager paycheck until something better comes along.

It's estimated that there are more than sixty thousand dealerships in the U.S. alone. A majority of sales advisors in these dealerships are sub-par, giving way to unlimited income and opportunities to a truly professional advisor. The average sales person lasts about three to six months, which means you as a professional have very low competition, you will never be unemployed again and you have job security.

What other career can you have where the only investment you make is in yourself? You don't need an expensive degree or training program. The advertisement is done for you, the product is there and the clients come to you. The opportunities available to a professional sales advisor are incredible.

It's Like Owning Your Own Business

I mentioned earlier that being a sales professional in the auto sales industry is like owning your own business. Your success or failure is solely dependent on you. Sure you have managers, but the ultimate responsibility is on you. The managers are there to keep you on the right track. The best thing about the dealership is that you don't have to own the inventory, you don't have to pay the bills or the overhead and you don't have employees.

The money is there, the clients are there, the inventory is there, the facilities are there and the services are there. All that is required of you to succeed is the drive and a professional attitude.

Reading this book is your first step to becoming a successful professional. Practicing the principles in this book is your second step.

If you opened your own business you would have to deal with a lot of things like rent, employees, overhead, buying inventory and making sure every aspect of the business is running like a well-oiled machine. How much do you think you would get paid for all that? $5,000 a month, $10,000 a month, $15,000 a month? The reality is that business owners in the beginning struggle and barely make anything, yet put in well over sixty hours a week.

If you've been in the car business for any amount of time, you know that the most successful sales advisors make anywhere between $10,000 to $25,000 a month. That's without making any financial investment into a business. The only investment they make is in themselves. You most likely will not be making that in the beginning, but you will in about a year when you've built up a book of business.

As a former business owner, let me tell you that any type of business ownership comes with a lot of headaches. It takes a special entrepreneurial spirit to put up with all those problems. For me it was worth it because I enjoyed many aspects of it, especially the freedom and responsibility. However, I did not like the large amounts of investment, paying out bills at the end of each month, eking out 10% after tax profits in some months.

The Future of the Industry

Some aspects of automotive sales will not change for some time:

- A vehicle is a necessity to most people. The need and want for vehicles will not change in the near future which is very good for the industry. Demand for vehicles will keep pace with the development of the world. At the writing of this book, it is estimated that there are approximately 1.6 billion vehicles worldwide.

- Most consumers will be shopping for a new or different vehicle every three years or so, depending on their changing needs.

- A vehicle will continue to be the second most expensive item people purchase in their lives after a home.

Changes on the horizon:

- The industry is slowly moving toward a one-price standard where the client will not need to negotiate on the price of the vehicle. Some dealers are hesitant to change as there will always people who don't know how to negotiate and are willing to pay thousands more than they should

- The internet has completely changed the industry as more and more information is available to the consumer. Gone are the days where the local population were limited to the advertisement in their local paper or to the dealerships in their vicinity. Dealers have to compete on a global scale now, where a consumer can buy a car on E-bay from overseas. Consumers have access to an enormous amount of information including pricing as well as competition

Who Needs a Sales Advisor?

The good news is that, even though people have access to enormous amount of information, they still need and want a sales advisor to assist them in picking out their next vehicle. Sometimes all that information leads to overload, which tends to make people forget a large percentage of information they've learned. They mainly remember their pain points or what their needs and wants are.

It's the sales advisor's job to bring out what the clients' needs, wants and pain points are. A true professional knows how to pinpoint the clients' pain points and how to customize their presentation to address those pain points.

Doing so will allow the sales advisor to match those needs and wants to their available vehicles. A professional sales advisor also needs to know how to build value in the vehicle so the vehicle is immensely worth more than the price. Clients on their own won't or can't do that.

Vehicles are the second largest purchase in a person's life after a house. Consumers would be very hesitant to spend that much money on a product as if it were a candy bar. They want someone to reassure them that they are making the right decision, answer their questions and make them feel good about the purchase. Purchasing a vehicle is an emotional decision as most people love and treat their vehicles better than they treat themselves.

If you've ever bought a computer, television or furniture costing several hundred dollars, you remember wanting someone there to answer your questions, reassure you that you were making the right decision and to make you feel good about the purchase. Now imagine going to buy a vehicle worth tens of thousands of dollars.

Buying a vehicle is not a simple process either. There are licenses, taxes, financing, servicing and maintenance to think about. There are features and benefits of the vehicle that most consumers won't be versed in. The consumer doesn't buy a vehicle every day. A typical client purchases a vehicle every three to five years.

The dealership also needs sales advisors to sell the dealership and all the services they offer. They need sales consultants to show value in more than the vehicle.

The difference between price and value is salesmanship!

A true sales professional is sought after by both the dealership and the client. Being a true professional means you'll never go hungry again.

Automotive Industry Statistics

Here are some statistics to mull over. These are according to NADA (National Automobile Dealers Associations) 2011 statistics found at www.nada.org.

- ❖ There are more than 17,500 new car dealerships in the United States, not including all the mom and pop, independent used car dealerships. When you add those, the total is well above 60,000 dealerships

    - ○ Once you hone and prove your skills, you can work for whomever you want making whatever you want

- ❖ The average annual sales for a new car dealer were $35 million 2011

- ❖ Total sales for new car dealerships in 2011 was approximately $609 billion. That's $609,000,000,000.

- ❖ New Car sales accounted for almost 54.4% while used car sales accounted for around 32.4% and service accounted for the remainder 13.2% of total dealership sales. These are figures of new car dealerships, not of independent dealers

- ❖ November, January and February are the worst months for cars sales: January being the worst for the whole year. If you're going to take a vacation, take it in January

- ❖ New car dealerships employee about 1 million people. Annual payroll is around $46 Billion

- ❖ More than 241 million passenger cars and light trucks are on the road in the U.S. alone

- ❖ More than 12.7 million new vehicles were sold and/or registered in 2011

- ❖ Approximately $12 million vehicles were scrapped in 2011

- ❖ The internet is the biggest advertising medium, followed by newspaper and television

As you can see from these statistics, the car market is huge. The auto industry is one of the largest industries in the world and has a profound impact on other industries like energy, service, transportation, mining, manufacturing, plastic, rubber and steel.

Vehicle sales also have a huge economic impact on the federal, state and local levels. Any city with an auto row can count on millions of dollars of tax revenue each year.

Some of the websites you should be checking out are www.nada.org, www.census.gov, www.naida.com and www.kbb.com These websites are invaluable in regard to pricing, industry trends and reviews. Your clients are looking at these websites and you should too.

The good news is that you can have access to all this flow of money, opportunity, goods and service without investing a dime. All you need is the drive to succeed and all you need to invest is time: time to become knowledgeable and a commitment to becoming a professional.

2a.   Basic/Relevant Terminology and Concepts:

MSRP: Manufacturer Suggested Retail Price. This is the price on the sticker or suggested retail price or sticker price. This is the amount the factory suggests the dealership should sell the vehicle. It is usually listed on a sticker called "The Monroney". All new cars must have this sticker on the vehicle prior to sale. The Monroney sticker must disclose the suggested retail price, standard and optional equipment of the vehicle, assembly point and dealer destination, safety ratings and fuel mileage.

Addendum: Next to the Monroney sticker will be another sticker that will show what else the dealer has added to the vehicle. If the dealer started with a basic new car retailing for $15,000 and added a stereo worth $1,500, then the addendum will show the MSRP price of $15,000 and list the details of the stereo added to the MSRP to give a final price of $16,500. Of course the client can negotiate down the price and tell the dealer to take out the stereo. Everything is negotiable. Some things cannot be removed like tint, pin striping or undercoating, but they are negotiable.

The addendum will also show if the dealer has marked up the vehicle even further. Vehicles with limited supply and high demand will usually get marked up by several thousand more than the suggested retail price. This will be shown as a markup on the addendum as a market adjustment.

Invoice: This is the amount the dealer paid for the vehicle, the cost of the vehicle to the dealership. It's not supposed to be general knowledge but if a client digs enough, they can usually get a good idea of what the dealer invoice really is.

Dealer Hold Back: Amount the factory pays the dealership for maintaining their vehicles until they're sold. This is usually a fixed amount. The sooner the dealer can sell the vehicle, the more of the holdback the dealer can recoup.

Mark Up: Difference between the MSRP and the Invoice, same as profit margin. If the retail price or MSRP of a vehicle is $20,000 and the invoice is $18,000, then the mark up or profit margin is $2,000.

> I have seen vehicles that sold way more than the MSRP only because there were shortages of that model so the demand was high. When the Tsunami hit Japan in 2011, the Japanese auto factories got damaged and there was a severe shortage of Toyotas and Hondas. I remember that they sold $5,000 or more cars higher than the MSRP, especially the Prius. This also happens when manufacturers roll out a very hot model like the new Camaro's that initially were selling for $5000 to $10,000 higher than MSRP. Just like any commodity, vehicles can also be subject to supply and demand.

Discount: Difference between the MSRP or retail price and the selling price. The MSRP is the starting point so the client wouldn't pay more than that for the vehicle with the exception of the add-ons or market adjustments on the addendum. If the MSRP is $20,000 and you sold the vehicle for $18,000, then you gave the client a $2,000 discount.

Gross Profit: Difference between the selling price and the invoice. Suppose you sell a vehicle for $20,000 and the invoice on the vehicle is $18,000. The dealership made $2,000 gross profit. This also applies to used vehicles after adding pack. Gross profit is what you get paid on so it's in your best interest to ask where to find the gross profit on the vehicles before you sell them. Any manager who tells you that he doesn't have access to that information or that he will tell you once you sell the vehicle is lying to you and getting ready to turn your deal into a mini no matter how much gross you keep in the deal. Ask the seasoned sales pros how to get that information.

Pack: This amount is added onto the cost of used vehicles to cover management fees, shop fees, overhead, labor and costs to run the dealership. If the dealership buys a vehicle for $10,000, then it will usually tack on another $1,000 to cover overhead, management fees and reconditioning of the vehicle. Now the cost of the vehicle is $11,000, and anything you sell over that is your gross profit. Some dealerships tell unsuspecting or green sales advisors that they shouldn't pack their vehicles or they should only pack it for $250 or less. This is a big fat lie. In actuality, the average pack is anywhere between $800 to $1,500. I might be wrong, you might be working at the only honest dealership in the country, but you'll see the amount you took in when trading,, the book sheet, the mark up and the pack. If you can't make sense of the numbers, try to ask one of your fellow seasoned sales advisors.

Some dealers will try to say that they don't pack their vehicles but don't believe them. Every dealership packs their vehicles.

So a vehicle that a dealer buys from auction for $10,000 goes through the shop for smog, safety, detail, overhead, management fees and other various fees that get added or packed, for another $1,000. Now the cost of the vehicle is $11,000. Therefore, you would need to sell this vehicle for more than $11,000 to make any gross profit or commission.

Mini: Stands for Minimum. It means it's the minimum amount a sales advisor will get for a sale. You either get paid a mini or a commission, whichever is higher. I've worked for dealerships that paid $75 minis and some that paid $350 minis. The lower the mini, the faster you should run from that dealership, unless they have other simple ways of making money like low number bonuses (a certain amount of money when you sell X amount of vehicles) or high back end. You shouldn't work for less than $150 minis. Making minis aren't your goal as a sales advisor, but if the dealership isn't willing to give a certain amount for each vehicle sold then they most likely will fool around with your money when you do make good gross. For a newbie, minis are going to sustain you until you get some experience under your belt. Also, most new car sales will be minis.

VIN: This is the *Vehicle Identification Number*. Every vehicle has a unique ten-digit number displayed on the dash board, the doors, door panels, fenders, engine, hood, truck or frame. .This is the vehicle's birth certificate number. The numbers are codes that represent the year of the vehicle, the make, model, type of engine and various other pieces of information that are usually specific to each maker. It is this number that you will use to get detailed information as to the value and history of this specific vehicle.

Vehicle History Report: There are several services out there that track the history of most of the vehicles in the marketplace (e.g. Carfax). They access DMV information as to the how many owners and status of the title, insurance companies records to see if it's been in an accident, law enforcement to see if the vehicle is stolen and dealership database to see the service records. These records are <u>not</u> 100% accurate but close enough They can't know everything but they do come pretty close. They can't know if you change your own oil, you got in an accident with your brother and the two of you settled it privately and fixed the vehicles yourself or if you took it in to your local garage to replace the engine. These are good reports to use when selling the vehicle if the records look complete and support your position that you're selling a great vehicle and also to reduce the value of someone's trade-in if there is bad information on the report.

UP: *Unsold Prospect.* These are fresh people who come to the lot looking to purchase a vehicle. In essence, walk-in traffic. These are people who have no prior recent contact with the dealership and have come in to see what you have for sale. This used to be the most common type of clients coming to the lot, but internet clients are becoming more frequent.

Book Sheet: This is a market report about a particular used vehicle. It's a one page report of the vehicles worth. It is usually generated by entering the VIN and various important options on the vehicle in question to get a market reported value. The report uses algorithms and historical information from other dealerships and auctions to come up with a market price. It's not 100% accurate, but it's a good ballpark.

Please refer to the image below as a sample of a good book sheet.

The figures at the bottom will usually tell you the retail and wholesale (auction) price of this vehicle. If someone is trading this vehicle at a dealership, you bet that the managers will try to get this vehicle way below auction price (the wholesale price) because you would not buy this vehicle for more than that unless you're going to offset that cost with the increase of the price of your vehicle. From my experience, most dealers will try to steal this vehicle for around $7,000 or $2,000 below the auction or wholesale price.

See below for sample book sheet.

Friday, October 19, 2012

Values are subjective opinions. We assume no responsibility for errors or omissions.

Retail/Auction Breakdown Blue Book
10/19-10/25

2009 Scion XB Sport Wagon 4D.. $14,225 / $9,775
VIN: JTLKE50E391854215

4-Cyl, 2.4 Liter..	Included
Automatic, 4-Spd w/Overdrive....................................	Included
FWD..	Included

*** Equipment ***

Traction Control...	Included
Stability Control...	Included
ABS (4-Wheel)...	Included
Air Conditioning...	Included
Power Windows...	Included
Power Door Locks...	Included
Cruise Control..	Included
Power Steering..	Included
Tilt Wheel..	Included
AM/FM Stereo..	Included
MP3 (Single Disc)..	Included
Dual Airbags..	Included
Side Airbags..	Included
Steel Wheels..	Included
Condition..	Fair
Total Value without mileage..	$14,225 / $9,775
Mileage adjustment (55101) miles...............................	($475)
*** KBB Retail/Auction Value....................................	$13,750 / $9,300

Like I mentioned, the book sheet pricing isn't 100% accurate. I looked up a similar vehicle on www.edmunds.com, it's trade-in value was $7,300 and retail was $9,300. This vehicle was selling for around $11,000 on Craigslist.

There are much more concepts and jargon to learn which I've attempted to cover in this book, but it is impossible to cover them all. Most of it you will learn in time and from your managers and fellow professional sales advisors. If you come across something you don't understand, you should ask one of the seasoned sales professionals or your manager. There's no shame in not knowing, only in not learning it.

You can also visit **www.autosalesadvisor.com** to get the latest tips and tricks to educate and motivate yourself.

There are many facets to the business of vehicle sales. Like a corporation has many different departments, so does the dealership. Each works together in generating income for the dealership. Each is connected to the other in supplying services and goods. By far the most important is the sales department. Why? Because:

Nothing happens until something is sold!

2b.　　The Dealership

Let's briefly look at an overview of each department:

The Sales Department: When the client/client first drives by your lot and sees something that catches their eye or just stops by your lot to see your inventory, the sales advisor is the first one to greet them and give them a warm fuzzy feeling of doing business with the dealership. It's the sales advisor's job to answer all their questions, build trust with them, find what their needs/wants are, present the vehicles based on those needs/wants and foster a long lasting relationship.

F& I (Finance & Insurance Department): Once the sales advisor has sold the vehicle and has come to an agreement with the client regarding price, payments and terms, then they are handed over to finance to finalize the deal and do the paperwork. Finance's job is to sell the client financial and insurance products as well as finalize the paperwork properly.

> **Service Warranty** – Depending on the year, make, model and mileage, a service warranty sells for somewhere between $700 to $5,000. Service warranties usually have limited coverage but are sold as a guarantee if anything should go wrong with the vehicle. The service warranty company will pay for the repairs. Since major repairs can cost thousands, it's worth buying on certain makes and models.

> **GAP insurance** – If the client is financing a vehicle and something happens to the vehicle and it's a total loss, the insurance company will pay the market value for the vehicle and not what the client owes on it. If he owes more than the market value at the time of loss, than the bank is going to want the difference from him. Gap insurance will cover the difference from what the client owes the bank and the market value the insurance company will pay, should the vehicle be in an accident or stolen and considered a total loss. This only applies to vehicles being financed.

Example: The client finances a vehicle that costs $20,000 and does not put <u>any</u> money down and one year later the vehicle is either stolen or involved in a severe accident where the insurance company deems it a total loss. Now suppose the client still owes $18,000 but the insurance company says the market value for the vehicle is only $15,000 and that's what they will pay. This means that the client has to cover the difference of $3,000. If bought gap then the gap insurance company will cover the $3,000. If he did not buy gap insurance, then he would have to cover the $3,000 or refuse to pay it, which will damage his credit in the process and leaves him open to litigation. It is best to offer gap insurance if there isn't a substantial down payment. Suppose the client did put down $3,000, then he is not financing $20,000. He is financing $17,000. If after two years he owes $15,000 when his vehicle got stolen, then the insurance company is going to pay $15,000 and he does not owe anything. GAP insurance is best when the client doesn't put any money down or has a low down payment.

Location Device: This is an aftermarket item installed on vehicles should they get stolen. If the car is stolen, the item can be activated and the car can be located quickly using GPS technology.

Paint Protection: A special sealant is applied to the paint every six months or so to prevent the paint from fading. It's basically a wax job.

Tint: The dealer will tint the windows and guarantee it for the life of the vehicle. If any rips, bubbles or scratches occur, the dealer will repair it for free for the life of the vehicle.

The average dealership has around three to six finance people, depending on the size of the dealership. Finance is also commission based and typically pays around 7% to 12% of everything sold. You might not think 7% is that much but when you consider an average dealership sells 150 units a month and <u>all</u> clients have to go through finance then it can add up fast. Each finance person see's 3 to 5 clients a day so they have and incredible opportunity to do business. This is the department that I would want to work in as soon as possible.

Service Department: The service department's job is to repair and recondition the dealerships as well as clients' vehicles. The job of the service advisor is to up sell more parts and service regarding the repair of the vehicles.

Repairing your vehicle at a dealership service department is extremely expensive because they are true professionals with certifications and have to go through continuous education. The dealership service department is usually the last resort for someone that's been all over town trying to fix their vehicle. The technicians at the service department are extremely good at their job only because they deal with the same problems and same types of vehicles day in and day out.

The service advisor gets paid a salary as well as commission on the total bill and mark ups on work they sell to the clients. This department is a huge profit center for the dealership. Not only do they charge an exorbitant amount to clients, but also to manufacturers when vehicles need to come in for recalls and warranty work.

Parts Department: The parts department's job is to stay stocked up on OEM (Original Equipment Manufacturer) parts for their specific make. These are the same parts that are used when they build the vehicle made to the exact specifications of the manufacturer and manufactured by the factory that supplied the original parts to the car maker.

There are many aftermarket parts makers for items like brakes, clutches and tires. The aftermarket parts makers will only make parts that they can sell at volume for relatively cheap prices. Aftermarket parts makers will only make parts that they can sell in volume. Most of the time parts stores will send you to the dealer for specific parts. Because of the huge secondary parts market, dealers don't sell high volume, so they charge incredibly high prices for a majority of their parts. It's not unheard of for dealers to mark up parts 100% to 150% or more. The parts department contributes a great deal of income to the bottom line in this way.

Desk Managers: Once the client decides that they want the vehicle that you so professionally demonstrated, displayed value in, and made them fall in love with, then you take them inside the dealership to talk numbers. Here, notify the desk manager that you have a client interested in vehicle X. The manager will then prepare a sales invoice for the vehicle for the client to purchase. The client can agree to make a counter offer thereby entering into negotiations. It's the desk manager's job to keep profit in every vehicle they sell, motivate the sales people, help close deals, manage the staff, manage the inventory and determine pricing and promotions. It is the manager who will make the final decision as to how much to charge the client in interest, how much down payment is required and how much the monthly payment will be: basically the structure of the deal. It is the manager and not the sales advisor who controls the price of the vehicle. This is something that needs to be communicated to the client early on.

Today, the computer is the boss. All the manager does is plug in numbers into that computer and the computer determines if the deal meets minimum profit requirements. The manager can override it but he better have a good explanation. Basically remember that it's the desk manager in charge of the approving deals. The Desk managers also get paid commission on every deal the sales advisor transacts so it's in their best interest for you keep as much gross income in the deal as possible. The rate of commission paid to desk managers vary but are usually based on units sold.

2c.   Types of Floor Systems

Traditional System

This is where the sales advisor will meet the clients on the lot and take them through the whole process up until finance. The sales advisor would usually present the vehicle to the potential client and them bring them into the show room and turn them over to a closer. There the closer would take over.

The disadvantages of this system are several fold.

There isn't much control as the client gets handed off like a football and made to feel like cattle. They don't have any loyalty to any one sales advisor. The other downside of this is that the sales people become lazy by relying on the closers abilities instead of reinforcing their sales and presentation skills. The clients are then turned over again to finance once the closer gets done with them. Another major problem is that the information gained by the sales advisor during the initial meet, rapport building and the presentation of the vehicle gets lost instead of used in negotiations.

The advantage of this system is that you have an experienced closer that can close the client and sell the vehicle. The other advantage is that the client is made sure that they are turned over to someone else and is touched by more than one person.

One Person System

This is where the sales advisor takes the client from greeting them on the lot to selling the vehicle, closing, financing and delivery. The client only deals with one person for the whole purchase of the vehicle.

The best part of this is that the sales advisor has complete control of the client throughout the whole system and the client only deals with one person.

The one drawback of this system that I've experienced is that the ASM's (Assistant Sales Manager) or the sales managers, get very lazy and don't touch the clients before they leave. There usually isn't a turnover to someone else before they leave. A system must be worked out where the ASM or a sales manager comes over and introduces himself to the clients either before they leave or even better, when the sales advisor and client first sit down. It makes the client feel important to know that another manager or someone higher is giving them some attention. The ASM or sales manager should also drop in periodically on the client during this whole process to make them feel even more important.

This does not mean the sales manager needs to talk about business, but rather chatting them up a bit, showing empathy, concern and making a friend. Even if the sales advisor is a pro and doesn't require any assistance, the sales manager should still come over and introduce themselves. Remember that it's a team effort.

In my experience, this system is best for the sales advisor as they have complete control and they also gets paid on any finance products they sells. This also helps increase the sales advisor's knowledge of the whole sales process, thereby making them him an even more efficient professional. The client also seems to really like this process as they only have to deal with one person, which makes them very loyal and trustful to this one advisor. Although the GSM or desk managers make decisions on the price of the vehicle, the trade-in value and terms of financing, the sales advisor still has tremendous control of the client throughout the buying process.

Whatever the system your dealership uses, know the strengths and weaknesses of them. To be a true professional you need to be proficient in all aspects of the sales process.

I very much prefer the one person system as long as the sales managers make sure to touch each client several times before they leave. This system also makes the sales advisor a more lean, knowledgeable and experienced professional.

I've worked for several different dealerships and by far the easiest and most successful was the no-haggle, no-hassle store. These were called a "One-Price Store". These dealerships usually pay their sales staff flats as opposed to commissions. The sales advisors at the one-price store were true sales professionals as they were also required to sell the clients financial products.

These are highly profitable dealerships and the clients loved them for it because they didn't negotiate on the price, as negotiations are one of the biggest fears clients have when buying a vehicle. No matter who came to the store, everyone got the same price: no negotiations.

The sales advisors were also handsomely compensated for each vehicle sold and financial product sold. The average pay at the one-price store was around $600 per vehicle. Just think how much your commission would be if you sold 10 cars a month.

If you can find a one-price store in your area or one that pays flats, find out their pay plan. In my opinion, these are the best places to work. The clients absolutely love these types of dealerships as they know that they won't need to negotiate like the traditional stores and they like it that they have to deal with only one person throughout the whole sales process, from picking out a vehicle to financing to getting the car delivered. The sales advisors are absolutely true professionals at these types of dealerships, since they're well versed in both sales and finance.

2d.   U.P. System – Unsold Prospects

U.P. is an acronym for *unsold prospects*. These are clients who come on your lot wanting to look at your inventory. Dealerships will usually have a way of approaching these prospects.

No System - In traditional dealerships, clients drive up onto the lot and start looking. The first sales advisor that approaches them and makes contact is responsible for that opportunity to make the sale. In this situation, the sales advisors watch the lot for any prospects that are looking for vehicles. The advisors have unwritten rules on who can and can't approach the client. Usually they go by the guy that has been outside watching the lot the longest who gets the next client who walks onto the lot. Once he gets his turn, then he goes back to the end of the line of the number of sales advisors waiting outside.

This is a good system as it rewards the hard workers. Those who want to work and make money will be outside all the time waiting for clients. Those who are lazy will just stay inside or play around on the computer all day. The sales advisor will have virtually unlimited clients to sell to if they work hard enough.

> The downside is that some sales advisors won't honor the rules and rush out if they see a good prospect, without any regard to who has been waiting out on the lot the longest. This causes a lot of conflict between sales advisors.

> Another downside is when more than five sales advisors decide to go outside to watch the lot they start to socialize more than look for opportunity.

> Another problem is that the sales advisors look like a bunch of vultures looking to pounce on the first client who comes on the lot. This usually scares away most clients from getting out of their vehicle and it also looks incredibly unprofessional.

U.P. System – There are many variations of having an U.P. system. I've worked for dealerships where the sales people took turns. One would watch the lot and another would answer the phones. If a client came on the lot, then the one watching the lot would greet them while the one manning the phone would move up and watch the lot and another advisor would come down and answer the phones. They all rotate until they all got a turn. The sales advisors not on the phone or with a client or watching the lot were required to make phone calls or were free to prospect for clients somewhere else.

Another dealership I worked required 2 sales advisors to watch the lot at all times. As soon as the first advisor went to meet a legitimate client, the second advisor became number one and another advisor would come and become number 2. A legitimate client was one who was actually looking for a vehicle and not one looking for service, parts or coming to meet for an appointment.

There are many variations but the main point is that approaching a client is organized.

The benefit of an UP System is that everyone is required to work and everyone gets a chance to get clients. It evens the playing field. The dealership looks more professional as there aren't packs of sales advisors waiting for a client. This system also gives all the advisors a chance at incoming phone calls or phone pops as well as internet leads.

The downside of this system is that it doesn't allow the sales advisor with the most drive adequate exposure to UPs. It forces the mediocre sales advisors to work and thereby blows away clients that a professional sales advisor could have closed. Believe it or not, the downside is actually a benefit to the dealership and the sales advisor because the sales advisor knows that they will only talk to a certain amount of clients a day. They won't have an unlimited supply of clients which makes them work harder with each client to get them to test drive, go into looking at numbers and closing them. They'll work extra hard knowing that their daily opportunities are limited.

I prefer a dealership with a UP system. It's more professional. The sales advisors are more focused on working and honing their craft instead of getting together and socializing. It also forces the sales advisors to figure out other ways of prospecting for clients besides getting UPs.

I instituted an UP System at my dealership as it helped the sales advisors think about other avenues of prospecting instead of solely relying on the fresh UP. It forced sales advisors to work every prospect they got to their fullest potential and work on improving their product knowledge and sales skills. UP's usually have a very low purchase rate as most clients won't buy just by visiting the lot. That is why it's very important to build up or cultivate your repeat and referral business.

2e.   The Life of a Professional Sales Advisor

If you've been in the car business for long you've noticed the incredible amount of turnover, meaning almost every month like clockwork a few sales people get hired and few quit or get fired. There are many reasons for this.

Unrealistic Expectations of the Business

Long Hours –Sales requires a virtually 24 hour commitment at the beginning. To be making $10,000 or $15,000 a month without a big book of clients is unrealistic. In the beginning to make that amount of money, you will need to realistically work, 55 hours a week or more. In the beginning, you're going to be working a lot of hours at the dealership. Most of it will be downtime unless you're a true professional. Most likely you're going to be working every weekend because that is when most of the people shop for vehicles, especially Saturdays. Sunday's are usually slow.

Even when your shift is over, you still get calls from clients asking you questions or wanting to stop by to look at vehicles. It would be very useful to live close by your dealership when a client does want to come by and buy something; otherwise a client that you've been chasing for a month will stop by when you're not there to buy something. Should another sales advisor help them, then this deal will turn into a half deal. Next to no deal, the half deal is one of the biggest irritants.

Half Deals - Half deals are part of the business, don't worry though. What goes around comes around. There will be plenty of time when you profit from another sales advisor's hard work, so just accept it as part of the business. It's controllable but unavoidable at times. It's irritating, but it's no big deal. Just make sure that that the other sales advisor pulls their own weight and make them do all the necessary follow up paperwork.

Under no circumstances do you let the other sales advisor take control of your client after the sale. Make sure you do all the follow up communication. Just because they bought from another sales advisor when you weren't there doesn't mean you lose them. Keep up with them when they buy again.

The whole industry is set up to cater to the client. The client, unless you've established an exceptional rapport with them will do whatever they want. In most cases, they'll come in to your dealership unannounced, usually when you're not there or when you're with another client.

It's part of the business and the sooner you accept that, the sooner you can move on and concentrate on what's important: the sales itself.

Lack of Commitment – By this I mean that the sales advisor doesn't want to put in the time necessary to learn all the nuances of becoming a successful sales advisor. They haven't yet learned how to keep gross profit in a deal and haven't mastered the whole sales process.

It takes time to master the sales process. You're not going to master it in a month. It takes a while to really learn to control your client and the entire sales process.

You need to put in your time. Sure you won't be making that much money in the beginning, but using the techniques in this book you'll be years ahead of most of the other green peas or newbie's or novices. Like I mentioned earlier, think of it as a career and not a job. A career is a long term commitment. It's important to find a dealership that you want to stay with, that will do what they say, compensate you appropriately, is reputable, and trustworthy. The grass will not always be greener at another dealership. You need to find a good dealership to work for so you will be able to better build your book of clients.

Conflicts with Management

Treatment/abuse - In my time there has been plenty of sales advisors who got into an altercation with the desk manager. I'm one of the guilty. In most dealerships, the desk manager deals with more than 10 sales advisors at a time and it's really easy for them to lose their temper. Managers are under a tremendous amount of pressure from upper management to increase sales and profit.

One day, you'll be one of the unlucky ones that they try to vent on and you'll find yourself at a crossroads of what to do.

a.   You can get hostile and give it right back, which most likely will get you fired

b.   You can also get violent and really give it back to them. This will not only get you fired, but also get you arrested as well as blacklisted from ever working at another dealership as most dealerships do a background check on their sales people for violence and other behavior that can potentially expose the dealership to lawsuits. This will also prevent you from getting any job that does background checks of any kind.

After all, you're going to be alone with most clients on test drives so nobody wants to hire a violent or unpredictable sales person

c.   The best course of action is just to let it roll off your back and just walk away because the other alternatives are even worse

Missing Pay – You'll know you're at the wrong dealership when you've calculated your pay for the period only to find your paycheck short. You've done your job and made the client fall in love with the vehicle, kept good gross income in the deal and made the client fall in love with you only to find that your paycheck doesn't reflect the commission that you've calculated. There can be legitimate reasons for this. When you confront management, you get nothing but excuses when you're only looking for your pay. The excuses they give you are so ridiculous that it's insulting. I've seen many sales advisors quit over this reason. There were always discrepancies over pay and never in the sales advisors favor. The sales advisors were always chasing their money every month.

If you encounter such situations, then you need to look into reporting the dealership with the commission board or other governmental agencies and look for another dealership to work for. If they do it once, they've done it before and will do so in the future. Most likely someone else has complained to the labor board. The more that people complain, the higher the chances that a case will be opened against them.

Don't be afraid to stand up for your rights and stand up for respect because if they do it once, they'll do it again and again.

One thing you must remember when working in the car business is that you must have a tough skin. Everyone is under enormous pressure to sell more every month. Even as you're getting pressure from the sales managers to sell, they're getting enormous pressure from the upper management to sell more vehicles. Upper management is under even more pressure by the owners to shape up or ship out.

I've worked with many former general managers who have run multimillion dollar dealerships. They've given up the high-paying and high-stress jobs to work as a sales advisor. They've told me that never a day goes by that a general manager doesn't fear for their job.

The point is, everyone in the sales process is under enormous pressure to perform and make profit. The higher you go in the sales chain, the better the pay, but the higher the pressure.

As a previous owner of a car dealership, the mounting bills, sales targets, profit margins and expense rolls were always in the back of my mind.

2f.   Stages of Typical Sales Advisor's Career

Stage 1 – Green Pea - The sales advisor is new to the business and is very motivated, has great enthusiasm, a great attitude and little product knowledge, but is willing to learn. Makes a great deal of money because they have a great attitude, enthusiasm and motivation.

Stage 2 – Novice - The sales advisor is becoming knowledgeable and enlightened with the process, clients, managers and products. Properly pre-qualifies. Questions the sales process and thinks about improving the sales process. Reassesses whether a career choice in sales is for them. Enthusiasm, attitude and motivation are waning due to realities of the car business.

To prevent being zapped in stage two, you need to focus on the basics: attitude, product knowledge and enthusiasm. Realize that anything you do successfully in life takes time and hard work to build your foundation. Keep in front of people, build a strong referral base and polish your basic skills.

Stage 3 – Seasoned – Has figured out costs, values and types of clients. Thinks they know everything they needs to know about the car business. Is extremely frustrated with the process as it doesn't conform to what they have in their mind. He becomes lazy, with a poor work ethic and habits. He has a bad attitude and lacks enthusiasm. He produces low earnings as he has given up on doing things a successful sales advisor does. He thinks he knows it all.

This is the crossroad stage. The sales advisor needs to figure out at this stage if a career in vehicle sales is for him or not. He needs to reassess his goals and plans in life. The grass is not always greener on the other side.

To avoid being crapped out in stage three, don't take rejection personally and surround yourself with positive and motivated people. Realize that failure is a learning opportunity. Maintain the process and do a proper follow up. Keep up your enthusiasm and attitude. You should already have good product knowledge.

There will always be problems with life. You, as a seasoned pro, should know this by now. You should also be able to prioritize those problems, their effects on you and remedial solutions. If a problem won't affect you a year from now, it's not that big of a problem. Can this problem be solved by selling more cars and making more money? If the answer is yes, then you have your solution. Sell more cars!

Stage 4 – The Professional – Realizes that their life and sales career are in their hands. Has control of their career. Has an excellent work ethic. Has accepted and mastered the selling process. Attitude and enthusiasm has returned like in stage one. Realizes the great income and personal potential in being a sales advisor. Re-assessed goals and plans and makes an extremely high income. Most likely a "by appointment only" sales advisor. Income depends on when they want to work. Money is there for the taking.

So what does it take be a successful sales advisor? Success in this business means a lot of repeat clients and referrals, which translate to more money. But, you can't make more money unless you have an excellent client base because it's these satisfied clients who keep sending your more and more clients. After a while, you won't have to do much work except pick up the phone and show a few vehicles.

So how do you build a happy and satisfied clientele?

If you don't learn anything else from this book learn this:

<u>Forget about selling a car and concentrate on making friends</u>

That's it. That's the secret. It's as simple as that. Nothing complicated at all. That is the open secret to almost all sales jobs. Are you going to make friends with <u>every</u> client you talk to? Not even a chance. Follow what I've outlined and I'll show you how to make as many friends as possible. Turn those friends into clients and turn their friends and family into clients.

Don't make it more complicated than that. Be more like your clients so they trust you. Keep their interests above all else and have fun with your clients.

2g.   Sales Advisor's Pay Plan

Commissioned

These are just simple examples of sales commission rates you should be expecting at most dealerships. Yet, they are not the only pay plans.

We're going to assume $2,000 profit on every sale and $3,000 worth of financial products (GAP insurance, warranty, paint protection, tint, accessories, add-ons) sold for demonstration purposes. Of course your deals will vary. It is good to get these numbers as soon as possible.

Units sold Retroactive	Front End Gross	Back end Gross (Financing)	(Mini)
Up to 10 cars	25%	3%	$150
Up to 15 cars retroactive	30%	5%	$200
Up to 20 cars retroactive	35%	10%	$250
Up to 25 cars retroactive	40%	12%	$300

What this chart says is that in a given month if you sell 10 cars, you will receive a 25% commission of the gross profit in the vehicle and 3% of the total back end or financing products. Should you fail to keep gross profit in the deal, then the minimum you will be paid is $150 per car. You are paid $150 or a commission, whichever is more, per vehicle. You should figure out the profits of each individual vehicle before you sell it to figure out what your commission threshold will be. How much can you negotiate on the price of the vehicle before the deal turns into a mini?

Given our assumptions above of $2,000 gross plus $3,000 back end gross on up to 10 vehicles sold, your commission would equal:

$2,000 * 25% = $500
$3,000 * 3% = $90
$640 per vehicle * 10 vehicles = $6,400 Total (Assuming you did the same amount on each vehicle you sold for demonstration purposes.)

Suppose you sell 14 cars? Your commission jumps to 30% on front end gross and 5% back end on all 14 cars, and not just on those above 10. It's a good incentive for the sales advisor to shoot for as many cars as possible.

$2,000 * 30% = $600
$3,000 * 5% = $150
$750 per vehicle *14 vehicles = $10,500 Total

What about if you sell 22 cars in that month? Your commission jumps to 40% front end gross and 12% back end gross retroactive to the first vehicle you sold.

$2,000 * 40% = $800
$3,000 * 12% = $360
$1,160 per vehicle * 22 vehicles = $25,520 Total

Of course, keeping $2,000 gross on every deal and selling $3,000 is hard, but not impossible. It is best to get all the numbers on the vehicle you're about to sell before you enter negotiations to figure out how far you can bend and how much gross you will give up every time you negotiate on the price. Not every car deal will be a winner and finance won't be able to sell everyone $3,000 worth of products. In reality, most monthly deals will have some minis, low gross, high gross, low financial products or no financial products.

Most dealers will pay $150 for a mini. If you ever get a position at a dealer paying less than $150 in minis then you really need to look at what else their offering. I've come across dealerships that were paying $50 to $75 in minis. Of course, minis aren't your goal as a sales advisor, but you will get minis once in a while, no matter how good you are. Without other incentives like high volume bonuses or high commissions, there really isn't a good way to make money at these types of dealerships. Needless to say, they only attract the inexperienced and naïve sales people who quickly leave once they figure out how little their paychecks will be.

Dealerships such as these don't care about the sales force and are considered a grinder dealership because they hire a sales force and put them through a grinder before they quit in a month or two. I recommended you talk to the sales people at the dealership, to get a good idea of what you can expect before applying.

You get paid either on the gross commission or a minimum amount, whichever is greater. I've seen good commissions turn into minis just because there were problems with the deal: finance moved the front end gross to the back end or management decided the vehicle needed further repairs, and that whittled down your front end gross. You better make sure the dealership has a good reason to whittle down your commission. You need to fight for every penny, because if they do it to you once, they'll do it to you again.

This commissioned pay plan is typical of a majority of dealerships. They might tweak it a little here and there to produce incentive for their sales advisors to work harder and give them more money, but they usually follow the guidelines as above. Making $2,000 gross per unit and finance selling them $3,000 worth of warranty, insurance, location device, paint protection, tint and other various items is typical of a seasoned sales advisor and finance manager. Most of the time, front end gross ranges from $0 to $5,000. The better you are at sales, the more likely you'll be living in the $3,000 to $5,000 range in front end gross. Financing is out of your hands so you'd better hope you have a good finance person to make you money. I'll discuss techniques on how to get a better rate of return from finance later in the book.

Volume or Base

In the volume/base pay plan, the sales advisor is either paid on volume or a draw. Once the sales advisor sells ten vehicles in a month, the commissions automatically go to $500 a vehicle. The commission increases $25 to $50 once the sales advisor has sold 13 vehicles, and even more if they sell more than fifteen. Should the sales advisor sell anything less than 10 vehicles, he would be paid a $2,000 base. It's a good incentive for the sales advisor to work to sell over 10 vehicles as well as earn a minimum standard of living. Obviously, should the sales advisor fail to sell 7 or 8 vehicles a month, for several months, the dealership will most likely let them go. This is great for the sales advisor as they won't need to negotiate that hard with clients, and only make sure the client likes the vehicle. This is one step closer, doing away with negotiations all together.

Flats

Flats are like minis. They're a flat amount paid on each and every sale. In a flat pay plan, the dealership will usually not negotiate on the price and the sales advisor will usually do the financing. This is usually done at one-price stores. This is the best deal for a sales advisor. There are variations but this is just one example.

Typical Flat Payment Plans:

Units Sold	New	Used	Financed	Warranty	GAP	Lo-Jack	Tint
Level 1 up to 12 cars	$250	$350	$50	$125	$50	$50	$25
Level 2 up to 18 cars	$300	$400	$100	$150	$50	$50	$25
Level 3 up to 22 cars	$350	$450	$150	$175	$50	$50	$25

Example of flat rates:

If you sell a used vehicle, you make $350. If the client finances the vehicle through your dealership, you make another $50. If you sell them a warranty, you get another $125. If you can sell them GAP insurance ($50), Lo-Jack ($50), tint ($25) as well, that's a total of $600 you can make on one car deal.

Here's the catch. It doesn't matter if you sell one car or 50 cars in one month, you still get paid on level one. If you do sell more than twelve cars, then the next month you'll be paid at level 2 pay, so instead of $600, you'll get $900 if you sell everything. Your current month performance determines you next month's pay plan.

Flats are the best way to go in terms of a pay plan because there's usually no negotiation on the price of the car. The store gives the client its best price and that's it. It's a great selling point because negotiations are one of the things that really stresses the client and turns them off to coming to a car dealership.

The only thing a sales advisor has to do in a flat rate situation is make sure the client likes the car, because they don't have any room to negotiate with. They really have to sell this point to the client and make them feel good about purchasing at the dealership.

Before you start looking for a position at dealerships in your area, call around and find ones that pay a flat rate instead of commission. Then look closely at their payment plan to make sure there isn't any kinky stuff going on. The best thing to do is to visit one of these dealerships during the week. Visit once in the morning and once in the evening. Park in the service or parts parking lot and tell the sales people or greeters that you're looking for parts. Once inside, kind of look around and find a sales advisor alone and really grill them about how it is working there, what the payment plan is, how the working conditions and managers are and any advice they might have in you getting a job there.

In a typical dealership there'll be 3 teams working. One team will be working in the morning and another in the evening with the 3rd team off. Typically all teams work on Saturday.

That's why you should go in the morning first during the week and grill someone on the morning team and then go again in the evening to grill someone in the evening shift.

Dealer Draw

Along with commissions/flats, dealerships typically pay minimum wage or a draw. At the end of the month dealers will pay their sales force either a commission/flat or minimum wage/draw, whichever is greater. The minimum wage is usually referred to as a draw. A draw can also be a set dollar amount like $2,000 a month. You are paid twice a month. If your commissions are less than your hourly/draw, then you will be paid the hourly amount. If at the first part of the month your commission is less than the hourly, then you are paid the hourly. If at the second half of the month your commission is more than your hourly pay, then the dealership will deduct the difference between your commission from the first half of the month and then calculate whether your commission or hourly is more.

Example pay plan using an hourly/draw:

First half of the month: 1st to the $15^{th.}$

Commission	Hourly/Draw	Difference	Paycheck
$800	$1,000	-$200	$1,000

Your commission is less than your hourly so you are paid the hourly/draw pay, which is $1,000.

Second half of the month: 16th to the 31st.

Commission	Hourly/Draw	Difference	Paycheck
$2,500	$1,000	$1,500	$2,300

Your commission is more than your hourly/draw so you are paid the commission less $200, extra the dealership paid you for the first half of the month.

If you look at the whole month, your hourly/draw would have been $2,000.

You total commission would have been $3,300. In the end you received your total of $3,300. Remember that you get either a draw or commission, whichever is more. The dealership paid you an extra $200 in the first part of the month because your commission was less than the draw, but then deducted the $200 on the second check so in the end, you received the $3,300 that you earned.

> **Caution** – If your commission is less than an hourly/draw for 2 months in a row, then you'll get fired. If this is the case, you need to really reassess if you're at the right dealership, if this business is for you or what can you do to be a better sales advisor.

Summary of Business of Automotive Sales

- Never refer to yourself as a salesman. You're more than that. You're a Professional Sales Advisor

- Being a professional sales advisor is like having your own business without any out of pocket investments. The only thing you need to succeed is the drive and a professional attitude

- Your main purpose as a professional sales advisor is to reassure the client that they're making the right decision by building trust in you, the dealership and your product

- People trust their friends. Making a friend should be at the top of your objectives in all interactions with people

- There are many departments in a dealership that work in tandem to make profit for the dealership. Know their roles and how they can help you succeed in your career, especially the sales department

- Being an Automotive Sales Advisor has many pitfalls as well as rewards. Make sure you're comfortable with both

3.   Target Audience – Fear of Loss, Hope for Gain

In order to fully appreciate and understand the buying process, one needs to understand the client. Who are the people who you're trying to sell to? What makes them tick? What are their fears, hopes and dreams?

It is said that the "fear of loss, hope for gain" is at the core of what motivates every individual.

The fear of making a bad decision, being taken advantage of, being unable to fulfill their commitments in terms of payments, receiving disapproval from friends and family, the fear of losing control and the fear of loss of options fall under this idea.

The hope of making the right decision, the hope for looking like a hero, the hope to win and the hope for value also fall under this idea

Stereotypical Fears

Misconceptions about the sales industry have conditioned clients to lie in order to not tip their hand in regard to the amount of money they have, capabilities or their likes and dislikes. Most clients have been conditioned to fear auto sales men, the profession of sales and the auto industry as a whole.

From the start, the sales advisor is starting from a negative position. There is the stereotype of a plaid jacket wearing, smooth talking, lying, double-talking, over-promising, under-delivering and dishonest car salesman.

There are countless television shows, movies, books and other sources of entertainment that reinforce these negative stereotypes of a car salesman. It's a source of humor as well as entertainment, but to an educated and rational professional these are just that, stereotypes. We have to contend with the other 90% of the population that fully accept these stereotypes without giving it a second thought.

Another negative stereotype a sales advisor needs to get over is that of the automobile sales industry. It's very common among the masses to think that the industry is designed to scam them out of their hard earned money. People think that there are numerous loopholes, fine print and schemes in the sales contract that are designed to nickel and dime them out of thousands of dollars. Countless articles are written about what to look out for at the dealership.

Most are unwarranted. The fact is that the auto sales industry is highly regulated so the consumer is very well protected.

The auto industry contributes an enormous amount of money to local, state and federal governments around the world. Without the auto industry, many world economies would grind to a halt. Almost everyone either needs or wants a vehicle. Without auto financing, most won't be able to drive a new or a good quality used vehicle. The auto industry employs thousands of people around the world from the sales staff, to parts suppliers, to assembly workers, to advertisers, to oil companies and shippers.

Are there unscrupulous dealerships out there looking to prey on the unsuspecting client? Of course there are, just like any other industry. Industries from banking to medicine to pharmaceuticals and construction have all been scrutinized and convicted of defrauding clients. Just look at the banking industry and the meltdown they caused around the world in 2008. Are industries as a whole responsible for a few companies preying on unsuspecting people? Of course not! The fact is, in almost all cases a few crooked companies give the whole industry a black eye.

These facts need to be communicated to the clients. People need to be educated to the fact that there are numerous crooked people out there waiting to take advantage of unsuspecting clients. Most importantly, you need to educate or communicate to your clients that doing business with you and your dealership is one way of protecting them from getting ripped off. You need to show them, one way or another how honestly you do business, either by awards you've won, third party sources or your sales policies.

This must be done throughout the whole sales process. Remember that most people don't buy a vehicle every day. They hold on to that vehicle for at least three to 5 years. They don't want to live with a mistake like that for many years.

So what is it that clients fear the most? What is it that clients hope for? It will become glaringly obvious to you once you've been in the car business for a while, but here are a sample of a few of clients' fears and hopes.

Fear	**Hope for Gain**
Paying too much	Paying the right amount
Being pressured	Good decision on reliability
Ability to make the payments	Good decision on safety
Reliability of the vehicle	Good decision on type of vehicle
Picking out the vehicle right for them	Approval of peers/loved ones
Losing approval of peers/loved ones	Making the right decision
Lacking proper knowledge	Looking like a hero

Being aware of what makes your target audience tick will allow you to dispel any fears they have while at the same time build on their hopes. This must be done throughout the sales process. This is the essence of the rapport building or friend making. You must be genuine when you do this.

Since most people who come to the dealership operate out of fear, you might want to include somewhere in your presentation: "You guys don't have to be afraid of me. I'm not trying to sell you something that you won't like. I've been doing this for a while now and 90% of my clients are from repeat or referrals. I treat everyone like they are my family and they keep buying from me and sending me clients, so you guys can feel free to ask or tell me anything you want."

You should address this fear early in the sales process to air it out and make them more comfortable with you. Acknowledge that you sympathize with what they're going through and tell them that you understand. Include that, "the more information you give me, the better I can help you achieve your goals. Help me help you."

Once a client leaves the lot, the chances of them coming back and buying from you drops substantially. That's why it's crucial for you to understand the concept of "fear of loss and hope for gain" when communicating your message to the client. Most clients operate out of fear, especially fear of commitment due to making the wrong decision.

You really need to think about some of the client's objections and hesitations going on in their mind, like the list above, so you can disarm it or overcome it before the client have a chance to bring it up. Make them feel at ease so you can build rapport and trust, and get them to see the benefit of buying from you.

The sales advisor also has a fear of loss and a hope for gain: a fear of losing the client and a hope for the sale or better yet, the sale and repeat and referrals from this client. That's why becoming adept at knowing what motivates the client and yourself and tailoring your message to address those fears and wants are crucial to becoming a professional in any career that requires social interactions.

It's your job to bring out these fears and dispel them by using proper trust building techniques so the client is more comfortable with you. You accomplish this by asking many questions, isolating objections, addressing them, finding common ground, being like a chameleon or more like them, sympathizing and empathizing with their plight. You must exude honesty, sympathy and empathy to come out as truthful.

One solid way to make this information yours is to put yourself in place of the client. Do you remember the last time you were shopping for a car? What were you thinking?

What type of vehicle were you shopping for? What did you hope to accomplish with such a vehicle? What were your hopes and fears? What was most important to you when shopping for a vehicle?

Safety – Airbags, seat belts, warning devices, special devices
Performance – Size of engine, quickness, sportiness, braking power, torque, power
Appearance – Appeal, image, design
Comfort – Road noise, leather, seats, shocks, engine noise, vibration, feel
Economy – Gas mileage, maintenance cost, resale value
Reliability – Proven track record, design, reputation, awards

Notice that the synonym for the above is S.P.A.C.E.R. **S**afety, **P**erformance, **A**ppearance, **C**omfort, **E**conomy and **R**eliability. Remember this acronym so you may use it when asking your clients, "What's most important to you? Safety, performance, appearance, comfort, economy or reliability?" I'll be referring back to this acronym throughout the book. Make sure you memorize the acronym, as it will be used in your fact-finding step when discussing the client's needs and wants.

Did you want a vehicle that was going to be viable for the next 3 to 5 years of your life? What were your plans for the next 3 to 5 years that necessitated a vehicle? How many miles were you planning on putting on that vehicle? What life changing events were you expecting in the next 3 to 5 years?

Did you fear being ripped off at the dealership? Making the wrong decision? Getting stuck in a commitment that you were less than 100% sure of fulfilling? That this vehicle might not last the term of the loan?

Once you're honest with yourself, you'll be able to get into the client's head and realize what they're thinking about when talking to you. Only then can you start to tailor your presentation and demonstration to address these fears as well as build up on their hopes. You can be selling the greatest vehicle in the world, but if it doesn't meet the client's needs or wants, it will quickly make that vehicle obsolete.

Doing a little research on the car maker that you work for to figure out what people are saying is an excellent way to find out people's hesitations regarding your brand. These are the fears they have. These fears can be turned around and transferred to hope if done properly. What types of clients are looking for the types of vehicles you're selling? What attracts the specific types of clients to your brand? After all, someone that's gas conscious probably won't be looking for a large truck or a fast sports car. Everybody buys based on their wants and needs, but who in particular is in the market to buy your product? This varies by the type of product your selling. People in the market for BMWs are different than people in the market for Hyundais. Their wants and needs will be completely different.

3a.   Types of Clients

There are as many varied types of clients as there are the various types of car models. All buyers have a type of vehicle in mind when they go shopping. Your job is to get them to reveal what's important to them and why. From there, you try to move them into a vehicle on your lot that best matches their wants and/or needs. Price and payments almost always come into play. People pick out a car with their emotions and buy based on logic.

> **Men –** Most men believe they know a lot about cars, financing and negotiations. Most men are logical so presenting them with their options with a practical explanation can win most over. Most men realize that this is a business and are willing to give in to negotiations. Men don't do as much research as women and usually go with their gut instincts on whether they like a vehicle or not. The major issue with men is that they need their wives to make a decision, especially a financial one. It is best to ask a man if his wife will also be needed to make a decision and what her preferences are before moving forward to discuss numbers.

Women – Women do a lot of research before buying a vehicle. So much so that most of the time they have information overload and their expectations become unrealistic. A lot of women come on the lot with a list of the different types of vehicles their looking for. They want to test drive five or six cars. For a salesman this will be a major waste of time as women don't make a decision right away. They have to think about if for a long time. Doing a thorough needs analysis is the best way to disarm this type of client and to keep from wasting your time test driving a vehicle she won't buy. Women buy 50% of the vehicles and have a say in 75% of the sales, so it's in your best interest to include women in all decisions as well as treat them with respect.

Families – Families with small children are one of the biggest challenges for any sales advisor. The kids are running around screaming and you really can't communicate properly with the buyers as to the benefits of the vehicle. Parents also bring kids along to see if the kids will be comfortable in the large SUV or minivan their shopping for. Kids are also a great excuse to use to tell the salesperson that they have a limited time at looking at vehicles to keep from committing to any sales decisions. A proper meet and greet and needs analysis should disarm most of the parent's objections and keep you from wasting your time. Never try to move the sales process forward without the wife unless the husband says it's okay. It's one of the things to ask during the needs analysis. Also ask if they have enough time to really look at all their options. If they give you excuses upfront about having to be somewhere in thirty minutes, then you know that most likely they won't want to test drive or talk numbers. In this situation, you need to do a great presentation so they make an appointment to come back, test drive and look at numbers.

Young People – Young people's main problem is lack of cash, credit and employment history. Young people know what they like and it's usually out of their price range. Style and performance are the main things they're looking for. A proper fact-finding as well as selling evaluation is needed to find these clients a vehicle they'll qualify for.

Older People – These individuals usually have excellent credit, good money down as well a reliable source of income. The key to selling to these types of clients is an excellent product presentation. They want to know that their dealing with a sales advisor who has excellent product knowledge and is a true professional. A little vehicle history also goes a long way with these types. Give these buyers good service and they'll buy.

Ethnicities – These types of clients have been in the country for about five years or less and are still unfamiliar with how business is done. They are from a third world country and they still have a third world mentality, meaning that whatever the price of the product is, they offer 50% of that price and go from there. Most actually think that the dealer is making $15,000 profit on a $17,000 vehicle. What their actually doing is testing the waters to see how far they can push you. Their favorite expression is "price too high". These types of clients already know exactly what they're looking for and it's usually a Toyota or Japanese vehicle. The key to dealing with these clients are good negotiation skills and a lot of patience.

Internet Clients – The internet has completely changed the car buying process. Information is at the tip of every client's fingertips. Internet clients like to only deal with the dealership through e-mail. They'll usually leave a phone number but are just looking for some information. The key to internet clients is responding to their e-mails within fifteen minutes. Also in your e-mail, you need to ask them a couple of questions so they respond and are engaged. The whole point is to get them to come to the dealership. With the ease of the internet, some internet sales leads will be dead leads because some people are just looking for information on a whim. It's your job to turn that daydream into a solid sale by building rapport and getting them into the dealership, even if that dream was a quickly fading day dream.

Phone Pops – Phone leads are an excellent source of sales lead. These clients took time out of their schedule to call in and seek information. A proper meet and greet is in order here first because that's all they know about you. You really need to set the stage and get them excited about the vehicle and/or dealership so they come into the store and test drive this vehicle. Like the internet client, your goal is to get the appointment for them to come and look at the vehicle.

What I used to do on phone pops was to get the clients phone number and then call them back about the vehicle they were interested in. "Yes, Mr. Client, I believe that vehicle is still available. We sell a lot of vehicles every day so I'm not 100% sure. Let me go to the lot and double check and I'll call you from the vehicle. I don't want you to drive all the way over here if the vehicle is sold. Is this number your calling from a good number to reach you?"

From there I would call them back on my cell phone and really build up the vehicle with all the features it had and the condition it is in. I would also ask about why they were searching for that vehicle. What else was important to them? I may be able to find them something comparable. I would always try to go for the appointment. The goal during the whole conversation is always to get an appointment for them to come in to the dealership because you can't sell a vehicle over the phone.

Illogical - Clients can at time be very self-centered, illogical, selfish, rude and have ulterior motives. There are many ways to handle these types of people but the most successful is to feed into their shortcomings.

If you notice someone being illogical, don't say "that's stupid" or "that doesn't make sense" or become sarcastic. This will only enrage the client and lose you the sale. Instead say things like, "I don't recommend that" or "most people come in thinking that way, but I've been doing this for a while now and I've found that this would work better." Make them feel smart and let them down that easily.

Selfish/Picky Clients – From time to time, you'll get clients who want this or don't want that...me, me, me....these clients are the most difficult to work with because they're so picky and have unrealistic demands in choosing a new vehicle. Worst yet, they have extremely unrealistic demands in choosing a used vehicle.

A used vehicle is what it is. You can't change the color, get a different trim or lower the mileage. There's a joke among sales advisors: "She wanted me to find her a car at the used car factory." If they want specifics on a vehicle, then you need to move them to a new vehicle. This will be the best way to get them as close as possible to everything they want.

Examples of objections and responses:

Client: *"I like this car but I wish it had leather."*
Sales Advisor: *"No problem, we can put leather in it for you, we have a wonderful shop that does great work."*
Client: *"For the same price?"*
Sales Advisor: *"No, but it won't be that much and we can roll it into the financing, this way you can get what you want."*
Client: *"This is the car I've been wanting but I want lower mileage."*
Sales Advisor: *"If we had the same exact vehicle with lower mileage, it would probably be several thousand more. If you look at the paint and interior of this vehicle, it has been very well taken care of. Don't worry about the mileage, whoever had it looked like they took very good care of it. Also all of our vehicles get checked out through the shop so you don't have to worry about any expected issues. If you want, you can have a mechanic take a look at it."*

Client: *"I like this model but I want the XLE trim."*
Sales Advisor: *"Why, what does the XLE have that this doesn't have?"*
Client: *"Sunroof, leather and a better stereo."*
Sales Advisor: *"If we had an XLE version, it would be a couple of thousand dollars more. Instead, we can have it installed for you at a fraction of the cost, and roll it into the financing."*
Client: *"The XLE also has a larger engine."*
Sales Advisor: *"If you drive this car you'll see that the current engine is more than adequate, and it gives you much better gas mileage."*

Or

Client: *"The other trim has a smaller engine, I want the gas economy."*
Sales Advisor: *"I understand, but what I've found out was that the difference in miles per gallon on this engine and the smaller engine are listed about two miles a gallon and the smaller engine's power isn't adequate for a vehicle such as this. In reality, you get better gas mileage on the larger engine because the smaller engine*

has to struggle to pull the vehicle around, while the larger engine doesn't need to struggle."

Rude Clients – At first, all you want to do to rude clients is to tell them to "get the hell off my lot." Not only will you lose all hope of making that sale, you'll probably get fired.

The best way to diffuse a rude client is to ignore their rudeness. Eventually in the car business, you'll get one of these below.

Client: "Look, we just want to be left alone and look. We don't need any help right now. If we need help, we'll come and get you."

Sales Advisor: "I understand, I truly do. The fact is the management doesn't like people walking around the lot unattended because we have stuff stolen all the time. So you guys look around and I'll be around in case you have any questions. We also have a bunch of cars in the back I can show you if you don't like anything you see here."

Client: "You car sales people are so shady. You'll say anything to make the sale."

Sales Advisor: "I don't know what your experience was with other sales people or dealers but a majority of my business is repeat or referrals from previous clients and this dealership has won numerous awards for client satisfaction. You can't get all that by being shady. I'm interested to know what happened to you to make you think like that?"

Clients with Ulterior Motives – Some of the really good negotiators will break down your vehicle to make it seem that they're not interested or that your price is way too high. They'll start this in the lot and test drive. The more they break down the more negotiating power they think they will have.

Remember, a smart sales consultant is trying to get the client to say "YES" and the smart client is trying to get the dealership to say "NO". By that I mean, you as a sales consultant are trying to get the client to agree to your price and terms by saying "Yes". The smart client is trying to find the lowest price you will go, the "No Price".

They'll do everything like telling you that they don't like the color, the trim, the interior or that they don't want a sunroof or leather. All the while, they really want the vehicle, but they are hiding their enthusiasm for it.

When you have multiple complaints about a vehicle and many remarks about how much they don't like the vehicle but are still willing to talk numbers and make an offer, you know you have an ulterior motive client. In this case, actions do speak louder than words.

Client: "I can get the same vehicle down the street for $2,000 less."

Sales Advisor: "Hmmm….(pause)….really, the same exact one? Same mileage and trim? No….we can't go down $2,000. I'll be happy to submit your offer to the management."

Here would be a good time to reiterate all the good selling points on the vehicle, as they'll quickly tell you everything they hate on it.

Client: "I don't like the color. I'd buy it in a heartbeat if it was red."
Sales Advisor: "Hmmm……(pause)….I understand, if I can make you a good deal, can you be color blind? Just kidding. It isn't a problem, we can paint it for you and roll the cost into the financing."

Client: "It rattles on the road."
Sales Advisor: "Hmmm….(pause)…..I understand, not to worry, I can have that taken a look at tomorrow. I don't think it's anything serious since all our cars go through a safety inspection."

Client: "I don't like the way it drives."
Sales Advisor: "What specifically don't you like about the way it drives?"
Client: "I don't know, all of it."
Sales Advisor: "Hmmm…(pause)…..I understand, Okay….maybe I can show you some other vehicles. Let's keep looking."
Client: "This is the only thing that catches my eye."
Sales Advisor: "Okay, but you must know that this vehicle has gone through a safety inspection as well as a road test and our mechanic did not find anything wrong with it. I can have them take a look at it again."

Client: "It has too many miles."
Sales Advisor: "Hmmm….(pause)…I understand, mileage isn't as important as the vehicle's history. As you can tell by the condition of the vehicle, it's been very well taken care of. Also if the mileage were lower, it would cost you several thousand more. Management priced the vehicle to reflect the mileage."

It's really important to acknowledge their arguments as genuine. Don't respond too quickly or you'll seem like you're a car salesman. Instead, keep silent for a moment and let them tell you everything they don't like about it. Let them really vent and play their game before responding.

When responding, don't forget to repeat what they've said so they too can hear it back and to acknowledge to them that you've heard what they've said. Respond, but always start with "I understand" or "you're right" or "fair enough" or "hmmmm….I can see that". Play into their game but try to overcome their objections.

If someone really tears your vehicle apart but he is still open to looking at numbers or pursuing more information on the vehicle, they're playing games to try to reduce the price as much as possible.

The most important thing to remember when dealing with clients is…….to never, never, never take it personally. It's just business. They're trying to get the best deal and your trying to get as much gross profit as possible.

There's nothing better than to sell a vehicle to someone that has many objections that you've overcome. Someone who has been rude, lied to you, played games with you, belittled your product and then ultimately, drives away in it.

"Success is the best Revenge"

Remember to keep your cool. This is a business transaction. Don't take it personally.

3b.   Universal Rules of Customer Service

When interacting with clients, a couple of things to keep in mind:

- **Treat them as a valued person** - Respect them as a valued human being, no matter how they are dressed or what they look like

- **Know and respect their needs** – Do a good fact-finding. Know exactly what they need and want

- **Spend at least 20 minutes with clients** – Some clients will seem very standoffish and not want to be assisted in any way. This negatively affects the sales advisor in many ways, including getting rid of them as soon as possible. The minimum amount of time you should spend with any individual is 20 minutes. Make any excuses you can to at least spend 20 minutes interacting and building rapport with them. This will allow you time to thaw the ice and get to their root objections or fears. You'll see that the 20 minutes quickly turns to one hour or more.

- **Exceed their expectations** –Treat them like family by going beyond what they expect. Under-promise and over-deliver.

- **Follow up** – Follow up with them every month to make sure they're happy with their purchase. This way they also keep you in mind if someone they know is looking for a vehicle. Following up just doesn't mean calling and saying "Hey what's up? How are you doing? How's the car?" You have to touch up on the notes you took of them when they were at the dealership. "Hey Mark, how have you been? Did you guys finally go on that vacation you were hoping for? How's Mary? Did she change jobs yet? You said you were selling your house, did you sell it?" Be a little bit more personal.

- **Do your best to fix any problems they may have** – Always be the go-to guy if the client has any problems.

- **Never take it personally** – Most clients are coming from a sense of fear. Never take it personally. They're just afraid.

3c.   Ethics

Like I wrote earlier, the image of the sales advisor in the automotive field is battered beyond recognition. This makes it very hard to build credibility and trust with the client.

If you want to become a professional, move up the chain, make that 6 figure salary and get that repeat and referral business that will catapult you to the next level, you're going to have to treat every client with dignity, respect and honesty. You're going to have to work toward the long term and build up your reputation.

Without repeat and referral clients, all you will ever do is take UPs. As anybody that's been in the business for a while will tell you, the selling rate of an UP is very low. Careers are built on repeat and referral business no matter which business you're in.

To build your book of repeat and referral clients, you need to treat everyone with honesty and respect. Never lie and never over-promise. In sales, the best course of action is to under-promise and over-deliver. If you just do this one thing, you can be assured that clients will have trust in you and your dealership for years to come. You also need to communicate to your clients that you don't intend to lie to them or promise them things you can't deliver.

A reputation of trust and honesty will go a long way toward furthering you career. A true professional is never dishonest or misleading or makes promises they know they can't keep. This is especially true in sales. To be successful in sales and especially in the role of an automotive sales advisor, your job is not to sell the vehicle to a specific client, but to all that clients' family and friends. The only way to do that is to give the client top-notch service.

I've worked at dealerships where sales advisors were making well over $250K a year from repeat and referrals alone. These sales advisors had built such a solid reputation within their community that they never took an UP and they would only work by appointment only. They were selling vehicles to generations of families.

If you want to become a true professional, make in excess of $100K a year and advance in your career, you need honesty and integrity to build a solid reputation of trust. You'll see in no time that clients will be calling looking to buy a car instead of you looking for clients.

Dishonesty also hurts the reputation of the dealership. There are many websites out there that track the reputation of various dealerships based on clients comments. You can use these websites to find dealerships that you want to work for as well as dealerships to avoid.

Summary: Target Audience – Fear of Loss, Hope for Gain

People fear dealers, that's why they over prepare before they come in to a dealership.

A vehicle is the second largest purchase in a person's life and understandably, they fear making a bad decision when it comes time to purchase one, like the time you were looking for a vehicle.

There are varied types of clients with varied needs and wants. Understanding them lets you customize how to treat them and address their fear, hopes, needs and wants.

In most cases, the client is operating out of fear. Never take what happens on the lot personally. It's business. The client is trying to quell their fears while the sales advisor is trying to build up on their hopes of a sale.

People want empathy to their situation. Empathy is understanding a client's feelings.

>   Listen – Give them undivided attention

>   Confirm – Ask Questions on important parts
>>   Summarize
>>   Rephrase
>>   Questions to clarify their feelings and situation and empathize.

>   Use words like "I understand", "I don't recommend", "That's smart", "You're right"

>>   Summarize "So you said", "If I understand you correctly"
>>   Rephrase
>>   Questions to clarify
>   Convey
>>   "I can understand that."
>>   "I can appreciate that."
>>   "I know what you mean."
>>   "I can see why you feel that way."
>>   "I see what you mean."
>>   "I understand how frustrating that can be."

Anticipate Objections. It's part of the business. Expect them.

To be truly successful, you must put yourself in the position of the client. Really think about what it's like to be sitting on the other side of the desk, the one making the commitment, the one that has to live with the choices they make in regard to picking out the vehicle.

4. Keys to Success – Attitude, Product Knowledge, Enthusiasm

In any business or profession, you need to be somewhat of a sale advisor. It doesn't matter the profession. If you interact with another human being, then you need to be able to sell. Sales permeates through all social interactions. Sell your ideas, knowledge, abilities, skills and yourself. To be successful in sales, especially a sales advisor in the car business, you need 3 very important attributes.

- **Attitude** – a professional attitude, a can-do attitude
- **Product Knowledge** – know enough about your product that you can match the features of your product to the wants and needs of your client
- **Enthusiasm** – nothing sells more than this skill. Enthusiasm for yourself, your product and your dealership are the emotions needed to build trust and excitement

A proper attitude, product knowledge and enthusiasm are the foundation of any successful sales career.

4a. Professional Attitude

What is attitude? The definition of attitude is "the mental or emotional position toward a fact or state." Therefore, what mental or emotional position should you hold as a sales professional?

The proper attitude would be to hold a professional attitude. A Professional is defined as "somebody with a high degree of skill or competence." Its synonyms are expert, skilled and, practiced.

A professional takes their duties and responsibilities very seriously. Success demands nothing less. This is your career and not just a job. You're working for long-term success and your attitude and actions should reflect that. Attitude as a professional sales advisor should convey confidence, competence and can-do.

No one wants to buy from someone who isn't confident, competent or able to get the job done. People want to deal with upbeat, positive, professional people. Attitude is part of your job. The client must know that their dealing with a professional. Your attitude will have a direct impact on your course of action in your career and life. You can either say, "Why me?" or, "No problem, I'll take care of it." That's your career. Your attitude should be to sell every prospect you come across. If they don't buy from you, then they'll buy from someone else. With a little determination, creativity and persuasion everyone can be sold eventually, maybe not today or tomorrow but someday.

A professional knows what is important, what their goals and objectives are and how to go about getting what they want. The goal and objective is a fulfilled and rewarding career. What's important is to work toward your goals and plans on achieving that rewarding career. The way to get that is to work toward being the best in your line of work. A professional also realizes all the pitfalls or obstacles from achieving those goals, like socializing instead of working toward your goal. Why would you show up to work for commission and waste away the time hanging out with the other sales people? You're there to make money. The only way to make money is to sell. The only way to sell is by talking to people who can buy.

That is the professional attitude you need to have. You know what you want and how to get what you want.

What are the attitudes that can catapult you past 99% of other sales advisors? What makes up a professional attitude?

Can-do Attitude: "No problem, I'll take care of it." You're going to come across problems in your life, career, marriage and family. Problems are a part of life. As a professional, you should already know that problems can be fixed if you concentrate on the solution and not the problem. You can't just throw your hands up and claim you're helpless. By choosing to concentrate on the solution instead of the problem, you're responding to the problem. When faced with a problem, ask yourself, "How can I fix, circumvent or go through this problem?"

We know the problem is there. Now what? When faced with a problem, asking yourself, "Why did this happen?" or, "How did it happen?" is unproductive. Okay, it happened. Now what? Instead, ask yourself, "What can be done to fix the situation so it never happens again?" or, "How can I make this right?" If you keep asking, "Why?" regarding a problem, you're concentrating on the problem. Instead, keep asking yourself, "What can I do to fix it?" or "How can I fix this?" or, "I will fix the situation!" or "I know I can fix this!"

These questions go through our heads all the time. Be more conscientious of the internal questions you're asking yourself every day. Change the question from "Why?" to "How I can fix this?" or, "What can I do to fix this?" or, better yet "I will fix this!"

In sales, you have to have an attitude that everyone is sellable if you can bring all the ingredients together. Your attitude should help you find which ingredients are missing. You need a "can-do" attitude. It's not, "Why can't I sell this person?" It's "What can I do to sell this person?"

Continuous Learning Attitude: You know that without knowledge there is no power. Just reading this book, you already know that you don't know everything. The world and the information within it are changing every day. A professional lives and breathes their career. In life and in the car business, to stay motivated, enthusiastic and to keep a winning attitude, you must never stop learning. Read motivational books, sales books and product knowledge books. Remember the last book you read? Did it open a flood gate of new ideas, imaginative scenarios and knowledge you didn't have before? Exercising you mind is fundamental to a successful life and career.

Continuous learning not only makes you a professional but also helps maintain your enthusiasm, motivation and product knowledge. Check **www.salesadvisor.com** for further sources of knowledge and experience.

Goal Oriented Attitude: You've come to terms that there many things in this world that are just distractions. If it doesn't affect your life and goal, it's not worth your energy. A professional has goals written down and actively work towards those goals. Properly written, achievable, track able goals motivate you to get up in the morning as well as tell you where you stand. Having something to work towards keeps you focused and motivated.

Positive Attitude: A positive attitude is crucial to a sales advisor In an industry where you hear "not now" from 75% of the people you talk to, it's very important to keep a positive attitude because you're not going to sell to everyone you meet right there and then, but if you have a positive and professional attitude, you'll sell to every one you meet; eventually.

Whether you're talking about yourself, a client or a fellow worker, always talk in positive terms and do your best to see the positive side in everything. Just this will make you appear to be much smarter and insightful than the next person. It will portray you in a more professional light rather than a whiner: a person who sees the potential in everything rather than the doom. It's very common practice and behavior to automatically see the negative in anything and everything. Being cynical is the norm these days. Don't shoot for common or mediocre. 20 years from now will you want to look back at mediocre or stellar?

When you see the positive in everything, you're training your mind to switch to problem solving mode. Practice by reading the newspaper every day and looking for the positive in every story. Positive speak is the language of the brain. Un-train your negative brain waves from thinking, "It is what it is" to, "It could be better If".

Responsible Attitude: Accept responsibility that it all depends on you and no one else. No excuses. "The only person an excuse satisfies is the one making it." No one else likes to hear an excuse. We are a product of our choices. So you need to decide: are you a victim or a success story? Successful people blame themselves and learn from their shortcomings or failures.

Attitude Toward Failure: In life and our careers, we learn through failure. Failure is never failure, but a learning experience. The only time it becomes a true failure is when we don't learn from it. It's a game we all have to play in life. It's not how many times you fail, but how much you learn from that failure. After a failure and/or success you have two options: quit or reassess how you failed and build on what you've learned to become even more successful next time. Learn to accept failure as part of your learning process. Recognize that it exists and prepare for it with every decision you make.

Genuine Attitude: In a sales advisor position, you must at all times maintain a helping and genuine attitude. Sales by its very nature is a service position. Not only is this good for your dealership, but even better for you. People aren't that stupid and can spot a fake person from a mile away. Be genuine as you are with your friends or family. Being fake or lying takes twice as much energy as being straightforward and real.

There have been many times where I was approached by a client to answer a question for them. In the course of the conversation, they mentioned to me that they were already working with another sales advisor. I proceeded to help them anyways because it was my job. Because I had properly tuned my attitude, product knowledge and enthusiasm, that client ended up coming back, asking for me and buying from me.

Big Picture Attitude: Being a professional requires more than having tunnel vision and only focusing on your needs. A professional also knows how to put themselves in the shoes of the client as well as their employer. By this, I mean that you must know what drives your clients. What their fears and hopes are? What drives them? As I mentioned before, knowing what your clients' needs and wants are allows you to tailor your message or pitch to the goals of your clients.

On the other side of the equation, you have to know what is expected of you from your employer as well. You must be able to see that this is a business, designed to make a profit not just for you but mainly for your employer. You should also know what their needs and wants are as well. What does an employer want in a sales advisor? They want a professional, someone who is reliable, dependable and smart, someone who will not only work hard to enrich themselves but also the business. Without a healthy profit, the business will die. If the business dies, then it will not need any managers, sales advisors or anybody else. At the very least, this is a business and you can't expect just because you're selling 20 cars a month that you deserve all the profit or all the attention. Even if you make enough money to open your own dealership, you can't ignore the needs of your client, your employees or the company's need for a healthy profit. As a business owner, in the beginning, you will need to be the one who has to sacrifice until the business takes off and can stand on its own two feet.

Understand the big picture: a business without clients, good employees and a healthy profit are doomed to an early death. Everybody in the organization needs to work toward making the organization as healthy as possible. This doesn't mean that you need to sacrifice your pay or let some unscrupulous manager steal your commission or accept being treated less than professional. Recognize that a lot of time, energy and resources have been put in place to open a dealership to make money. You being a great professional will be seen as an asset as opposed to being a liability.

How do we maintain our attitudes? – Doing all the above will help you maintain your attitude, which will have a direct impact on your life and career. We all have and always will have problems in life. It's our responses to the trials and tribulations that make us who we are.

Keeping good company is a sure fire way of maintaining your success. The top sales advisors are always the ones who have the best attitude, which helps them gain excellent product knowledge, which in turn affords them a high level of enthusiasm in their professions. Good attitude, product knowledge and enthusiasm are all contagious. It's one of the core tendencies of the overachiever. Stay away from people with bad attitudes. The saying, "You're a product of your environment" can't be truer than in the car business. Successful people flock together. Keep a proper attitude by associating with successful people. Attitude can be contagious. Don't associate with negative sales advisors or ones with a bad attitude.

Attitude is not an accident; it's a conscious decision we make each and every day of our lives to either live a successful life or a mediocre life.

Attitude breeds activity, which breeds income, success, accomplishments, enjoyment and a career.

A bad attitude will sway you to take actions that will lead to negative results because you don't perceive any benefits to them. A good and even great attitude will lead to positive actions, which will lead to positive, goal-oriented and professional results leading to success.

Bad attitude people constantly ask themselves questions that indicate that they have no control like, "Why is this happening to me?" Good attitude people ask, "What can I do to remedy this situation?" "Who do I need to talk to, to fix this situation, to meet my goals?" "How can I fix this?" Notice that the language changes to take on responsibility. This is the type of internal talk you need to have when dealing with problems. This type of dialogue will help you take on responsibility for your actions and outcomes and your life.

Use words that give <u>you</u> responsibility and **power** to your actions.

Live consciously!

It all comes down to <u>you</u>!

When you're in front of a client, you're on! Meaning, it's your time to shine. You must have a positive/can-do/genuine attitude at all times in the presence of a client. Your attitude determines your environment and your success and not the other way around.

This reminds me of a story:

One day a little boy was having a rough time with his classmates at school. He came home crying to his grandfather. After hearing his troubles, his wise grandfather put three pots of water on the stove. In one pot, he put an egg, in the other he put a potato and the other he put in a spoonful of coffee.

After 10 minutes, the pots started to boil.

He called his grandson over and he said, "In life, there will always be hard times. It is these times that make us who we are. It's up to us to choose which course of action we will take."

"You see in this pot I put in an egg. An egg is very liquid and soft but when it goes through hard times it becomes hard." Just like a person will become hard, anti-social, ornery, jaded or bitter when tested through hard times.

"In this other pot I have a potato. A potato is hard but when it encounters the hot water it becomes soft and even falls apart." This business requires a tough skin. A "some will buy, some won't, so what's next" attitude can help you go a long way. You can't let rejection get you down. Like the potato, some people will become soft and quit when faced with hard times instead of persevering.

The grandson looked at the third pot puzzled.

"In the third pot I have coffee. The coffee reacts completely different. Instead of becoming hard or soft, the coffee actually changes its environment instead of letting his environment change him."

"You see son, we decide how we react to our environment and not the other way around."

It's very convenient and easy to play the victim instead of taking responsibility in your life. Giving up responsibility and control is the much easier than thinking, planning and taking action. Words like destiny, fate and luck take away power from you to control your own future.

There is a saying that I've taken to heart in my life.

You deserve the life you have!

The point is, wherever you are in life, it was your <u>choices</u> that lead you to here and now. It <u>wasn't</u> destiny, fate or luck. To change things, you need to take responsibility and action.

Make or control your own destiny or fate

You can also log into **www.salesadvisor.com** to keep yourself motivated, educated and keep up your attitude. I will be posting up a motivation app where the program will download motivational material relevant to the car business daily to your phone or email.

## 4b.	Product Knowledge

In order to properly sell something, you need to know as much as possible about the product you're selling. More specifically, what are the benefits and features of your product and how do those features benefit the client? Imagine if every answer you were asked about a vehicle was, "I don't know."? Do you think the client will have confidence in you? In your product? In your dealership? Would you buy from someone who knew nothing about the product they were selling? Of course not.

A professional attitude is a can-do attitude showing that you can help clients with whatever they need. Product knowledge builds confidence in you, your dealership and your brand. This is where you connect them with the vehicle that will meet their every need and want. Your product knowledge will help address their fears, concerns and hopes.

There will be times when clients will stump you with a question: exact gear ratio of a model, size of the brakes or the material the seats are made of. It's important that you don't lie when stumped. Instead just tell them, "Good question, I'm not 100% sure about the answer to that but I'll find out for you." You don't want to lose credibility by lying.

Extensive product knowledge is necessary to build trust and confidence and to properly match the client with a product that will benefit them the most.

Most dealerships require new advisors to go through some sort of product training, usually consisting of watching some videos and then taking a multiple choice test. In my experience, these training tools were insufficient at the least. Most of the questions were very basic and common sense. They gave some information, but not much detail.

Obviously in the beginning, you can't know the specifics of each and every model. The best course of action in the beginning is to talk to your manager and the other seasoned sales advisors.

1. Which models are the dealerships bread and butter? For example, if you're selling Toyotas, the top selling models are the Camry, Corolla and the Prius because gas mileage is becoming such a huge issue.
2. What are the typical questions people ask regarding these models?
3. Is there anything special that you need to know about these specific models?
4. Are there any specific financial incentives on these models?
    a. Typically all dealerships should give you a sheet of financial incentives for various models each month. It's a great selling point.
5. What are the biggest selling points of the various models? What features and benefits are the typical buyers of these models looking for?

You should ask these questions first of your managers and then of the seasoned sales people. Don't be shy and don't think that you'll look dumb. You're just reinforcing your own knowledge and you'll look like a true professional in front of your managers and coworkers.

Obviously, if you're working for just a used car dealership then your product knowledge would consist of what you have in your inventory, price, mileage and the condition of the vehicles. You will use this product knowledge along with good fact-finding on the client's needs and wants to sell your vehicles.

The point of having a high-level of product knowledge is to properly match the client's needs and wants with your product. How do those features benefit the client?

Product knowledge also means knowing your inventory, knowing what used vehicles you have on the lot, which ones your dealer received in trade as well as some choice selling features like condition, year, mileage and trim.

Here are other sources to help increase your product knowledge. Keep in mind that the client is also doing research on most of these places so it's to your benefit to know what they're looking at.

Company Website – the maker's website is the best source you will find on each model's specifications. They also make it very easy because they have side-by-side comparisons of each model's various trims. You can easily figure out what the difference is between the "S" trim, the "LE" trim and the "XLE" trim.

Consumer Websites – The client will be doing their research on more than one website. They may start at the company's website, but they usually migrate to other independent sites like www.cars.com, www.edmunds.com, consumer reports or www.autotrader.com. These websites not only have articles about the various makes and models, but also pricing

47

information, which will give you a good idea of what the client is thinking about when negotiating.

Competitor Websites – Looking at other similar dealerships' websites can give you a good idea of what other dealers in your area are selling their vehicles for. You bet that the client is also looking at all the dealer's websites in your area before deciding where to go to buy one. It's to your advantage to know the deals being offered by your competition. Read the fine print on these sites because there is always a catch to low prices that you can use to overcome the price objection to potential buyers.

Brochures – Every new car dealer has brochures that they give out to clients. Most older car buyers don't like to use the internet and rely more on printed material. Study the brochures of the various models to learn the verbiage you should use in your presentation and demonstration. They're also a great source of information on vehicle specifics. They also serve as an excellent visual aid source during the negotiation phase. You can open one in front of the client while you're in negotiations to remind them of the features and benefits again as well as review the pictures of the vehicle.

Review Websites – Any website that has articles on vehicles will usually have a review section. The review section will probably have a rating system like stars, so a specific model might get 3 out of 5 stars. It's useful to read these reviews to see what people are saying about your make and specific model. There are sites that not only rate the make and model of vehicles, but also sites that rate specific dealerships. You should really read the comments on these websites to see what the specific models best selling points are as well as their weaknesses. Google Maps and Dealer Rater are 2 sites that come to mind that review specific dealerships.

Test Drive – Sometimes to really understand something, you need to experience it yourself. When it's slow, get yourself a dealer plate and test drive the various models on the street and freeway. Go for a ride. Put the vehicles through their paces in a safe area. Test for things that an average client would be looking for. Test the various engine sizes, the various bells and whistles and trim.

Experienced Sales Advisors – This is your greatest source of information. Find the top sales advisors in your dealership and casually ask them some of the questions outlined above. Befriend them, take them out to lunch and hang out with them. They say you are a product of your environment, so keep good company as if your career depended on it. Also ask them what objections they hear the most and how they address those objections.

I urge you to make a spreadsheet of the models you sell by breaking down the different types of trim that they offer and note down what makes them different in regard to exterior, interior, safety and price. This way, you can get a good feel for the major differences each model has in regard to the various trim. Make a note of the major differences for each sub category, like fog lights only come standard on one trim, a bigger engine comes in the 2 highest trims, etc.

For example, you might put together a worksheet of what the highlights or major selling points are of certain models as well as some common facts. Spend some time of your downtime on the websites to build your education and expertise. You'll be investing in your knowledge and career.

Used vehicles are similar to new vehicles when it comes to product knowledge. Of course you don't need to be as detailed or thorough as you do with new vehicles. It would be a waste of time to check the details of every used vehicle you have on the lot. These are steps you need to take for the top 5 or 10 used vehicles you have on the lot.

Review Websites - You still need to look up to see what other people are saying about that particular vehicle. Test driving all the vehicles will be impractical because you will only have one of that kind. Test-driving is practical if someone is coming in to look at that particular vehicle and you want to make sure everything works properly.

Pricing – You still need to do research on what similar vehicles with similar conditions and mileage are selling for to figure out where your vehicle stands. Find websites or ads that reinforce your price so you can use it in the negotiating phase.

History Report – If you have access, try to find the history report of the vehicle. Look for positives in the history like one owner, lots of maintenance records and no accidents. Find any information you can to support your position that it's a great vehicle.

Inspection Report – This report will give a detailed report of what was done on the vehicle before it was put on the lot. Most dealerships as part of their safety and refurbishment process will send used vehicles through the shop to fix major problems, especially safety issues. The shop will generate a report that will document all their findings. Any vehicles that you think still have major issues should be presented to the management for repair. Any vehicle with major issues that the management won't take care of should be avoided in presenting to the client or disclosed fully.

This will also tell you that the dealership that you're working for is not conducive to a sales professional if they allow shoddy vehicles on their lot. Any dealer that tries to sell vehicles in need of repair is risking their client's safety and should be reported to the proper authorities. These types of dealerships don't stay in business for long and you shouldn't work for them either.

Inspection – You should personally inspect the vehicle for any odors, stains, present ability or bad sounds. You don't want to try to move the client to a particular vehicle only to find out that the seats have stains and it smells like someone smoked in the vehicle, or worse that the vehicle smokes.

In order to build confidence with clients, you must know what you're talking about. Product knowledge is vitally important in building confidence and trust. A true professional not only knows everything about their products but also more importantly, knows how those features can benefit the client.

4c.   Enthusiasm

Defined as "passionate interest in or eagerness to do something". The key word in the definition is "passionate". It's what keeps love affairs hot, artists creative, business people leaders in their industry, arguments heated and happiness in life.

I mentioned earlier that attitude, product knowledge and enthusiasm are the cornerstone of every successful sales advisor. Enthusiasm is the heart and soul of every sale. It's the emotion or passion in your presentation. It's the excitement in your presentation.

This one attribute can catapult you past even the most experienced and seasoned sales advisors. Enthusiasm in one's self, dealership and product is contagious and can permeate through the entire sales process. Making it a big part of your pitch gives credibility and excitement to your sale.

It's the open secret of all sales people. It communicates your belief, trust and pride in your product. This lets your client know that it's the best product out there and you, as a knowledgeable sales advisor, have done your research and whole heartedly believe it to be the best in the market.

Enthusiastic sales advisors are unforgettable to their clients. When they're ready to buy, they'll buy from you. You've built enough excitement and trust that they remember when the time comes to make that purchase.
When you first start at a dealership, everything seems new to you. You take in the motivational talk of the managers, the promise of high income, the ease of selling a vehicle and the promise of special sales incentives that can push you over the six-figure salary mark. All you have to do is go out there and sell.

"That's all?" You ask yourself. Seems easy enough. You get out of bed running. You can't wait to get up. You can't wait to go on a test drive. Your first month you sell 15 cars and you think to yourself, it wasn't easy but I got there. I worked for it. Next month I'll hit 20.
Slowly and surely, you start to talk to other 5-car-a-month sales advisors about how crappy the pay is, how crappy and unfair the management is, how crappy the clients are, how bad the sales people are treated at that dealership, and how much greener it is at other dealerships.

Slowly all this negative talk creeps in and you soon find yourself selling only cars a month. What happened? You went from 15 cars to 5 cars. You used to look forward to work. You couldn't wait to sell, now it's a slough to get into the dealership.

The difference between the first and second month is that the first month, the sales advisor had tremendous enthusiasm and was fearless in their attitude to selling a vehicle. The second month their enthusiasm waned in the face of criticism and negativity. The first month the sales advisor was just excited about the position and imagined all the money he was making as well as he was excited to talk to people. The second month, all the negativity of his fellow sales people crept in as well as the attitudes of some of the potential clients.

What happened is, you let your environment zap your enthusiasm. You didn't associate with best people. You kept bad company with the negative sales people. You weren't positive.

Who do you blame for all this? You blame yourself. This was a product of our choices and you allowed all this negative talk to interfere with your passion, attitude and motivation.

When clients don't see enthusiasm in your selling and in your product, then they won't be so excited about purchasing from you or your product.

Every green pea experience=s this enthusiasm drain without realizing it. To be a true professional, you need to realize that to get people to trust you, you must convey high levels of enthusiasm in yourself, your dealership and your product. Enthusiasm sells trust and confidence by using emotion.

The major benefit of enthusiasm is that it sells what you're saying.

I've hired many sales advisors that I managed to motivate to go out and sell like mad to make a great income. The first month their numbers were through the roof, selling an above average of 15 cars or more. After the first month, their numbers settled to that of an average sales advisor. What happened was that they allowed all the negativity, the stress and the politics creep into their heads. They went from taking this as a professional career to a job, an $8,000 a month position to a $2,500 a month position. The difference was that they weren't as excited as they once were for the position, which showed in their presentation, attitude and product knowledge to clients. Their enthusiasm had dropped significantly.

When that happens, there are only 2 things to do.

1. Lay them off
2. Somehow increase their enthusiasm or motivation

I didn't like to lay anybody off who had potential, especially, If I saw professionalism and a good work ethic.

Increasing motivation was another matter entirely.
Several things can be done to maintain or regain your motivation and enthusiasm. These can also help you maintain your attitude.

1. **Keep Good Company** - Stop associating with the mediocre and negative sales agents. They'll bring you down as well as negatively affect your attitude. They've already demotivated themselves and it shows in their numbers, which means that they won't be at the dealership much longer.

2. **Continuous Learning** – This is a great way to regain your enthusiasm, attitude and motivation. Keep this book handy and refer to it at least once a month on the various subjects to get you back on track. You don't just have to read on car sales. Educating yourself about anything that interests you will help you increase your enthusiasm for life and your work. When you learn, you get motivated. Motivation leads to enthusiasm. Enthusiasm leads to a better attitude. Attitude and enthusiasm lead to an increase in performance in life and in your occupation. When you learn, your creative juices begin to flow, your imagination gets sparked, your hopes and dreams begin to

develop and your self-worth increases. Check **www.autosalesadvisor.com** for the latest on maintaining your enthusiasm and attitude.

3. **Perspective** - We're all going to get stressed and unnecessarily worry about things that don't affect us or things we can't change. When stressed, you need to take a step back and gauge the importance of the stress factors, how they affect you and how you can remedy those stressful situations.

    Pinpointing your stressors is the first step.

    What is causing you so much angst?
    How does this affect your life in 1 month, 6 months, 1 year? If it doesn't affect your life in 6 months, then most likely it's something you don't need to stress about.
    What is the remedy to this stressor? Can this stressor be resolved by selling more vehicles? By making more money? Go get your enthusiasm up and sell more cars.
    Have problems with fellow coworkers? Let management deal with it.
    Jealous of another sales advisor? Sell more cars.
    This also includes being abused by management.

4. **Motivational Speakers** - Get yourself pumped up by listening to motivational tapes and seminars. These days with smart phones, mp3 players and CDs, we can listen while driving, working out or just relaxing at home. Look up motivational speakers on the internet and find out which ones are good and find their tapes, CDs or mp3 files. Get a new perspective on life and your occupation to get you out of the rut that you're in. Look up some great motivational speakers on YouTube.

5. **Fake It Until You Make It** - Forcibly, up your enthusiasm when with clients. It's a great skill to have to turn this skill on and off when need be.

6. **Take a Break** - People get burned out in any job they do if they do it for long periods of time. Your paycheck is dependent on your enthusiasm . If you're burned out, it means you don't have any enthusiasm left. Take some personal time to recharge, reflect and reorganize, and redirect your energy toward what's important in your life. Put things back in perspective. If something isn't going to affect your life a year from now, then maybe it's not worth worrying about.

7. **Change Your Attitude** - Your attitude encompasses everything in the sales process. A good professional attitude will help you realize that losing your enthusiasm is dangerous to the selling process and that it's essential to a successful sales advisor.

8. **Set Goals** - With goals you have a road map, markers and a destination. Your progress toward your goals can be used to increase your enthusiasm. Working toward achievable goals that you can track can really help you maintain your enthusiasm and

attitude because at any given time, you know where you stand and what you need to do. Not only do you know where you are heading, but you also know what you need to do and the consequences of not meeting your goals.

9. **Have a Slogan for Yourself** - Example: "If it doesn't make me money, it doesn't matter." This way at any given time, you could chant your slogan to regain your perspective.

10. Log on to www.**salesadvisor.com** to see what other successful sales advisors are doing to increase their motivation, attitude and enthusiasm.

Enthusiasm makes you memorable and leaves a positive impression, more so than the product. Enthusiasm is contagious to the client. Like a performer on stage, you're on. When in front of the client, the successful sales advisor is ready to perform and sell themselves, the dealership and the product. Enthusiasm can turn a green pea into a superstar and lack of it can turn a superstar into a mediocre sales advisor. Enthusiasm is passion: passion for your product, your job, your life and your career. It's the open secret weapon of the sales process.

It's the key attribute all sales advisors must have to successfully get to the next level. It's management's job to know how to build enthusiasm in their sales force.

Enthusiasm is that push that some clients are looking for in making a decision to buy from you rather than someone else. It helps build trust and confidence in you, the sales advisor, by showing them how excited you are about your product and showing them that they'd be fools not buy this vehicle. It conveys a message to them that this person is in the business and knows what he's talking about.

Enthusiasm builds conviction into your pitch and selling points. You need to utilize it in your presentation especially when talking about how the features benefit the client's needs and wants. The number one reason people buy is because they like the sales person. Enthusiasm builds emotion into your relationship.

4d.   Other Keys to Success

Although there isn't one key to success, most of these tips and rules below fall under having a professional attitude, product knowledge and enthusiasm. Your experiences will direct you to what works and what doesn't in life and your career. These are the foundation of success and should be added to, based on your style, experience and talents.

1. **Always Be on Time for Work** - Nothing shows professionalism in the eyes of ourselves, clients, management and coworkers more than being on time and having a respect for someone else's time. Being early for your shift shows that you care for your job and displays professionalism. "If you're not 10 minutes early, your 10 minutes late." This is a mantra I tried to instill in my sales force.

Being on time or early shows pride in your work and your career. This shows initiative, responsibility, value and maturity to your management.

I knew a very young kid at one of the dealerships that I worked who was always early to his shift and left a little late after his shift. Management noticed this kid's promptness as well as his dedication. His numbers weren't that great but he was solid when it came to work ethic. When it came time for management to hire a new assistant sales manager, people who had been there for years were passed up and this kid was promoted, all because of his work ethic. Just think, if you owned a dealership and needed a sales manager to keep an eye on things, would you promote the slackers or someone you can depend on?

Most will tell you to be 30 minutes early so you can walk the lot, review your daily schedule, organize your calls and to talk to management. 30 minutes is a little overkill unless you work at an incredibly busy dealership where you won't have time to walk the lot, talk to management about new inventory or organize your day.

I too recommend 30 minutes prior to your shift but 10 minutes should suffice. You'll have plenty of time to walk the lot after the sales meeting and to talk to management during the sales meeting.

2. **Time Management** - As a sales advisor, your job and paycheck depend on you driving sales. While at work, you need to spend as much time as possible driving sales, prospecting and building up your pipeline. Whatever tasks you're doing, you need to ask yourself how they are increasing your sales. How does this expand your pipeline? How does this coincide with your mission statement? Any time used to generate sales as well as making a sale is considered a very good use of your time.

3. **Prospect Each and Every Day** - Your job is selling. To do that, you need clients. You must get in the mindset of thinking a week or 2 in advance. Just because you sold 2 cars today, doesn't mean the battle is over. What have you got going on tomorrow? You can also prospect from people you just sold a car to. "Do you know anyone else looking for a vehicle?" You must put together a plan on bringing in potential clients every day. You can't rely on walk-in traffic. Walk-in traffic is not very dependable or reliable. It's your business and you must prospect to find sales every day. You can't wait for things to happen because that's what a newbie does. You must participate and take action. Take to heart the prospecting section in this book as a good starting point.

4. **Know Your Inventory** - Every successful sales advisor knows exactly what their selling. The major difference of the car business is that inventory changes every day. Out of eighty cars on the lot, 10 to 15 cars get sold every day and another 10 to 15 become available for sale. You as a professional must check your inventory every day to keep on top of the changes, so when a client says, "I'm looking for a manual truck with low miles," you can say., "I just got one in, let me show you."

5. **Plan and Prepare to Sell Every Day** - There are days in a month. Plan on selling a vehicle every day. Doesn't mean it's going to happen, but tell yourself that you're going to do it. After a while, you'll see that you'll get closer than anyone else in the dealership.

6. **Review the Day** - At the end of very shift, sit and ponder what happened with the people you talked to. What could you have done differently to close the sale or sell them a vehicle? What could you have done to make them your special friend so they want only do business with you? Why didn't they buy? Why did they buy? What could you have done to change the outcome? What did you do to make the sale? What did you do right? What did you do wrong?
What step in the process did you get to before the client left? This is called a post mortem.

7. **Follow Up** – Follow up with everyone you've talked to during the day. What happened to the people you talked to last week or last month? Did they buy or are they still in the market? If you got their contact information, be sure to call them up and thank them for coming in and let them know to contact you if they have any questions or concerns. There is plenty of opportunity in former clients.

8. **Continuous Learning** - Information is constantly changing. To be a true professional, you must be ahead of the curve and educate yourself of information that can achieve your goal. Continuous learning has so many benefits, but the most important is that it keeps you motivated and enthusiastic; 2 traits that are key to a successful sales career and life. Log into **www.autosalesadvisor.com** to increase your learning knowledge, motivation, attitude and enthusiasm.

9. **Contain Your Bad Habits** - We all have bad habits that aren't detrimental to anyone but ourselves.

> Cursing – Eliminate this bad habit from you daily life. Cursing may make you feel better, it may be a good avenue of release from your stress, help you connect with other co-workers or may make you feel more masculine. It does nothing to your image as an articulate, smart, professional sales advisor: not to your fellow workers, managers and definitely not to clients.

> Smoking – I would say that over 60% of sales advisors I have come across smoke. I don't know what it was, either because they had the freedom to go outside whenever they wanted to, the stress, the long stretches of time between clients or because sales people used it as a social way to get together. I would also say that 98% of the clients didn't like the smell of cigarette smoke. Even if you smoke one cigarette a day, that smell stays with you all day and clients can smell your morning cigarette late into the evening. Covering it up doesn't help. This is a tough habit to give up, but do your health a favor and quit for at least a week and soon the urge becomes less and less pervasive. Keep in mind the overwhelming power tobacco has on an individual. It is a drug and should be respected as a drug. In all cases that I've come across, tobacco was much stronger than the individual. It is better

never to start, but if you do smoke, respect the power of this leaf. Quit for a week and you'll notice the urge getting less and less. Respect it to the point of never picking up another cigarette again.

<u>Talking Loudly</u> – In a dealership clients are within earshot of the sales advisors all day. Imagine a client overhearing you talk about how you worked over another client, or about last night's adventure at the bar or how you engaged in an illegal activity and got away with it. Sales advisors become comfortable with each other and tend to treat the dealership like a social club. It's very unprofessional for clients to hear such things, it makes the dealership look even worse.

10. **Love the One You're With** - Another key to success is knowing and believing that each and every opportunity you have must be exploited to its utmost. What this means is the client that you're with is the one who you should give your most undivided attention. It's better to spend five hours with one client who is going to buy, rather than thirty minutes with ten clients who can't or won't. Imagine if you sold a car a day. You would have thirty sales or more a month. Now realize that you get to talk to around five people a day; each individual should get your undivided attention until they say no, or no thanks, or not now, or walks away. Even then, if you've spend any considerable amount of time with them, you know that you've left an impression that you can later call them to touch base with them. Although some say thirty minutes is too long when you know someone can't or won't buy, I say it's a good number to shoot for, to be memorable and leave an impression on someone.

Make sure that you spend at least 20 to 30 minutes with each person regardless of their situation or ability to purchase at that moment. Doing so will leave a good impression on them and make you that much more memorable. Find any excuse you can to spend at least 20 to 30 minutes because some clients will come on the lot in a hurry to view your inventory and leave in about 10 minutes giving you no time to make an impression.

11. **Appearance Does Make the Man/Woman**
Be properly dressed – dressed for success. Look and act the part of a professional.
Stay in shape - This helps with your appearance as well as your overall health and energy.

Head up and proper posture – Talk and walk like a confident professional.

Smile a lot – People like to be around positive, happy people.

Get enough sleep - Always appear fresh. It's hard, but you have to get enough rest.

12. **Proper/Professional Attitude** – People like to be around positive, successful people. Even if you haven't made a sale in 2 weeks, you still have to stay completely positive. Whenever a client asks you, "How's business?", your response will always be, "Great, never better. We're having a hard time keeping stock of vehicles on the lot." Being positive like this works to your advantage in many ways.

One is that people like to deal with upbeat, positive people. People like to work with winners because they know that they can get things done. Negative people are stuck too much in the mundane and they give up too easily and in most people's minds, are a waste of time to deal with.

The second reason being positive helps is that when it comes time for negotiations, the client won't think that the dealership is desperate to take any low ball offer. They know that if business is good, the dealership isn't in a rush to sell and can afford to wait for a better offer on their vehicles. Even if they don't ask you, "How's business?", you should still bring up how great business is. Even if it's garbage, you need to stay positive. It's part of your job to make the client feel good about the dealership, about you and most importantly about the vehicle that their picking out.

The third is that you can use this along with "the big sale" to change the client's perception that there isn't a better time to buy than right now. You, the client, are the luckiest person in the world and you're at the right place at the right time. You'd be a fool not to buy right away.

13. **Have a Nickname or an Easy-to-Remember Name** – Having a name like Mir was very hard when I was selling vehicles in Phoenix, AZ where most of the people weren't open minded and they didn't like people who didn't meet their specific mold. Easy-to-remember names helps someone become more memorable and can be used to associate with something happy and positive like the nickname "Coach" or "Griz". You don't have to change your name, but having a memorable easy-to-remember name can help you sell and become more endearing to various clients. You can derive an easy-to-use name from your current name or a name that can be tied to something positive by shorting your name or finding something similar to your name.

14. **Proper Product Knowledge** - How does the vehicle that you picked out for the client meet the client's wants and needs? What are the benefits of the features to the client? Is your client looking for high gas mileage? Why does showing them a V8 truck benefit them? Why does a hybrid benefit them? Your client also mentioned safety. What safety features does the vehicle have and how do they benefit him and his family? How can this vehicle improve his life? How does your vehicle meet or better yet exceed their needs so that they can't live without it? A little knowledge or education can take you a long way.

15. **Use Stories** – Stories can be used to connect with your clients on a deeper level, to build rapport and to build trust. Keep them simple but full of emotion. Make yourself stand out from the other 20 salesmen who they've talked to or will talk to. Use stories from your childhood or from previous clients. The key is to find common ground, build rapport and trust. Stories remind the clients that we, as sales advisors and sales managers, are normal people just like them. We're just doing our jobs. We have families, responsibilities, dreams and ambitions. During the meet and greet and fact-finding, we find out whether the clients has kids, a wife, a house, family, animals and where they're from. We can then use these bits of information to quickly tell a story that our life is similar to theirs. Be genuine. Don't

go overboard with your indulgences or you'll be found out as a fake. Learn to tailor your stories to the situation. This is a big part of rapport building.

16. **Have a Plan and Set Goals** - You and everyone else has heard of the mantra, "If you fail to plan, then you plan to fail." And, "People don't plan to fail, they fail to plan." In anything you do in life, you must have some sort of a plan. Having a goal and a plan on achieving those goals can help you stay motivated and on the right track. Sit down and write your long term (5 years or more) goals. Then break those down by priority to achieve your long term goal. You can even break the year plan to a monthly plan so you can always see where you are on your road map. There are tons of tools on the internet that can help you track your goals and plans. Goal setting is the subject of the next section.

17. **The Right Employer** – In chapter 2 we discussed the business of automotive sales. Every dealership will be different in how it conducts its business. Some dealership groups like to hire, chew up and spit out sales advisors like they were sun flower seeds. Other dealership groups like to foster talent because they know that going through sales advisors is very expensive in terms of training, lost clients and lost sales. You must conduct your due diligence in terms of reputation of your employer, otherwise you'll be jumping from dealer to dealer, all the while starting from scratch every time. It's best to go and interview the sales advisors at various dealerships before applying. In order to be successful, you should first find a dealership that you can grow with. Jumping from dealership to dealership resets everything you've worked for at the previous dealership, including you building your book of clients, reputation with management and product knowledge.

    You should first find the make of vehicles that you like to target dealerships in your area that sell that brand. Do an internet search as to the reputation of these dealerships. After that, go to these dealerships you're most interested in, once in the morning and once in the evening to grill a couple of sales advisors to get insight on working there. If you can help it, find dealerships that pay flats, that you can make at least $500 per unit or more. Choose dealerships that have huge inventories or access to lots of vehicles, especially used. Some dealership groups are better than others in the way they treat their employees. Stay away from dealerships that chew up and spit out sales advisors because no matter the pay plan, you'll be chasing your money long after you leave that dealership.

    Look for a dealership that you can grow with and succeed in. You can't be much of a success jumping from dealership to dealership as you will be starting from zero every time you do.

    How do you choose what to sell and to whom? What type of client demographics is your personality best suited for? Who do you want to sell to? Low income, mid income, high income clientele? Buy here, pay here, low credit type people? Average credit people? High credit score people? Economy brand or high line brand? What is the image of the dealership you want to work for?

Look them up on the internet: www.dealerrater.com is one. Any particular brand that you like? During the writing of this book around mid 2013, Hyundai was the hottest seller on the market as they had a tremendous warranty, stylish vehicles, very reasonable prices and a solid reputation for quality. It might take 6 months to a year until you figure these things out. There's always a learning curve when someone is new to an area or industry. Talk to as many sales people as possible to find the right fit for you.

Although lower income buyers only care about the payments and not necessarily the cost of the vehicle, they are a lot harder to finance and will usually qualify for 20% or higher interest on their loans. Higher income or high line buyers are a lot savvier. Although they have better credit, they also know how to deal. They will usually beat up the dealership to within pennies of the invoice of the vehicle. High line buyers usually have better credit scores and are easier to finance, but they're a lot smarter and know their value.

What brands do you like? What brands sell in your geographic area? What about gas and energy prices? I doubt BMW or Mercedes will sell well in rural America, with nothing but farms around. It's also not realistic to be successful in selling Chevy Trucks in San Francisco.

Do your research on the internet of the reputation of the dealership you're interested in. Really dive into the clients' comments. Does the dealer service department get good or bad reviews? What about the sales department? Researching what the clients say is one thing but what does the employees say about working there? The dealership can be a great dealership to its clients but can treat its employees in a less than professional manner.

I worked for a dealership that had extremely high client ratings but when it came to its employees, it had extremely high turnover, was constantly making up revenue lost on deals from the sales advisors pay, had a reputation for screaming and yelling during sales meetings and had a degrading management attitude toward its employees. This dealership group was notorious among sales people of treating their employees the worst. It was part of their business model. They had the worst reputation in the industry and when talking to any sales person at any dealership, they would warn against working for that dealership or that group of dealerships. Last, I checked if that dealership was looking for salesmen under general labor on Craigslist, as most professional sales people avoided them like the plague.

Visiting with the dealerships you're thinking about working for and talking with several of the sales advisors is a sure way to avoid working for a dealership or dealership group like the one above. Make several visits and talk to several sales advisors to get a good feel for the dealership. Ask them how they like working there. How many sales advisors do they have? How many cars does the dealership sell a month? This will give you a good idea of what you can expect to sell by the average each sales advisor sells. If they sell two-hundred vehicles a month and they have 20 sales people, that means that each sales person should be averaging around 10 cars a month. Not all sales people will sell that many, maybe a few will sell a lot but most will be average, meaning 8 to 10 cars a month or less in this situation. Remember that the average sales percentage is around 12% for mediocre sales advisors and 20% to 35% for stellar sales advisors.

What's the pay plan like? What do you get paid on?   What is the management like?

Who gets the internet leads? The internet has been a growing source of sales and leads for most dealerships. It's to your benefit to get as many internet leads as possible. If the internet leads get sent to a special internet department, then that's the department you want to go into. These leads are much better than UPs or walk-in's, as these people are doing research and are in the market.

I never understood why dealerships had a separate internet department and a floor sales force. These are basically the same sales people. The timeliness of the response can easily be managed by sending out the lead to available sales members and making sure management is tracking response time. The only drawback to spreading out the internet leads to the general sales force is that the managers will usually give the leads to their favorite sales people so new advisors who haven't yet proven themselves with the managers will usually feel neglected, which results in a breakdown in group cohesiveness and a political environment.

Who gets phone leads? Phone leads are another source of hot leads, hotter than an internet lead. This also tends to become political if not handled properly.

What's the dress code like? Do you have a wear a long sleeve shirt, pants and a tie or do they allow you to wear shorts? Do you always have to wear a jacket? It's important to be comfortable since you are running around all day, but even more important is to dress for success. Be neat, clean, proper and professional. Dress for success.

How are commissions calculated? Front end profit, which is the selling price minus invoice, minus dealer pack, plus/minus trade-in allowance? How much does the dealership pack their used vehicles? Pack is the overhead cost the dealership attaches to every vehicle or reconditioning, clean up and maintenance while on the lot. Invoice is the amount paid for the vehicle. Trade in allowance is the profit or loss on the trade-in. Suppose you sell a vehicle for $20,000 and the invoice on the vehicle is $17,000, so you now have $3,000 in profit. The pack is $1,000, so now you have $2,000 in profit. If there is not a trade-in involved, then at 25% commission you just made $500 on this deal. But if there is a trade-in involved, then if the trade is valued at $5,000 and the owner sells it to the dealership for $4,000, then that's an extra $1,000. So now you have a total of $3,000 in profit, but if the owner wants $6,000 for the trade-in, then you just lost another $1,000 in profit and so now you only have $1,000 in profit and your commission goes to $250. Commission on $3,000 is $750.

How much does the dealership pack each vehicle? Some tell the sales advisor, "We don't pack any vehicle." Don't believe them. All dealerships pack vehicles. Some give you ridiculous numbers like we only pack vehicles $250. The range is somewhere between $800 to $1500. The higher the number, the faster you should run from this dealership.

How much does the sales advisor get from the back end profit? Back end profit is the profit from financing. The sales advisor usually gets a small amount from the back end: usually around 3% to 10%. If finance can sell the client products with a profit of $1,000, then the sales advisor will usually get anywhere from $30 to $100.

Is this a finance store? What this means is that the dealership business model is to make most of its money from financing. How that affects you is that this dealership will take the front end profit and rework the numbers and turn the front end profit into back end profit. So instead of 25%, you get 3% commission. They don't do this on every deal, but they do it enough where you get robbed out of most of your commission. Ask them how often they do this. Most dealerships will do this from time to time to meet profit goals and if they do it to you, you had better make sure you fight for your money.

4e.   Goal Setting

What is your plan in life?

Are you going to wing it or work toward some goal?

What are your short-term goals to achieve your long-term goals?

Are your goals specific or general or vague? "I want to be rich." Isn't specific.

Are your goals achievable?

Can you track your goals? Can you measure them? Things must get done at certain dates.

All successful people set goals and work to achieve them. Setting goals isn't enough; you must also put together a plan to achieve those goals.

Find the passion in your life and work.

You must have written goals.

First, think back 10 years, 5 years and 2 years.
If it's financial goals you're after then write:

- What kind of work did you do 10 years ago, 5 years ago, 2 years ago?
- How much money did you make 10 years ago, 5 years ago, 2 years ago?
- How much money did you have in your savings account for each period?
- If you knew then what you know now, what would you have done differently?
- What happened at each of those time periods that caused you to miss your ideal life?

- What significant events caused such problems or success and how did you respond to them?
- Rate your scale of happiness at each of those periods on a scale of 1 to 10.

Make another adjacent list showing 2, 5 and 10 years into the future.

- What are your goals for those time periods?
- Knowing what you learned from the last 10 years, what needs to be done to reach your 2, 5 and 10 year goals?

All goals must be:

Specific – The definition is "precise and detailed, avoiding vagueness". What is your goal?

Motivational – A goal that you can, given your personality really achieve.

Achievable –Realistic goals and not a pie-in-the-sky dream.

Relevant – Logical to your work or being.

Track able – Measurable, specific targets needed to achieve to move to the next level.

There are guidelines in place to setting goals and the acronym for them is S.M.A.R.T. Keep that in mind.

Keep these guidelines in mind when setting goals and planning your strategy to achieving your goals. Your goal must be specific. It's a goal that you actually want and keeps you motivated to achieve. The goal must be achievable. The goal must be relevant to your needs and desires. You must be able to track your progress to reassess from time to time your strategy and overall goal.

Goal Setting Worksheet
Make copies of this page and use it to fill out this page.
Carry you goals with you so you're reminded every day of what's important.
S.(specific), **M.**(Motivated), **A.**(Achievable), **R.**(Relevant), **T.**(Track able)

1. **What is your Main Goal (Specific)?**_____

Remember…it has to be <u>measurable</u> and <u>achievable</u>.

2. **What is the time period of your Goal (Track able)?**

_____

Be realistic because the next step depends on it.

3. **Broken Down by Year/Month/Week/Day.**

_____

**4.   Given your Personality/Limits/Schedule/Responsibilities/Resources, Can you stay <u>Motivated</u> to <u>Achieve</u> _____?
If no, rework and rethink Steps 1 to 3.**

Be realistic. You know yourself better than anyone else. This will also help you come to terms with unproductive habits and behaviors. You're not being graded, but you will be responsible to yourself for achieving your goals and dreams. You can only get a grade A or a grade F in this exercise. Only you have to live with failing to meet them.

Daily/Weekly/Monthly/Yearly Plan to achieve each step

There is no one else out there who cares for or knows you better than yourself. It's up to you to really sit down and think out every step. It will be you who needs to be held responsible for achieving all the steps needed to achieve you goals, that is why it's essential that you carry this around with you at all times and take a look at it at least once a day.

You also need to think of all the other ways needed to achieve your goals. Like they say, "There are many roads that lead to the same end." You must think of other routes you can take to meet you weekly, monthly and yearly goals.

A purposely-built plan for achieving your goals and dreams is paramount to the outcome of your success.

Remember your goals have to be achievable. Your goals need to have baby steps all the way to achieving your long-term goals. Don't set yourself up to fail because doing so will demoralize you deeply. Be realistic. You can't become a doctor in 2 years or with a low GPA and you can't go from being a green pea at a dealership to a GM in a year. Also don't keep your goals too easy. Keep them challenging. Setting a goal of selling 8 cars a month should not be a challenge to someone who follows the lessons in this book.

Be honest and do some serious soul searching. One way is to start at the 10 year goal and work backward to the 2 year goal. To reach your 10 year goal, what has to happen at the 5 year goal? And to get to your 5 year goal, what has to happen at the 2 year goal? You can also break it down by year if need be. Really give it some thought. Where do you want to be in 10 years? Besides goals, you might want to consider what would happen if you don't meet these goals, what would you do to get back on track?

No one else can do this plan for you and no one else cares for you or knows you like you do. After all, you're going to have to live with the consequences, and no one else.

Keep these goals handy and look at them every day or week. One way is to keep them on your smartphone and set reminders of things that need to be achieved every month, 6 months, every year, every day, etc. Keep these goals handy and refer to them regularly. This is your blueprint for your financial career or your life. You can set one up for other aspects of your life too and finally meld them all together for a truly successful life.

You also need to periodically evaluate your progress or lack of it. Have you met, exceeded or have fallen short of your written or planned goals? What is the problem? There should not be any excuses. What needs to be done to get you back on track?

Below is a sample monthly vehicle goal that I used to have my sales advisors fill out. I would sit with them and work out these numbers. The reason I did this was because I wanted them to know that I was holding them accountable for meeting those goals. Not only did this help the dealership, but it also made the sales advisors realize what was expected of them and their potential.

Sample Vehicle Selling Goal: The underlined parts are where you can input your information.

Goals for _March_ 2013

I _Mike Waters,_ am committing myself to a sales production level of _7_ new vehicles and _8_ used vehicles for a total of _15_ vehicles sold for the month.
In order for me to produce _15_ units new and used, I will need to have a minimum of _45_ manager confirmed appointments.

In order to achieve my goal, I will need _100_ opportunities, and have a closing ratio

of _15_%.

Mike Waters
Sales Advisor

M.I. Seka
General Sales Manager

After we agreed with the numbers, we both would sign and I would give them a copy. At the end of the month, we would then sit down to assess our numbers. Why did we miss the target numbers? Why did we fail? Why did we succeed? To be truly professional, we need to monitor our progress as well as our strengths and weaknesses.

Goal Setting Formula for Vehicle Sales = OTDB X Closing Ratio.

My <u>June 2013</u> Goals

My Dollar Goal is to earn   **$7,000**

Divide $ Goal by Average Commission

<u>**$7,000**</u> ÷   <u>**$250**</u>   = <u>**28**</u> **(# of Units Needed)**
Goal   Average Commission

# of Units Needed X 110% = <u>**31**</u> **(# of Written Deals)**

<u>**31**</u>   ÷   .35 =   **89**
Written Deals Needed   **(# of OTDBs Needed)**

Based on 90% demo. 75% write up to demo, 35% sold/closed

<u>**89**</u>   ÷   **25**   =   **4**
OTDBs Needed   Selling days this month   OTDBs needed Daily

Sales are actually vehicles delivered to clients.

O.T.D.B. is an acronym for *Opportunity To Do Business*. This is actually the number of opportunities we have to attempt to sell a vehicle.

Closing ratio is the number of OTDBs divided by number of sales. If you talk to 100 people in a month that you attempted to sell a vehicle to, and then your OTDB is 100 and out of those 100 you sell 15 then your closing ration is 15%, which is pretty average.

If the average commission is $500, then we have all the necessary information to set realistic goals for yearly income. In reality, the more experience you have and the better you get in sales, the higher the average commission. $500 is very low for a seasoned sales advisor.

This is a typical goal sheet at the dealerships. If your goal is to make **$7,000** in a month given that the average commission will be **$250** per unit sold, then you need to sell **28** units. During the month, you will see that some of your deals will need to be unwound for some reason or other. The dealership or the client could not get the deal done, so to protect yourself you would need to sell **31** units.

Based on how good you are at your job as a sales adviser, you would be expected to close **35%** of your write-ups. To close **31** deals, you would need to talk to **89** clients, clients, UPs or OTDBs. Thirty-five percent of 89 is 31. Therefore, that means that you would need to talk to 89 clients a month.

You would then need to check with your schedule to see how many days you are scheduled to sell for that month. If you are scheduled to be at the dealership for **25** days that month, that means that you need to talk to four clients a day to meet your target of 89 clients by the end of the month. The calculation comes out to 3.5, but you need to round up.

Of course, the better you are at your job as a professional sales advisor, the higher your average commission will be and the higher your closing ratio. This means you will need to talk to less people. Then again, the better you are at your profession, the more people you talk to, the more money you make.

Imagine that you've gotten good at your job and your average commission is $500 per deal. How will that change the numbers? Do the math. You can see that you'll need 14 units to make $7,000 and you will only need to talk to two people a day to hit your target. What will your goal look like if your average commission is $800 a unit, $1,000 a unit? Do the math so you can see for yourself how much better things get the more professional you become.

Suppose your top goal is to make $100,000 in one year in the car business.

This is based on S.M.A.R.T. This goal is Specific, Motivational, Achievable, Relevant and Track able.

All that's left is to break it down so we can be able to track it.

$100,000 Divided by 12 months is $8,333. Therefore, to achieve your goal of $100,000, you must make $8,333 a month.

Next, we look at the average commission to come up with how many sales we need.

$8,333 divided by average sale of $500 is 17 cars, rounded up.

The longer you are in the business, the easier it becomes. If your closing ratio is that of an average sales person at 15% and you need to sell seventeen cars, you would need to have an OTDB of one hundred and fifteen people a month.

$$Sales = OTDBs \times Closing\ ratio$$
$$17 = 115 \times 15\%$$

We work backward to get to 115. We know that 15% of 100 is 15 units sold, so we have to have OTDBs of more than 100 and 115 is perfect OTDBs.

So in order to hit 17 sales a month given that we sell to 15% of the people we talk to, we have to talk to 115 people a month. Seems like a lot, but you'll talk to many more people than that.

What does this mean about what we have to achieve daily?

115 OTDBs divided by 25 working days = 5 (rounded up). Meaning, we have to talk to people a day to meet our income goals.

You must plan on going out every day to talk to prospective clients. I'll show you how to put yourself in front of even more people in the prospecting section.

You must break down all goals you set out for yourself, whether they be for income, sales or project management.

Annual income needed ___$100,000_____

Annual income divided by 12 to get to monthly income needed
$100,000/12 = $8,333

Monthly income divided by the average commission = number of sales needed in a month
$8,333/$500 = 17

OTDBs needed X closing ratio = number of sales needed in a month
115X15% = 17

Monthly OTDBs divided working days = daily OTDBs needed to reach income goal
115/25 = 5

In summary, you need to talk to 5 prospective clients every working day to achieve your goal of $100,000 a year given that you sell 15% of the people you talk to. The higher your closing ratio, the less people you have to talk to and the less you have to work. This will come with time and experience.

4f.   Daily Routine

- Check with management about new leads and your to-do list

- Call all hot prospects to check on their status: clients who needed time to think about it or who are still searching. Check up on them and keep in contact

- Set goals. Depending on your closing ratio, how many people do you need to talk to today?
- Stay focused on your goals
  If your goal is 15 cars for the month and your closing ration is 15%, then you need to talk to 100 people, which is about 4 a day. The more you study this book, the higher your closing ratio, the less people you have to talk to and the higher your income

- Walk the lot daily. Know your inventory. Keep a note with you of all the clients you have who are looking for a specific vehicle. Know what their requirements are in case you come across one on the lot. Walk your used, new and trade- in inventory every day

- Call all your unsold prospects. Find a reason to call them. Stay fresh in their minds. Contact your sold clients at least every three months. Call prospective clients from service, old clients and any other leads you can find

- Email at least 10 people

- Learn to pick up clients in the service department. Walk service and chat up at least two people. Try to talk to them for at least 15 minutes and give them your card

Get to know service people as best as you can. Service deals with clients all the time and they know clients who are looking to upgrade or to change out of their vehicles. They can be a wealth of referrals. Give them some money for referrals and make sure everyone there knows that you'll share your commission with any referrals they send you. You can also tell them that you'll half your commission with them. Increasing your numbers as well as selling to that referral's friends and family is worth more than half your commission.

Your daily activity should be all about prospecting every day and getting in front of potential clients, whether they be from service, clients that are actively searching or people in your dealerships database. You, as a professional, need to make things happen and can't wait for things to happen.

Summary of Keys to Success

3 attributes are the foundation of a successful Automotive Sales Professional.

> **Attitude** – A professional attitude. This is your career and not a job. You must work on becoming an expert on every facet of the position. You need to work on becoming the go-to guy when problems arise because you're a problem solver.
>
> **Product Knowledge** – Although it seems like common sense to know about your product, you must go further than that and know exactly how the features of your product benefit the needs and wants of the client.
>
> **Enthusiasm** – This is the excitement built into your presentation and in the interaction the client feels when in your presence. It sells your presentation on an emotional level.

Under these three attributes are a multitude of other attributes that support the top three that you need to succeed, but they all come down to being a professional and finding ways to make the sale.

Goal setting is another major factor in your success. It will give you a road map of where you need to be, how to get there as well as consequences of not meeting those goals since it will affect your other goals.

Take this as your career and be serious about it. Only you have to live with not living up to your truest potential.

Statistics:

> Prospects who bought within a week: 80%
>
> Closing ratio for first time clients: 12%
> > This is an average. Once you go through this book, you should reach 25%.
>
> Closing ratio on be-backs (Clients who tell you they need to think about it and say, "I'll be back."): 70%
>
> Closing ratio on referrals: 60%
>
> Closing ratio on repeat clients: 70%

Given the statistics above, you can see why following up with prospective clients is so important. It's estimated that an average sales advisor follows up with only 30% of the clients who visit the store after they leave. As a professional sales advisor, it's not only your job but in your financial interest to follow up with every client who you talk to. You must also keep in constant contact with former clients. I don't mean calling them every day, but have some kind of communications with them at least once a month. A simple email or post card is enough, but they should hear your voice at least once every 3 to 6 months.

Talk to every client you can, regardless of what your impression of them is. I've had the biggest sales from clients who looked like they couldn't afford any of the vehicles or had bad credit. Just based on the fact that they're on your lot speaks volumes about their interest in purchasing a vehicle. Even if they do have bad credit and you did a good job of selling, they can still find a cosigner or they might be cash buyers or they have a big chunk down.

Be in it for the long haul. It takes time to master all the aspects of sales. Time will reward you. It is not unusual for a professional sales advisor to make $8,000 to $15,000 a month and a successful general manager to make $20,000 or more a month. Successful and professional sales people make much more than the average doctors or lawyers without hundreds of thousands of dollars of school debt.

Focus on what's important: the number of units sold and amount of gross you kept in the deal. Everything else will fall into place once these numbers have been hit.

Learn to listen.

Be in the right mindset when approaching a client. Think of every sale or success you've ever had when approaching a client to get you in the successful mindset.

5. The Sales Process – Going from "Hello" to "Thank You for your Business"

Every dealership has their own way or process of selling. The process has specific sales steps outlined, from meeting the client to delivering the vehicle. The aim is to make the client feel comfortable, find out what their needs are, match those wants and needs to the dealerships vehicles features, sell them a vehicle that you have in your inventory and make them want to do business with you and your dealership.

Purpose: The purpose of the sales process is to keep control and keep moving in the right direction. After all, if the sales process isn't moving forward, then what's the sales person doing except chit chatting and wasting time.

Keep in mind that the large amounts of money, energy, effort and time spent in setting up a dealership or any other business is to make money, not only for the dealership, but also for you the sales advisor.

The process has been set up by experienced and capable management that knows how to turn shoppers into buyers so make sure that you're familiar with your dealership's process and to follow it

We'll discuss the individual steps further in the next few chapters, but it's beneficial for you to familiarize yourself with the whole process first. Get the whole picture or to see the forest from the trees of the selling process.   Here we'll look at the all the steps in the process so you can connect them with one another to make sense of the whole selling process.

We'll look at the various details of the steps in the next few chapters.

<u>You can't skip a step. Every step of the sale process becomes the foundation for the next.</u>

Each successive step in the process of selling is meant to nudge the client slowly from a looker to a committed buyer. The way you nudge them is to isolate all their fears and offer information that will negate these fears while building up their hopes.   What those fears and hopes are will be evident from your interactions and the proper qualifying questions you ask of them.

The process usually follows this routine. Not all dealerships follow this model exactly, but most have guidelines similar to this.

1.   **Meet and Greet** – How to approach the client properly when they step on the lot to your dealership

2. **Fact-finding / Needs Assessment /Qualifying** – Wants and needs of the client. Getting information about who are the decision makers, what the client is looking for as well as what they're driving now and why they want to switch

3. **Selling Evaluation** – Figuring out what vehicles we have that would fit the client's needs

4. **Product Presentation and demonstration** – Building value. Showing the client the features of a vehicle that matches closest to what they're looking for and selling the benefits of that particular vehicle. Includes the test drive. Building value is crucial in this step. Make the vehicle worth immensely more than the price tag. How do the features benefit the clients want and needs?

5. **Setting the Stage** – Using various trial closes to mentally help the client own the vehicle. Root out any objections they may have preventing them from buying the vehicle today. Turn them from a shopper to mentally owning the vehicle

6. **Write Up of Deal and Approaching the Desk Manager** – Gather necessary information from the client to aid the client in making an offer on the vehicle as well as assist the desk manager to prepare the paperwork. Helping the client make an offer for the vehicle

7. **Negotiations** – Getting the client to commit financially to purchasing the vehicle. Going from mentally owning the vehicle to financially owning the vehicle

8. **Vehicle Delivery** – Ensure the client is familiar with all books, features and accessories of their new vehicle. Vehicle is free from any and all defects. Ensuring the client is happy with their purchase and experience

9. **T.O. (Turn Over) to a Manager** – Ensure that the manager has had their chance of communicating with the client on the benefits of the dealership by using their wealth of experience to help in closing the deal. If at any step the client does not want to proceed any further in the process and is about to leave, you need to bring in a manager to assist in closing the deal or have the manager talk to the client before they leave

10. **Log in Your Efforts and Follow Up/Persist** – Learning from your mistakes and or success. Record all information regarding client and the deal, and follow up with clients to try to get them back in the store to purchase from you. Includes holding a post mortem on every client you deal with. Asking yourself why the deal happened or why the deal didn't happen and how you can prepare or to deal with the objection the next time it comes around

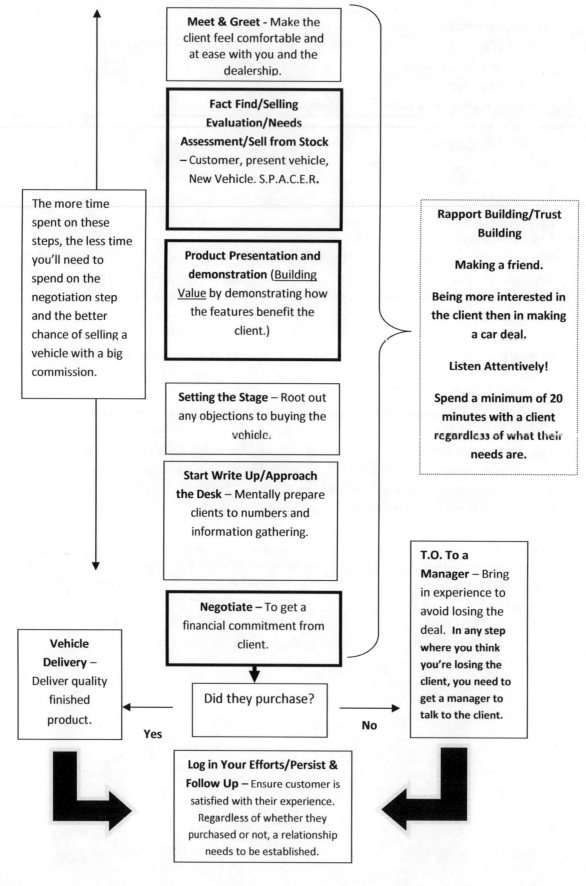

Meet & Greet - Make the client feel comfortable and at ease with you and the dealership.

Fact Find/Selling Evaluation/Needs Assessment/Sell from Stock – Customer, present vehicle, New Vehicle. S.P.A.C.E.R.

The more time spent on these steps, the less time you'll need to spend on the negotiation step and the better chance of selling a vehicle with a big commission.

Product Presentation and demonstration (Building Value by demonstrating how the features benefit the client.)

Rapport Building/Trust Building

Making a friend.

Being more interested in the client then in making a car deal.

Listen Attentively!

Spend a minimum of 20 minutes with a client regardless of what their needs are.

Setting the Stage – Root out any objections to buying the vehicle.

Start Write Up/Approach the Desk – Mentally prepare clients to numbers and information gathering.

T.O. To a Manager – Bring in experience to avoid losing the deal. In any step where you think you're losing the client, you need to get a manager to talk to the client.

Negotiate – To get a financial commitment from client.

Vehicle Delivery – Deliver quality finished product.

Did they purchase?

Yes

No

Log in Your Efforts/Persist & Follow Up – Ensure customer is satisfied with their experience. Regardless of whether they purchased or not, a relationship needs to be established.

73

Other variation of the process:

1. Meet & Greet
2. Selling Evaluation
3. Sell From Stock
4. Product Presentation and demonstration
5. Setting the Stage
6. Start Your Write-Up
7. Approach the Desk
8. Negotiate
9. T.O. to a Manager
10. Log in Your Efforts
11. Persist & Follow-Up

Process on a One-Price Store:

1. Meet & Greet
2. Philosophy Disclosure (Why we don't negotiate)
3. Take a Tour of the Dealership
4. Fact Find/Needs Assessment
5. Vehicle Selection
6. Product Presentation
7. Road Test/Trial Close
8. Service Walk
9. Prepare the Write Up
10. Equity Analysis
11. Explain the Client's Options
12. Financial Services Overview
13. Doc Finalization
14. Vehicle Delivery
15. Log in Your Efforts and Follow Up

In a perfect world, the process would go exactly as outlined above. Since we don't live in a perfect world, clients will force you to jump ahead in the sales process. Knowing where you are in the sales process will allow you take control of the sales process. Suppose a client walks on the lot looking at a vehicle and asks you, "What's the best price you'll sell me that vehicle?" Looking at the steps of the process, you can see that the client skipped all the steps including the meet & greet and jumped right into the negotiations step.

A green sales advisor will probably be thrilled because he didn't even have to sell anything or do any work, but in reality this client is not serious or is just looking for information he can use to negotiate at the next dealer. This person hasn't seen the value of the vehicle or the value in you or your dealership.

It's important to realize that the sales process is in place to assist both the sales advisor as well as the client. The sales process is in place so the sales advisor can control the sales process as well as make sure that all the clients' objections or issues have been properly dealt with before proceeding to the next step. The sales process also helps the client slow down and think carefully about their wants and needs as well as how this vehicle will benefit them.

Rapport Building

Although the process has been put in place to help you keep track of where you are in the sales steps, what hasn't or can't be taught is how to build rapport with the client. Rapport depends on the individual sales advisor's personality traits and style. Rapport building is an art in itself. Rapport building in essence is friend building or being likeable. I've laid out some guidelines for you to follow to build rapport, trust and to make a friend. In time, you will find your own style based on experience, but these guidelines should be followed until you find your way.

- Be genuine, take an interest in your clients lives, their want, and needs
- Ask open ended questions, questions that require more than a yes or no answer
- Find common ground. Ask them about themselves and find things you have in common
- Eye contact
- Share a common experience and stories with them
- Empathize with their life and experience. Any time they tell you a story, share a similar experience you've had, your friends had or your clients had. Have stories ready that also give you're plight and show that you empathize with them
- Concentrate on making a friend

By building rapport and trust, you get the client to open up to you and communicate what it is that they're actually looking for and their pain points. An important part of rapport building is to let them talk and you listen.

Rapport building is in essence building a trust with your client.

Rapport building starts with the meet and greet but never ends. Even if they buy from you, you still need to periodically check up on them and keep in contact with them to sell them or their family another vehicle. Keep them in your pipeline. Increase their commitment to you and you alone.

To show them that you empathize, you must use stories that give similar experiences of someone else who you know that went through the same thing. Use language to show that you understand how they feel, appreciate how they feel and know how they feel.

Imagine yourself on the car lot. You see some people on the lot looking at cars. You approach them. It's a man and a woman. They look like they're married. You introduce yourself and confirm that their married and looking for a vehicle because their family is growing.

Therefore, you already know that the decision makers are present and you know that their pain points are that they need a bigger vehicle, but you also know that they want safety for their family. Have you built trust yet? No, that takes time. You have to find common ground. You have to bring yourself up or down to their level. If they're in business for themselves, then you talk about how you once had your own business or know of someone that had a similar business and obviously, you talk about your own family and kids and all the problems with having kids. If they're paying cash because they have bad credit, then you also discuss yours or someone close to you who also is in the same situation.

5a.   Sample Scenario

It's a nice hot summer day in Phoenix. Currently, it is 90 degrees with an expected high of 102. You've just landed a job at a dealership. You don't know that much about their various models or makes except that they are a new and upcoming company, have gotten tremendous reviews and have won many awards and accolades for reliability, craftsmanship, fuel efficiency, style and affordability. You obviously haven't done your homework on which dealership or brand to work for.

The names of the models aren't important. What is important is how each class benefits the client.

- A compact vehicle that's good on gas
- A full size sedan with room for five
- A hybrid model that gets 60MPG
- A mid-size truck with decent gas mileage on 4 cylinders
- A full-size truck
- A small SUV
- A full-size SUV

You're on the front line waiting for a client when a car pulls up and parks in the sales parking lot. The clients slowly start to get out of their vehicle and look toward the sales lot. At this point, you approach the waiting clients.

Meet & Greet
Sales Advisor: *"Hello…..how are you folks doing in this hot weather?"*
Clients: *With a smile, "Fine and yourself?"*
Sales Advisor: *"I'm good. My name is Mark. Is there something I can help you with?"*
Clients: *"Were looking for a car for my wife."*
Sales Advisor: *"Okay, I can help you with that, what were your names?"*
Clients: *"I'm Steven and this is my wife Mary."*
Sales Advisor: *"It's nice to meet you both."*
He shakes hands with both of them.

This was the <u>basic</u> meet and greet.   Not all meet and greets will go this smoothly, but this example will help you see how and why the process was set up.

Fact-finding/Needs Assessment
Sales Advisor: *"Mary, are you looking for new or used?"*
Mary: *"New, I always buy new."*
Sales Advisor: *"So Mary, what are you driving now?"*

Mary: "I have an old sedan that needs replacing."

Sales Advisor: "What do you use that car for?"

Mary: "Just errands and we take a few long trips a year in it."

Sales advisor: "Okay, so a small SUV or a full-size sedan would work for you?"

Mary: "Yes, I guess but I also want something that gets good gas mileage and is comfortable."

This was a basic fact-finding scenario. Not all clients will be forthcoming, but this is designed to give you a general overview. Some clients already know the model their looking for; this doesn't make your job any easier. You must constantly be asking questions because you might have another vehicle, new or used, that would work better for their needs. Notice that I didn't delve too much on their wants and needs, which is a big mistake. This step is crucial to finding their wants and needs.

Sell from Stock

Sales Advisor: "Great, I have some really nice ones over here, follow me. Are you guys from the area?"

Steven: "No, we're planning on moving to the area. We're in town to buy a house here."

Sales Advisor: "You'll really like the area. There are some spots to avoid, but on the whole, it's a great area."

Your product knowledge really comes in handy in this step because you must know what you have in your inventory to match the client's wants and needs. Notice that during the whole interaction I'm making small talk as well as asking questions. Building rapport is a big part of sales. I also communicated to them that I know the area and can be a big help in directing them toward which neighborhoods to avoid as well as which ones to look at.

Product Presentation/Demo Drive

Sales Advisor: "This is the SUV2000. It has room for five and gets 30 mpg."

Steven: "We don't like this color. We kind of wanted leather. We wanted an automatic."

Sales Advisor: "Oh...what else did you want?"

Steven: "We also wanted a 4 cylinder. Do the back seats fold down?"

Sales Advisor: "I think...let me see. Yeah, they do. Hop in and let's take it for a test drive."

Steven: "No, we don't like this model."

Had the sales advisor done a proper fact-finding, he would have known their needs and wants much better. Most important is the fact that he didn't build value into the vehicle. But, I'm just giving you the basics so let's pretend that they did want to go on the test drive. In addition, he would have presented the vehicle much better if he knew what they were looking for.

On the Test Drive

Sales Advisor: *"Make sure all your mirrors, seats are adjusted the way you want, and your seatbelts are fastened. Take a right out of the lot, then take a left if you want to go on the freeway or right if you want to drive around the streets."*

Mary: *"This drives nice. What does this light mean?"*

Sales Advisor: *"That's the overdrive light. It means that the vehicle is in overdrive."*

Mary: *"Oh, okay."*

Sales Advisor: *"Steven, do you also want to drive it?"*

Steven: *"No, It's okay. It's her car."*

Sales Advisor: *"Oh...Okay."*

This sales advisor didn't use any trial closes, meaning he didn't ask them questions to make them feel as if they already owned the vehicle. Questions like, "Will you register this vehicle in this state or somewhere else?" and, "Will you both be registered on this vehicle?" The sales advisor also didn't ask any questions about the clients to keep building rapport or to make himself feel like it would be an asset to know him. He also didn't connect how the over drive light benefits the client.

Setting the Stage

Sales Advisor: *"Okay great, come inside and we can discuss the price."*

Mary: *"Hold on, we need to think about it. We still have some questions."*

Sales Advisor: *"Oh, sorry. What else do you want to know?"*

Steven: *"We're just not sure right now."*

This sales advisor has done a poor job so far at rooting out any objections these clients have to purchasing this vehicle. He's also done a poor job at building rapport and trust. He clearly hasn't made a friend. Let's pretend that they decide to come and take a look at some number anyway.

Start Your Write Up/Approaching the Desk/Presenting the Numbers

Sales Advisor: *"Okay, I just need some information to present to the managers."*

Mary: *"We don't want our credit run yet. We just want to know what the payments are."*

Sales Advisor: *"I just need to run credit so I can give you proper numbers."*

Steven: *"No I don't want our credit run. Just give us the payments as well as how much our trade is worth so we can get a better idea."*

This sales advisor still has not build trust and rapport with this client. By not building trust, the clients will become hostile toward you and your dealership.

Negotiating

Sales Advisor: *"Okay, here are the numbers. The new car costs $25,000 and I'm willing to give you $2,500 for your trade, so with tax and license the total cost is around $26,500 and will cost around $450 a month."*

Mary: *"Wow.....that's a lot. I don't think we can afford that much."*

Sales Advisor: "What if I can get your payment down to $400? Can you afford that?"

Steven: "No, we were thinking of $300."

Sales Advisor: "Okay, sign down here and I'll see what I can do."

Most training programs at dealerships will tell you to keep lowering your price until the client says yes or commits. This is what is called "getting the commitment." You're not actually going to give them the vehicle at that price but you just want a signature so management knows that they're serious and that they've moved from looking to being serious about buying. This is a very old school and outdated technique. By doing this you lose all credibility with the clients as well as looking manipulative when you come back with totally different numbers. The sales advisor also failed to justify his numbers, holding no credibility in the first place. Because he didn't build rapport and trust with the client or build value in the vehicle, the clients have no loyalty toward him or the vehicle. When there is no trust or value in the vehicle, then the price is the only thing left to negotiate. Let's pretend that they bought anyway.

Vehicle Delivery

Sales Advisor: "Here's is your new vehicle. Do you have any questions?"

Mary: "Yeah, where is the spare tire?"

Sales Advisor: "I think it's underneath the trunk. Hold on, let me see. Yeah, there it is."

Steven: "How do you program the radio?"

Sales advisor: "Let me get someone from service to help with that."

This would be a good vehicle delivery if the sales advisor was going to quit right after this sale because these people will never buy from him again and neither will their friends and family. To retain these people as future clients and use them for referrals and references, you need to treat them like family. If these clients gives a bad CSI (Client Satisfaction Index) report to the maker that they were treated this way, this sales advisor will most likely get fired or have his paycheck docked.

Let's pretend that they didn't buy the vehicle and decided to leave during the negotiation phase.

Turn Over to a Manager

Steven: "We need to think about this. I don't think you or your dealership are very professional."

Sales Advisor: "Why do you say that, we've helped you every step of the way. Hold on, let me get the manager so he can help you answer any questions you may have."

Anytime the client wants to leave or has major issues with you, your vehicle or the dealership, then you need to bring in your sales manager to address the issue. The sales manager has a wealth of experience to a call on to close the deal. Most dealerships have rules that the manager needs to talk to every client before they leaves.

Log in Your Efforts/Follow Up/Persist

Sales Advisor: "They said they want to think about it."

Manager: "Did you do a good presentation?"

Sales Advisor: *"Sure."*

Manager: *"Did you find out what they really wanted?"*

Sales Advisor: *"Sure."*

Manager: *"Did you build trust in you, your dealership and your brand?"* *"Did you build value in the vehicle?"*

Sales Advisor: *"Yes."*

Manager: *"If that's the case, then why didn't they buy from you?"*

Sales Advisor: *"I don't know why."*

Manager: *"I want you to call them tonight and thank them for coming in and then call them tomorrow to see if you can get them back in here to look at another vehicle."*

You can't sell every client that you talk to, but if you're good, you will be able to sell to a majority of the clients you talk to. Follow up is very important. It keeps you and your dealership fresh in the clients mind. It shows that you still think of them and value them as a client. You should keep contacting them until they ask that you don't.

5b.   The Three Major Factors of Selling

You are a sales advisor and being a successful sales advisor, not matter what you sell entails three crucial factors.

- **Who are the Decision Makers?** – Finding the person who will be using the vehicle is the first step in any sales process on the car lot. It's not hard at the dealership since they're there and most likely the decision maker or makers will be present. If they aren't, then you're most likely dealing with only the information gatherer. You give everything to the information gatherer except the final price because unless the decision makers are there and their committed to making a decision, there's no use in negotiating with the information gatherer.

- **Build Trust** - After finding the decision makers, the first thing that needs to be done is to build trust. This must be done skillfully when we first approach them during the meet and greet and throughout the sales process by being more interested in them then the car sale.

  By building trust and befriending the buyer, they will more receptive to your message. Once they trust you, then they can open up about what it is they need and what it is that is causing them to find another vehicle. Building trust is not one step. Building trust isn't achieved once, you must continually do this throughout the whole time the client has a relationship with you. This can be summed up in one statement and that is you need to make a friend.

  Be genuine, otherwise, the client will figure you out as a salesman instead of a sales advisor or a friend. This will allow the client to open up about what it is that they are really looking for.

- **Build Value** - Once you know the pain points of the client, their wants and needs then you need to build as much value into the product that you are selling that matches closest to their pain. Build so much value that price will not be an issue. "The difference between price and value is salesmanship." It's your job to make price insignificant to the buyer compared with what they are getting.

Building trust takes time and can't be rushed. Clients coming to a dealership usually have their guard up and won't put them down as soon as someone says, "Hello".

To build value, we first need to know what it is that the client is looking for in a vehicle. What are their wants and needs? The only way to do this is once we've built some trust with them is to ask questions. What's the point of selling them a truck when in reality the client wants an SUV or a minivan? Asking questions also keeps you in control of the process.

When at the vehicle, have the clients walk with you and gently tell them to "touch this", "smell this", "open this", "feel this" and "look at this". This is all part of control, but remember to include why that item benefits them and especially if it's something that will meet their needs.

The one asking the questions is the one in control!

The one asking the questions is the one in control. Keep asking them questions and keep them engaged and interested. Keep getting more information to use in your presentation. Ask questions that will get their imagination going about owning the vehicle. "Where will you go first with this vehicle?", "Who will you show this vehicle off to first?", "Who's name will this vehicle be registered under?" Give them mental ownership. These are called trial closes, best used on the test drive. More on these later.

One of the most basic reasons this all falls apart is that the sales advisor falls for the "making a friend" part too. He starts to think that he's made a friend too and counts on an easy sale. The sales advisor starts to think that he already has the sale and acts accordingly only to see things fall apart.

The sale doesn't end until the client drives away with the vehicle.

Never discuss price or financial details of your vehicle on the car lot. There will be plenty of time to talk about money during the negotiation. Your main concern is to make a friend and match the clients' needs and wants with a vehicle that you have on the lot. Their wants and needs will also encompass their financial limitation they may have like, "We only have $500 down" or "We can only make $200 a month in payments" or "We don't have any money down". This information is okay to gather so you may match them up with relatively priced vehicles you have on the lot. It's a starting point.

The client may bring up money or the car, which is fine. Not everyone will be easy. The client has their own baggage, concerns and fears to deal with. Address as much as the client wants but tell them that it makes no sense to discuss anything else until you find a car for them that they like. "Let's find you a vehicle that fits your needs before I quote payments and terms; there's no point in getting into all that until you've found a car that you like or works for you."

When shopping for a vehicle, it's natural for clients to visit at least 4 or 5 lots. One of the tricks that some buyers will try to pull on a sales advisor is to try to compare your vehicle that they like to another one they saw on another lot. Of course, the other vehicle will be newer, less mileage and a lot cheaper. Of course, your vehicle is crap compared with the one they saw at the other dealership.

This is a no-win situation for the sales advisor to get into.

You don't know if the client is telling the truth, 98% of the time they won't be. You don't know the condition of the other vehicle and if the other vehicle is so much better and cheaper, then why is this client here and willing to take a look at your vehicle? Like I said, this is a no-win situation. If a client brings up that they saw a certain vehicle at another lot that was better and cheaper than yours, don't insult them by saying, "Then why didn't you buy it?" Instead calmly tell them, "I don't know about the other vehicle, the only thing I can do is find you a vehicle that matches your needs and wants to what you like. After you have all the information, then you can make a better-informed decision. Sound fair? Even if you don't buy from me, at least you get the necessary information and you'll feel more confident about buying the other one. Sounds fair?" "Buying a car is a long-term commitment and I don't want you folks to get stuck with something you aren't going to be happy down the road."

Be confident when saying this, as the client will sense a sale pitch if you sound weak. Most objections can be easily neutralized with logic. Come back to the steps and continue talking up your vehicle and all the positives you know about your vehicle.

Remember, we're not trying to deceive the client or be sneaky in anyway. We're simply trying to proceed forward without any of the fears and trepidations people have about car salesmen. This way the client can concentrate on other aspects of the sale, like what are their needs, requirements and wishes are. They can relax about thinking about being taken by the sales man and can put their trust into the sales advisor.

5c.   Communication

In all aspects of business, sales and social interactions, there is communication. Here I briefly touch upon 2 types that you need to be aware of when interacting with prospective clients. The 2 types of communication in the car business are verbal and non-verbal.

It's very important to recognize these 2 as there is a saying in the car business and that is, "Buyers are liars", implying that all buyers will lie about their wants, needs and capabilities in order to get the best price and terms possible. Both the verbal and non-verbal in tandem communicate the real intentions and feelings of a buyer. In time, you will become versed and put together these two forms of communication to figure out exactly what the client is saying.

Don't take this as an insult, but treat it as part of the game. Understandably, a buyer will try to protect as much of their money as possible. In the meantime, you, the sales advisor, are trying to hold as much gross profit as possible so you can make a bigger commission. The better your demonstration and sales skills, the easier your closing skills will become. We discussed in the previous chapters about putting yourself in the target audience's position.

The first thing you need to learn is the real meaning of a client's words and body language. Don't take the lies personally as it's part of the game. The client is trying to save as much money as possible while you're trying to increase your commission as much as possible. Clients have been conditioned over the years that all sales people are liars and that they should keep their guard up whenever dealing with sales people.

I can't go into detail of how to tell if someone is lying or not because I myself don't know but keep a few guidelines in mind.

Actively Listen – means that you engage and prod whenever a client has an objection or a barrier to what is being discussed. By actively asking questions, you can uncover the real source of the lie or objection and then you can address it. Someone who gives you lots of stories instead of a yes or no answer when that is all that is required is usually lying.

Body Language and Mood – A client who isn't in a good mood will usually signify that he has his guard up and most likely will tell you anything or lie. On the other hand, a friendly client is much easier to work with but may also not be as committed to buying anytime soon and is only looking for information.

A client who avoids eye contact or plays with their mouth or nose is usually lying.

Here are some body language overviews you should be looking for. To become well-versed in body language, watch T.V. with the voice down, every night for 3 weeks in a row. You can develop the skills needed to read body language properly.

- People who avoid eye contact or look to the side a lot are either distracted or lying
- Dilated pupils means the person is interested unless they're on drugs or had an energy drink
- People mimic body language to build rapport with others. If your client is mirroring your body language then they're very interested in you and interacting with you. You should mimic all your client's body language to help you build rapport and trust
- Crossed arms usually signify that they don't want what your selling
- Rubbing hands together or touching their body signify that your client is uncomfortable with you
- Touching the back of their neck or head means that they're open
- Hands on hip signify impatience
- Hands clinched signifies anger or irritation
- People point feet toward where they want to go
- Confident people have prolonged eye contact
- The face will show involuntary uncontrollable twitches when something happens that changes the persons mood
- Watch for quick changes to body language instead of the body language itself to tell you if something has changed

- Breathing patterns also give lots of information on the status of the person's state. Long breaths indicate relaxed. Short, quick breaths indicate nervousness
- People tend to touch the nose and mouth a lot when lying
- People sweat more when lying
- When we lean in, it means we are telling the truth. When we lean away, it means we're lying
- A person who is lying usually is trying to clear their throat
- People who lie tend to avoid normal hand gestures
- Knuckles of liars turn white as they grab something while lying

There is a lot more to know. Do a quick search on the internet for body language. Use that information to find what you can do to become more trustworthy to your clients like mirroring their body language, leaning in and using an open body..

Experience – most of this intuition or skill will come from experience. At first, you'll need to go with your gut instinct, but as you become more seasoned you'll be able to recognize for yourself if someone is lying, telling the truth or has a genuine concern that you did not address in your selling process.

Remember that clients are also evaluating you to see if you're lying. Always keep good eye contact, actively listen, have an open body language and always check your attitude before approaching the client. Recognize that most clients are operating out of fear and never take things personally, as the client is acting out of fear. All you can do is present what you have.

Although I present you with ways to go about selling a vehicle, you're going to have to custom tailor your own message and your own style of presenting and selling, one that is most comfortable to you. You have to customize you presentation to each individual buyer but the process is the same for everyone. Start with the first step and continue to the last without skipping a step, otherwise you're going to work harder on the last and most crucial steps: negotiating.

Each step in the process will have its own set of objections that will prevent you from proceeding. I've touched on the most common ones in the next chapters, but it's important to accept that there will be objections at each and every step. Over time, you'll see that there are only a few common objections and you'll develop skills to isolate and overcome them.

Summary of the Sales Process

Every dealership has a process on how to deal with prospective clients to ensure that the sales advisor maintains control and that all the clients' concerns are addressed, designed to move the client from a looker to a buyer. They are similar to the samples I've given previously. Know the dealerships process.

The process benefits both the client and the sales advisor. It helps the sales advisor keep the sales process moving forward, address any objections and build trust. The process helps the client to slow down and think about their options, get all their questions answered and objections addressed.

In all sales, you first need to find the decision maker, then start building trust throughout the whole process, and then build value in you, your dealership as well as your vehicle beyond the price. Asking questions, actively listening, being genuine and aiming to make a friend are all part of rapport building.

Never take anything in the sales process personally. It's a game most people play. You won't be able to sell to every prospective client you meet, but with time and skill, you'll be able to sell to a majority of them. In time, you'll learn to make the process work for you, but in the beginning follow it step by step.

Keep in mind that 93% of communication is non-verbal. It's important to recognize this to address any underlying concerns your clients might have. Look for visual non-verbal questions.

"Car sales is a numbers game" is a mantra you'll hear again and again in the business. Meaning, the more people you meet, the higher your chances of making a sale. I believe that everyone goes by 13% as the average closing ratio, so if you talk to 100 people a month, you should make 13 sales. I don't believe this to be true. The really good sales people have a much higher closing ration somewhere north of 25%. This means that they're good at what they do. Skill is definitely involved: skill to build rapport, skill to build trust, skill to find common ground and skill to make a friend to buy from you and only you.

---

6. Meet and Greet (the first 30 seconds)

Purpose: This first step in the sales process is called the meet and greet. The Purpose of a proper meet and greet is to make a good first impression, make the buying experience with you and your dealership unique and to put the client at ease so you can begin to build trust and rapport.

This happens in the first 30 seconds to a minute of meeting the client, either on the lot or in the dealership showroom. This is the first impression the client gets of you and the dealership.

There are various ways of approaching the client depending on your personality type, how you read the client and other parties involved. You can either use a one-size-fits all approach or tailor each meet and greet to each client, depending how you read them. In the beginning, use the one-size approach until you feel comfortable with your own approach. There is more on the various approaches later.

Some dealers have a process they use in the meet and greet where they require the client to fill out a guest sheet, while others want the sales advisor to bring them in and fill out information about them on the computer. Both are equally ridiculous. These two requirements breeds even more fear than the clients initially had. Needless to say, 99% of the sales advisors either refuse to or ignore this rule. No client is going to want to come in and give their personal information to someone if your dealership doesn't have what they're looking for.

Fear and Hope
Almost everyone walking onto a car lot is operating out of fear. What are those fears? It is the job of the sales advisor to uncover them. By building trust, you reduce most of their fears so that they can let their guard down and open up about their fears. Recognizing that people operate out of fear is a major factor in deciding on how to get close to someone. You have to acknowledge this fear and empathize with your client so he does not worry, your dealership will be there for them and you will be there for whatever the reason they require. We discussed earlier that, to be successful in sales, you need to put yourself in the place of the client to figure out what motivates them and what concerns or fears they may have.

You need to get into their world. Become like them. Be a chameleon. What motivates them, their passions and their pain points? Their fears and hopes?

The Fear of:
- Making the wrong choice of vehicle
- Future events beyond their control, like losing their job and being unable to fulfill their financial responsibilities
- Gas prices
- Insurance rates
- The future in general
- Disapproval of family and friends

The Hope for:
- Making the right decision
- For the future
- Winning
- Approval of friends and family

Be a chameleon but be empathetic.

Dealerships and particularly the car salesmen have a very bad reputation. Most of these impressions are false and based on the media. This is a big fear that most clients have of the dealership and especially of the sales advisors. Keep these fears in mind when approaching clients so you can isolate them and overcome them.

In today's technological world, the client has access to the same information that the sales advisor does, if not more. It's important to remember these big hurdles that we need to overcome in the meet and greet.

6a.   Meet and Greet Basics

Today's sales advisor needs to be confident, make strong eye contact, have a firm handshake, smile and have a professional appearance. These are some of the tools we need to use in the meet and greet to build trust and confidence in ourselves and our dealership.

Eye contact is the key to any successful meet and greet. It tells you gobs of information about whether the client is a serious buyer or a looker. It also determines the type of greeting you'll use. Lack of eye contact means the person is not that serious or doesn't want or need help. Strong eye contact denotes seriousness, someone who thinks they're superior to you, meaning they know exactly what they want, and approachability, meaning that they are open to being assisted.

A **firm handshake** denotes respect, confidence and competency. A limp handshake denotes weakness, disrespect and laziness.

A **friendly smile** puts all parties at ease. A smile allows both parties to open up about what they expect to get out of the interaction. People like people who smile a lot. People like to be around happy and positive people. A smile conveys honesty, happiness and friendliness.

A **professional appearance** conveys a professional attitude, mentioned earlier, and competence.

Get the **Client's Name** and use it often. Once you exchange names, use their name in a formal way. It's Mr. Brown and not Joe. People really like hearing their name, especially in a formal way.

These are the cornerstones of a good meet and greet.

- Always make eye contact – make a note of everyone's eye color

- - - Take off your sunglasses so the client can also see your eyes
- Use a Firm Handshake – rarely will some clients not want to shake hands for various reasons. No problem. Ignore and keep moving forward. Nothing personal
- Be properly dressed
- Smile a lot
- Give appropriate personal space – don't crowd the client
- Have Confidence – Be happy you have an opportunity to make money
- Get the client's name and use it often. People love the sound of their name
- Introduce yourself to all parties
- Use formal language. Mr. Wilson and not Jim
- Be sincere and appreciate this opportunity to do business
- Don't be overly aggressive

There are certain things you need to do to effectively have control, establish common ground and establish trust.

The type of meet and greet you use will also be determined by the way your potential client behaves. The meet and greet is the first contact you will have with the client, so the message needs to be tailored to your client's behavior, body language, demeanor, attitude and eye contact.

6b. Sample Dialogues

Wait until the client gets their bearings and figure out what and where they want to go. Don't be overbearing, it turns people off. Don't ask them, "Can I help you?" because they'll just tell you that "Their just looking. Instead, beat them to the punch by asking, "How are you guys doing today, are you guys looking around?"

"Hello Folks. My name is Steve, how are you guys doing today?"

"Hello Folks. My name is Ernesto, how you guys doing today? That's a nice truck you guys came in on; are you going to trade it in?"

"Hello Folks. My name is Richard. Weren't you guys here last week?"

"You guys look familiar. Anyway, I'm Richard." Hold out your hand for a handshake.

"Hello Folks. Welcome to ABC motors, my name is Mark. And you are?" Hold out your hand for a handshake.

"Hello, welcome to national Ford, my name is Mark, you guys looking around today?"

"Hello, my name is Mark and you are?"

"Hello, my name is Mark, are you here for the big sale?"

Some managers want you to stand by their car as soon as they pull up on the lot. Don't do that. It's just common sense. Doing so makes you look hungry, unprofessional and overbearing. Remember, you're building rapport and trust and you're there to help them find a vehicle and not sell one. Don't be overly aggressive or use high-pressure sales tactics.

The client just got out of their vehicle and is looking around. Wait until they get their bearings before approaching.

Sales Advisor: *"Hello, can I help you guys?"*
Client: *"No, were just looking."*
Sales Advisor: *"Okay….well, let me know if you need anything."*
Client: *"Okay, we'll come and get you as soon as we find something."*
Sales Advisor: *"Okay…"*

This is an example of a complete rookie performing a meet and greet. The rookie doesn't want to make the client feel awkward, easily gives up, and does what the client wants instead of trying to guide the client in the direction of the sales advisor's choosing.

One of the greetings you can use is, "Hello, my name is Mark. Welcome to River Auto. Are you guys here for the big sale?" Saying, "Are you hear for the big sale?" not only separates you from all the other sales advisors they've probably talked to, but will also peak their interest as to what the big sale is all about. From here, you can continue about what incentives, mark downs, liquidations or anything else you can use to entice them further.

This statement will also, on a certain level, make them think, "Wow, we have good timing. We didn't even know there was a big sale and we got lucky that we were in the right place at the right time." Try using this line in your meet and greet to separate yourself from the pack.

This line is also helpful later on to instill a sense of urgency to the deal in negotiations or throughout the buying process. "Management is willing to do such and such because of the big sale. There are only a few days left." Remember, there is always a big sale going on at your dealership because every month the manufacturer or management rolls out new incentives.

The clients just got out of their vehicle, looked around and headed into the lot.

Sales Advisor: *"Hello, welcome to ABC Motors. My name is Matt. Are you guys here for the big sale?"*
Client: *"Maybe, we're just looking."*
Sales Advisor: *"Okay….we'll let me help you look. My name is Matt and you are?"*
Client: *"I'm Jack and this is my friend Bill. You guys are having a sale?"*
Sales Advisor: *"Nice to meet you both, yes, we currently for a limited time have extremely generous rebates on our trucks and vans. Are you looking for new or used?"*
Client: *"Used."*

Sales Advisor: *"Okay...our used vehicles are this way. Follow me. Have you been to ABC Motors before?"*
Say this as you're walking toward the used car lot.
Client: *"No, but we drive by here all the time."*
Sales Advisor: *"Oh really. A little about us: we've been in the valley for more than thirty years. I've been working here for more than five years. We're the top dealer in the state. We've won the top company service award for 5 years in a row. We're ranked in the top 1% in service by autorater.com in the whole country. We have more than four hundred new and used vehicles. A very good mix of all types of vehicles."*

This is an excellent meet and greet because the sales advisor mentioned the "big sale", peaking the clients curiosity and kind of hinted at a sense of urgency where they need to take advantage before the sale is over.

Manufacturers usually have tremendous amounts of incentives on their new vehicles and they change every month. Therefore, there is always a sale going on. This response is tremendous because the word "sale" implies "for a limited time". Time is of the essence.

The sales advisor also built trust in himself and the dealership by stating a little of the awards they had won as well as the number of vehicles available. By saying you've been working somewhere a long time and that the company has been around for a long time hints at competence, a good reputation, professionalism and client service.

As you read the above conversation, you might be thinking, "Wow that sounds like such a sales pitch." Or, "I can't say that, the client will see right through it as a sales pitch." It might sound like a sales pitch, but don't worry, it's just the foundation of your rapport building. You could sprinkle in some questions about them, their vehicle or anything else before jumping into the history lesson. It'll become better once you're in the fact-finding and throughout the sales process. In the beginning, use it until you find your own voice and style.

Another good tip is to write down the client's name on a piece of paper as the average person quickly forgets. Asking it again doesn't look too good for the sales advisor's professionalism. I used to carry around a clipboard with a list of our entire used car inventory as it changed daily as well as our incentive sheet for that month. This way I could show the clients our incentive sheet for the big sale as well as having something to write down the client's name and contact information.

6c.   Types of Greetings

Casual – Language and body language used when we meet a friend of ours, siblings, close associates. "Hey Paul, how you doing?" and "Nice ride dude, what did this set you back?" shows openness and lowers their guard a little.

Laid Back – Language used by really close friends or best friends. Similar to a casual greeting, but much less formal. "You ready to get a smoking deal at ABC Motors?" and "Let me guess, you're looking for a truck?" I don't recommend this type of greeting since you don't know what type of personality or mood the client is in. If they're in an extremely good mood then yes, but you don't know. I've seen it used effectively but I wouldn't recommend it at all. It shows openness, but brings up a slimy sales person image. It is only to be used with someone you've already established some rapport and history with.

Formal – Language reserved for people of importance, superiors, parents, strangers. "Hello Sir, welcome to ABC Motors, how can I help you?" and "Hello, my name is Mark. Welcome to ABC Motors, How may I serve you?" and "Hello Sir, thank you for coming out to ABC Motors, how can I assist you today?" shows respect of the clientele and professionalism of you. This is highly recommended.

Jokey – Language used to illicit a laugh and get the client in a good or happy mood. "Wow, your car looks like it's on its last leg, do you want me to shoot it?" This is not recommended at all as people's sense of humor are varied and can be taken as offensive. In addition, you don't know what mood your client is in.

Commenting – Commenting about something you notice about the client or clients, usually about the vehicle they arrive in or their appearance, because that's all you have to go on in the beginning. "What's that license plate say? Lover? Nice." Suppose you see a religious sticker on their car, in this case a cross. "How can I help fine Christian people such as yourself today?" Maybe they are a large family. "Wow, look at this large family, life's been good to you guys." This shows interest in clients without trying to sell them anything. It also opens up some dialogue later on that you can come back and touch.

There are other variations than those listed above. You'll find your own way and find greetings that work for you. In the beginning, stick with the safest greetings. The best ones will be to mix of formal and the commenting greetings. This will show clients that you respect them and show them that you've noticed something about them and have a genuine interest in them. You don't know what mood or where in the buying process your clients are, so use the formal greetings until you get some experience.

Whatever greeting type you decide, be confident, make eye contact, be sincere and be direct.

Keep in mind that your objective is to have effective control, establish a common ground and mutual trust, save time by being to the point. You're earning the clients respect, trust and confidence.

6d.   Types of Client Behaviors

Avoidance or salesmen Adverse – These clients come on the lot and don't want any help. They don't even look toward the dealership at all. They beam right for the new car or used car section without even looking back. These buyers have usually gone to many dealerships, have been treated very badly and are now salesman adverse. Good thing you're a sales advisor. Judging by the body language, you instinctively know that they want to be left alone and don't want any help. This is going to be a tough sale. Any of the greeting approaches will work, depending on the mood you're in. If you're in a good mood and you've realized that clients such as these are part of the job that neither you nor anyone else can avoid, then use the jokey greet, but always keep it clean and have fun with it. It's best to use the jokey or laid back greetings for these types of buyers because you want to try to get them to feel at ease and let their guard down.

If a client does beam straight into the lot without even looking back:

Sales Advisor: *"Hello my name is Mark, can I help you guys find something?"*
Client: *"No, we just want to be left alone."*
Sales Advisor: *"Okay…no problem, let me save you some time. Are you looking for new or used?"*

Now here you will see how salesmen adverse they are.

Client: *"Look, we just want to be left alone!"*

They are very salesmen adverse.

Sales Advisor: *"Okay, I understand, it's just that we have a lot of stuff stolen from vehicles all the time, so feel free to look around and I'll just hang back. I'm also here if you have any questions. New vehicles are over there, new trucks are over here, used cars and trucks are over there."*

Here you would follow the clients around at a distance and out of their way. Be close enough to answer any questions they may have or to inject something to build some rapport.

Typically, management doesn't want people walking around the lot unattended, so you need to stick with people when they come on to the lot whether they want it or not.

By hanging with them, you have a chance to let them look around while being available for any questions. You can also chime in every so often if you hear a question being asked or make a comment about something you overhear them talking about. Remember, it's not personal, it's business. People that behave like this usually have high credit scores and are immediate buyers.

If the clients respond with:

Sales Advisor: *"Hello my name is Mark, can I help you guys find something?"*
Client: *"No, we just want to be left alone."*
Sales Advisor: *"Okay, no problem, let me save you some time. Are you looking for new or used?"*

Somewhat averse.

Clients: *"We're looking for used."*

Sales Advisor: *"Okay, no problem. Used vehicles are over there, feel free to look around. I have to go inside for a second but I'll be right back to answer any questions you may have. We also have a lot of trade-ins in the back we just got that I can show you too if you don't find anything you like out here."*

This response is good on many fronts. It gives the clients some room to look around and discuss between them what they like and don't like; it keeps you from looking overbearing which turns off most clients. It also puts in their mind that there is another section of the dealership full of vehicles that they can see but will need your help to access. Remember, hope for gain, fear of loss. You can also use this type of rebuttal or response for clients that are very sales adverse. Give them a few minutes on their own and then check back with them on any questions they may have.

Give the clients a few minutes to look around and then come back with either a list of your vehicles or bottles of water. Preferably both.

Sales Advisor: *"Did you guys find anything that you liked?"*

Best case scenario.

Client: *"Yes a few, can you get the keys to these vehicles?"*
Sales Advisor: *"Okay, by the way what are your names?"*
Clients: *"John and Martha."*
Sales Advisor: *"My name is Jason. I'll be right back."*

When you come back, you would then go into the second step in the process of fact-finding because there might be something else you have that they haven't considered.

Worst case scenario.

Client: *"No, nothing really catches our eye."*
Sales Advisor: *"So what is it exactly that you're looking for? Well first of all, who's this vehicle for?"*

You would then start with the second step in the process of fact-finding, but not before getting their names and giving some information about you and your dealership.

Fact-Finding Clients – These types of clients are looking for information. They're not necessarily looking to buy today, but are just scouting for information and to look and compare vehicles. These clients will get out of their vehicles and look around a bit before moving toward the lot. They will usually look considerably at the dealership before moving toward the lot. These types of buyers will be in the market for a vehicle in a few weeks.

Sales Advisor: Hello, my name is Mark, are you here for the big sale?"
Client: "I want to see some minivans."

Sales Advisor: *"okay, no problem. What was your name?"*
Client: *"Robert."*
Sales Advisor: *"Okay, Robert, nice to meet you. Are you looking for new or used?"*

Here, you can use all the greetings except jokey and casual. This person has taken time out to do some research. This is a serious buyer, maybe not today, but soon.

Here you will go into step 2 of fact-finding. In fact-finding, you get to the bottom of the time period for this purchase.

Serious Clients – This client is at the end of their search and has finalized the type of vehicle, as well as trim, color, and price. They're ready to buy and at this point of their buying process, they are more knowledgeable than most of the sales people out there. These clients have been to many dealerships, online research, manufacturers' websites and the internet. They know exactly what they want and how much they're willing to pay. When they get out of their vehicle, they make a beeline to the first sales advisor they see.

Sales Advisor: *"Hello, my name is Mark. Is there something I can help you with today?"*
Client: *"Yes. I've done my research and I'm looking to buy a Camry SE with sunroof, leather, upgraded stereo, cylinders and in a dark grey. I want to pay invoice for it. Can you help me?"*
Sales Advisor: *"Of course I can, would you like to drive it first?"*
Client: *"No, I've driven a couple of them and I know what they drive like."*
Sales Advisor: *"Okay, come on in and let me see if we can meet your requirements."*

It's not typically advisable to skip steps and go from meet and greet straight to negotiations. When you approach the desk manager, the first thing they will ask is if they've test driven the vehicle. The answer will be "yes", but not here. They've been to other dealerships and test driven them there. Since the buyer has told you that he is willing to buy makes it somewhat okay.

The reason you don't want to skip steps is because if you follow the steps of the process, not only do you find a vehicle that will match their needs, but more importantly, your building rapport. You're building a relationship with them. The more time you spend on building rapport, the less time you will need to spend on negotiations, thereby giving you a larger gross and paycheck.

In this case, you would take this client inside, sit them down, run their credit, then go into the negotiations phase.

I would use the formal greeting as well as call them Mr. or Miss when talking to them. You should make them feel important and smart.

I've Already Test Driven This Vehicle, Let's Talk Some Numbers Clientele - This is similar to the serious people. At first, you might be thinking this is going to be an easy sale. The truth is, they're shopping you. They've been to other dealerships and have given such ridiculous offers for vehicles that the other dealers didn't want to or couldn't do business with them, so they're here looking to see how much you'll bend or break. These clients are all about the negotiations. They want to go from your first step in your process to the negotiation step.

Your job was just made harder because you never got a chance to do a presentation of the vehicle in question and build value in it. Another negative is you didn't spend enough time with them to build rapport and make them like you.

Sales Advisor: *"Hello, my name is Sam, what can I get you information on today?"*
Client: *"Hello, I'm Steve. My brother-in-law has this model and I've driven it a few times. I'm ready to buy so I just need to see some numbers."*

REMEMBER TO USE THE WORD "WHY" TO PROBE THE REAL REASONS BEHIND THEIR CHOICES.

In this scenario, no value has been built into the vehicle to justify the price. The higher the value built into the vehicle, the less justification needed for the price.

Sales Advisor: *"I understand Steve, but no 2 cars are the same. I really think you should take it for a spin just to make sure you like it and it meets your needs and requirements."*

This way, you have a chance to build some value in the vehicle during the test drive and find out more about Steve and his needs. "I just don't want you to waste time getting numbers on a vehicle that you don't like in the end or make a mistake in choosing a vehicle that's not suited to your needs."

If Steve agrees, all the better for you because you have a chance to build value in the vehicle as well as to go down the steps in the process of fact-finding.

If Steve doesn't agree, continue on into the dealership and quickly ask him during the walk some qualifying questions.

Who's this car going to be for?
  "Me" – *"Okay, no problem."*
  "Wife" – *"Where's your wife? Will she come to finalize the deal?"*

What do you like about this vehicle? **S.P.A.C.E.R.**

- **Safety** – Airbags, seat belts, warning devices, special devices. Safety for your family?
- **Performance** – Size of engine, quickness, sportiness, braking power, torque, power
- **Appearance** – Appeal, image, design
- **Comfort** – Road noise, leather, seats, shocks, engine noise, vibration, feel
- **Economy** – Gas mileage, maintenance cost, resale value

- **Reliability** – Proven track record, design, reputation, awards

Do you have any other vehicles that Steve will be happy with?

The point is to keep Steve's options open in case he doesn't qualify.

Do you have a trade?

> *"No." – "Okay, no problem."*
> *"Yes." – "Where is it?"* Take time to evaluate his trade to slow him down and get more information from him as to exactly what he's looking for.

Have you been to other dealerships?

> *"No." – "Okay, no problem."*
> *"Yes." – "What happened? Were you trying to buy the same vehicle? What* happened?"

Are you paying cash of financing?

> *"Paying cash." – "Okay, no problem."*
> *"Financing." – "Do you mind if I run your credit?"* If he's ready to buy, you have to run credit.

What do you hope to accomplish today?

> *"Buy a vehicle" – "Excellent."*
> *"Just get some information." – "What type of information do you need?"*

Just Looking Clientele

Client: *"I'm Steve and this is my wife Mary. We're just looking."*

This is the most common objection or answer you'll receive as a sales advisor. It keeps the client from getting pinned down on a vehicle or in most cases, is the truth because as a shopper you scout the market first and then make a decision.

Sales Advisor: *"Okay, no problem, I'll help you look and get you some information and if you don't see anything you like here, I can show you some new units we just got in in the back. This way you have your options open."*

These people have just started their car search. They have a rough idea of what their looking for but are mainly going on something that catches their eye. They haven't bought a car in a long time and they are afraid of making a mistake. They probably won't be buying another car in a long time so they want something that lasts, is functional as well as look nice and will be up to date for a long time.

Their biggest fear is being talked into something they don't want by a slick sales advisor. Formal greeting is best used on these types of clients.

They usually prefer to be left alone to look without any help. You most likely will be just background noise to them. You will need to educate these client as to what they're actually looking for and what you have to offer.

Sales Advisor: *"Hello, my name is Justin. How can I help you today, sir?"*
Client: *"Were just looking, we'll come and get you if we need you."*
Sales Advisor: *"Okay, sir. Not a problem. Are you looking for new or used so I can point you in the right direction?"*
Client: *"Justin, like I said, we don't know what we're looking for and I don't want to waste your time."*

At this point, you have choices.

1. Let them wander the lot by themselves. Most likely, they'll look around and leave without getting any information from you, about the vehicles or about the dealership. There goes your opportunity. So the first choice is not a choice

Sale Advisor: *"Okay, let me know if you need anything."*

2. Stick to them so you can slow them down and get some more information so you can turn them around and help them make the decision to buy from you, also, to build rapport, trust and make a friend.

Depending on how hostile their attitudes are toward you, you have two responses. The more hostile they are toward you, the more you need to educate them that by talking to you, not only are they saving time but you are also keeping them from making a wrong decision.

If they're really hostile, the chances of them buying from you are very slim so the best response would be:

Sales Advisor: *"Look, I understand. I'm just here to answer your questions and help you find a vehicle that meets your needs, but I understand. The thing is that we have things stolen from the vehicles all the time, so I'll just walk with you guys and you can look as much as you want. You won't even know I'm here unless you have a question."*

Some say that this response is the same as accusing them of being thieves. All you're doing here is finding an excuse to help them, because at this point you don't have anything. In my experience, clients who wandered the lot by themselves usually got back in there vehicles and left, so the sales advisor never engaged them about their fears and hopes. You can leave the "stolen from our vehicles" part out and just say, "I'll walk with you and you won't even know I'm here" instead. Letting the client wander the lot by themselves will prevent the client from building trust, rapport and excitement with you and your dealership. Letting the client wander for extended periods of time by themselves is not an option. They're not buying furniture, they're buying a vehicle.

This way, you're giving them a chance to look and walk with you without a commitment and you tell them that you're cool with that. This way, it brings their guard down a little. From here if they talk to you, talk about everything but the cars and don't seem too excited about them picking out a vehicle.

Or

Sales Advisor: *"Okay, I understand. I've been doing this for more than five years and I'm not here to sell you anything, just to show you what we have that matches as close as possible to what your needs and wants are. We sell more than three hundred vehicles a month, so we get a bunch of trade-in's every day and I can show you those too before anyone else has access to them. Sound fair?"*

This is a better pitch because you've built trust by giving them your background of five years of experience, you have built trust in your dealership by telling them you sell more than three hundred vehicles a month and you've built a hope for gain and a fear of loss by telling them you can show them vehicles in the back that most clients don't have access to.

Another option would be to bring them a list of your inventory or a copy of your monthly incentive sheet. This way, you give them some time alone to look and have an excuse to talk to them again.

If they seem nice, but just don't like sales people:

Sales Advisor: *"I understand. You guys don't like sales people. I've been doing this for a long time and I come across clients like you all the time. They don't want to deal with anyone and rush through without getting all the information they need and end up making a really bad decision. You guys need to slow down, get all the information and look at all your options. Even if you don't buy from me, at least you know what you're dealing with, what your options are and you learn something. Slow down, you'll have this car for years to come. It's important to get as much info as possible before making a decision."*
Here you have them slow down and really start thinking that they can only benefit by talking to you. They open up and bring their guard down. This way, you have a chance to move on to the next step in the process of fact-finding so you can match their needs to what you have for sale, which is the selling evaluation. You also gave them an out with, "even if you don't buy from me", so it is a double bonus.

You can even use this for the hostile clients because you have nothing to lose with them.

Tailor your message to stress the point of *"**Fear of loss, hope for gain**"*.

98

With this rebuttal, you've addressed their fear of loss, which is making a bad decision and a hope for gain for slowing down, getting the right information and making an informed decision.

Typically, you won't have one or the other type of a client but a mix of averse and serious, fact-finding and averse or any combination.

This may sound silly but you should rehearse some of these lines in front of the mirror so you can get your expression, body language and eye contact just right. Body language is very important and to be a true professional, you're going to need to rehearse the parts you're going to play. Role-playing in front of the mirror or with other sales advisors can also bring out places that you look weak or places you need help.

Look for body language to tell you how to greet them.

6e.   Body Language

7% human communication is through language. 93% is in body language or non-verbal communications. Learning to read body language accurately can help you expose the root of many objections.

A **handshake** should be straight and firm. If you shake hands with your hand outstretched and on the bottom, then you're in a position of weakness. If you offer your hand palm down, you're in a position of strength, which could be offensive to the client subconsciously. The best way to shake hands is straight and firm: straight as it conveys mutual respect and firm as it conveys strength and respect as opposed to if it was limp, which conveys weakness.

Make strong eye contact while shaking hands as it conveys interest. Make a note of everyone's eye color.

You should emulate your client's body language to seem more like them. Be a chameleon. You need to be conscious of your body language to convey trust. Have an open body, not hiding behind the body by crossing your legs or your arms, as this signified defensiveness.

Smile, look them directly in the eyes with a firm handshake and bow your head slightly forward to display respect to the client. The bigger the smile, the higher they perceive enthusiasm. Have good posture with your back straight, shoulders back and chest out; this conveys confidence. Have an open body, meaning don't hold your hands or be fussing around with your hands or have your hands in your pocket, which means you're hiding something.

Touching or rubbing your hands together means that you're nervous and assuring only to the sales person. This doesn't convey confidence or competence. It also makes you feel distant.

Remember, most people buy because of how they feel about the sales advisor. They're looking for someone they like who they can trust. Someone that's a professional, competent and honest.

Don't be higher than the client. When they're sitting down in the vehicle, you should either be sitting next to them or on your knees explaining the features to them or at least crouched down. Standing higher than them conveys dominance and say's that you are better than them.

Be genuine. Work to make your body language natural and not fake. Clients can see through the fakeness, either consciously or sub consciously.

Through it all, you're building rapport. What rapport is in its essence is you communicating to clients that you're similar to them, you understand them and you empathize with their feeling. You have nothing to hide and they can trust you. Find common ground.

Give the clients your undivided attention and look them directly when talking to them.
How to read the body language of the clients is also of immense advantage to you: how they walk, dress, eye contact and hand gestures.

There are 7 universal expressions: happiness, sadness, anger, fear, surprise, contempt and disgust. According to Dr. Paul Ekman, these are universal to every human being regardless of culture. Therefore, when someone expresses something other than what's natural, it should tell you that they're not being truthful.

Eye brows that go up and come down to a corner conveys fear. The brow and forehead convey loads of information as well as reinforce what the client is saying. Your voice should also be solid and not shrill. You should control your voice to be more convincing and to convey confidence and competency.

Body language works in a package like gestures, eye contact, facial expressions and sounds of the voice, all working together to send a message of comfort, trust and competence.

6f.   Scenarios

Just Looking: Here they are trying to avoid any high pressure because they only want to be there for a short amount of time and want to avoid making a decision right now. They're just looking for information. Your goal is to build trust in you, your dealership and to get them to commit to an appointment, unless you have something in your inventory that they will absolutely fall in love with.

> **Jeff:** "Let's just stop by and have a look around. If a sale guy comes by, just tell him we're looking around and we're three months away from purchasing."
> **Maria:** "Okay, also tell him that we have an appointment in half an hour."

They park, get out their vehicle and find their bearings.

> **Sales Advisor:** "Hello, My name is Mark. Are you guys here for the big sale?"
> **Jeff:** "My name is Jeff and this is my Maria, we're just looking right now. Were three months away from buying anything."

Sales Advisor: *"Okay, no problem Jeff and Maria. What's happening in 3 months?"*

Maria: *"We'll be done with our current car payments and we will be looking to trade it in."*

Sales Advisor: *"Sounds good. Have you guys been here before?"*

Jeff: *"No."*

Sales Advisor: *"Okay, a little about us, we're the 2nd largest Toyota dealership in the valley but number one in client satisfaction. We've sold more than four-thousand new vehicles last year and more than thirty-five hundredd used vehicles, and you can't do that if you don't get good client satisfaction. Look it up if you want.*

I've been selling cars for nine years now, so I too know what I'm doing. I'm here just to show you around and answer any questions you might have. Are you looking for a car, truck or an SUV? Is there anything in particular you're looking for?"

You really need to build value in yourself and your dealership. You need to give them a reason to do business only with you.

Maria: *"Car."*

Sales Advisor*: "Okay. .I have tons to show you. Do you guys have time right now?"*

Maria: *"No, we have to be somewhere in half an hour."*

Clients will usually use this ploy to try to get as much information without anything else or just to get their feet wet.

Your job is to keep the sales process moving forward. There's nothing worse than spending 2 hours with a client showing them various vehicles and test drives only for them to make up an excuse that they have to go somewhere and the dreaded question of, "Do you have a card?"

Sales Advisor: *"Maria, when will be a good time for you guys to come back and really look around? I don't think I can show you much in half an hour. Also you don't want to make a decision on an item such as a car without really checking it out, test driving it and looking at numbers. You're going to make a mistake. Don't worry, I'm not here to pressure you or to sell you something that's not right for you. My job is to answer your questions and find a vehicle that suites your needs."*

This is one way to disarm the *"I'm just looking, I have to be somewhere soon"* excuse.

Husband: *"Oh...it won't hurt to just look around a little. We'll just tell them we're just looking. We're not buying."*

Wife: *"Okay, you do all the talking, I don't want to deal with any pushy salesman."*

Sales Advisor: *"Hello, welcome to ABC Toyota. My name is Mark. Are you guys just looking around?"*

I don't like phrase. "What vehicle are we shopping for?" "who are we shopping for?"

Husband: *"Yes, were just looking."*

By now, you already know that this is going to be a tough sell or is it? You job is to continue the sales process.

Sales Advisor: *"Not a problem. Nobody buys the first time they come on a lot, most people look around, find a vehicle they like, get some number and go home and think it over. They usually take a few days to think about it and come back in a few days and make a purchase. Is that what you guys were thinking?"*

With this approach, you've taken the pressure off the client and given them an out so they don't have to buy today. It's okay to discuss numbers, open up about information, and let their guard down, because like most people they don't have to buy right now. Right?

We've Just Started Looking and We Don't Know What We Want: Here, the buyers are trying to avoid being pinned down and are letting you know that you might be wasting your time by assisting them because they just don't know what their looking for. These buyers also fear making the wrong decision so a little sympathy can go a long way.

Sales Advisor: *"Hello, Welcome to ABC Motors, my name is Mark, what can I get you information on today?*
Husband: *"My name is Jeff and this is my wife Maria, we're looking for a vehicle for her but she doesn't know what she's looking for. We'll know it when we see it."*

These clients will really drive you nuts because you can't satisfy them. They don't know what they want and are extremely picky. They'll nitpick everything.

Sales Advisor: *"Okay, not a problem. I've been doing this for more than nine years and a majority of my clients are repeat and referral, so I understand how difficult it is to make the right choice in selecting a vehicle. After all, it's a decision that will be with you for many years. Right Maria?"*
Here, you're sympathizing with the client on the difficulty of looking for the right vehicle as well as her fear of living with her decision for years to come.

Sales Advisor: *"We have a tremendous inventory of new and used vehicles to choose from. If I don't have it, I can get it as we have numerous other dealers that we can get vehicles from. We also get a lot of trade-ins daily so we'll find you what you're looking for. Let me ask you this Maria: what will this vehicle be used for?" "How many miles a year do you drive?" "What's most important to you? Style? Comfort? Fuel efficiency?,".(S.P.A.C.E.R)*

Now this goes into later chapters of the needs analysis: finding out what the client is really looking for. This person does need a vehicle but doesn't realize what and why. She's an impulse buyer.

Summary of the Meet and Greet

Tailor your greet and message to each individual client. Keep the idea of hope and fear in your messages. Hope to get a great deal and fear of making a bad decision by not conducting business with you and your dealership. The purpose of a proper meet and greet is to get the client to relax and feel welcomed so you can move into the rapport building or trust building.

You shouldn't pick and choose clients based on the ones you think are going to buy, most closely resembles you, seem more in the market to buy, ethnicity or some other qualifying item you subconsciously use to pick your clients. You should approach as many clients as possible. The more the variety the better. This will make you a better and a more professional sales advisor. You never know who's buying and who's looking unless you talk to them and build trust with them. If they're on the lot then they're in the market. Maybe not at the moment but soon. If you're a good sales advisor and build trust in them, build rapport and have confidence and enthusiasm, you'll make the sale whenever they're ready to buy.

Smile, use eye contact and a firm hand shake.

Mirror their body language, mood, actions and verbiage, but keep it clean.

No matter what the client is like, aim to spend at least 20 to 30 minutes minimum with each client getting to know each other. Anything less will not be sufficient to build rapport and trust with your clients.

Keep in mind that your objective is to establish common ground, trust and to start to build rapport with clients. Clients are operating out of fear and hope. Acknowledge and address these fears while at the same time build up their hopes.

7.   Fact-Finding /Needs Analysis (Establish Trust by Listening)

Purpose: To uncover clients' needs, wants, wishes. To continue to build trust, build rapport and to find common ground with client. In this step, we're digging for what the real wants and needs of the client are as well as continuing to build rapport and trust with the client.

This is one of the most important steps in the whole process!

So many other steps in the process depend on this one step, because how can you build value, trust or enthusiasm in a vehicle if it's not what the client is looking for? I recommend you refer to this chapter from time to time as you might get too comfortable or in a groove and ignore other fruitful techniques. Fact-finding, product presentation and negotiations are the most important steps in the sales process and must be studied at some length to grasp the concept of the sale and process.

The more information you get from the client, the better you can match their needs and wants with what you have on the lot and the easier it will be to build value in your vehicle, build trust in yourself, the dealership and the vehicle, and the less time you will need to spend in negotiation. Information gathered in this step has implications throughout the sales process so it's vital you ask questions that can help build value in the vehicle, to prepare for objections later on and to match the client's wants and needs with the available vehicle at your dealership.

> *Sales Advisor:* *"Hello, welcome to ABC Motors, are you here for the big sale?"*
> *Client:* *"Hello. Big sale? No, I'm just looking."*
> *Sales Advisor:* *"Yes, were currently having our huge yearly sale. My name is Jake and you are?"*
> *Client:* *"David. Nice to meet you."*
> *Sales Advisor:* *"Nice to meet you David. We currently have huge incentives on our sedans, trucks and vans. We've also discounted our certified pre-owned inventory. Are you looking for new or pre-owned?"*
> *Client:* *"I'm looking for a used vehicle."*

Safety – Airbags, seat belts, warning devices, special devices

Performance – Size of engine, quickness, sportiness, braking power, torque, power

Appearance – Appeal, image, design

Comfort – Road noise, leather, seats, shocks, engine noise, vibration, feel

Economy – Gas mileage, maintenance cost, resale value

Reliability – Proven track record, design, reputation, awards

> *Sales Advisor:* *"Okay, I'll be happy to show you around. Our pre-owned inventory is this way. Anything in particular you're looking for David? Car, truck or SUV?"*

Client: *"I am looking for a commuter car because I just got a job and I'm going to be driving a lot."*

Sales Advisor: *"Okay, we have really niece pre-owned gas efficient vehicles over here.*

David, have you been to our dealership before?"

Client: *"Yes, I helped my sister buy a car here last year."*

Sales Advisor: *"Okay, great. So you're familiar with our dealership. You know about the award winning reputation as well as our competitive pricing policy?"*

Client: *"Somewhat."*

Sales Advisor: *"I've been working here for about three years and I would say 85% of our clients are repeat or referral clients such as yourself. How is your sister doing with her vehicle?*

Client: *"Good so far. Haven't really heard her complain."*

Sales Advisor: *"Excellent. So you're looking for a commuter, so I guess gas mileage is important to you?"*

Client: *"Somewhat."*

Sales Advisor: *"Somewhat? Okay, out of Safety, Performance, Appearance, Comfort, Economy or Reliability...what is the most important to you?"*

Client: *"Sorry, say again?"*

Sales Advisor: *"Safety, Performance, Appearance, Comfort, Economy or Reliability." The Acronym is S.P.A.C.E.R.*

Client: *"I would say Appearance first then, Reliability and then Economy. I know safety is important but now a days most cars are pretty safe."*

Sales Advisor: *"True, especially the vehicles produced by our company. What else will you be using the vehicle for?"*

Client: *"I might need to haul some equipment but nothing big."*

Sales Advisor: *"Sorry for asking so many questions. It's just that I want to save you time and help you find the vehicle that will best fit your needs and wants. Like I said I've been doing this for more than three years and giving great service to my clients is very important to me."*

Client: *"No problem, I understand and appreciate that."*

Sales Advisor: *"So David, what kind of work do you do that you require equipment?"*

This scenario goes into the initial meet and greet as well as some fact-finding. Notice that the sales advisor initiated an approach that help pique the interest of the client as well as briefly touch on the reputation of the dealership and himself. This way he established that the dealership as well as he can be trusted in assisting the client in the purchase of his next vehicle. The sales advisor will go more into detail about the reputation of the dealership when he takes the client through the tour and will sell his own skill and reputation throughout the whole sales process.

Also notice that the sales advisor is the one asking the questions, thereby keeping control of the sales process. There are many ways of going about this and in time, you'll find a script or technique that best fits your personality. Get the client's name and use it often as if you're close friends.

As always, it's to their benefit to listen and answer your questions because you can help them save time, money and help them make an informed decision.

> **Sales Advisor:** "I don't want to seem pushy by asking you all these questions but I just want to save you some time and help you to make an informed decision on your next purchase. The more I know what your needs and wants are, the better I can find a vehicle that will work best for you. Sound fair?"

7a.   Asking Questions to Build Rapport

The Person asking the questions is the one in control but the one that actively listens builds trust.

Most of the time the client doesn't know what they're looking for and are just going on instinct or something that catches their eye. They have an idea but can be easily swayed. At this point, the idea is to get them to relax and build trust in you. Always hold the carrot of other vehicles in the back you can also show them. The only way to really uncover what the client needs is by asking properly worded questions: non-threatening, non-confrontational, open ended questions. The more you know about their wants and needs, the better you can match that to your vehicles.

The more you get them to talk, the more information they'll give and the better idea you will have in fitting them in a vehicle that meets their needs. People like to talk and hear themselves talk. People also like to talk about themselves. Open ended questions allow them to give you information on their lives, their needs and wants and it makes them feel like you're interested in their lives more so than if you just ask closed ended questions. Ask questions but listen intently. Use this information by asking questions not only about what kind of vehicle they're looking for but about them in general.

Always avoid the topics of sex, politics and religion. These topics should be reserved for close friends or family.

Finding common ground with everyone is one of the most important skills a sales advisor can develop. Not only will this skill help you on the job, but it will help you in life in dealing with others to be more likeable. Finding common ground means appearing more like them and empathizing with them. It's one of the most important aspects of friendship building. You must also be genuine, as most people will see through deception.

We all have common things in life and a great skill to develop is to find those common things we share with people that are completely different from ourselves.

On way of doing this, is to ask non-threating and non-judgmental questions.

Always ask open ended questions. Open ended questions are questions that require an extensive explanation. A closed ended question only requires a yes or no answer. Avoid any questions that can have a yes or no answer. Questions starting with who, what, when, where, why and how are a good starting place.

Questions like: "Tell me more?", "That's interesting, and then what happened?", "Wow, how did you feel about that?", "Then what happened?", "Wait, I don't understand. Explain how that works again?", "What do I have to do to be more like you?", "When will be the next time that will happen?", "How can I be more like you?"

Say statements like: "I never thought of that", "It's a good thing you were there, I would have gotten scared and left?", "Wow, you did that?"

Every client is different. Tailor your message to each individual client. If they seem standoffish and don't want to discuss the vehicle, then just accompany them and make friends with them by talking about everything but the vehicle. The more you get them to talk about themselves, the more comfortable they'll get and the more important they'll feel. Spend at least 20 to 30 minutes with each client, regardless of if they're looking seriously or not.

7b.   Three Key Topics to Discuss

- Questions about the client - Why they're there, personal life, etc.....make a friend.
- Questions about their current vehicle - Age, make, model, mileage.....try to assess why they want to get rid of their current vehicle so you know what they liked about it and what they don't. What don't they like about their old car? Why are they looking for another vehicle?
- Questions about what their looking for - S.P.A.C.E.R.

S.P.A.C.E.R.
Safety, Performance, Appearance, Comfort, Economy, Reliability

Sample Questions:

About the Client:

What brought you to our dealership?
What kind of work do you do? How Long? What type of industry are you in?
Do you live in the area?
What is the size of your family?
Are all parties here that will be using the vehicle or making a decision on the purchase?
Who will be driving the vehicle and who will be the principal driver?
What lifestyle change has occurred since your last car purchase?
Do you have enough time to look at all your options?

What do you hope to accomplish today?

About their present vehicle:

What do you like/don't like about your present vehicle?

How long have you had it?

Where did you buy your present vehicle?

How much was the price of the vehicle when you bought it?

Was it new or used when you bought it?

How has your present vehicle treated you?

What's the most important things in your next vehicle? Safety, Performance, Appearance, Comfort, Economy, Reliability? S.P.A.C.E.R.

What other vehicles do you currently own?

What vehicle they are looking for?

What do you plan to do with the vehicle?

Will this vehicle be the primary or the secondary vehicle?

Who else will be driving this vehicle?

How many miles do you drive?

What is the most important feature of your new vehicle: Safety, Performance, Appearance, Comfort, Economy or Reliability? S.P.A.C.E.R.

What do you hope to accomplish with this visit?

When asking these questions remember to let them talk as much as they want or can. You should just listen. Listen with your eyes and ears. Notice their body language as well as their words. The more they talk the more time they spend with you and the more information they reveal as to what makes them happy in life, family and in a vehicle. Listening is one of the most important aspects of fact-finding.

Nod your head a lot and give them the sense that you're paying attention, reiterate their answers and make them feel that you're interested in what they have to say. You should be. Every minute they talk gives you more ammunition when it comes time to negotiate about their likes, dislikes and capabilities. Actively listen. Be genuine as you might be found out as fake, eliminating any trust that you've built up.

7c.   Questions to Avoid During Fact-Finding and Why

What color do you want? Most likely you won't have the color their looking for, especially in a used car. Avoid this question. Instead, ask if they are looking for a light or dark color.

Would you like to drive the car? It's too early for them to drive the car. You have to really sell the features and benefits before they drive the vehicle.

What have you been offered for your trade? Most likely they'll tell you some outrageous price that can't be true just to get you to up the trade value. Leave that up to the management.

<u>What do you think your trade is worth?</u> Again, they'll think it's worth what their selling it for at the dealer next door. They'll get a figure solidified in their head that their car is worth all the money. Should they ask you, "What do you think my trade is worth?" The best answer would be "I don't know, my manager needs to appraise it, but because of our sale they're giving some crazy numbers for trades."

<u>How much?</u> Never discuss price of your vehicle in the lot. You're only concerned with meeting their requirements and needs at the moment and if they are looking for Safety, Performance, Appearance, Comfort, Economy or Reliability.

> Most dealerships these days have prices on the windshield. These prices are typically overinflated to compensate for the client wanting to negotiate. Keep this in mind if a client balks or comments on the high prices of the vehicles. Everything at dealerships is negotiable except at the no hassle stores. During your fact-finding, you undoubtedly will need to get what their financial limits are. Knowing how much they have for a down payment, credit rating, income and monthly payment requirements are all useful information you need to find them a vehicle that not only meets their needs but also one that they can afford. There will always be wiggle room to the limits to get the deal done.

<u>Would you take $$$$ for your car?</u> It's too early to ask. We must first find them a car to fall in love with. The rest is just logistics.

7d.   Fundamental Questions to Ask

These are general questions. In time, you'll know when and where to use these questions. You have to tailor these questions to your own style. For now just stick to the script until you get some experience.

Who is this vehicle for? If the client is present whom this car is for, then you will need to devote a majority of your time to this person's needs and wants. If the person is not present, then continue like they are. Sometimes people will say it's for their partner just so they have an out. You should ask when will be a good time for the decision maker to come by and take a look for themselves. What's the point of going through the process with someone who isn't the decision maker? Never sit down and discuss price and terms with someone other than the decision maker. It's only the decision maker who can say, "Yes" or "No", so why would you waste time negotiating with someone who doesn't have that authority?

What will this vehicle be used for? This is a very important question to ask because it opens up their option to other vehicles you have on the lot so you can show them a couple of different vehicles. If gas mileage is most important, then using your product knowledge you know at least 5 or 6 vehicles on your lot with great gas mileage. This will also give you insight into body style, number of doors, hatchback, coupe or convertible. Every client knows what they will use the vehicle for; it will all depend on you to bring out their true needs and wants. There are other factors at play here like price, comfort, reliability, appearance and safety to find something that will fit their needs. Condition and mileage will also play into it, but we're just interested with how they will use this vehicle with this question. This is where your product knowledge comes in handy. In addition, if they will be driving a lot then you may want to move them to a newer vehicle and plant the seeds for a warranty.

Are you interested in new or used? Most people are open but some are only looking for a new vehicle. Although the commission is better on a used vehicle, you can try to move them to a used if they seem like they are open to it. If you're working at a used car dealership only, you would skip this question as all your vehicles are going to be used.

What are you driving right now? This gives you insight as to what they're not looking for. Always comment, "I hear that those are nice vehicles." They'll tell you if they like it or not. Never put down a client's vehicle. People have an unusual attachment to their vehicles as you do to yours, no matter how bad of a vehicle it is. A good follow up question would be, to ask why they are looking to trade out of it. This way you know what they don't like about their current vehicle. It could just be mileage.

> **What did you like or dislike about your last vehicle?** This is a big question. This will give you a great idea on their wants and needs, especially what their dislikes are. The new vehicle has to meet or exceed their old vehicle, which it should. This can be used later on during negotiations where you highlight the benefits of their new vehicle over their old one.

> **Are you going to trade it in?** Here you'll know how serious they are as they've already committed to getting rid of their last vehicle. Some see the trade-in and purchase of their new vehicle as separate transactions, but you, as a professional, know it's the same. It's just another piece of the puzzle to the deal.

> **Do you owe money on it or own it outright?** This will give you a glimpse into their credit as well as how much in monthly payments they are spending right now. A client who owns it outright will be an easier deal because you don't have to deal with negative equity in their current vehicle. Did you bring the title with you? If they brought the title with them, it is even better, as this indicates a serious buyer. Clients who still owe money on their vehicle are almost always upside down, meaning they owe more money on the vehicle than it's worth. That's another huge hurdle to jump over in the negotiation phase.

What are the most important things in your next vehicle? S.P.A.C.E.R. Safety, Performance, Appearance, Comfort, Economy, Reliability. This question will help you sell the vehicle that you pick out for them as you'll continually hit on their preferences on the vehicle you pick out. These are the client's wants and needs or hot buttons. They can pick out more than one. Ask them to rate it from most to least important. Keep in mind that your product knowledge will be crucial in selling why this vehicle is safer, has high performance, is comfortable, economical or reliable.

Do you have a budget in mind in regard to price or payment? In previous sections we said that you shouldn't discuss price on the car lot. This still holds true. The questions you will be asking will be on budget and payments for them and not on the price of the vehicle. Here, were trying to see what our limits are in terms of price and payments. If someone says that they're trying to be at $200 a month, then you already know that with good credit the most they can buy is around a $13,000 vehicle, that's including tax and license, so a vehicle that is retailing for around $11,500 or $12,000. If you show them anything more expensive, you're going to have to reduce the price and give away your gross and extend the terms of the loan to meet that payment. A couple of ways out of this is, even though they say $200 a month, you can most likely bump them up depending on how good of a sales advisor you are. You should always ask how they came up with that number regardless of what they say. Most of the time, clients are misinformed on how much they qualify for or their financing options.

These questions are designed to bring out the client's wants, needs, motivations and expectations they have in the buying process. We want to address and build up all their wants and needs in the new vehicle and how the new vehicle matches what they're looking for in terms of motivation and expectations.

The answers to these questions will be used later on to present the vehicle, demo the vehicle and close the client.

You should provide small talk to clients. Rapport building requires that you find common ground with your clients. To do that, you have to ask a lot of questions about them and their lives. Take an interest as to how their life is going. You can only find common ground with them if you know about their life. Find similarities between your life and theirs. This is one of the ways of finding common ground and building trust.

Make them feel better about themselves and their lives. If they tell you that their child gets in trouble in school or is unruly, then you would also share a similar experience of your niece, nephew, son or daughter who acts much worse than their kid to make them feel better or to reassure them that it's not that bad. Be genuine; don't make things up as people can see through it, which blows your chances of making them a client for life.

7e.   Addressing Fears and Hopes

I know that I've brought up the fears and hopes topic many times but the reason for that is because it is important; you need to keep it in the forefront of your communication and thinking. It should be addressed at every step in the process.

Sometimes people act in a rush going to a dealership because their acting out of fear and you might want to address these fears by divulging somewhere in your presentation, "You guys don't have to be afraid of me. I'm not trying to sell you guys something that you won't like. I've been doing this for a while now and 90% of my clients are from repeat or referrals. I treat everyone like they were my family and they keep buying from me and sending me clients so you guys can feel free to ask or tell me anything you want."

Addressing this fear somewhere in the sales process, preferably early on, airs it out and helps put the client on a higher comfort level with you so you may get to the root cause of their wants and needs. Acknowledge that you sympathize with what they're going through and you understand. Include that, "The more information you give me, the better I can help you guys achieve your goals."

Some clients will come in with some ridiculous requirements that they're looking for in a used vehicle that can in no way be met, like lots of power with high gas mileage or a cheap low mileage vehicle. Some think that they are actually is a "Used Car Factory". The question to ask is, "Why?" After you get that, then you can apply the "why" to something you already have on the lot. The question uncovers many of the hidden objections or hang ups that will come up later on. Get in the habit of asking "why" a lot to uncover some underlying issues that at client may have that will come up later on.

> **Client:** *"I only want the color white in a vehicle."*
> **Sales Advisor:** *"Why only white?"*
> **Client:** *"Because I read somewhere that insurance rates are lower on white cars."*

> **Client:** *"I'm just looking right now. I can't buy for another 3 months."*
> **Sales Advisor:** *"Why, what's happening in 3 months?"*
> **Client:** *"I don't have any money right now but I am starting a new job in 3 months."*
> **Sales Advisor:** *"I don't think any of these vehicles will be here in 3 months. What kind of job will you be starting?"*

> **Client:** *"I'm trying to only spend $200 a month in payments."*
> **Sales Advisor:** *"Only $200? Why only $200?"*
> **Client:** *"Because I only want a 36 month loan."*
> **Sales Advisor:** *"That's going to be tough, let me show you some options you may have."*

This way we can isolate the reason behind their hang up and then address it.

7f.   Scenario

> **Sales Advisor:** *"Hello, my name is Mark. I'm a sales advisor here at ABC Motors. How are you folks doing today?"*
> **Client:** *"Hello Mark, my name is Steve and this is my wife Mary. We're just looking."*
> **Sales Advisor:** *"Okay, not a problem. I'm currently showing vehicles, so it works out perfectly. Let me save you some time. What are you looking for? New or pre-owned and who is this vehicle for?"*
> **Client:** *"Pre-owned and this vehicle is for my wife Mary."*

Sales Advisor: "All right Steve and Mary, our pre-owned inventory is this way, follow me. Have you guys been to our dealership before?"

Client: "No, this is our first time."

Sales Advisor: "Okay, a little about us, we've been around for more than thirty years and we've been at this location for around 20 years. We've won the president's award for service for 5 years in a row. We sell more than three hundred vehicles a month so we get a lot of trade-in's and I've been selling vehicles for more than ten years and have been with this dealership for a little over 4 years, so you're in good hands. A majority of my clients are repeat or referrals. Quick question. Why are you looking for pre-owned?"

Client: "Because vehicles depreciate so drastically, I'd rather just buy a vehicle that has already taken the depreciation."

Sales Advisor: "What if I told you that a new one sells close to the price of a used one? The reason for that is that our make of vehicles have such a great reputation that our used vehicles are going at a premium. Something to think about. I can show those later. Are you looking for a car, truck or SUV?"

Client: "Okay, we can take a look at those later. We're looking for a car."

Sales Advisor: "Who will be the primary driver of the new vehicle?"

Client: "Mary will be the primary driver."

Sales Advisor: "Mary, what will be the primary purpose of this vehicle?"

Client: "It'll be primarily be used for errands, as a kid carrier, and occasionally on long trips to Florida to see our relatives."

Sales Advisor: "Nice. How many kids?"

Client: "3 kids and a dog."

Sales Advisor: "I have 2 kids and a dog. With all their stuff I need a SUV just to cope. Won't a car be too small for you with 2 kids, a dog and cargo?"

Client: "No, I don't think so; it just has to accommodate a car seat and a booster seat."

Sales Advisor: "What are you driving now?"

Client: "We have an old station wagon that needs to be retired."

Sales Advisor: "Is it here so I can get you a trade-in price?"

Client: "Yes. It's the brown one over there."

Sales Advisor: "Okay, let's find you a vehicle to drive home in before I price your trade."

If the trade is there, that's good news because it says that they are serious about doing business today.

Sales Advisor: "Mary, what was it about that vehicle that you really like?"

Client: "It was really comfortable. It fit like an old shoe."

Sales Advisor: "What was it that you really hated?"

Client: "Gas mileage. It was old so the gas mileage wasn't that great."

Sales Advisor: *"Sorry to be asking you so many questions, but I'm trying to figure out what's the most important thing to you guys so I can show you relevant vehicles."*

Sales Advisor: *"What is the most important thing to you: Safety, Performance, Appearance, Comfort, Economy or Reliability?" S.P.A.C.E.R.*

Client: *"Well with our family, Safety always comes first, I guess then comes Reliability, Comfort and then Economy. Appearance would be nice but we don't need performance."*

In this scenario, we know who the decision makers are since we asked. Asking who the vehicle is for is one of the fundamental questions that needs to be asked in fact-finding so we can tailor our message to the end user, and most likely they will be the decision maker. People who shop for a vehicle without the end user are just trying to gather information for that person. It's important to give these people as much information as possible and sell the vehicle but never go into negotiations or talk price unless the decision maker is present or involved. You'll be wasting your time as well as giving away vital information to the deal.

In time, you will develop a sense of what type of questions to ask and when. To be successful in the fact-finding step, you will have to develop a sense of asking the right questions at the right time, learning to listen effectively with your ears and eyes and fully realizing that the person asking the questions will be the one in control. Become a master of open ended questions. Also communicate with them that you are there to help them make an informed decision.

Summary of Fact-Finding

The fact-finding step in the process is one of the most important steps in the whole sales process. Gathering information to use later on as well as addressing objections later on is the goal of information gathering.

Since most people operate out of fear when shopping for a vehicle, they must be put at ease and their fears need to be addressed.

Some basic questions to ask of clients during the fact-finding step are:

Current vehicle: What they like and dislike

Themselves: Who are they? What makes them special? Make a friend. Why are they shopping for a new vehicle?

What they're looking for: Use of the new vehicle, preferences? S.P.A.C.E.R.

Always ask "why" to get to the bottom of any objection or preferences. This question can unveil what is really driving the choices the client is making.

Make a friend. Sometimes the best way to go about selling a vehicle is to talk about everything but the vehicle. Pretend you just met the client at a park and have no other agenda aside from getting to know them better. Once you build trust in you and your dealership, the client's wall will come down revealing exactly what is driving their choices.

Remember: slow the client down by asking questions to continue the client to the next level of picking out the closest vehicle you have to meet their needs, that they will fall in love with and one that they will test drive. In slowing them down, you will also do the most important thing any sales advisor can do and that is to MAKE A FRIEND.   Use this information by asking questions not only about what kind of vehicle they're looking for but about them in general. Let them go off and feel important, needed, liked and interesting. You too have the same needs and wants but you're currently a sales advisor and your job is to listen and to make the client feel important and interesting.

8. Sell from Stock (Best Fit for Immediate Gratification)

Purpose: Select the perfect vehicle or vehicles on your lot based on the client's needs and wants gathered in the fact-finding step. Several reasons why you need to sell from stock for both the client and sales advisor:

<u>Benefits to the Client</u>

1. Immediate transportation for the client. He doesn't need to waste time searching all over town when we have the perfect car for them
2. The buyer can see, touch, feel, drive, finance, purchase and smell the vehicle right now. The buyer can fall in love with the vehicle right now
3. Top trade-in allowance today. Vehicles depreciate around $40 a day, so their trade will be worth $40 less tomorrow or $160 less in a month
4. Time. No need to waste any more time. You can get the job done right now

<u>Benefits to the Sales Advisor</u>

1. Saves time and effort. You have the client there and you don't want to tell them to come back until you get what their looking for. Chances are, they're going to go somewhere else and purchase something else. You need to make them fall in love with what you have in stock
2. Commission sooner.
3. Faster turnover of stock. The more you sell, the faster that newer stuff comes into inventory, giving you more options of things to sell
4. Less possibility of cancellation. By this I mean that if you get a deposit on a vehicle that's coming from another dealer, then the client will have too much time to reconsider the deal and potentially cancel on you. Making a big buying decision always starts the "what if I can't afford it" wheels in their head. Their fears can get the best of them. Better to have them get a car now instead of waiting for it later
5. Getting your sales numbers up. Add to your numbers to get to the next level
6. Get them to the next level of the test drive

If selling used vehicles, you have no choice but to sell from your own stock. I haven't heard of too many dealerships letting other dealers sell from their used car inventory unless they had the same parent company or some sort of partnership, which is rare.

New cars are a little different story. Most dealers that sell the same make usually will have an agreement with each other, where they'll trade with each other if they have a client looking for a specific model and trim. If one Toyota dealer has a client looking for a new dark grey Camry with leather and sunroof and the only Toyota dealership that has it is 30 minutes away, then the first dealership will contact the second dealership and do a trade for another new model that they have on the lot. Of course, this will take time and energy and most dealerships won't take the time unless the client is very serious or committed. In a dealer trade situation it's essential that you show them a model as close as possible to the one they want so you can get a commitment. You must also involve your manager as they're the one that are most likely going to call to make arrangements for the trade.

Most manufacturers make models that have the same exact engine and transmission and drive exactly the same. The only difference will be the specific interior trim and maybe a body kit and rims. If that is the case then you can have them test drive a similar vehicle to make sure they like the drive and feel of the model before contacting the other dealers for the specific trim your client is looking for.

The point is, just because you don't have the exact trim that your client is looking for doesn't mean you skip the test drive step in the process.

By now, if you've followed what I've laid out for you on fact-finding and needs assessment, you have a very good idea of what the client's needs and wants are. With your excellent product knowledge in your inventory, you can find them a vehicle on your lot that not only meets their needs but also one that they can fall in love with.

You need to refer to your needs assessment section regarding what the client was looking for, especially when you kept asking them, "Why?" Asking "why" will root out their root needs, wants and desires to allow you to move them to other vehicles on your lot that will meet their wants and needs.

8a.   Product Knowledge

Product knowledge is the key to selling from stock. Product knowledge just doesn't mean knowing the features and benefits of various models, but also your available inventory. Even though they said they're looking for used, you can still show them some new vehicles that'll fit their needs. Don't forget to mention all the manufacturer incentives that your dealership is offering. Change your attitude. You're an advisor. Your job in this section is to use your fact-finding skills to match the client's needs to any available vehicle you have on the lot, new or used.

Also be prepared to show them sedans, if that's what they requested, but also show other models that will work out for them even better.   You're an advisor, so feel free to advise if you think they'll be better off in a different model.

> **Sales Advisor:** *"Okay good, I have a couple of vehicles that will fit nicely with what you're looking for that'll give you years of use and enjoyment. Follow me."*

Show them at least 3 vehicles: one that comes closest to what they're looking for and others that almost come close to what they're looking for, so when you come back after the test drive you could ask them if they want to take a look at that vehicle too. This will tell you how committed they are to this one.

When you do find several vehicles that would fit your client's needs, start with the most expensive one first and work your way down to the least expensive one. You can justify the price by comparing it the lower end or cheaper model, and the client will usually sell themselves on the higher priced one as they do not want to picture themselves in a cheaper vehicle.

8b.   Unrealistic Demands

Many times clients will give you ridiculous demands for what they are looking for:

> *Client: "I'm looking for a low mileage, cheap, Japanese vehicle."*

There is no such thing.   A low mileage vehicle means that the price will be somewhat high, besides, what's cheap?

> *Client: "I'm looking for a high performance vehicle that gets at least 40mpg."*

High performance means one thing and that is a big engine. How fast a vehicle goes is in direct proportion to how fast it can burn gas. You don't buy a full size truck for the gas mileage and you don't buy a compact for its towing capacity.

> *Client: "I'm only looking for a low mileage vehicle around $5,000."*

We would not sell a low mileage vehicle for $5,000 unless it's was over twenty years old. Believe me when I tell you that this client will scoff at a twenty-year-old vehicle.

When you get ridiculous demands from clients, the question, "Why?" is your best weapon. You're still in the fact-finding phase because we don't have anything in our stock that will even come close to their wants, so we need to probe their needs.

Let's see how we can turn some of these ridiculous demands into a client that is more reasonable. By the way, this is just a summary; you still need to ask them about their current vehicle, their likes and dislikes of their current vehicle, about them as a person and more about what they will be using this new vehicle for.

> *Client: "I'm looking for a low mileage, cheap, Japanese vehicle."*
> *Sales Advisor: "Okay, well let's see what we can find for you. We sell more than two hundred cars a month and we do get those cars on occasion but their usually sold before they're brought to the front and their usually not that cheap unless they're really old because everyone is looking for those vehicles."*
> *Sales Advisor: "What's low mileage?"*
> *Client: "Around 30,000 or less."*
> *Sales Advisor: "Now why must this vehicle be Japanese?"*
> *Client: "They have a good reputation for reliability."*
> *Sales Advisor: "Well all the manufacturers are making better vehicles these days. Why must this vehicle be cheap? Are you trying to hit a certain monthly payment budget?"*

Client: *"Yeah. I can only pay $200 maximum a month in payments."*

So now we've gotten to the core of the objections and that is they can only afford $200. Now we know what we're dealing with. We now need to show them vehicles that would fit their needs. Our horizon is a little wider now. We now need to get over the Japanese vehicle hurdle.

Here we can show them a couple of vehicles that would fit their needs even if they are not Japanese or have more than 30,000 miles. We need to show them vehicles close to this range of payments. Even if the vehicle your showing them is a little more expensive, it keeps their options open. Also, finance can play with the numbers by extending the term of the loan to get to $200 a month in payments. Or, if we can make them fall in love with the vehicle, they'll find a way of bumping the payments up.

We need to sell them on the reliability of the vehicle as well as any other savings that they might get for buying the vehicle like better gas mileage, newer model, better trim and anything that is a plus of the current vehicle.

If they are looking for a cheap, low mileage, Japanese vehicle and all we have are domestic vehicles with over 50,000 in mileage, and priced around $15,000, then we need to justify why they should be interested in our vehicles and not anything else. You can use condition of vehicle, history report, third party sources confirming your sales pitch and the drive and feel of the vehicle.

Don't be afraid to tell it the way it is. Clients like these need to be educated and brought to reality. You can't get a low mileage, cheap, Japanese vehicle or any cheap low mileage vehicle. They're being way too picky. They have champagne taste on a beer budget. You'll hear that a lot in the industry.

> *Client:* *"I'm looking for a high performance vehicle that gets at least 40mpg."*
> *Sales Advisor:* *"Okay, Let's see what we can find. Now why are you looking for a high performance vehicle?"*
> *Client:* *"I like driving hard sometimes."*
> *Sales Advisor:* *"If you drive hard you know you won't get good gas mileage."*
> *Client:* *"I know, but when I'm driving normally, I'd like to get good gas mileage."*
> *Sales Advisor:* *"Okay, we have several sport cars I can show you."*

Even though sports cars with a lot of power don't get high gas mileage, it seems like performance is more important to this guy than gas mileage. Show him good performance and sell the vehicles gas mileage even if does get 24mpg.

> *Client:* *"I'm only looking for a low mileage vehicle around $5,000."*
> *Sales Advisor:* *"Why $5,000, are you trying to hit some monthly payment budget?"*
> *Client:* *"No, I want to pay cash. That's all I have, so the out-of-the-door price has be $5,000."*

> **Sales Advisor:** *"Okay, let's see what we can find for you. You do know that with tax and license you're looking at about a $4,200 vehicle. We get those in from time to time. "How soon are you looking buy something?"*
> **Client:** *"Within this month."*
> **Sales Advisor:** *"We have many good vehicles, but most of what you're looking for is around $8,000. Would you be willing to finance a portion of your new vehicle? Although it will be a little bit more expensive, you're getting a newer model, lower miles and better condition. It will be better peace of mind."*
> **Client:** *"Maybe, which vehicles are you talking about?"*

If you don't have anything that they are looking for, you still show them something as close as possible to what they are looking for but also ask them what their time frame is in purchasing something because you can get their contact information just in case you do get something that they're looking for.

You also go in and ask your manager if they have any ideas on what to show them.

If you don't have anything even close to what they're looking for, you always go for the contact info just in case you get something in that fits with what they're looking for and to build your sales pipeline.

> **Sales Advisor:** *"Okay, the closest thing I have at the moment is this vehicle for around $10,000. Like I said, we do get those vehicles in here from time to time, so I can get your information and contact you when we do. You said you're looking for something within a month time span?"*

These scenarios were a little brief and oversimplified but it just illustrates how important the fact-finding step is. You still need to ask them about their current vehicle, about them as a person to build rapport and about what their needs and wants are. The main purpose of this step in the process is to use your fact-finding information to find them a vehicle on your lot. It seems like common sense but the step is necessary to illustrate how to go about this.

You're not always going to have exactly what the client is looking for. Before you tell the client that we don't have what you're looking for always ask your manager before you cut them loose because it's your one shot of earning their business and the manager, with their wealth of knowledge and experience, may be able to find something similar for you to suggest to them. It's important to match their needs to your inventory as close as possible. At the very least, get the contact information in case you do come across something.

I used to carry a clipboard with me with a list of all our used vehicles, mileage, price, year, make and models. This way I was sure to find them what they needed as well as a couple of other similar vehicles that would fit their needs. I would also use the back of these sheets to write down their names, numbers, what they were looking for, time frame of their purchase and price ranges. I would then enter this information in our CRM system to keep track of clients looking for vehicles. I would also write the acronym S.P.A.C.E.R.

Safety – Airbags, seat belts, warning devices, special devices

Performance – Size of engine, quickness, sportiness, braking power, torque, power

Appearance – Appeal, image, design

Comfort – Road noise, leather, seats, shocks, engine noise, vibration, feel

Economy – Gas mileage, maintenance cost, resale value

Reliability – Proven track record, design, reputation, awards

This is to show clients visually what was most important to them.

Just imagine selling a vehicle a day for 30 days. Selling 30 cars a month is rare. Most average to mediocre sales people sell 8 to 10 vehicles a month so there are many days where they don't sell a vehicle. Worst yet is spending all day with a client and not selling a thing for one reason or the other. By getting their contact information, you increase your sales pipeline of buyers. Now all you have to do is find them something that closely matches their needs even if you have to upsell them a little bit.

8c.   Continue Trust Building

We've discussed in the previous steps that you need to make a friend and the car deal will come. This is true 100% of the time. By building trust and making a friend with the client, it allows you to show and sell them vehicles that they never considered and to think a little beyond their capabilities.

Most people shop for a vehicle by going from dealer to dealer in the hope of finding the perfect deal. By building trust with them, you can sway them to your way of thinking. You must slow them down and find them a car that you have, that best fits their needs. You must give them 100% of your attention and effort to get a car deal done. You only get one shot.

Summary of Selling from Stock

Product knowledge of your inventory should quickly match the client's wants and needs to what you have in stock. Selling from stock benefits both the client and the sales advisor.

Based on what you've learned, show them at least three vehicles that match as close to what their looking for as possible. Start with the most expensive and work your way down.

Building trust, rapport and friendship with clients will allow you to show them vehicles that you, as an advisor, think will benefit them the most even if they haven't even thought about it.

The question, "Why?" allows you to get to the root of many objections of any deal. Finding the reason behind sticking points is important in making deals work.

9.   Product Presentation and Demonstration – Building Value

Purpose: To present the features of the vehicle and their respective benefits to the buyers, demo the vehicle, and to tailor your presentation toward the wants and needs of the client. Doing these exceptionally well builds value into the vehicle, which in turn will justify the price of the vehicle.

The difference between price and value is salesmanship!

What this mantra is saying is that the price of a product does not matter as long as the client believes that the price is justified and worth it and that the features built into the product are worth immensely more than what is being charged for. That is the main point of the presentation and demonstration step in the process is to build as much value as possible to make price a non-issue, making the negotiation phase a breeze.

9a.   Building Value

Attitude, product knowledge and enthusiasm are all equally important in this step. This is where the rubber meets the road in the sales process. This is where we use the information we gathered in the fact-finding step to build value and make a sale.

How do we build Value?

When presenting and demonstrating the vehicle, remember to not only explain the features, but customize your presentation to show how the features benefit the client. The best way to do this is by using the word "so".

Keep going back to what you learned in the fact-finding step of the process and tailoring your presentation to that.

> *"You said you were looking for a vehicle with good gas mileage, this vehicle gets 29 city/35 highway, **so** this vehicle will almost pay for itself with the gas savings you'll be enjoying."*

> *"You said safety was important. This vehicle has Bluetooth standard, **so** you don't have to fumble with your phone while driving, you don't have to risk getting a ticket or have sound issues because the sound comes in right through the speakers, **so** you can keep your eyes on the road, keeping you safer from being in an accident."*

Bluetooth is great to have but, you have to show the client why it is great. How does it benefit the client? Every feature has a benefit for the client, that's why the manufacturer put it in there, but the client needs to be made aware of it so they can mentally visualize themselves using the feature. The more you explain how the feature's benefit the client by using the word "so", the more the client sees themselves in action using the feature or benefiting from that feature.

Start out with the hot button you learned in the fact-finding step first. You can always mix in hot buttons at every aspect of the demo. If they're interested in safety and reliability, then when you open the trunk you can explain how and why the rear end is made to make the vehicle safer in a rear end collision, why the sides have special beams that protect as well as the side airbags. Connect the client to the features by helping them see how it benefits them. Keep remembering the hot buttons. Don't forget about the other positive and nifty options the vehicle has.

The more features and benefits you can show them, the more value you're building into the brand. The more you can show them that they can't live without this vehicle, the more value you've built into the vehicle.

Without getting too technical, explain in layman's terms how something works. The more the client knows about the inner workings of something, the more confidence they will have in the product as well as the comfort of the product. Product knowledge is key in this area. This will also build up your brand so if they don't like the model you're showing them, then they'll be easier to move up to another model. Of course, the more ingenious or even simple a feature is, the more you're going to explain to the client that its exclusive to your brand. My favorite was when I would explain how the airbags worked on the Camry:

> *"Our vehicles come with a patented ingenious airbag system that has small tubes in the bumper of the vehicle with little ball bearings in them. If the vehicle hits a speed greater than 20 miles an hour, the ball bearings will be shot forward because of the momentum, thereby triggering the airbag system. The bumper will take most of the damage but airbags will also deploy because the energy of the hit will reverberate through the vehicle and into the occupants causing them to jolt forward as well. The reason they use this system is because it is extremely reliable and long lasting because a ball bearing being moved by momentum doesn't have any electronic parts, because others use switches that can go bad over time or anytime. So, what that means is that your airbags are always ready to go should they be needed, which makes for a safer vehicle. Also, the airbags deploy in a split second, long enough to absorb the occupant's forward momentum and they deflate right away so they don't get in the way of a quick exit."*

Going through this type of explanation communicates to the client the amount of research, development, engineering and thought that went into your brand. The more knowledgeable they are about how the features benefit them and how those features work, the more value will be built into the vehicle. It's to your benefit to learn how these safety features work so you can fully explain them to your clients. Do you think the next dealership they stop at and ask the sale advisor, "How does your airbags work?" they'll get a satisfactory answer? Definitely not. Set yourself apart for the mediocre. Find out what makes your vehicles special.

You might want to hang out with the mechanics and learn the inner workings of the vehicles and various models as to their features, reliability, power, strength and weaknesses so you can more easily build them up or overcome them and be more knowledgeable.

Don't gloss over anything, know your vehicles. Most safety features are standard on all vehicles a manufacturer makes, so it's not that hard to learn the safety features. Same goes for the creature comforts. You need to know these inside and out. The specific features of what makes a model stand out from other models is also of great importance. Why is a Honda Civic a Honda Civic? How is it different than a Corolla? Why is a GMC Yukon a GMC Yukon? How is it different than a Tahoe? They all have the same safety features. The civic might have better gas mileage, better reliability or resale value, and Yukon might have towing capacity, seating capacity, power ratings and torque rating.

Keep thinking about the hot buttons of your client and keep hitting those and addressing those to build value.

> "This vehicle has a leather interior, **so** it always looks great, is easier to clean, and doesn't stain like fabric."

Other good points to make are the warranties and guarantees the manufacturers have on a set of vehicles you're showing them. Nothing is better at putting the clients' fears at ease than warranties and guarantees. That's one less fear that we have to deal with thanks to a reputable car maker.

In this step of the process we:

- Let the vehicle sell itself
- Show the features of the vehicle
- Show how the features benefit the client and their needs
- Build value in the vehicle
- Have the client mentally own the vehicle, meaning the client is seeing himself driving this vehicle in his own mind
- Demonstrate the vehicle in action
- Get the client involved
- Increase the client's desire for ownership
- Strengthen negotiations-if the client falls in love with the vehicle, then they will be less inclined to negotiate hard for the vehicle
- Obligates the client to the sales advisor-the more time you spend with them the more attached they become to the sales advisor and the more likely a deal can be struck
- In your presentation, you can use trial closes to solidify in their minds that they own the vehicle. Ask questions like, "Where do you plan on taking a trip in this vehicle?" and, "Whose name will this vehicle be registered in?" These are trial closes and conjures up a picture of ownership in the client's mind.

Remember to show features and explain how those features benefit the client based on what you learned in the fact-finding step.

S.P.A.C.E.R.
Safety, Performance, Appearance, Comfort, Economy, Reliability

9b.   Mental Ownership & Time

Transfer mental ownership by talking in terms of *"your new car"* or *"your new truck."*

Get the buyer emotionally involved by touching, smelling, opening, closing doors, trunks and hoods. Emotional involvement is essential to building value, creating urgency and reducing price resistance during negotiations. Try to use all the senses of the client.

- **Sight** – "Notice the quality and beauty of the paint of your new car."
- **Listen** – "Hear how quite the engine sounds?" "Hear how powerful your new engine sounds?"
- **Sound** - "Listen to how quite the cabin is when driving around in your new car."
- **Touch** – "Feel the smooth ride of your new car." "Feel the smooth leather of your new vehicle."
- **Smell** – "Smell the new car smell of your new vehicle." "Smell the interior cabin; there is not any funky smell of your new vehicle." "Can you tell that your new vehicle doesn't generate any smells while running?"

Try to incorporate all their senses so they get a better sense of ownership. Get the client involved to own the vehicle mentally and to do that they must see the features as beneficial to them.

There's nothing in the sales process that will incorporate all their senses more than the test drive, which we'll talk about more later in the chapter.

Time

Don't take any shortcuts. Spend as much time as possible with the client in the lot. The more time you spend with the client, the more obligated they will be to buy from you and you alone and the less time you'll be haggling on the price. The more time the client spends with the vehicle, the more mental ownership he builds up.

Avoid car business jargon or lingo as it tends to confuse people not in the industry.

One of the ways to spend as much time as possible and to incorporate mental ownership is to go on a test drive. Test drive their new vehicle.

9c.   Sample Dialogue:

Sales Advisor: *"Bill, This is the first vehicle I want to show you. This is the Bell Air 55S. You had said that you were looking for a vehicle that was Comfortable, Safe and Reliable (S.P.A.C.E.R). This model has extra heavy duty shocks and springs to absorb all the bumps on the road, <u>so</u> you won't hear or feel them in the cabin, which makes for a more comfortable ride. The frame also has special rubber mounts to absorb the road vibrations, <u>so</u> you won't feel any road or outside vibrations, which makes for a quieter ride. The engine also has liquid filled mounts to dampen engine noise and vibration, <u>so</u> you won't feel any discomforting noise or vibrations from the engine. These rubber stoppers and motor mounts were the result of 5 years of research by our company, <u>so</u> the drivers and passengers of this vehicle will be able to drive in complete comfort. It's as quiet and smooth as a recliner in your living room. The seats have special contour foam designed to grip and cushion your body for extra comfort. The seats are also made specifically large to not only absorb the remaining vibration of the vehicle, but also to give you the maximum comfort possible. The material and shape used in the seats are the same as some high end massage chairs and made specifically for our manufacturer and this model, <u>so</u> it was designed to not only be completely comfortable like a recliner, but also to eliminate driver fatigue on long trips which you said you like to take from time to time.*

"Also, if you sit in the seat, you notice the large gauges and dials which are also designed to eliminate eye fatigue for the driver, <u>so</u> you don't have to worry about your eyes getting tired on trips. The layout of the dash has been tested using more than five hundred test subjects to make it as intuitive and efficient as possible, <u>so</u> once you own the vehicle for a short amount of time and get used to the layout, you won't be fumbling for the controls as much, which will keep your attention on the road.

"Also, if you notice the large windshield, it was designed to mimic air plane windows <u>so</u> you get as much visibility as possible. The windshield has also been coated by a patented layer of sunscreen to block out harmful UV light, <u>so</u> the windshield protects in other ways beside wind, bugs and road debris."

Client: *"Hmmm...the seat does feel comfortable."*
Sales Advisor: *"What about the windshield?"*
Client: *"Yeah...that is big and I think I can get used to the controls. Let's take it for a drive."*
Sales Advisor: *"Okay, let me explain to you about the safety and reliability you mentioned."*

Notice that I referred to the information gathered in the fact-finding step: that the client was looking for comfort, safety and reliability. For every attribute the client said they were looking for, I had at least 5 features and benefits to use. You can and should use more, but clients tend to only remember about 3 so put extra emphasis on the most relevant and specific to your make.   Since they had told me that they were looking for comfort, I used the fact that this vehicle had:

1.   Special shocks and springs
2.   Special rubber stoppers on the frame
3.   Special liquid filled motor mounts
4.   Special seats
5.   Windshield and layout of the dash board

It also helps to mention that these attributes are only specific to your make and can't be found on other makers' vehicles, which is true in most cases because your make is specifically designed for their type of clientele.

To build value, you can't just list all the features of the vehicle, you must connect the benefits of those features to the client's needs and wants. That's how you build value. You have to communicate to them how those features benefit your clients, like I did in the dialogue. You can only do this if you know what the client's needs and wants are if you've done a proper fact-finding by asking "why" a lot.

Just because the client told you that Comfort, Safety and Reliability is what he looks for in a vehicle doesn't mean that you ignore Performance, Appearance and Economy. You also need to touch on those after building up the comfort, safety and reliability. In reality, you need to be well versed in all aspects of S.P.A.C.E.R. for each vehicle regardless of the individual client. Concentrate more on their hot buttons but also discuss the other aspects, as this will also sell your enthusiasm for your vehicle.

When looking at new vehicles, take the key to the one they want to look at and the keys to a lower model. Show them both models and tell them the difference. Let them see the lower model and let them sell themselves up to the higher model. This will help sell the higher model. Don't belittle the lower model by calling it the "basic model", "standard model" or "lower model". Call it by its factory designation, "the S model", "The LE model" or "the LTE model". This will give them an out if they figure out they can't afford the higher model.

9d.   The Product Presentation Using a 5-point Presentation Technique

When presenting a vehicle, most will tell you to start at the engine and work backward. I like to start at the trunk and move forward and end it with the interior. That's because to most people, the appearance of the vehicle is more important than trunk space and interior is more important than the style of the vehicle. People by nature have poor memory, so end the presentation with the interior because that's the last thing they'll remember and once you get them inside, it's easier for them to go for a test drive.

Also, you don't want them to sit in the vehicle and then get out to check the outside. Once they're comfortable inside, let them stay there while you get the keys or make a copy of their license to go on a test drive.

As always, tailor you message to what you learned during the <u>fact-finding</u>.

<u>Position 1</u>. <u>All around the vehicle</u>. Before starting the presentation, walk around the vehicle giving tailored information based on what they are looking for. Pop the hood and the trunk. "This the 2012 Studebaker, completely redesigned with increased gas mileage, room for five, very comfortable and spacious."

<u>Position 2. Trunk area.</u> Rear trunk space, easy loading, ground clearance, styling, cargo space, spare tire and foldable seats. Benefits of safety, space and convenience.

<u>Position 3. Passenger side.</u> Right side styling, roominess of interior, fabric, paint, safety features, shoulder room and unitized construction. Suspension, comfort, safety and luxury.

<u>Position 4. Front.</u> Talk about the engine, chrome accents, safety bumpers, fenders and glass area. Benefits of power, fuel economy, durability, performance, reliability, cost of maintenance and styling. Battery, double latch hood, crumple zones, braking system and computer.

<u>Position 5. Driver side and interior.</u> Have them sit in the driver's seat, close the door and get in the passenger side. Have them look at the instrument cluster and controls, inspect the leg room, ease of entrance and pedals. Benefits of ease of use, comfort, convenience and safety.

Position 1: All around. When showing a vehicle, first approach the whole vehicle and walk them all the way around so they get a feel for the whole vehicle. Now keep in mind of what you've learned during the fact-finding because you're going to have to touch on what they've told you during the fact-finding. While doing this, pop open the hood, trunk and all the doors because we always want to explode the vehicle as much as possible and end up in the rear of the vehicle by the trunk. Most people will jump right inside the vehicle as soon as you open it. This can't be helped as most people want to see what the inside looks like. You can unlock the whole vehicle, but get them to follow you to the trunk first by stating, "Let me show you what this vehicle has to offer." It is best to unlock the trunk first and have them follow you around and end in the driver's seat.

New car regulation requires that there be an MSRP sticker (Monroney) on the vehicle detailing the trim gas mileage, model and other specifics. This sticker is like a magnet to the client. This is the second thing they look at right after the overall look of the vehicle. Make sure you're there when they're inspecting the sticker and point out the model, trim, gas mileage, safety, package and any discounts that they've given the client on the sticker. It's important that they know that they're already getting a discount, so later on you can tell them that they're already getting a discount. Of course you would point out information on the sticker that reflects what you've learned in fact-finding; for instance, if they told you that gas mileage is of the utmost importance to them, you would make sure they know that this vehicle gets 40 miles per gallon or more.

Position 2: The trunk. Review what you've learned in the fact-finding, for instance, if they told you they need a lot of trunk space, safety or carry a lot of cargo.

>   The benefits of the trunk are Safety and Convenience.

>   Also cover:
>>   Trunk space
>>   Easy loading features, rear bumper
>>   Cargo space and location of spare tire
>>   Folding down of rear seats, if an option
>>   Emergency trunk release, safety bumpers
>>   Special crumple zone of rear trunk/bumpers

Position 3: Passenger side. Review what you've learned in the fact-finding if they told you they need a 2 or 4 doors, styling or safety.

>   The benefits of passenger side would be styling, beauty, comfort and safety.

>   Also cover:
>>   Paint and finish
>>   Styling of window and glass area
>>   Easy access for the passengers
>>   Quality construction/manufacturing tech
>>   Rear seat space
>>   Safety features for passengers
>>   Side door beams to absorb impact

Size of the large windows
Visibility

Position 4: Front/Engine. Review what you've learned in the fact-finding if they told you they needed power, reliability, gas efficiency, performance, economy, durability or safety.

The benefits of the front would be the styling, comfort, luxury, safety, performance, reliability, maintenance costs, economy and durability.

Also cover:
Styling of the front hood and grill
Engine power and advanced technology
Accent features
Safety features
Reliability of engine and components
Special crumple zones of frame in case of frontal impact
A hood that folds in on itself to protect the occupants from flying glass

Position 5: Interior. Review what you've learned in the fact-finding if they needed roominess, comfort, safety or convenience. In this step, you would have the buyer sit in the driver seat while you sit in the passenger seat. This way, you can point out all the benefits and features as well as how they apply to the consumer.

The benefits of the interior are luxury, convenience, styling, comfort and safety.

Also cover:
Easy access
Quality construction and manufacturing tech
Interior colors, fabrics, carpeting
Shoulder, head, and leg room (roominess)
Instrument cluster and controls
Options like leather, convenience controls
Sound system/navigation
Safety features – airbags, crumpling steering column, side and knee airbags, energy absorbing head rests, 3-point seatbelts
Electronic safety features like ABS

Keys to a successful vehicle presentation/demonstration:

- Learn a good 5 point presentation. Have 3 features and benefits at each point. Start with the trunk, to passenger side, to the front of the car, to the driver's side and finally the interior
- Explain the features but sell the benefits. Why does this matter to the client? How does this benefit the client?
- Be enthusiastic. It's contagious. Get excited about the car and so will the client
- Get the client involved

- Don't use too much jargon or technical language as it tends to confuse and distract the client

After the client is sitting in the driver seat looking at the vehicle, you would then ask them, "Is this vehicle equipped the way you like it?" If they say yes, then proceed to ask them for a driver's license so you can get the keys and/or a dealer plate to go on a test drive.

9e.   Product Presentation Dialogue

Sales Advisor: *"Bill, from what I gathered, **Safety, Reliability and Comfort** are features that are most important to you."*

Client: *"Yes, like I said, I have small dogs as well as children, so definitely safety. I don't like being stuck somewhere so you're right, reliability is also high on my list. Also comfort since I told you I spend a lot of time in my car due the nature of my job."*

Sales Advisor: *"Bill, follow me. I have several vehicles I want to show you. This is one of them. This is the 2014 Saturn Commuter. Notice that it has a very nice stance and a very appealing look to it."*

Client: *"Looks aren't that important, but it looks nice. How much is it?"*

Sales Advisor: *"We'll the Monroney sticker is over here. Notice that it has gotten 5 stars for safety and 4 stars for reliability. Because of our sale I mentioned earlier, we're currently giving a $2,000 discount off of MSRP. Also notice that this vehicle gets around 35 mpg, so this vehicle can save you tons of money in fuel costs alone."*

Client: *"That's nice. As long as it's safe, reliable and comfortable."*

Sales Advisor: *"Hold on, let me get the keys and I can show you more."*

Client: *"Okay, I'll be here."*

Sales Advisor: *"Hey Bill, I got the keys. I know you're anxious to look at the inside, but let's start with the trunk. Notice the size of the trunk. They've made it huge, <u>so</u> you have plenty of room for your stuff on long trips and for your job. Also notice that the deck is low, <u>so</u> you don't have to struggle getting things in and out of the trunk. They've also built the frame surrounding the trunk in a way to absorb rear end collisions, preventing it from spreading to the occupants, <u>so</u> to keep you and your loved ones safe. The frame actually collapses in on itself, should you get hit in a rear end accident."*

Client: *"Good to know."*

Sales Advisor: *"If you follow me to the passenger side, you'll see that they've given you large side windows to increase your visibility, <u>so</u> you are better able to monitor your surroundings while driving and changing lanes, preventing you from getting in an accident.*

"The doors have also been reinforced with extra side beams to protect you and your loved ones, should you be involved in a side accident. Our manufacturer uses a special patented design as well as materials to absorb a majority of the energy in a

side impact, _so_ to prevent harm or injury to your occupants. You also said comfort was important, so look at the large rear seats that this vehicle comes in. The seats recline and have their own climate zones, _so_ to keep your occupants comfortable on long rides."

"This model uses special extra thick window rubber to fully seal the doors and windows from most of the outside noise, _so_ as to keep you and our occupants quite comfortable. There is also front, side, curtain and seat airbags all the way around to absorb any energy from accidents to prevent any harm to come to your loved ones.

"Our manufacturers' special crumple zones along the patented materials and design and airbags help absorb almost all the energy associated with an auto accident, _so_ as to keep you love ones free from harm."

Client: "Yeah...safety is very important to me."
Sales Advisor: "I know, that's why I'm showing this vehicle. It's one of the safest sedans on the market and has won numerous awards of which I can show you later. If you follow me to the front of the vehicle. The engine on this vehicle is the same type that they've been using for more than ten years now."

"It is extremely reliable, durable and very low maintenance. It has more than two hundred horse power and can do zero to 60 in 6 seconds, which is phenomenal for a vehicle in this class. The engine has the power when you need it and the gas efficiency when you don't."

"This engine has been in use in many different models because of its reliability and durability, but I think you already know this. The engine alone will help you save lots of money over its lifetime in maintenance as well as keep you from getting stranded somewhere."

"This model also comes with special shocks and motor mounts to help absorb most road and engine vibrations, _so_ to keep you and your occupants comfortable and make the ride extra smooth. The engine is a 4 cylinder that has great low end torque, _so_ you'll have power when you need it, yet it gets 35 mpg. The engine is designed in a way not only to be reliable, but also to be accessible, _so_ maintaining it will be relatively easy."

"The frame surrounding the engine was specially designed to not only absorb a majority of a front-end accident, but also to absorb a majority of the road vibrations, thereby keeping you and your occupants safe and comfortable. If you notice the shape of the pillars as well as the frame itself, you can see that if something hits it at great speed, it will collapse in on itself, absorbing a majority of the impact energy to help keep you and your occupants safe. The hood is also designed to collapse in on itself to prevent flying debris from going through the windshield."

Client: *"Wow, really? Seems like they've put a lot of attention into it."*

Sales Advisor: *"You have no Idea. This vehicle has won many awards on some truly unique innovations, which I can show you later. Follow me to the driver's seat. Have a seat and I'll get in on the passenger side."*

Client: *"Okay."*

Sales Advisor: *"The first thing you'll notice is that the seats are made up of a special patented foam designed to mold to the shape of your body. The seats are wide like a recliner to give you the best of comfort and tension like a massager. This model comes with a special airbag system, with airbags in the steering wheel, side of the seat, curtain, pillars and one for the knees. They thought of everything. So, should you be in an accident, you and your occupants are encompassed fully in airbags, seat belts and crumple zones."*

"Also notice the layout of the dashboard. This manufacturer has done more than 5,000 hours of testing using more than five hundred individuals, not only on the reliability of the components, but also on the layout to find the most comfortable and intuitive design. So, you won't have to take your eyes off the road while looking for the climate control, radio or any other controls, and this keeps you and your loved ones safer."

"The windshield on this model uses a special patented sheeting that not only gives you great visibility as you can see, but also reflects harmful UV sun rays to protect you and your loved ones. Feel the controls. Notice that they've been made with special materials so as to help you find and memorize where they are. Smell the new car smell. Nice huh?"

Client: *"Very nice."*

Sales Advisor: *"I can talk to you for hours about this car, but you're going to have to experience it for yourself on the road. Let me get your license so we can go on a test drive."*

Client: *"Okay, you've got me excited about this car. I hope your sales pitch holds up to the performance."*

Any claims or facts you throw around like awards, safety, patents or designs need to have some sort of supporting documentation attached to it. Most of these will be found on the internet or brochures, but make sure you have them handy on the off chance that the clients wants proof. Otherwise, you'll look like a sales man instead of an advisor.

9f.   Test Drive

The purpose of the test drive is to demonstrate the vehicle in action as well as help the client mentally own the vehicle. It's very important that you don't skip this step. Some clients will say, "I've driven these before and I know how they drive, let's go and talk numbers." To solidify mental ownership, the client needs to take a test drive.

Remember, the more time you spend on the lot, the less time you will spend in the negotiation phase. If the client elects to skip the test drive, that means you'll have a harder time in the negotiation phase, **so** you'll have to grind out a smaller profit.

If you want to double your income and double your sales, then you need to increase the amount of test drives you take. Drive everyone. The more people you drive, the higher your sales numbers will be. It's a known fact that most people who take a test drive come in to look at the numbers. The more people who look at numbers, the higher the chance of them buying. "Car sales is a numbers game" is a mantra you'll hear again and again in the business. Meaning, the more people you meet, the higher your chances of making a sale. Thirteen percent is the average closing ratio, so if you talk to one hundred people a month, you should make thirteen sales. I don't believe this. The really good sales people have a much higher closing ratio, somewhere north of 25%. This means that they're good at what they do. Skill is definitely involved: skill to build rapport, to build trust, to find common ground and to make a friend that will take a test drive with you. The professional knows that a good product presentation ends with a test drive. The better you are at presenting and demonstrating the vehicle, the higher the test drives will be.

Regardless of what a client says about the money, hesitations or fears, get them to take a test drive.

Make it logical. "Come on, you're here already. Drive it to get a better sense of what you want to do, to make a better decision. Even if you don't buy here, at least you have a better idea of what you want to do." "I have nothing else to do, let's take a drive." This statement gives them an out, so they are not committing to anything except taking a joy ride.

- Before the test drive, you need get a copy of the driver license. This not only proves the client has a valid driver's license, but you're also getting detailed information on the client that you can use to enter in your computer system. A proactive manager would already have done this for you while you're on the test drive
- Make sure the client adjusts their seat, mirrors and seat belt before leaving the lot. Make sure you and the client obey all local traffic laws
- Explain to the client how to adjust their seat properly, with the mirrors fixed and the seatbelt on. Make sure he knows where the turn signal and lights are with the proper gear selected. Make sure he is comfortable. While on the drive, make sure that the vehicle is in proper gear. Just because he looked like he shifted in drive doesn't mean it's in drive. It could be in third gear. I've had that happen to me several times before
- The sales advisor should drive first by taking it out of its parking space. Explain the vehicle's safety features again, and show that you're in control
- The test drive should be on a preplanned route avoiding rough roads, traffic jams and other dealer lots. Nothing is worse than driving by other dealerships on the test drive, which have

- signs of cheaper prices, more selection, easy financing or other incentives. Also, consider places to pull over in case your client's spouse wants to drive
- Pick a route where the streets are smooth, with places they can pull over and get out to either change drivers or to look at the outside of the vehicle again. Most drivers will want to take the vehicle on the freeway. Make sure you have a route for the freeway that's smooth, uncongested and has proper on and off ramps
- Always go on the test drive. The client may not know the area or not know what a particular noise is or not familiar with functions of the vehicle. There will be times when a family of five or more show up and they all want to go on the test drive. Insist that you go. Take two test drives if necessary
- Keep quite on the drive and let the client drive. They'll usually talk among themselves while the passenger pushes and pulls all the buttons. Give them silence for at least the first half of the drive unless they have questions or problems arise. Give them directions regarding where to go, remind them of the speed limit and places they can pull over
- Some sales people tell you to drive them off the lot and find a place to switch. I prefer to have them drive off the lot. One reason is that the car dealership lot is usually well paved and smooth, so they can feel the vehicle smoothness and can contrast it if your route ends up on a rough street. Another reason is, I like them to feel the feeling of driving their new vehicle off the lot
- The test drive should last as long as it takes the client to fall in love with the vehicle
- Trial closes need to be used during the test drive to get the client thinking and imagining owning the vehicle Trial closes are statements to get the client to own the vehicle mentally during the test drive

  - "Whose name will this vehicle be registered in?"
  - "Where is the first trip you'll take in your new vehicle?"
  - "Who will you show your new car to first?"
  - "Do you plan on modifying this vehicle?"
  - "Is this vehicle equipped the way you want it?"

You will get a good sense if the client likes or dislikes the vehicle on the test drive. Sometimes they don't like a vehicle because they don't have a working knowledge of the vehicle. That's why it's important to ask midway through the test drive if they like the vehicle of they don't.

I remember one client who was very quiet during the test drive So finally I asked, "So do you like your new truck so far?" He quietly said, "No. It's not smooth, lacks power. It doesn't seem to be shifting." Upon closer inspection, I noticed that the client had the vehicle in 4th gear the whole time and the vehicle was an automatic. They had set the gear to 4th instead of drive. "Oh….you have it in n 4th gear." Once I put it in drive, the vehicle smoothed itself out, shifted very smoothly and changed his whole impression of the vehicle. They also felt kind of stupid, but that was on me to notice those things beforehand.

If there is more than one person, ask the other people if they would like to drive the car. Get the whole group involved. The more people fall in love with the vehicle, the easier it will be for you to negotiate a good price and up your commission.

If during the test drive they tell you, "No I don't like this vehicle", and they give you a lot of reasons that can't be explained away, like the size of the windshield, blind spots, power and the general feel of it, then there is no reason to continue the test drive. Have them turn around, go back to the dealership and find them another vehicle.

Most likely, they will like the vehicle because a majority of the objections with the vehicle will come up when presenting the vehicle. When and if they do like the vehicle, upon returning to the dealership, have them park next to their vehicle so they can see their new vehicle next to their old vehicle that they're trading in. Get them to see mentally that they are trading in their old car for a newer or new one.

If their vehicle is parked too far away or isn't convenient, then have them park near your service department, if you have one. This way, you can give them a tour of your dealership on your way to show them numbers.

After the test drives, some managers will have you park in a designated sold area. You're supposed to tell them to park there and tell them that's the sold area. This puts fear into their eyes because they think you already consider them sold without any consideration to them, and most people are afraid of making such a big commitment.

Other managers will have you park next to their old car so they can compare and contrast with their old car, so they can see how much better the new car is compared to the new one. I like this and it should be done if it's convenient, but sometimes people park very far away and it's not very convenient. We can look at their old car later and use it in our sales approach.

I prefer to park next to the service bay, if you have one, so you can walk through service and give them a tour of your dealership, selling your dealership some more. Alternatively, you can park next to the closest door into the dealership if you don't have a service bay.

9g.   Test Drive Dialogue

> *Sales Advisor:* *"Okay, make sure your belts are fastened and your mirrors are adjusted. We're going to go out there and take a right. Watch out for people walking on the lot and once we get on the road, you can go either right to drive on surface streets or left to go on the freeway. After that, you can go where you need to."*

For the first half of the test drive the sales advisor should remain silent. This will allow the vehicle to sell itself as well as help the client make an honest evaluation. You should only speak if they ask you a question. Even though you told them that they can go anywhere they want, you should direct them toward a route with little traffic and smooth pavement.

> *Sales Advisor:* *"So, how do you like it?"*
> *Client:* *"It's nice, except that the engine is a little too noisy. Also it's a little too rough."*
> *Sales Advisor:* *"This is typical for this class of vehicles. We can find you a different model or higher model that will be quieter and smoother than this model, but you*

said you wanted high gas mileage and a compact vehicle. The other models will have lower gas mileage and will be quite a bit larger."

Client: *"Yes, I've driven the other makes and it's about the same as this one."*

Sales Advisor: *"Also don't forget that this model was voted the best in its class as well in comfort and reliability."*

Client: *"Yes...I read that somewhere."*

Sales Advisor: *"Yeah...you said you take a lot of road trips so you need something reliable as well as good on gas. Also the warranty will allow you to go to any of our dealership across the country and the your vehicle history will be accessible to all the dealerships you go to so you are covered. The gas mileage alone can save you a lot of money on gas."*

Client: *"Yeah..I guess."*

Sales Advisor: *"Where's the first trip you're going to go with this vehicle?"*

Client: *"Probably going to see my parents in Florida."*

Here, the client needs to be reminded of what they told the sales advisor during the fact-finding, that gas mileage and cost was the highest item on their wants and needs list. When you throw in facts on reliability as well as warranty, it can negate any issues they may have on noise and comfort.

The sales advisor also mentioned what he learned on the fact-finding that this client likes to take a lot of road trips. He used this to help the client mentally own the vehicle. By mentioning the road trip and asking, "Where will you go with the vehicle?", the sales advisor put it in the client's mind a picture of the client driving down the road or highway in this vehicle. This is called a trial close when you help the client mentally own the vehicle. This is usually done in on the test drive, but can be used at other steps.

Summary of Product Presentation and Demonstration – Building Value

The product presentation and demonstration phase is vital to building value into the vehicle by showing the features and selling the benefits to the client. Specifically, show the features that benefit the client the most that were the hot buttons you gathered in the fact-finding.

In terms of S.P.A.C.E.R., just because the client only specifies that 3 out of the 6 qualities are important doesn't mean you're to ignore the other 3. The other 3 qualities are a bonus to the client and must be touched on during the demonstration and presentation. All qualities must be addressed, but emphasis must be put on the ones the client desires the most.

The more time you spend on demonstrating and building value in the vehicle, the less time you will need to negotiate.

To build value, you need to use the word "so" often to connect the client's needs and wants to the vehicle's features and benefits. Spend as much time as possible demonstrating the vehicle, including going on a test drive. Get the clients to mentally own the vehicle by asking them questions and using language as if they already own the vehicle and all that's left is some paperwork.

The more people you test drive the higher your sales numbers. Test drive everyone who has any interest in the vehicle. To get to the test drive, you first need a good needs assessment so you can tailor your product presentation and demonstration to help you build value in your product, thereby compelling your clients to take a test drive.

10. Setting the Stage – Overcoming Objections to the Vehicle and Asking for the Sale

Purpose: In this stage, we're trying to root out any real objections the client may have to purchasing the vehicle. We're trying to get a mental commitment so we can work toward a financial commitment in the negotiation phase. This is done after returning from a test drive.

After the test drive when pulling up to the dealership, you should have a very good idea if the client loves the vehicle or not. Statistically, the majority of clients who take the test drive will be invested enough to take a look at the numbers, which is one of the reasons you need to have as many test drives as possible.

As the client is pulling up to the dealership after a test drive, you have to decide which will be a good place to park their new vehicle. If the client came in with a vehicle that they want to trade-in, then most managers will tell you to park next to their trade-in so they can see how nice the new vehicle looks next to the old one.

Others will tell you to direct the clients to park in the sold section. This will be kind of presumptuous and might be looked upon as gimmicky, which it is. This might also instill commitment fear with the client.

In my opinion, the best place to park is near the service department so you can give the clients a tour of your dealership should they wish to proceed in looking at numbers. Where you park will depend on your style and methods. This is a good place to remind them of what they've told you regarding what they're looking for as well as some key features of the vehicle that will enhance their ownership.

After the test drive, recap all the features and benefits that match their hot points as well as warranties, road side assistance and service that comes with the vehicle. Present it in a way that the only bad decision they can make is not to purchase the vehicle. Keep the clients' fears and hopes in the forefront of your mind. Some will stick out more than others when your building rapport and trust throughout the whole process up to this point.

Point out the S.P.A.C.E.R. qualities the client deemed important and then add on the others like they are icing on the cake.

> **Sales Advisor:** *"Mr. Edwards, are you prepared to take delivery of this vehicle and take it home today?"*
> **Client:** *"No, I want to think about it and check a few other dealerships."*
> **Sales Advisor:** *"Why Mr. Edwards? You had told me earlier that you wanted a vehicle that has **Safety**, is **Comfortable** and **Reliable**. Right?"*
> **Client:** *"Correct, it's just that I want to keep looking. This is the first place I stopped."*

139

Sales Advisor: *"Hmmm……I understand, but I did show you how safe this vehicle is with all that our manufacturer has put into it like the airbags all the way around, crumple zones as well as the materials and design incorporated into it. You also saw for yourself how comfortably the vehicle handled. I described how comfortable it was but you experienced it for yourself. Right?"*

Client: *"True."*

Sales Advisor: *"You already know the reliable reputation of this vehicle along with the free warranty we offer. I don't even have to tell you about that. Right?"*

Client: *"No, I know about the reliability."*

Sales Advisor: *"So not only is this vehicle Safe, Comfortable and Reliable, this vehicle also has a quick engine that has plenty of power so **Performance** is also built into it as well as being **Economical** because it gets such good gas mileage. In addition to that, the vehicle has a very **Appealing** design to it. A lot of people find this design very attractive, so when the time comes to sell this vehicle or trade it in, you won't have a hard time getting all the money for it. Our manufacturer tries to make vehicles not just for today, but vehicles that can be viable for years to come."*

Client: *"Yeah, I do like the design of it."*

Sales Advisor: *"So you not only get **Safety, Comfort** and **Reliability**. You also get **Performance**, nice **Appearance** and **Economy** on top of it all. I mean, you like the vehicle, so let's see if we can make the financials work. If they do, then great, you have a great new vehicle that will serve you for years to come, And if we can't, we'll just part as friends. Fair enough?"*

Client: *"Okay, I'll look at some numbers, but it doesn't mean I'm buying."*

Sales Advisor: *"Not a problem, come inside and I can show you how easy it is to do business with us."*

Once you get out of the vehicle after the test drive, this is the time to set the stage. Meaning, you attempt to root out any objections they may have with the vehicle and proceed forward.

10a. Sample Closings

Some sample closing questions to ask to get clients to proceed to the next step:

Sales Advisor: *"Do you like the vehicle?"*
Or
Sales Advisor: *"Do you like the vehicle well enough to own it?"*
Or
Sales Advisor: *"Is this vehicle equipped like you want it?"*
Or
Sales Advisor: *"Do you like this vehicle enough to drive it home?"*
Or
Sales Advisor: *"Have I earned your business today?"*
Or

Sales Advisor: *"Are you prepared to take delivery of this vehicle and take it home today?"*

Or

Sales Advisor: *"Can I schedule delivery of this vehicle for you?"*

Or

Sales Advisor: *"If we can work out all the details to your satisfaction, can we earn your business today?"*

Or

Sales Advisor: *"Come inside and I can show you guys what the numbers look like. This way you have all the information you need to make an informed decision."*

One of two things can happen when you ask a closed ended question where the only response is "YES" or "NO".

> *Client:* *"Yes, if only it was another color."*

If It's a new car

> *Sales Advisor:* *"Not a problem, I can find any color you're looking for. Come inside and I can see what I can do."*

If it's a used car

> *Sales Advisor :* *"Not a problem, we can paint it for you. Just kidding."*
> *Here you will need to remind them of all the other aspects of the vehicle that they liked.*

It's hard to overcome major problems with the vehicle, but we as dealers can modify vehicles in repainting, adding leather, Navigation, Bluetooth or repairs. The client needs to be aware of such available modifications as well as the fact that they will need to pay for them, because we as dealers can't go around modifying vehicles on a chance that the client will like it. They must pay for them when they're paying for the vehicle.

If they say no

> *Client:* *"No, I don't like the way it handles.", "No, I don't like the blind spots.", "No, I don't like the noise level inside the cabin."*
> *Sales Advisor:* *"Not a problem, I have a couple of other vehicles I can show you that might work out better."*

Remember, you only have one chance to earn this client's business. You must show them everything you can.

10b. Objections: Specific & Non-Specific

No, I want to think about it.
No, I need to do a little more research.
No, I want to look around some more.

Non-specific objections are avoidance objections like, "I want to think about it", "I don't know", "I want to look around some more." Real objections are specific objections like, "The payments are too high, I want more for my trade.", "The price is too high.", "I don't like the color.", "I don't like the look of it."

Clients use avoidance to keep from going to the next step. You have to uncover the real objection. It is much easier to address a true objection than an avoidance objection.

When you do get avoidance objections or non-specific objections, the thing to do is first pause like it's no big thing, but you're trying to figure out what went wrong. Then empathize and tell them that you understand. Then try to clarify what the specific objection is.

Empathize: "Oh...Okay, I understand. But you said you were looking for this type of vehicle with these types of features. So do you not like the vehicle? Is it the price? Is it me? Do you not like me?"

> *Client: "No...it's the vehicle."*
> *Sales Advisor: "Okay, what is it about the vehicle that you don't like?"*
> *Client: "I don't like the look of it."*
> *Sales Advisor: "What specifically don't you like about its looks?"*
> *Client: "I don't know, I don't like the way the head lights are shaped."*
> *Sales Advisor: "Okay, let's see if we can find something else you might like."*

In this scenario we're trying to get to the heart of the matter or the real objection.

Remember, to be a true sales professional, you must realize that you can't let a client go until you fully exploited every option of selling this client a vehicle. You can't make much money by letting clients go just because they don't want to make a decision. Of course, you don't want to pressure them either. Your only option is help clients figure out what they're really objecting to and overcome that. If you can't get them pinned down, tell them, "Okay,. no problem. Let me go and get you a card from inside." In this case, you should leave the keys with them so they can play with the vehicle some more to keep them there until you come back. This is where I tell the manager to come out and schmooze them or turn them while I get a card. I explain everything that happened to the manager and have them take a turn.

Do a post mortem. Ask other managers how they would handle it. What can you do so you don't run into the same objection later?

If the client says, "Maybe", then clarify what maybe means. It could be that their significant other isn't there and they need that other person to make a decision. Probe a little to find the real objection to turn the "No" or "Maybe" to a "Yes".

Some clients don't want get committed from the beginning, so they make up excuses that they have to be somewhere soon. They equate looking at numbers with making a commitment to purchasing. Which is fine. You should have asked this in the fact-finding step, but that doesn't mean you don't take the client on a test drive. Never show numbers to clients who aren't serious about purchasing today or committing today. Why go through negotiations when the client isn't ready to commit? It's all part of the game that clients like to play and we must play along, but that doesn't mean that we're going to be at a disadvantage. It's nothing personal, most clients are operating out of fear.

If the client says they like the vehicle but doesn't want to look at numbers, then you can try to figure out by asking, "Why"? Rationalizing this can help you move many clients to the next level.

> **Client:** *"No, we have to be somewhere in half an hour."*
> **Sales Advisor:** *"Why? When will be a good time to come back so I can show you some numbers?"*
> **Client:** *"Well, how long will it take for you to get me some numbers."*
> **Sales Advisor:** *"It'll take at least half an hour and get a solid number on your trade. Just be a little patient, you've spent this much time picking out a vehicle that you like. What's another half an hour?"*

It doesn't take that much time to get the numbers, but people who are in a rush rarely if ever do a car deal. If the clients don't seem that serious in buying this vehicle, then you don't want to go through all the motions with people who aren't serious. If the client says they don't have enough time:

> **Client:** *"No, we don't have any time right now."*
> **Sales Advisor:** *"Why? When will be a good time to come back?"*
> **Client:** *"I don't know....let us have your card and we'll call you."*
> **Sales Advisor:** *"Okay...let me go and get you a card."*

Always make an excuse to get them a card from inside so you can notify the manger of what's going on.

Before they leave, make sure you tell your manager that they test drove the car, but now they say they don't have the time to talk numbers. Most likely your manager will want to come out to talk to the clients before they leave and tell them the exact same thing and ask them when a good time will be to come back to look at numbers.

You should always notify your manager before a client leaves for any reason. Not only is this required in many of the sales process of any dealership, but this also allows the manager to use their wealth of experience to assist you in getting the client to move forward in the sales process.

10c. Sample Scenario

> *Sales Advisor:* "That's a nice shaded spot…..park over there. Well,. did you like the way it drove? It was smooth right? You said you wanted comfort and handling. Also this vehicle comes with such a huge manufacturer's warranty that you won't have anything to worry about for at least 3 years. Are you prepared to take delivery of this vehicle and take it home today?"
>
> *Client:* "Maybe, depending on the numbers."
>
> *Sales Advisor:* Okay, why don't you come in so I can show you some numbers regarding your new and old vehicle?"

If they say, "No we didn't like it", then you need to figure out what they didn't like and why. From there, you need to either isolate the objection and overcome it or move them to better vehicle. Try to get to the root of their objections before moving on.

> *Client:* "No, I don't really like it."
>
> *Sales Advisor:* "Hmmm……you don't? You said you were looking for comfort and reliability and economy. This vehicle gets over 30 mpg as well as has the highest rating in terms of reliability. You even said on the test drive that it was comfortable. Right?"
>
> *Client:* "Yes, but I just don't like it."
>
> *Sales Advisor:* "Well, what is it specifically that you don't like?"
>
> *Client:* "Well…to be honest after second thought, I don't think I can afford it."
>
> *Sales Advisor:* "Hmmm…..is that all? We deal with all types of financing. I'm sure we can make something happen for you guys. It's not a big deal. Come inside and let me show you some options that are available to you. But in terms of the vehicle, you do like it? It does exceed all of your expectations right?"
>
> *Client:* "Yes we like the vehicle; we're just concerned with the payments."
>
> *Sales Advisor:* "Okay, don't worry about that. We have a very professional finance department that can help almost any buyer with their budget. I'll see what I can do to help you guys take this vehicle home today. I just need to gather some information from you and present you with some numbers. Fair enough?"

We're trying to overcome any objections or perceived objections they may have in regard to the vehicle only. We're only concerned about the vehicle at this point. We're preparing ourselves for the negotiations phase. We want to make sure the utility of this vehicle has no bearing on the negotiations. We don't want to go through negotiations only for them to say, "Actually we don't like the vehicle." We want to make sure they like the vehicle before proceeding. We don't know anything about financing at this point because we haven't gathered all the necessary information.

At other times, the client will want to think things over before coming in to look at the numbers. In the previous chapters, I mentioned that most people are operating out of fear and equate looking at numbers to committing to buying or being subjected to pressured sales tactics.

> *Client:* *"Well, we like the vehicle, but we want to think about it."*
> *Sales Advisor:* *"Okay, I understand. But what is it that you don't like about the vehicle?"*
> *Client:* *"It's not the vehicle, I just don't know if we can afford it."*
> *Sales Advisor:* *"Oh...I see. Well, why don't you come in so I can show you some numbers. This way you can get some accurate numbers to chew over. Sound fair?"*

The highly competitive nature of the car business requires the sales advisor to work every client to the best of their abilities because once the client leaves the car lot; chances are that they won't come back. The sales advisor needs to keep moving along the process and get to the next step. In this step, we're trying to overcome any objections they may have with the vehicle so we can get to the next step of them looking at numbers in the negotiations phase.

Try to isolate each objection to find the root cause. You can't push too hard or you'll blow any chance you have of them coming back.

> No, my husband has to look at it. "Okay, where is he? Let's take the car to him right now."
> No, my banker has to approve it. "Let's call them right now."
> No, it's the first place I stopped. "Make it the last place. You saw that this vehicle meets all your wants and needs to a tee. I just don't want you to make a mistake. This vehicle seems perfect for you."

There is no real reason to go further if the client doesn't like the vehicle, all individuals are not present in making a buying decision, they don't have enough time to complete the deal or they are irritated for some reason because this could completely fall apart with no explanation.

We're trying to figure out if they can do business today. If they can't, then we need to communicate to them a sense of urgency: they may lose this vehicle, expiring incentives and discounts or saving them time and energy looking for similar vehicles. These should have been planted at the meet and greet and fact-finding.

There is an exception to the "all parties need to be present to make a decision and document signing." This happens when the buyer's cosigner is in some other state, area, city or elsewhere. In this case, the buyer will make the decision regarding buying the car and agreeing to the financing while the paperwork will be sent overnight to the cosigner to sign. In most cases, the management will want the vehicle gone with the buyer if there is a substantial down payment, because a deal has a stronger chance of being finalized if the client leaves with the car and in most states the vehicle isn't considered sold until it leaves the lot with the buyer. Once a client leaves with the vehicle, legally it's theirs unless the financing falls through.

If the client says, "Yes, we like this vehicle. Let's look at some numbers.", then proceed to take them on a tour of your dealership.

10d. The Tour

The tour gives you an opportunity to build more trust in your dealership as well as remind them of the trust you already built in the dealership in the meet and greet. Some processes leave out the tour of the dealership as being too gimmicky, where the client sees right through it. However, I believe that the tour is extremely important for several reasons.

1. **Sell the Dealership:** During the meet and greet, you sold yourself and your dealership. Lip service alone won't help your cause; you need to show the clients that doing business with your dealership is a wise and safe decision. Make sure you have a list of all the major awards your dealership has won or if you're a small dealership or a non-franchised dealership, make sure you have on hand anything positive about your dealership like client satisfaction, number of people you've helped get into a vehicle, number of repeat clients, prices, how you make sure your vehicles have good quality and experience in business. This includes anything that will help put the client's mind at ease that dealing with your dealership is a safe bet.

2. **Slowing Down the Client:** The tour also helps slow down the client. Most of the time the client is anxious to get the numbers and leave. The tour helps them slow down, relax and put their guard down a little. After the tour the client will be more inclined to really look at the numbers and talk it over a bit more.

3. **Make Them Feel at Home:** Psychologically, the tour will help the client feel at home at your dealership, especially if they meet some friendly and charismatic people. Knowing where all the amenities are and the layout of the dealership helps the client get a feel for their surroundings.

The extent of your service walk depends on you. You don't want to go into detail on service if your clients seem uninterested, pressed for time or have been to your dealership before.

You can go even further and walk them through the service department to point out the state-of-the-art equipment they use, the certified factory technicians, body shop, shuttle service, loaner cars, competitive pricing and dealer commitment to quality service. Show them where the parts department is and show them any accessories available for their vehicle. Show them around the showroom.

Most importantly, show them where the bathrooms are. They need to be as comfortable as possible before looking at the numbers. Get them a bottle of water even if they didn't ask for one and show them where the free snacks are.

You should have some data on your dealership that can help you sell the dealership to use during your tour of your dealership.

> **Client:** *"Yes…we like the car, now let's see if the numbers will be to our liking."*
> **Sales Advisor:** *"Okay, great. Follow me. This is our award winning service department. They've won the president's award 5 years in a row in client*

satisfaction. This is our showroom. Our dealership is ranked 1st in the state for
client satisfaction, repeat business and referrals. There are refreshments right over
here. Would you like a soda, water or some sweets? The bathrooms are right over
here. Let's find a nice quiet desk where I can show you your options."

The tour is the time to get them a bottle of water, some popcorn or a cookie, if your dealership offers such things. In these modern times, I don't see any reason why they wouldn't. People are more in the buying mood if they have some nourishment, snack or comfort food. Prices of these items are negligible. If you must, buy them a soda or a snack. "I'm having a soda, would you like one?" or "I'm having a cola, what would you like?"

The reason for the tour is get the clients to slow down. Slowing down the clients will allow you to get your message out more affectively so they can see how they benefit by doing business with you and your dealership. This also allows you to remind them again of the trust built into the dealership.

Summary of Setting the Stage, and Asking for the Sale

Any objections the client has need to be isolated and overcome. Many times the client is just afraid of proceeding because they believe in doing so, they are committing to the sale.

Should the client like you, the dealership and the vehicle, then there shouldn't be any reason for them not to proceed. Ask them, "Do you like me?", "Do you like the dealership?", "Do you like the vehicle?". If they say yes to all 3 of the questions, then why wouldn't they proceed any further?

Keep asking questions until you get to the real reason they don't want to proceed.

If they have no problem proceeding, then you need to sell the dealership again with a tour. Keep some facts and figures on hand to upsell the dealership. The tour helps to slow the client down and it gets them in a numbers processing mood.

Always make sure your client:

1. Likes the vehicle well enough to take it home today
2. All decision making parties are present at time of negotiations and document signing. (This should have also been asked in the fact-finding phase)
 3. The client has enough time to complete the deal. (This should have also been asked in the fact-finding phase)
4. Clients are comfortable and relaxed prior to talking numbers by getting them a beverage or snacks and by showing them the bathroom

Isolate and address any objections.

11. Start your Write Up /Approaching the Desk/Trade-In Evaluation

Purpose: Obtain all the necessary information to present to management as well as mentally prepare the client to financially purchase the vehicle. Go from mentally owning the vehicle to financially owning the vehicle.

To get to this step, you've done a great job in the rapport building phase and the client seems to like you and your dealership. You've conducted a world class presentation and fully explained the features of the vehicle the client is interested in as well as how the client will benefit from those features. You've made sure all parties making a decision are present, they have enough time to complete the deal and have gotten them some water, soda or snacks so they are comfortable.

The first step is to take the client information and enter it into the system. You can get most of the personal information from their license they gave you before taking a test drive.

By now, you should already know if they are planning on paying cash or financing. If they are financing, they will need to fill out a credit application; make sure they sign it.

11a.　Starting the Write Up

Most dealerships have their own way of writing up the client so you should be familiar with it. The following is a general process of starting your write up and approaching the desk.

Find a quiet and out-of-the-way desk to seat your clients.

It's always beneficial to explain the buying process to the clients before you go in or before taking their information to mentally prepare them as well as build some credibility that you're truthful and forthcoming. Explain to them that you will go in and notify the management that they're interested in purchasing the vehicle they've chosen. The management will use the information they provided to present them with their options.

Try not to mention negotiations, price or financing. Keep that out of your vocabulary.

By them acknowledging this procedure, they are in a way, committing to purchasing.

Scenario:

The client has test driven the vehicle and likes it enough to look at numbers. You've given them a tour and brought them some refreshments. You need to gather some information about them to further the sales process. You already have a copy of the driver's license before you went on the test drive, so that is the first piece of information you would enter in the computer.

> *Sales Advisor: "Okay, Mr. Stevens, I'm just going to enter some information in the computer to note what we've talked about, and then I will notify management that you are interested in purchasing the vehicle. After that, management will use the*

information I enter in the computer to present to you your various options.   Just bear with me. It won't take long."

Mr. Stevens: *"Okay, but I don't want my credit run until we have some solid numbers."*

Sales Advisor: *"Okay, but I can't give you exact numbers without knowing your credit rating, because the finance department uses your credit score to quote you a finance rate which will affect your payments."*

Mr. Stevens: *"My credit won't be a problem. It's in the high 700s, so don't worry about that. I don't know exactly what it is, but it's up there."*

Credit is very important when putting together a deal because for one, it gives us accurate information on the possibility of this deal. Second, it's part of the three C's which is **cash, credit and commitment**. Getting clients to give you permission to run credit is a big commitment on their part that they are willing to do business with you today. It's very important to the management that you get a credit application filled, as this signifies the seriousness of this buyer. Another reason is, if the client has poor credit, then we don't need to go any further because we can't finance him on a vehicle unless he can come up with a cosigner or a big chunk as a down payment.

Unfortunately, a majority of time people don't want their credit run, as running it too much affects their short term credit score. This is understandable.

If you were a client shopping for a car, would you like to have your credit run every time you looked at a vehicle? Probably not, unless you wanted to purchase the vehicle, which is why getting a credit app is important. Don't take it personally. People who want to protect their credit are usually very responsible, mature and have a high credit score, so take care of clients like that, as they have a good ability to do business.

Any client who doesn't want his credit run should be treated like a good prospect. Just take his word for it when he says what his credit score is. 4 out of 5 times, these people will be good clients who are responsible and mature.

Under no circumstance should you run someone's credit without him picking out a vehicle that they really like and are willing to purchase. It doesn't make sense to run credit when a client hasn't picked out a vehicle.

Sales Advisor: *"Okay, no problem. We'll ball park it for now. Is this your current address? What's a good number to reach you? We use the phone number to look people up, don't worry, we're not going to be calling you or sharing your number."*

Mr. Stevens: *"Yes that is my current address and my number is 480-123-4567."*

Sales Advisor: *"Mr. Stevens, how much have you budgeted for a down payment?"*

No matter what they say, you shouldn't react because you're just getting the information down.

Mr. Stevens: *"I've got about $5,000 down."*

Sales Advisor: *"Okay, how long of a payment term are you looking to get into?"*

We don't want to ask them how much monthly payments they want to pay because no matter what they say, it'll be way too low and that will be another hill for you to climb. I've found that most clients' will blurt it out anyway during their visit.

Mr. Stevens: *"I don't want anything longer than a 5-year loan."*
Sales Advisor: *"Okay, sounds good. Do you have a trade?"*

You should already know from your fact-finding if they have a trade-in. If they do, then you would start to enter all the information regarding their trade.

You would then also enter in the notes section the stated credit score and other pertinent things about the client that you have learned so far. You would also enter information about which vehicle the client is interested in, usually the stock number.

Most clients will ask about terms, payments and rates. Give them ballpark figures. You can give them some numbers, but not too low that they get excited only to be pissed off when they get the real numbers and not too high that they decide right there and then to leave because it's no use to discuss any further, it's way more than they budgeted for. Besides, no matter which numbers you give them, they'll always ask for less. The best way is to not get into that game in the first place. Just say, "Well, it all depends on the buyer because of credit, income and down payment" Then ask, "Where are you trying to be?" This will tip their hand as to where their starting place will be because all clients will want to be as low as possible in regard to price, payments and down payment.

If these clients have a trade-in, then continue to gather information about their trade. If they don't, then excuse yourself to talk to the desk manager about this deal.

11b.   Trade-information

At this point, we're only interested in the trade-information and not in the trade evaluation. If there is a trade-in this deal, you will need to enter the pertinent information into the computer. In order to do this, you will need to get a trade-in evaluation sheet or bid sheet, which is a small form used to write down all the details of the trade-in. Some basic information we'll need are: make, model, year, mileage and condition. In over 70% of the cases there is a trade-involved. Bring back the sheet to the desk and quickly ask a couple of questions on the sheet as well as questions not on the sheet like:

1.   Has this vehicle ever been in an accident?
2.   Where was this vehicle serviced?
3.   Are you the first owner?
4.   Is there anything wrong with this vehicle?
5.   Do you have the title present?
6.   How much do you owe on this vehicle?

This question is tricky because most will tell you to assume a zero dollar amount for the payoff because the payoff has nothing to do with what the car is worth. But the desk manager will ask you this when their preparing a payment structure. The reason for this is because if they owe more than the car is worth, then the extra must be put on the vehicle financing that you're trying to sell and most banks won't finance more than 120% of the value of the vehicle. (More on this later)

7. How much are your payments?
    a. How is your credit? Average, good, excellent?
        i. Do you know what your credit score is?
        ii. Would you like me to check your credit?
8. When is your next payment due?
9. How much are you expecting to get for the vehicle?

You might want to write the answers to some of these questions on the back of the vehicle bid sheet. These questions are meant to gauge the sentiment of the client regarding their vehicle.

We need to know how much they owe on the vehicle as well as monthly payments because most people want to be very close to their current monthly payment. Clients are almost always upside down on the value of their vehicle, meaning they owe more money than the vehicle is worth, unless they put a lot of money down at the time of purchase.

Don't ask the mileage because in my experience, 99% of the clients were way off to knowing what the mileage was. You might want to ask if the vehicle has a sunroof, power seats and alloy wheels. All this information is moot because you're going to have to go to the vehicle with your manager and see for yourself. This is just to get the client involved a little bit so it seems like they have some control in appraising their trade.

You never want to ridicule their vehicle, any of your vehicles or any other vehicles with different makes and models. It's not professional and you don't know what kind of feelings the client harbors toward any of those models.

I remember I was showing a married couple a Toyota Tacoma. The lady loved it but the husband wanted to see a Dodge truck next to it. I showed it to them but commented that Dodge wasn't a good make as it had a really bad reliability rating. Since the woman was doing most of the talking and the vehicle was for her, I didn't do a proper fact-finding on the man. Turns out, he was a dodge mechanic at another dealership and took great offense to that comment. Needless to say, this made my job that much harder. I eventually sold the wife on the truck but it took more than three weeks of communication.

11c. Approaching the Desk

Sales Advisor: "Okay, good. Can I have the keys to quickly check out your vehicle? Like I said earlier, for me to give you accurate numbers, we're going to have to check credit sooner or later. Here is a credit application you can look over while I'm *appraising your trade; all I need is the first 5 lines filled. You can fill it out if you want, it is something to think about."*

Even if they don't want their credit run, they can become familiar with the form so running credit doesn't look as scary when the time comes.

Although we asked them some information about their vehicle, we still need to see the vehicle to confirm that information as well have the used car manager evaluate it.

> **Sales Advisor:** *"Okay, I have everything I need. I'm going to need the keys to your vehicle so my used car manager can take a look at it and appraise it. You can come along if you wish."*
> **Mr. Stevens:** *"It's okay, I'll wait here."*
> **Sales Advisor:** *"Okay, I won't be long. Help yourself to any of the refreshments."*

If there isn't a trade-in involved, then you would skip the whole trade-in section. Let's pretend that there is a trade-in involved.

After entering the necessary information into your computer database, you will need to talk to the management about your clients so the management can prepare an offer. That's why we need as much information as possible in the computer before approaching the desk.

You will then need to come and give the bid sheet and keys to your manager so he can do a proper appraisal. Since the manager will be responsible for making an offer for the trade-in and not you, the sales advisor, they will want to appraise it personally.   In most cases, your manager will want to go out with you to check the vehicle so he's comfortable with its condition.

Make sure you fill in the evaluation form completely.

Some systems tell you that the client should be there when you're assessing their trade so they can visually see all the imperfections. Also, if they are present, you can use some closes like, "Have you owned this vehicle for the whole eight years?", "Did you do this?" (feeling out any and all imperfections), "What's happened here?" (pointing to any stain or dents or rips), "Will you get this fixed?" (pointing to any damages).

This is very effective in bringing the client down to earth as to the value of their trade. They start to realize that maybe their vehicle isn't such a gem as they once thought. Many imperfections that most people overlook on a daily basis about their vehicle now seem to stand out. They start to think that whatever the dealership offers them for their vehicle will be satisfactory to them.

If the client doesn't go out to the vehicle while you're getting it appraised, then you would point out any damage or imperfections when you get back to the desk. In no terms are you to make fun of the client's vehicle. Even if they hate their car, only they are allowed to make fun of it. Most people have an unusual attachment to their vehicles. Like their family members, even if they don't get along with them, they'll rally to their defense if need be.

Sales Advisor: *"Mr. Stevens over there is interested in the 2013 Toyota Camry."*

Manager: *"Did he drive it?"*

Sales Advisor: *"Yes."*

Manager: *"Does he have a trade?"*

Sales Advisor: *"A silver 2003 Accord. Here are the keys."*

Manager: *"Did you get a credit app?"*

Sales Advisor: *"No, I asked but he doesn't want his credit run. He says that it's in the high 700s."*

Manager: *"Any down payment?"*

Sales Advisor: *"I think around $5,000."*

Manager: *"You think or do you know?"*

Sales Advisor: *"Yeah...he said around $5,000."*

Manager: *"What kind of payments are they thinking for this vehicle?"*

Sales Advisor: *"I didn't ask. They wants a 5 year term though. Nothing more."*

Manger: *"How much in monthly payment are they making on their current vehicle?"*

Sales Advisor: *"Paid off."*

Manager: *"Okay, let's go and take a look at their trade."*

The reason the manager asks so many questions is to make sure that you did your job as well as figure out how much wiggle room they have in putting this deal together. The manager is trying to get as much information as possible to make this deal as appealing as possible. Remember that the sales manager also gets paid on the number of vehicles they sell so they also have a strong vested interest in selling as many vehicles as possible.

11d. Trade Evaluation

The purpose is to evaluate the vehicle based on its condition and not on its value. One thing to remember is that at this step, all we're doing is getting a condition report of the client's vehicle. We don't present them with numbers just yet. All we're doing is evaluating the vehicle for any and all defects, damages, dings, dents and mechanical problems.

The Important thing to remember is that we're going to use this information in the negotiation phase, so keep in mind that the trade-in value is a number that we will come back to. But at this point, we just want to assess the condition of their vehicle.

Most clients know what their vehicle is worth by checking comparative vehicles on the internet. They use this information as a negotiation tool and want to get as close as possible to this price on their trade-in value. The smart ones know that they can't get retail for it so they check what the trade-in value of their vehicle is using one of many vehicle sales websites like www.car.com or www.autotrader.com or www.KBB.com. These websites are hopelessly out of date and usually give the value of their trade based on mileage, make and model, a much higher number than the current market.

When at the vehicle, make sure you write down the VIN, start the vehicle and write down the mileage and run the AC. Also make a note of the condition of the interior, noting anything that might need repair. Check all the windows to make sure they go up and down in a smooth manner. Open all the doors, trunk and hood and check for any damage or missing VIN tags. Listen for any noises or unusual things about the vehicle. Feel every tire to gauge the depth. Run your hands along the edges of the back of the hood by the windshield, checking for sharp edges indicating that the vehicle has been painted. Note any differences in the gaps between body panels.

The most important information pieces are any dents in the body, any signs of an accident, mileage, does the A/C work, do the windows work, VIN, condition of the tires and any weird noises coming out of the engine or transmission. Note any smells, dents, repairs needed, noises, imperfections with the exterior and interior and condition of the tires, anything that we'll need to have repaired before putting the vehicle on the lot for resale.

We need to find any and all imperfections to use during the negotiation step in case the client objects to the amount management is willing to give for his trade. We're going to need to use these imperfections to justify the amount we will offer for his trade.

The desk or used car manager will most likely use the information he wrote down on the evaluation sheet including the VIN, condition of the vehicle, imperfections and other options the trade-in has to find the market value or book sheet, similar to the one below.

As you can see from the book sheet, this vehicle with all its options and high mileage sells for around $3,953 at the dealer auction, so this is the maximum we'll offer for the vehicle. These numbers are an estimate because this vehicle is ten years old and similar vehicles are selling for around $2,500 on www.Craigslist.org and Edmunds prices this vehicle trade-in value at around $2,700. Most likely, the manager will offer them $2,500 for the trade.

2003 Honda Accord Sedan - What Your Car is Worth

Pricing Details for a 2003 Honda Accord Sedan
EX V-6 4 door car

	Trade-In	Private Party	Dealer Retail
Mileage Adjustment - 183,851 miles	$-1,172	$-1,172	$-1,172
Condition Adjustment - Average	$-1,508	$-1,754	$-2,072
Total	**$2,717**	**$3,471**	**$4,533**

155

Tuesday, December 04, 2012
Publication for Arizona: 12/7-12/13
Values are subjective opinions.

Retail/Auction Breakdown
12/7-12/13

2003 Honda Accord EX Sedan 4D.. $9,553 / $4,978

VIN: 1HGPP47843A091243

V6, VTEC, 3.0 Liter..	500 / 375
Automatic...	Included
FWD..	Included

*** Equipment ***

ABS (4-Wheel)...	Included
Air Conditioning...	Included
Power Windows...	Included
Power Door Locks..	Included
Cruise Control..	Included
Power Steering...	Included
Tilt Wheel...	Included
AM/FM Stereo..	Included
CD (Multi Disc)...	Included
Premium Sound...	35 / 25
Navigation System...	235 / 175
Dual Airbags..	Included
Side Airbags..	Included
Dual Power Seats..	35 / 25
Leather...	165 / 125
Moon Roof...	Included
Alloy Wheels..	35 / 25

Condition..	Fair
Total Value without mileage.......................................	$10,558 / $5,728
Mileage adjustment (183851) miles................................	($1,775)
*** Retail/Auction Value..	$8,783 / $3,953

156

Some say that you should write down or note all the problems with their trade on the book sheet below so should the client object to the value your placing upon the trade, you can pull the book sheet out and show him all the notes you or your manager have taken in regard to their trade. You can also go as far as noting estimated costs of repair for each item to get to your offer. I don't recommend this as you shouldn't show the client the book sheet at all because in most cases, the dealership will be using Kelly Blue Book sheet and Kelly Blue Book is notorious for overvaluing vehicle prices because they want to attract individual clients more so than the dealerships. Also, this may force the client to reconsider trading in their vehicle, complicating things even more. It's better to find alternative third party sources to show the real market value of their trade like www.Edmunds.com.

This way, the dealership can try to sell this vehicle for around $3,900 at the auction. In reality, this vehicle will probably sell for around $3,000 or less at the auction.

The used car manager will probably call around to some of his wholesalers to ask them how much they'll buy this vehicle for to gather additional information and to properly price this trade. The manager will also run a history report on this vehicle to see if it's been in any accidents, salvaged or flooded. This bit of information should also be kept with you so you can use it in the negotiation phase.

While the management is looking at the trade or preparing an offer, log into a few auto pricing websites and take a look at the trade-in values for their vehicle. Also, keep in mind the imperfections of this vehicle to justify your prices. This would be a good time to check a few 3rd party websites such as www.Craigslist.org, www.Edmunds.com, www.Autotrader.com or www.Cars.com and check the prices of the vehicle you're selling.

Note the sites with the lowest price for trade-in values as you might have to pull these up in front of the client. Websites like www.Craigslist.org and www.Edmunds.com are usually the most realistic. The reason you need to do this is because if the client balks at the trade-in value, then you can show them on the computer as to the worth of their vehicle from a 3rd third party source. If your price is significantly lower, then you need to figure out other ways to justify your price like condition, mileage, car history, color or trim.

I like to use www.Edmunds.com to show the value of their vehicle as it's the closest to real world values of used vehicles.

No matter what, you need to find the lowest value you can use to justify that price for their trade for several reasons:

1. If their vehicle trade-in value is $10,000 and your used car manager offers them $8,000, then you have $2,000 worth of gross profit in this deal already. Giving them a lower number keeps some gross in this side of the deal. At 25% commission rate, you just made $500 on the trade alone

2. No matter what you say, most clients will want more for the trade. Some want way more than the retail value and most want more than the trade-in value. So If their

157

trade is worth $10,000 and you tell them it's worth $10,000, then in most cases they'll want more because they think you are trying to rip them off. If they want $10,500, then you have lost $500 on this deal from the start. At 25% commission rate, you've just lost $125 on the trade alone

3. You have to start out low for their trade so you have room to negotiate and so you can keep some gross in the deal. If their vehicle is worth $10,000 and your used car manager offers them $8,000, then you have $2,000 to negotiate with. If at the end of the negotiations you give them $9,000 for their trade, it leaves $1,000 in gross profit in the deal. At 25% commission, you just made $250 on the trade alone

Almost all vehicles that are taken in as trade need some reconditioning if the dealership is going to sell them on the lot. Vehicles that don't meet minimum requirements that are too old, have too high of mileage or are the wrong make or model for the dealership are automatically sent to the dealer auction.

While the management is preparing the first offer, you need to figure out where your limits are on the price of the vehicle, trade and payments. By this, I mean figure out where the profit targets as well as commission rates are so you know how much you are losing for every price drop on your vehicle or increase in the trade-in. Suppose we're selling a vehicle for $10,000. Total cost including pack on this vehicle is $8,500, so that leaves us with $1,500 to play with. At a 20% commission rate, you know that if you sell this vehicle you'll make ($1,500*20%) = $300 or $100 for every $500 you hold on to. If the client wants the price dropped to $9,500, then at 20% commission, you'll make $200 on this sale, maybe on par with your mini. You should be aware of these numbers to mentally work out what you'll be making as well as how much you'll be losing.

The offer that the management will have prepared for you will be in the form of the starting selling price, plus any add ons (tint, paint protection), less that trade, tax, title and final price.

What you need to make the client understand:

1. You're giving them the trade-in value based on the condition of the vehicle
   a. Any faults that you find with the vehicle need to be communicated to the client without insulting them to justify the value that you're assigning to it

2. The value you're assigning to the trade is the value that this particular vehicle is selling for at the wholesale market or at the dealer auctions

3. All vehicles taken in on trade require some reconditioning. As soon as the dealer takes in a trade, it has to sink in some costs to make it presentable, whether it be mechanical, body work or interior.... There are costs involved in bringing a used vehicle up to par to dealer and safety standards

4. The sales advisor also needs to make clients understand that we, as sales advisors, have nothing to do with assigning a trade-in value for their vehicle. The used car manager is

the one who values their vehicle based on market values. This way we shield ourselves from looking like the bad guy if our value is nowhere near what they had in mind.

As seen below:

Terms	Down Payments			Retail Price of Vehicle	
Rate of 2.9%	$2,000	$5,000	$10,000	Retail Price	$21,995
36 Months	$557 a month	$470 a month	$325 a month	Discount	-$2,000
48 Months	$424 a month	$358 a month	$247 a month	Selling Price	$19,995
60 Months	$344 a month	$290 a month	$201 a month	Options: Tint, Pin Striping, Paint Protection	$649
				Subtotal	$20,644
				Fees	$336
				Doc Fee	$500
				Sales Tax (10%)	$2,200
				Trade-in Allowance	($2,500)
				Net Sale Price/Amount Financed	$21,180.00

Some states charge you tax on the price of the vehicle while other states deduct your trade-in as well as your down payment before assessing tax. I've assessed tax on the purchase price before all the discounts. It varies by state.

Management: *"Here's the offer…..now go and get me a commitment."*

Sales Advisor: *"You're only giving them $2,500 for the trade?"*

Management: *"It's worth around $3,000 maximum, but I have given you some room to negotiate with should you need it."*

Sales Advisor: *"Okay."*

Sales Advisor: *"They said they don't have any more money down."*

Management: *"They all say that, just present them with these numbers and we can adjust it later on."*

Sales Advisor: *"Okay."*

Remember that the desk manager leads the deal. Follow their lead and instructions.

To be continued in 12D: presenting the numbers in the next chapter on negotiations.

Summary for Start your Write Up /Approaching the Desk/Trade-In Evaluation

The goal here is to prepare for the negotiations, specifically by entering all the pertinent client information into the computer system so your manager can present an offer to the client.

The client's credit information and trade-in information are very important in this step.

Doing research on the price of the clients' trade-in from a 3rd party website is crucial to justify your offer.

Researching prices of the vehicle you're selling is also important while waiting for the management to prepare an offer. Use these 3rd party sites to justify the price of your vehicle when the time comes to negotiate.

Gathering information on the amount of gross profit on the vehicle you're selling is also very important in helping you negotiate. This way you can see how much room you have to negotiate with as well as how that will affect your commission.

Fact-finding, product demonstration and negotiation steps in the process are so important. Refer to these three chapters frequently to keep yourself from becoming stagnant.

12. Negotiations - Presenting the Numbers, Negotiate the Offer, and Closing the Deal

Purpose: The purpose will be to turn the client from mentally owning the vehicle to financial committing to owning the vehicle. Up to now, the client has only imagined seeing themselves driving this vehicle, showing it to their family or taking a road trip. We're going to try to turn that into reality.

The key thing to remember in negotiations is getting the client to agree to a price, terms and a payment. The better you get at negotiating, the more gross income you can keep, which directly reflects the amount of money you make.

In order to get to this step, you've done a great job in the meet and greet, found out what their pain points are and found them a vehicle from your inventory that matches closest to what they are looking for. Made sure all the decision makers are present, and they have enough time to look at all their options. You have conducted a world class product presentation and demonstration and built value into your product. You overcame all the client objections in regard to the vehicle as well as properly sold yourself and your dealership. It is now time to finalize all your hard work and turn this client from mentally owning the vehicle to financially owning the vehicle.

This is another important chapter that must be studied multiple times for one to really grasp the concepts. Fact-finding, product presentation and negotiations are the most important steps in the process and must be studied at some length to grasp the true concept of the sale.

Most sales people who have issues in the negotiation step of the process actually have major issues in the steps leading up to the negotiation, like fact-finding and product demonstration. In order to be successful in negotiating, one must know what the client is looking for and build value in the product based on those needs and wants. After that, negotiation become simple.

The more time you spend on the fact-finding and product presentation, the less time you will need to spend on the actual negotiation. The more time you spend on getting to know the client, building trust, building rapport, building value and test driving, the less time you will need to spend in the actual negotiation.

Think about it, how hard do your friends need to talk you into doing things? Not that hard because you trust them and you value their interaction and suggestions. The only difference is that we don't have that much time to build friendship, trust or rapport. This is where we need to become like a chameleon and be more like them, empathize with them and impress them with our professionalism, product knowledge, attitude and enthusiasm. These will all become evident once you spend a week or 2 on the job.

The whole process has been set up to make this step as painless, effortless and as fruitful as possible. It's been said many times earlier in this book: the more time you take on the lot making them fall in love with the vehicle and building value, the less time you'll spend in negotiation.

12a. The Commitment

The 3 C's - Most dealerships will tell you that the sales advisor will be in much better shape before the negotiation if they get the 3 C's (Cash, Credit, Commitment).

> **Cash** – A down payment of some sort including a trade-in and/or a check or cash
>
> **Credit** – A completed Credit Application with permission to check credit
>
> **Commitment** – The client stating seriously that they want the vehicle, usually done by signing on the X on the bottom of the offer sheet.

At this point of the negotiation, all we have is our client willing to look at the numbers. They haven't committed to anything yet. What does it mean for them to commit?

Commitment comes when the client says, "I will buy from you." or "I will buy it at this price and terms." Although the request may be incredibly farfetched and mathematically unsound, when they utter that concept, it's a commitment. What they're actually saying is that they're ready to buy today; they're committed to making a buying decision at a negotiated price.

If they give you a cash, check or credit card for a down payment, then that is a good indication that they are willing to buy and it is a great commitment. If they let you run their credit, then that is also a great indication of commitment. Once you present them the numbers and they are okay with them and say yes, then that is the best commitment. That is a sale.

Specifically, the 3C's mean that you must get a <u>commitment from the client to buy **NOW**!</u> It communicates the seriousness of their offer for the vehicle. Keep hammering away until the client says yes. One technique that I was taught when I was green was when clients get comfortable after you gathered and entered their information into the computer, take a piece of paper and write, "Mr. and Mrs. Jones will take ownership/delivery of the 2012 Black Corolla S model Vin #XXXXXXXXXX if the numbers are agreeable. This vehicle meets/exceeds all their needs and wants." Draw a line with an X next to it and have them sign it. Tell them this doesn't mean anything, it just tells the manager that they are serious about allowing us to earn their business today. What this actually means is that the client is making a more solid mental commitment, a more solid financial commitment because we use the term "numbers". If the client refuses to sign it, then no big deal. Just keep moving forward.

I don't like using this technique because it communicates to the client that there is a large room for negotiation and that it takes the control away from the sales advisor and gives it to the client because it says that "if the numbers are agreeable" or similar verbiage.

Feel free to use this technique; it might work for you, but it did not work for me as some of my clients became defensive and it came off as gimmicky. Sometimes you just have to feel out your clients and customize your presentation for each client.

12b. Negotiation and The Close

To some, negotiating comes naturally, they inherently know that two parties are coming together for the sole purpose of coming to an agreement over an issue. They're also keenly aware of what each other is seeking in the negotiation and on how flexible each is in regard to meeting their needs.

I wish I was one of the natural ones, but I had to develop this skill over many years. Figuring out what management wants and how flexible they are is the easy part. Figuring out what the client wants is the hard part. You'd think that both want as much money as possible, but money is not always a driving force in negotiations.

In my long career, I've witnessed some really sharp negotiators who commanded attention and respect and I've witnessed some really weak negotiators like myself when I first started in the business.

Negotiation is a skill that can be mastered. The first step is to know what level of skill you are and to learn the rest from seasoned professionals by hanging out in the tower or the manager's office when deals are being worked. Another way is to ask the seasoned pros or managers after you've lost a deal as to how they would've handled it. **Ask for feedback.**

You can also ask your fellow coworkers to role play with you. By role playing, you and your fellow advisors can bring up reasons for failed negotiations from your past and figure out how you should have handled it. Also by hanging out at the tower when you're not with a client or times when it's slow, you can pick up some valuable Information on how the seasoned pros do it because the manager will always give advice on how to present the numbers, next course of action and expected results.

In the car business, you truly hear a few varying objections to the purchase of a vehicle that I've outlined throughout this book, such as:

> Price/payment too high
> Not enough down payment
> Monthly payments are too high
> Just looking
> Want to think about it
> Want more for the trade
> Upside down on their current vehicle

It's good to understand these objections so you can address them early on or find ways to isolate and address them individually.

Another valuable tool, which I talk about later, is to reassess everything that happened with your last client on what went wrong. What could you have done differently? What went right? You should reassess especially when you sold a car. What did you do to sell that vehicle? Did you make money on the vehicle or was this another mini? Do a post mortem on every client you interact with. Keep a log of everyone you talked to and the contact information so you can figure out at what stage in the sales process you lost them.

Another important tip is that once you're in the tower with the manager looking over the offer, either mentally or jot down all the negatives and positives of this deal, including the negatives and positives of your vehicle, the client's trade, client's credit, down payment, 3rd party justification of your price and their trade and the likes and dislikes of their trade, anything that can be used to justify your prices and assist the client to own the new vehicle.

Start off with a running balance of the negatives and positives of this deal, like their credit, job time, whether they like the vehicle, down payment, year of the vehicle, their trade, their immediate needs, cosigner, loan to value, debt to income and monthly payment requirements. Also send them to the ceiling and then peel them off by showing them high numbers first and then bring them down to reality.

A lot of the skill will come from experience, but I will try to outline some general rules when going into a negotiation. Remember that negotiations are part of the business and any objections or hesitations that a client has shouldn't be taken personally.

12c. Various Types of Clients

This is a short list of some of the common type of clients who purchase a vehicle at a dealership. You'll have a good idea on the lot but you'll know better when you get to the negotiation.

Lay Down or Flop – These types of client are the most sought after of all the clients. These clients don't want to haggle too much. They just want to be treated with honesty and respect. They'll usually only want about $500 or less of a discount on a vehicle, if that, and be on their way with their new vehicle. Be careful though, sometimes the lay down are bad credit in disguise. These people can't buy a vehicle because of their credit, so they won't haggle on the price too hard because they don't want to ruin their chances of not getting financed.

The know it all – This client has been around the block a few times and knows how a dealership operates. They supposedly know of all the fees and hidden profits dealers make. They know much more than you. They're only concerned with finding the right car and low balling you to a mini. You can turn it all around on these types of buyers by conducting an exemplary presentation and demonstration.

I'm just looking to get some numbers – This client doesn't want to go through the process and they know exactly what they want and need. Most likely they've already test drove and liked the vehicle in question and told the sales advisor they were working with at the first dealership that they will "think about it" or they will "be back" or possibly that they were on their way to the first dealership to buy the vehicle except they wanted to stop at another dealership to get a price to use in the negotiation at the first dealership because they've already picked out the vehicle they liked.

Most dealers, including myself, wouldn't want anything to do with these types of clients because they're just going to use your numbers to shop other dealers. Any client that you don't have a commitment that they're buying today should not be shown any numbers or terms except the sticker price. The reason for this is if you jump through hoops to get them a good deal on their vehicle, on their trade or qualify them and they leave to go to another dealership to buy, they are using your figures as a negotiating tool.

Usually clients who don't give you a chance to take them through the process so you can impress them with the vehicle and make them fall in love with the vehicle will not be that committed. Only when the client is committed do you go into the negotiation phase. What's the point of showing a client numbers when he doesn't even like the vehicle, or all the decision makers are not there, or they don't have the time to sit down to talk numbers.

Some managers don't want to turn these clients away. They want the sales people to still work them. The idea behind this logic is if someone comes to the dealership and wants the price of a certain make, model and trim but doesn't want to drive it or look at it that means that he has already looked at the vehicle, gone home done some more research and is serious about buying but wants to get a second opinion on the prices before going to the first dealership to buy the vehicle. They're pretty loyal to the first sales advisor or picked out a vehicle they liked at the other dealership but still want to get a good deal. The managers want the sales advisor to spend as much time as possible with these people to build a relationship with them, anything to stall them and spend as much time with the sales advisor as possible so the sales advisor can make the client switch loyalties from the first sales advisor to them. The advisor would talk at length with them, ask open ended questions and get them numbers for their trade.

Rarely did this ploy work, mainly because the client was always in a hurry. They just wanted to get the best price you could give them and move on. They rarely stayed more than an half an hour, no matter how much the advisor tried to stall them.

You could try either way. Sometimes you need to go through this to learn. It might work for you but from my experience, if the client isn't committed to buy a vehicle, then there is no point in showing them numbers unless you're working at a dealership that doesn't negotiate on the price at all, in which case everyone gets the same price.

The Final Offer Client - During the first or second round of negotiations they flatly tell you, "This is what I'm willing to do, you can either meet it or you can't." "If it's not meant to be, it's not meant to be." These clients don't seem to show any connection to the vehicle. They're buyers for sure but they're offer is so ridiculous that it's not even worth discussing with the managers. It's a mini for sure, but it's a sale none-the-less. These clients really take a lot of work to bring their price up to acceptable levels. Every time you show them new numbers you have to sell the vehicle again and again until you make them see reason. The only thing you can do is present the numbers to management and have them decide.

Clients that bring in support – Some buyers will bring friends or family members along with them for support or out of fear of being taken advantage of. These assistants don't have any economic interest in the transaction and they're there to keep the clients company. Engaging the assistant early on in the fact-finding, rapport building and product demonstration is the key to winning over the assistant. As a sales advisor, you should always be addressing the whole group anyway. Don't alienate anyone. Even if the parents are there with the kids, the kids will influence the buying decision.

165

The assistant can also be used to close the deal by asking them to assist you in finding ways to close the deal, like having them cosign, loaning the buyer a down payment or helping with the payments. Some assistants will try to put up opposition to the deal and they must be addressed as if the buyer is putting up the opposition. Don't lose patience, your cool or your professionalism. It's all part of the game.

12d. Presenting the Numbers

Terms	Down Payments			Retail Price of Vehicle	
Rate of 2.9%	$2,000	$5,000	$10,000	Retail Price	$21,995
36 Months	$557 a month	$470 a month	$325 a month	Discount	-$2,000
48 Months	$424 a month	$358 a month	$247 a month	Selling Price	$19,995
60 Months	$344 a month	$290 a month	$201 a month	Options: Tint, Pin Striping, Paint Protection	$649
				Subtotal	$20,644
				Fees	$336
				Doc Fee	$500
				Sales Tax (10%)	$2,200
				Trade in Allowance	($2,500)

There are various forms or presentations from using a 4 - square (which we'll discuss below) to using a purchase order like this, to bringing up a computer screen to show what the numbers look like. Although the visuals vary, the underlying concepts are the same.

The way to present the numbers is similar to this:

> **Sales Advisor:** *"Okay...I have the offer from management."*
> **Client:** *"Okay, so how does it look?"*
> **Sales Advisor:** *"The retail selling price of the silver 2013 Camry is $21,995, we've given you a discount/rebate of $2,000 to get to a selling price of $19,995. We have options of tint, pin striping and paint protection for $649 for a subtotal of $20,644. There are license fees of $336, doc fees of $500 and sales tax of $2,200; our used car manager has determined that the fair market value for your vehicle is $2,500, which comes to a net sale price of $21,180. Given an annual percentage rate of 2.9% based on what you told me your credit score was, with $5,000 down, your payments would be $470 a month for 36 months, $358 a month for 48 months or $290 a month for 60 months. Similarly, if you wish to put down even more, then those are the respective monthly payments. Please circle the payment plan that appeals to you the most and sign at the bottom and I'll get the car all cleaned up for you."*

You would then draw a line at the bottom of the sheet with an X next to it for a place for them to sign.

X _____

You would use a pen to point to every number on the presentation.
You would then put down your pen and the sheet in front of them and keep quite while they absorb all the necessary information and come to a decision as to which payment plan would best work for them.

Don't use the work "ask" when discussing the price of the vehicle you're selling, as in, "The asking price is $21,995." "Ask" implies that you're willing to negotiate. "Ask" also communicates weakness.

If you have not run their credit, then you're manager has built the deal using the credit score that the clients have provided. It's a good idea to mention that. "Based on what you told me your credit score is, with $5,000 down, you payments for 60 months would be $290."

The signature by the X is vital to the negotiation phase. It is the commitment. It signifies that the client is willing to do the deal today. The client is mentally moving from a looker to a buyer.

All we have to do is come to an agreement on the price and terms.

This will be required and discussed in every step of the process. Just keep in mind that signing by the X is a mental commitment by the client and not a financial or legal one.
At this point, the client will likely do one of two things:

1. They sign on the line by the X which is great because they've accepted the offer and are willing to buy at your stated numbers., a lay down
2. They look over the offer and want to make a counter offer by changing several things

It is rare that they circle the best pay plan for them and sign at the bottom. This is called a flop, where they flop right down and want the deal done without any negotiation.

Most likely they'll want one or more of the numbers changed. Either the price of the vehicle, the payments, the price of their trade or the down payment. These are the objections.

The manager should already have the trade-in information, the information regarding the vehicle that they are interested in, the credit information from the clients themselves and the down payment information. The first offer or first pencil will usually incorporate all of these into a presentation above. It's important to know that management will usually not change the original price of the vehicle here at the first pencil. If the price of the vehicle is $10,000, then that's going to be the first offer. It's up to the client to negotiate down. Every time they negotiate the price down, they win. Everybody likes to win and the client is no different. Every time they get their way, they feel like a winner.

There really is no reason at this point to reduce the price of the vehicle. We present the numbers as they are and let the client negotiate down. Don't let their expectations be too unrealistic. Do this whenever price comes up like when talking about trade, payment and down payment. The price of the vehicle is at its highest possible because the client will want to negotiate down to feel like a winner. The down payment requirement is at its highest possible because the client will want to negotiate down. The trade-in value is at its lowest possible because they will negotiate up. The payments will be at their highest possible because they will negotiate down, even though payment is a byproduct of price, value of the trade, down payment and term of the loan.

12e. Objections

It's rare that you get a client that doesn't want to negotiate on the numbers. A couple of things to remember when dealing with objections are:

- Never give objections too much power – they may be real or they may not. Test the validity of the objection. Have the client elaborate. Ask why

- Never take an objection personally – it's a game all clients like to play

- Never handle more than one objection at a time – address one objection at a time

- Never make verbal proposals – write everything down

- Never abandon negotiations because of an objection due to the reasons above

- Never think the objection will keep the client from buying

- Never ignore the objection

- Never interrupt the client while they're making an objection
- Never write down what they want for them to see. Only your numbers matter. Only write down your numbers and proposals

- When expecting and overcoming objections, keep in mind, **"What is in it for them?"** If they say the price is too high then, "What's in it for them?" to pay a high price for the vehicle. Maybe you've built so much value into it that the price is justified. It saves them time because this is the perfect vehicle. This will keep their family safe, save them money in maintenance and fuel and they look nice in this beautiful car.

No matter what the objections are, keep a few things in mind:

- **Act surprised** – you're giving them a good deal after all from the beginning
- **Defend your position** – justify your position without seeming too defensive. It's all part of the game
- **Create room for counter offers** – don't give them everything they want, only a little bit at a time. Giving them everything they want will make you lose credibility by seeming easy and that it's all part of the game
- **Test the validity of the objection** – "Oh...I can get the same vehicle down the street for $5,000 cheaper." Go ahead and get me one too. Always ask the client to elaborate on the objection. "The same vehicle, with the same mileage, trim, condition, model?"
- **Never...ever take it personally** - Everybody plays the game
- **Keep up your attitude and enthusiasm**
- **Listen attentively** - give them time to explain without butting in
- **Use language** that doesn't imply the buyer is lying
- On used vehicles, **ignore** all the numbers the client is throwing around, for instance, that he can get one just like it for $2,000 less or he can get more for his trade elsewhere because they have nothing to do with your vehicle and it's all a game they all play

The key word for any negotiation is **justify.**

- Make sure to reiterate all the features and benefits to the client on the vehicle should they have an objection or try to counter offer you. You need to justify all your numbers. Before presenting the numbers to the client, mentally justify the values on the sheet to counteract any objections they may have. Using a 3rd party source like the internet or publications gives your justification even more legitimacy

The better you become at justifying your position the better negotiator you will be.

- One strategy to use when an objection comes up is to ask, "Compared to what?" Price too high? Compared to what? My trade is worth more. Compared to what? Payments are too high. Compared to what? Just like you're justifying your figures, this allows the client to justify theirs. Otherwise the client will be pulling down numbers from thin air making you justify that they're wrong

- **"Compared to what I owe on my trade"**. The explanation is that what you owe and what the car is worth are 2 different numbers. The fact is, the longer they keep the vehicle, the less the value will be of the vehicle compared to what they owe. This is a case where the owner is upside down on their vehicle, meaning that they owe more than the vehicle is worth

- **"Compared to what the dealer next door will pay for my trade."** Most likely they're comparing the value for their trade-in on a different vehicle than yours where the other dealer has more of a profit margin and can play with the numbers. But most likely they're lying about it. It happens all the time that buyers will go through a good song and dance to get the price they want. Maybe there are rebates involved. Don't even get pulled into this game because you don't know what they're comparing it to or even if they're telling you a lie. In this situation you need to tell them, "Sir, I don't know what the other dealer's games are or what kind of things they're not disclosing, but this vehicle you picked out meets all your needs, right? It drives great? Fitted the way you like it? Right? Okay, what if I can get the manager to increase the value of your trade by $500, do we have a deal then?" Mark a line with an X on it and have them sign

- **"Compared to what other dealers who are selling vehicles like my trade."** Here you need to explain that the price they're referring to is the retail price. Explain that the dealership can't pay more than what they can replace the same vehicle at a wholesaler or at an auction. Show them websites to the actual price of their vehicle in the condition that it's in. Educating them on how business is done at a dealership is the key to overcoming this objection.

When an objection does come up, one of the ways to deal with it is to draw up a traditional 4square. A 4 square is a simple visual aid to show where the numbers currently are.

You would draw up underneath the numbers that you presented, like the numbers above, a large "plus" sign. In each quadrant you would enter "Trade-in" and underneath it the amount that you're sales manager is willing to pay for their trade. In another quadrant you would enter the word "Down", which is the amount the client is willing to put down. In another quadrant, the selling price and amount of the selling price of the vehicle. In the last quadrant, the monthly payment and the amount. Similar to below:

Trade-in	**Down Payment**
Selling Price of New Vehicle	**Monthly Payment**

Trade - is the value of their trade-in.

Down Payment - is the amount of down payment they can come up with in about a month.

Selling Price – is the price of the vehicle the client wants to purchase.

Monthly payment – is the amount of their monthly payment after tax, license, doc fee and other additions.

These are the 4 elements that we, as sales advisors with the approval of the desk manager, can adjust to make a car deal work. In order to maintain a descent commission, we want to avoid adjusting the value of their trade-in and the selling price of the vehicle since our commission is directly based on the amount of profit we keep in the deal. Always be thinking when talking to clients which one of the four squares can you adjust to make this car deal work. Always aim to get the client to increase the amount of their down payment, monthly payment or the right side of the quadrant. The term of the loan is another factor that a manager may be able to adjust to affect the payments, but not all vehicles will qualify for longer terms, like used, high mileage or old vehicles.

Given the scenario above, you would fill in the 4 square as such. Payments are based on 60 months:

$2,500 Trade-in	**$5,000 Down Payment**
$19,995 Selling Price of New Vehicle	**$290 Monthly Payment**

Most dealerships will teach you to draw the 4 square, but I've always taught my sales advisors to be aware of the 4square, but not to draw it. The concept of the 4 square is much more important than the visualization of it. The big issue I have with it is it reminds the clients about all their options of negotiations. Once they have a problem with payment, they see that they can also adjust the price, the down and the trade-in value. They usually won't be satisfied until they touch on all 4 items on the 4square.

It is far better to work on one objection at a time. Suppose they have an issue with payment. Only write the amount of the payment in question and work on that alone. Drawing up the other items such as price of vehicle, down payment and trade will only remind them of what else they can negotiate on.

Concentrate on adjusting the down payment and monthly payment squares first and foremost. If a client is saying they can only afford $200 a month and nothing more, then you know from that bit of information that you're looking for a $10,000 vehicle. That is the first place you should search for when looking for a vehicle. This should have been done in the fact-finding or selling from stock step. If another vehicle would be perfect for your client but is a little bit more expensive, then you as a sales advisor need to be persuading the client to increase their monthly payment budget before anything else.

Use these reasons when appropriate at every level of the negotiation phase.

Reasons to Buy Now

Dealer Incentives	Resale Value	Factory Warranty or Extended Warranty	Expired/Expiring Plates
Book Change on Trade	Repairs or Expense of Trade	Reliability	Personal Investment
Price Increases	Ego, Prestige, Image	Possible Payment Delay	Performance
Supply and Demand	Lease Incentives	Economy	Safety
Lower Payments	Technology	Lower Maintenance	Dependability/Reliability

Don't write down anything that they say, only write your numbers down for them to see. Writing their numbers, wants and needs give them weight. Only your numbers carry weight.

Look at the whole deal, all the plus and minuses. Reducing the price of your vehicle or increasing the price of their trade will reduce your commission.

When thinking about adjusting the numbers, you need to look at the whole deal and not one aspect of it. Business is a plus/minus game where we're trying to increase our overall profit any way we can and trying to reduce our costs any way we can. Keep this in mind when in negotiation, because if you reduce the price in one area, you will need to make it up in another if possible. A professional advisor needs to look at the whole deal rather than only one aspect of it.

For example:

2011 Cadillac SRX retail price		$40,000
Dealer Cost		$35,000
Total Profit		$5,000
Trade-in: 2003 Nissan Altima		
Wholesale Price	$4,000	
Client Asking Price		$6,000
Total Profit/Loss on Trade	-$2,000	
Total Gross Profit	$3,000	

As you can see, the dealer total cost on the selling vehicle, which is a Cadillac SRX, is $35,000, which retails for $40,000. So the total profit will be $5,000. Now suppose someone interested in the Cadillac wants to purchase it and has a trade. If the trade's book value, meaning that's what it's worth in the wholesale market is $4,000 but the client insists that that it's worth $6,000 and he will not take anything less, then the dealer will be losing $2,000 on the trade and will offset this loss by applying to the profit of the new vehicle. So now the profit on the Cadillac, which currently is $5,000, is less; we're losing $2,000 on the trade, so it ends up being only $3,000. You, as a sales advisor, would get paid on the $3,000.

This is a very good reason to find the dealer costs and profit margins on all vehicles you're selling. You need to know your limits as well as your commission thresholds.

As a sales advisor, I will take deals like this all day. A 20% commission on $3,000 is $600. The problem is that some clients are more savvy than that and will want to also negotiate down the price of the vehicle. They'll want to drop the price of the Cadillac from $40,000 to $37,000. In this case, there is no profit left for the sales advisor since there will only be $2,000 profit on the Cadillac and a $2,000 loss on the trade to net out to zero, which means that this will be a mini for the sales advisor.

This is a call that your manager will need to make but in most cases, they will take it because the vehicle has already been padded with dealer profit, called packing, like we discussed earlier. All vehicles get padded about $1,500 for sunk costs, overhead and management fees. Most dealers will say that they don't pack their vehicles but I haven't seen any dealer that doesn't pack their vehicles.

So keep the whole deal in mind during negotiations. A change in one number will usually affect the other numbers in the deal. Trade-in value and price of your vehicle directly impacts your commission.

The scenario above is most likely a new vehicle, but I've incorporated some examples like it's a used vehicle just so you can get your head around the whole sales process.

12f. Objection: Trade-in

Obviously, all objections regarding the trade mean that they want more money for it. The only way to overcome the trade objection is to justify as best as you can the trade-in value your manager is offering.

Keep in mind all the negatives about their trade-in vehicle so you can use them later on to justify your position.

Assess the condition, mileage, age, model, make, history report and tax savings on the new vehicle by trading it in, time (it is worth less in future), needed repairs, noises, smells and the prices that you looked up when the manager was preparing an offer.

Main client trade objections:

- Not enough money for the trade
- My car is still in good shape
- I can get more from the dealer down the road. I'm no longer interested in trading
- I owe too much
- I would rather sell myself
- I would need at least X for my trade

Objection: "I can get at least $4,000 for my trade if I sell it on my own."

Act surprised, defend your position and numbers, keep up your attitude and enthusiasm and listen to the client's explanation.

Pause for a second and look over the trade-in sheet as if you're trying to make sense of their objection. Keep in mind all the negatives you've learned about their vehicle.

Samples of ways to justify your position:

1. **Sales Advisor:** *"I can understand that, Mr. Client, but your vehicle is about 10 yrs. old. We can't give you retail for your vehicle because we can get a similar vehicle at the auction for around $2,000 and we're willing to give you $2,500 to earn your business."*

2. **Sales Advisor:** *"We also can't sell a vehicle of that age/mileage/condition on our lot. We're going to need to ship it straight to a wholesaler."*

3. **Sales Advisor:** *"I can understand that, Mr. Client, but your vehicle has well over 100K miles. It's tough to sell vehicles with that mileage for that much money."*

4. **Sales Advisor:** *"I can understand your position, but your vehicle also has had an accident in the last couple of years from the vehicle history report."*

5. **Sales Advisor:** *"I can understand your position, Mr. Client, but that make isn't that popular and it's a hard sell with all the problems they're having right now. You have had the vehicle for a very long time before you tried to sell it, reducing its value. We have had similar vehicles such as yours and we ended up selling it at an auction because of lack of interest."*

6. **Sales Advisor:** *"I can understand your position, Mr. Client, but your vehicle is in need of some repair, some as much as $3,000. Why not save yourself that money and headache of selling it on the street. Why would you have these repairs done on a vehicle with more than one hundred thousand miles?"*

7. **Sales Advisor:** *"I can understand your position, Mr. Client, but by trading your vehicle in, you are also saving an extra $250 in taxes, so were actually giving you $2,750 for your vehicle." ($2,500+$250)*

> Some states base the sales tax on the price of the vehicle, less incentives and trade-ins, so if you're buying a $10,000 vehicle and the dealer will give you $6,000 for your trade-in, then you pay tax on the difference or $4,000. You also need to use this fact that the total amount they are getting for their trade is $6,000 plus $600 savings in taxes given a 10% tax rate for a total of $6,600 for their trade. In this case, the selling price of $21,995 - $2,500 = $19,495 @ 10% tax is $1,949 which is about $250 less than $2,199 tax of the original amount. ($21,995*10% = $2,199 tax. $19,495*10% = $1,949 tax. A difference of $2,199-$1,949 = 250 in tax savings.)

8. **Sales Advisor:** *"I can understand your position, Mr. Client, but if you wait, your vehicle won't be worth that much later on, so if you come back later we'll probably give you $2,000 for your vehicle. Vehicles depreciate at around $50 a week."*

9. **Sales Advisor:** *"I can understand your position, Mr. Client, but the vehicle doesn't seem to running too well. It has something major wrong with it."*

Give 2 reasons that defend your position and to bring the buyer back into reality.

Don't write down anything that they say, only write your numbers for them to see. Writing their numbers and wants needs give them weight. Only your numbers carry weight.

Sales Advisor: *"Now, what if I can get you $2,800 for your trade, would that earn your business today? Now I can't promise anything because it's in the hands of management, but I can present this to management and see what they say. Just sign by the X below and I'll present it to management."*

Client: *"No, I said I can get $4,000 on the street, I want more for it."*

Draw the 4 square with the boxes filled in. Again, I would only write down the item in question or what we're negotiating and leave the other parts out as I don't want to give the client an idea of what else they can negotiate about. I've left the whole 4 square in place so you can get a better idea or bigger picture of the process.

~~$2,500~~ Trade-in $2,800	$5,000 Down Payment
$19,995 Selling Price of New Vehicle	$290 Monthly Payment

Pause for a second and look at the trade-in sheet and zoom in on anything that you can use as ammunition to devalue the trade, like repairs needed, mileage, make, model, color, age and unpopular accessories and options.

While the management is preparing the numbers, check a few websites to educate yourself on the trade-in value of this vehicle. Also note the websites that had the lowest trade-in price just in case you needed to use it. It is here that you need to use it. Log into the website that had the lowest trade-in price and pull it up in front of the client to show them values from a third party source to justify your position.

Of course, if the websites showed a higher trade-in value, then you would keep that to yourself and find something else to use to justify your price.
You know that during the "approaching the desk" step when the management prepared the numbers for you they said that the trade was worth $3,000, so to get $4,000 is going to be a stretch. By now your only option is to get the client back to reality. This is where your internet research comes into play.

> **Sales Advisor:** *"Mr. Client...if you look at this website, you can see that your trade is worth a lot less than we're paying you for it. This is the reason; I can't give you that much for your trade."*

> **Sales Advisor:** *"I can understand your position, Mr. Client, but by trading your vehicle in, you are also saving an extra $300 in taxes, so were actually giving you $3,100 for your vehicle." ($2,800+$300)*

> **Sales Advisor:** *"What if I can get you $2,950 for your trade, do we have a deal then? Now I'm not promising anything, all I can do is present this to management and recommend that we proceed."*

Give 2 reasons justifying your position and reduce the price again.

~~$2,500~~ Trade-in ~~$2,800~~ $2,950	$5,000 Down Payment
$19,995 Selling Price of New Vehicle	$290 Monthly Payment

Sales Advisor: *"Also remember, Mr. Buyer, that your vehicle is considerably older than the new one, which will also increase your reliability, save you on maintenance fees as well as your gas mileage."*

Sales Advisor: *"Also remember that you'll also be saving on the tax of $300, so you're actually getting over $3200 for your trade." ($2,950+$300)*

Sales Advisor: *"You can see that I've brought up the price of your trade by $450. I think that's a fair price for your trade, don't you?"*

Client: *"No, you're going need to do a little more, I just put new brakes on it."*

Sales Advisor: *"I don't know...I've might have already gone too far by increasing the price of your trade by $450, which will reduce your payment as well as your down payment requirement as well as your taxes. We are looking at a high mileage, older vehicle with some badly needed repairs that will need to be wholesaled at a loss to us."*

Sales Advisor *"What if I can get you $3,000 for your trade, do we have a deal then? Now I'm not promising anything, all I can do is present this to management and recommend that we proceed."*

If you noticed that at the first objection I increased the value of the trade by $300 (from $2,500 to $2,800). At the second objection I increased it $150 (from $2,800 to $2,950) and the last objection I increased it by $50 (from $2,950 to $3,000). In increasing the value of the trade I have to increase by smaller and smaller increments so the client can visually see that the increases are coming to an end. Similar to a funnel. This is called the funnel or step down method. The funnel method is where you start large like the mouth of a funnel and gradually go smaller and smaller. Use the same principle when dropping your price or down payment requirements or payments.

$2,500 Trade-in (crossed out) $2,800 (+300) (crossed out) $2,950 (+150) (crossed out) $3,000 (+50)	$2,000 Down Payment
$19,995 Selling Price of New Vehicle	**$290 Monthly Payment**

In this case, this can go in many directions from here:

1. **Client:** *"No....I want $4,000 and nothing less for my trade."*

   a. In this case, the management won't likely want to do business with this person since the vehicle is only worth $3,000 and he wants $4,000 which is $1,000 more. This might be able to work if no other numbers on the 4 square need to be negotiated on like selling price. Giving $4,000 for his trade will change his payments as well as amount of down payment. It depends on how badly the management wants a deal. Regardless, you're going to have to get a manger to approve this deal

   b. In this case you would ask, "Okay, Mr. Client. If I can get you $4,000 for your trade, do we have a deal?" Get as much information as you can get on what other numbers he wants to adjust but keep in mind that his payments will go down or change. Then you need to talk to your manager about what to do next. Most likely your manager will want to come out and talk to this client. If the client agrees that if he can get $4000 for his trade he'll buy the vehicle then most likely the management will oblige him but if the client also wants $4,000 for his trade and a discount on the price of the vehicle as well as reduction in the interest rate, then most likely the management will pass on this deal. In the end, it is a business and the dealership must make money or no one gets paid

2. **Client:** *"Yes....that sounds good, now let's talk about changing some of the other numbers."*

   a. In this case, your manager won't be happy with giving him a lot of money for his trade and adjusting all the other numbers like selling price and payments. In case they want to adjust the other numbers, then just follow the other scenarios on dealing with objections for the other squares. **Get the signature below for the commitment**

3. **Client:** *"Yes....that sounds fair, I'll sign below."*

a. This would be ideal since basically you got the commitment to proceed with the deal. It doesn't mean that the deal is done. The management still needs to analyze this deal before approving it

Another strategy that I used very effectively at my dealership was that when the sales advisor was finished inputting the most basic information about the client's trade-in, as a sales manager, I would take over. I would go over and talk to the clients, chat them up a little, build rapport and trust. I would then ask them a little about their vehicle, their use, why they wanted to trade it in, condition and get a gauge of how much they liked their vehicle. I would then ask them to go out with me to look at the vehicle. It didn't matter whether they did or not but it was a great excuse to meet the clients and acknowledge their importance. I would then prepare the numbers and offer for them. During this whole time, my sales advisor would be doing research on third party sources as to the value of their vehicle so they could have some information to justify our offer.

Either my sales advisor or I would present the numbers, but I preferred to do it as the numbers now carried some weight that a manager was presenting them. I would usually do this for the new sales advisors or the ones that needed help in closing. My seasoned sales advisors would take the client all the way through, but my green peas needed some special coaching before I cut them loose.

This strategy works great, especially if the manager needs to come back and touch the client at another objection later on like price, payment or down.

12g. Objection: Price

Obviously the main purpose of this objection is to get the new vehicle as cheaply as possible. Altering the price of your vehicle will have a direct impact on your commission.

This objection should have been anticipated and nullified with a good presentation and demonstration. When you showed the vehicle, you should have built so much value in the vehicle that the client fell in love with it and found the asking price more than fair.

The difference between price and value is salesmanship.

What this mantra is saying is that the price of a product does not matter as long as the client believes that the price is justified and worth it and that the features built into the product are worth immensely more than what is being charged. That is the main point of the "Presentation and Demonstration" step in the sales process, which is to build as much value as possible to make the negotiation step a breeze. Value can only be built by a professional and enthusiastic sales advisor. Only proper attitude, product knowledge and enthusiasm can help the client see that what their getting for the price far exceeds the price.

Keep in mind all the positive aspects of your vehicle to justify the price, which you will need to remind the client from time to time to prevent them from objecting too much on the selling price.

The value of the trade and the price of the new vehicle have a direct impact on your commission. The lower you get the trade for and the closer to retail you sell your vehicle for, the higher your

179

commission. Instead, you might want to focus on the payment, since a majority of buyers are payment buyers, meaning they're only concerned with how much they can pay a month.

Client: "The selling price is too high; I saw a similar vehicle down the road for much less."

Pause a moment and look at the price sheet as to make sense of their objection. Also remember everything you've learned from them in the fact-finding step of what's important to them and how this new vehicle meets those requirements.

Don't write down anything that they say, only write your numbers for them to see. Writing their numbers and wants needs give them weight. Only your numbers carry weight.

Give 2 reasons to defend your position and drop the price by a nominal rate.

Sales Advisor: "When I first talked to you, you stated that the most important thing you're looking for was safety and efficiency. Well, this is the safest sedan on the market as well as the most gas efficient for its size."

Sales Advisor: "There are similar vehicles on the internet selling for $2,000 more. The vehicle you saw at the other dealership couldn't possibly have the same miles and be in the same great condition as this one."

Sales Advisor: "Hmmm...I understand your concern, but as you can see we're already giving you a $2,000 rebate off the original MSRP. We've done this because we don't want to play games with our clients. We gave you the discount upfront. Don't you think that's fair?"

Sales Advisor: "What if I can get the price of the vehicle dropped from $19,995 to $19,495? An additional $500? Will we have a deal then? Now I'm not promising anything, all I can do is present this to management and recommend that we proceed."

Draw the 4square. Again, I prefer you only write down only one item out of the 4.

$2,500 Trade-in	$5,000 Down Payment
~~$19,995~~ Selling Price $19,495	$290 Monthly Payments

Client: "The other vehicle is priced at $17,000 and it's in similar condition."

Give 2 reasons to defend your position and drop the price by a nominal rate.

Sales Advisor: *"That vehicle must have high mileage or a bad history because these vehicles are retailing for $21,995 and we've already given you a $2,000 discount to get to $19,995. So there's already a huge discount in the price."*

Sales advisor: *"I've worked here for a while now and we never overprice our vehicles. Our prices are very competitive with the market. We can't overprice them because banks won't finance vehicles with large markups. Now what if I can get the management to lower the price a bit more, to say $19,245? Do we have a deal then?"*

$2,500 Trade-in	$5,000 Down Payment
~~$19,995~~ Selling Price ~~$19,495~~ $19,245	$290 Monthly Payments

Client: *"I checked out the other vehicle; it has low miles and it's in better condition than this one."*

Never give an objection too much weight and never be afraid to play the game because the client is doing the same. If the other vehicle was lower priced, with lower mileage and in better condition, then why is this guy here negotiating on this one? In most cases it comes down to price.

Sales Advisor: *"I don't know what to tell you Mr. Client, I haven't seen too many of these vehicles as clean as this one. Look on Craigslist and KBB on how much they're selling for."*

Sales Advisor: *"There has to be something wrong with the other vehicle to be discounted so deeply."*

Sales Advisor: *"I don't know what to tell you Mr. Client, I've already dropped the price by $750 to earn your business as well as a $2,000 discount upfront. Do we have a deal if I can get the price dropped to $19,145? This will also reduce your monthly payments."*

$2,500 Trade-in	$5,000 Down Payment
~~$19,995~~ Selling Price ~~$19,495~~ ~~$19,245~~ $19,145	$290 Monthly Payments

Notice that I started with a $500 ($19,995-$19,495) discount at first and then went to a $250 ($19,495-$19,245) discount and then to a $100 ($19,245-$19,145) discount. I reduced the price by smaller and smaller increments so the client can see that the discounts are going to zero very fast.

After the third drop and you still can't get the client to sign the commitment at the bottom, then you need to figure out what the client actually wants.

The commitment is what we're after so after the 3rd attempt, write what the client wants and tell them, "Okay, sign by the X so management knows you are serious and I can present it to my manager." Now this doesn't mean that we're agreeing to this, but we're trying to get the client to move from being a shopper to a buyer.

Another strategy you should always be using is:

Sales Advisor: *"I can recommend in the spirit of fair trade and client service to the management that we should go to $19,145. Like I said, I can't promise anything, I can only recommend. We've given you a $2,000 discount right out of the gate and now were giving you another $850 on top of that. You've got to help me out here, your making out like a bandit."*

Whenever you're talking about numbers that benefit, the client you should write them down on the sheet so the client can see them visually in **big bold** numbers. The numbers $2,000 and $850 above need to be written down and added so you can show them that their saving a total of $2,850. Then circle the $2,850 and write **savings** underneath to remind them of how much they are saving.

$7,500 Trade-in	$2000 Down Payment
~~$19,995~~ Selling Price	$252 Monthly Payments
~~$19,495~~	
~~$19,245~~	
$19,145	

$2,000 Rebate
+$850 discount
_____
$2,850 savings

People remember and comprehend things much better if they see it in writing or illustrated on paper.

In this case, this can go in many directions from here:

1. **Client:** *"No....I won't pay any more than $17,000 for this vehicle."*

   a. In this case, you would cross off all the price drops for the price of the vehicle and write in $17,000 and have them sign by the "X" below. You'll need to present this offer to management for their approval. Most likely, management will want to come out to renegotiate a higher price and hammer away at reasons why. Get the commitment first and then management will work out the details later

2. **Client:** *"Yes....that sounds good, now let's talk about changing some of the other numbers."*

   b. In this case, your manager won't be happy with reducing the price of your vehicle and probably adjusting the trade-in value, payments or down requirements. In case they want to adjust the other numbers, then just follow the other scenarios on dealing with objections for the other squares. **Get the signature below for the commitment**

3. **Client:** *"Yes....that sounds fair, I'll sign below."*

   c. This would be ideal since basically you got the commitment to proceed with the deal without adjusting any other numbers. The management still needs to analyze this deal before approving it

12h. Objection: Down Payment

In my experience, I would say about 70% of people didn't want to put any money down, excluding a trade-in. Since a majority of car buyers are payment buyers, meaning they only care about how much the payments are, we need to figure out a way to keep their monthly payments down while at the same time maintaining a decent profit in the deal to make a decent commission.

One way is to talk the client into putting some or more money down. More money down only benefits them.

Benefits to the buyer of a larger down payment:

Less Cost – The vehicle will cost less to the owner over the life of the financing or loan due to the interest paid out.

Instant Equity – The more money a client puts down, the more the vehicle will be worth compared to how much they owe on it. They will have equity in the vehicle should they choose to trade the vehicle in at any time during the life of the loan.

Shorter Trade Cycle – The client will be able to pay off the vehicle sooner and can trade it in for a better vehicle sooner. With the equity they have in it, they can trade up sooner.

Smaller Payments – The more you put down, the less you finance, the less your payments will be.

Bank Requirement – Banks are always trying to reduce their risk and one way they reduce risk is by requiring the client to put some money down on a purchase of a vehicle so the buyer has some vested interest in making the payments. Having some skin in the game.

Financing Tax & License – Clients who don't put any money down will have the tax and license rolled into the financing, which means that they will be paying interest on the tax and the license fee. It makes no sense whatsoever to pay interest on tax and license if you can help it.

Necessary to Get Financing – Clients with subpar credit, which is below 600, will need a lot of money down for the banks to finance them at a decent interest rate and terms. You either have credit or you buy your credit. Buying your credit means putting a lot of money down, thereby financing a lower amount.

It's very important to remember these selling points and to communicate these points to the client and how it benefits them.

<u>Sources of Down Payments:</u>

Emergency Cash Deposit	Money Market Fund	Credit Cards	Security
Insurance Policy Advance	Next Car Payment	Pawn Shop	Payroll
Family	Friends	Personal Loans	Tax Return
Second Mortgage	401K Policy	Insurance Settlement	E-Bay
ATM	Bonuses	Stocks & Bonds	Garage Sale
Sell Stuff on Craigslist		Anything Morally Right	

This is not an exhaustive list, nor is it a list that most people will take seriously, but the point is that there are many ways where someone can get some extra cash to put down on the vehicle. Dealerships can usually give the client about a month to come up with a down payment so it is feasible to sell things, borrow from friends, somehow come up with the extra cash. It gives them something to think about like a garage sale, Craigslist or emergency cash.

The best one is the "next car payment". When purchasing a vehicle, the buyer usually has 45 days to make the first payment so they can use the next car payment on their current vehicle or trade-in to use as a down payment.

Since most buyers are payment buyers, to keep their payments under control, the first thing we should be looking to adjust is the amount of their down payment. As most people will resist putting down more money, the benefits really need to be communicated to them.

Every $1,000 change in the price of the vehicle, down payment, or value of their trade affects their payments by about $20 a month. So if we can get an extra $1,000 as a down payment, we can reduce their monthly payments by about $20, respectively for every $1,000 we don't get, we increase their monthly payments by $20.

$2,500 Trade-in	$5,000 Down Payment
$19,995 Selling Price	$290 Monthly Payments

Client: "After second thought, I don't have $5,000 for a down payment."

Don't write down anything that they say, only write your numbers for them to see. Writing their numbers and wants needs give them weight. Only your numbers carry weight.

Sales Advisor: "Hmmm….I understand Mr. Buyer, but you have to realize that the total cost of this vehicle will be a lot lower if you have some money down because you're financing less and paying less overall interest on the loan."

Client: "I know, but I have some bills coming due very soon and I need all my cash for them."
Sales Advisor: "The amount of the down payment also affects your monthly payments tremendously. For every $1,000 you put down, we can reduce you monthly payments by $20."

Sales Advisor: "I can give you a month to come up with the down payment if that's what holding you up. You can also use your next car payment on your current vehicle as a down payment, since we'll be taking your trade and paying it off so you won't have another car payment."

Client: "Really? My next car payment is in 20 days. I was hoping to use that to make my first car payment on this new vehicle and to skip making a car payment on the old one."

Sales Advisor: "No, you have forty-five days from today to make a payment on your new vehicle so you can use the money you were going to make a payment on your old vehicle as a down payment."

Client: "Let's see what we can do without any money down."

Sales Advisor: "A couple of reasons that putting some money down makes sense for you is that you don't want to finance the tax and license. It doesn't make sense to pay interest on taxes and license fees. Does it?"

185

Sales Advisor: "Also due to your credit, it makes it a whole lot easier to get you financing. Banks typically like to see some down payment as it reduces their risk exposure. Now can you borrow some money from somebody, sell some stuff on Craigslist, have a garage sale, right?"

Sales Advisor: "It'll make your monthly payments a lot more manageable, the more you put down. Like I said, for every $1,000 you put down, you can reduce your payments by $20, not to mention the interest savings over the life of the loan."

Sales Advisor: "So can you at least put down $2,000?"

$2,500 Trade-in	**$5,000 Down Payment** **$2,000 Down Payment**
$19,995 Selling Price	**$290 Monthly Payments** **$350**

If payments are $290 with $5,000 down and we increase/decrease payments by $20 for every $1000 of down payment, then if we take away the $5,000, we would have to increase the payments by at least $100 ($20 for every $1,000), which would take their payments to $390. If we can get at least $2,000 down, then we can reduce the payments by at least $40 and bring the payments to $350. It is the same as reducing the down from $5,000 to $2,000 or by $3,000. $20 for every $1,000 change will have a net effect of $60 ($350-$290 = $60).

Sales Advisor: "As you can see, if you reduce your down payment from $5,000 to $2,000, your payments will go up by $60 to $350."
Client: "I might be able to since it affects my payment that much."
Sales Advisor: "We can't go on 'might', it's going to be in the contract so I need to know for sure. If I give you a month, can you come up with the whole $2,000? Look, I'll try to get this done either way, but it benefits you tremendously to put as much down as possible."
Client: "I'm not sure; I have a lot of bills coming up but I also want to keep my payments as low as possible."
Sales Advisor: "Okay......I'll just put down that you have a $2,000. You should think about selling items you have no use for anymore to free up some cash. I can give you a month to come up with it."

At this point, you don't want to pressure the client too much or you'll lose them. The best you can do is educate them on how much it benefits them to put something down. Given the fact that a majority of people don't want to put anything down, getting something is a great achievement considering a lot of people don't want or have anything to put down.

Sales Advisor: *"Okay....just sign by the X and I'll tell management that you only have $2,000 down."*

The commitment is what we're after so keep at it until they agree and sign. Now this doesn't mean that we're agreeing to this, but we're trying to get the client to move from being a shopper to a buyer.

12i. Objection: Payment

A majority of clients are payment buyers. In reality, most buyers know that the down payment, price of the car, interest rates and term of the loan affects the monthly payments. It's the monthly payments that most clients are looking at because they are wondering if they can afford to make these payments month after month, are they going to have a job for the term of the loan, what will be left over after all their expenses including the car loan and how far is this payment from what they have been budgeting for.

Payments can affect someone's life tremendously. It could mean a great Christmas or a lean Christmas, dinner out 3 times a week or 1, car payments at the expense of other expenses.

Payment objections will be the most common objection. In reality, the only way to remedy a payment objection is to reduce the price of the selling vehicle, interest rate and/or increase the financing term, increase the down payment or increase the value of the trade.

For our purposes, we don't want to decrease the price of the vehicle because that's what we get paid on. We want to focus all the attention on the term and the amount of down payment the buyer is bringing to the deal. During the fact-finding step in the process, you should have had a good idea of the amount of payment the buyer was budgeting for and showed them vehicles within that range.

The price of the vehicle is the last thing you want to play around with because your whole gross income is in the price of the vehicle. If the price of the vehicle is $15,000 and the cost of the vehicle to the dealership, including pack, is $12,000, then you have $3,000 in gross. At a 20% payment level, you're earning $600 in commission. For every $500 you discount the price of the vehicle, you, as the sales advisor, will be losing $100 in commission.

The price of the trade also adds to your gross, as most dealers will bid on a vehicle $1,500 to $3,000 below wholesale book. Which means, that if a wholesale book on a vehicle is $10,000, then the dealer will bid $8,000 so they can have about $2,000 to play with. That's a $2,000 profit or gross you can make on this deal which translates to $400 commission on a 20% commission rate.

Whole sale book is the price that a dealer can get this same vehicle with the same mileage from a wholesale source like a dealer auction.

Of course a mini is much better than nothing but keeping gross in a deal is much, much better than a mini.

The first thing you'd want to do on a payment objection would be to try to increase the down payment because the more down payment they have, the lower they will be financing, the easier it will be for the banks to finance them as they see it as vested interest in the loan and the less interest they will be paying over the life of the loan.

In explaining this to your client, you should draw this diagram to illustrate the benefits of a higher down payment:

People remember and comprehend things much better if they see it in writing or illustrated on paper.

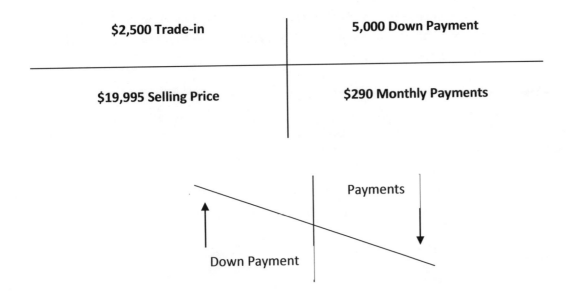

Client: *"I love the car but I just can't afford the payments. It's much more than I've budgeted for."*
Sales advisor: *"Hmmm...well, how much did you budget for?"*
Client: *"I think the most I can do is $200 a month."*

To get from $290 to $200 we're going to have to either increase the value of the trade by approximately $5,000 or reduce the price of the vehicle by approximately $5,000 or get them to increase their down payment by about $5,000 or a combination of all three. Remember the $20 increase/decrease for every $1,000 change. We don't want to do any of this lightly as it will directly affect our commission. Increasing the value of their trade or reducing the price of our vehicle is the last thing we even want to think about.

Sales Advisor: *"$200? Why only $200? Hmmm...well....one way to reduce your payments would be to increase your down payment. See, the higher your down payment is the lower your payments are. It's of great advantage to put down more money. You can also get financed easier, save money over the term of the loan and build instant equity,"*

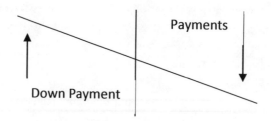

Client: *"I just don't have any more money to put down right now."*
Sales Advisor: *"What if I gave you some time to come up with a down payment? How much more can you come up with in a month?"*
Client: *"I don't know....maybe a $1,000."*
Sales Advisor: *"We'll I have to know for sure because it'll be in the contract. So If I give you a month to come up with an additional $5,000, can you give me $2,500 in 2 weeks and another $2,500 two weeks after that?"*

Most dealerships will delay the down payment provided that they receive something in 2 weeks and some more 2 weeks after that depending on credit. As long as they receive something within 2 weeks. If they've put some money down already and talk about additional money, then you can give them the full month to come up with the additional money.

Client: *"No, I don't have any money. $1,000 extra is all I can afford right now for a down payment."*

$2,500 Trade-in	~~$5,000~~ **Down Payment** **$6,000 Down Payment**
$19,995 Selling Price	~~$290~~ **Monthly Payments** **$270**

Give 2 reasons to defend your position and drop the payment by a nominal rate.

Sales Advisor: *"Okay....Mr. Client. That's going to be a tough stretch without a good down payment. I really want to earn your business and will do everything I can to help. Now you do know that the newer vehicle will have better gas mileage, lower insurance and lower maintenance than your old vehicle so there's some savings there. Now $270 isn't that far off from your mark but can't you find a little more money than $200 a month to make this deal work? Can you help me out a little bit by figuring out where you can find some money from your daily expenses to make this work? Can you meet me half way?"*

$2,500 Trade-in	~~$5000~~ Down Payment
	$6,000 Down Payment
$19,995 Selling Price	~~$290~~ Monthly Payments
	~~$270~~ Payments
	~~$250~~ Payments

Sales Advisor: *"What if I can get your payments down to $250 a month? Do we have a deal then?" "You have to help me out here. I'm trying to make this work. If we increase the loan from a 60 month loan to 72 month loan then we can get there. It doesn't mean you have to keep the loan for 72 months, you can pay it off as fast as you want and most people don't keep vehicles more than 3 years anyway."*

Client: *"No, 72 months is a long time, I don't like to keep my vehicles until the wheels fall off so 72 months is a very long time. I don't want to go any higher than 60 months. I can only afford $200 at the most at this time."*

Sales Advisor: *"So is there any way of increasing your down payment more than $6,000? Is there anything you can sell within a month to come up with more cash?"*

Client: *"Sorry, no...that's all I got."*

Sales Advisor: *"Is there no other way of making a payment of more than $200 a month? I know you like the car but I think we might be on the wrong vehicle."*

Client: *"No....I like this vehicle. It's the only one I want on your lot."*

Sales Advisor: *"Okay......sign by the X below and I'll propose it to my manager."*

This scenario should never have been played through if a good "fact-finding" step had been performed. Obviously the client was shown a vehicle that is beyond their means and now were either going to have to reduce the price of the vehicle, increase the term of his loan or increase the value of his trade.

You shouldn't go back and forth more than 3 times. After the 3rd time, the manager needs to come out and talk to the clients directly and tell them that this is all you can do. Going back and forth makes you look weak and unprofessional and makes the dealership lose credibility.

To reduce monthly payments:

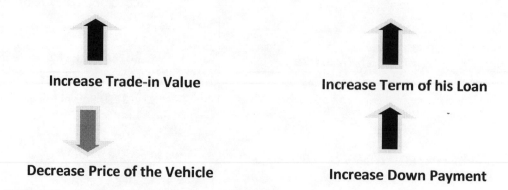

Increase Trade-in Value   **Increase Term of his Loan**

Decrease Price of the Vehicle   **Increase Down Payment**

The value of their trade has to go up, the term of the loan needs to be increased, the amount of down payment they have has to go up and the price of the vehicle can also go down to reduce monthly payments.

Obviously, we want to stay away from adjusting the trade-in value and the price of the vehicle. We want to concentrate on the down payment and the term of his loan.

Either way, if the client is stuck on one payment and that's all he can afford and we can't persuade him to come up to our level or get him to increase at all, then this becomes a management call. Management needs to come out and try to persuade them or cut them loose.

We need to notify management of the situation after we make sure he's comfortable with his trade-in amount and down payment. The management will need to make a call of reducing the price of the vehicle to make this deal work.

The commitment is what we're after so keep at it until they sign at the X at the bottom of the page. Now this doesn't mean that we're agreeing to this, but we're trying to get the client to move from being a shopper to a buyer. Sometimes a mini is better than no deal at all. You'll see and experience for yourself working with a client for 5 or more hours with no car deal.
That is the worst case scenario.

12j. Closing Techniques

What make a good closer?

- Listens attentively
- Handles objections well
- Doesn't take objections personally
- Creates mental ownership
- Maintains trust and confidence
- Flexible
- Genuine
- Wants the deal

- Keeps up their enthusiasm and energy
- Sincere and believable
- Persistent
- Communicates to the clients hope for gain and fear of loss
- Translates the benefits to the client

A close is a natural end to a good presentation; a close with a good gross is a natural end to a great presentation.

Various types of objection handling:

Feel, Felt, Found Method: In this method, no matter what the objections are, the sales advisor communicates to the client that they understand how the client _feels_, uses other clients who _felt_ the same way and _found_ that by doing what the sales advisor wants them to is the right course of action.

> *Client: "The price is too much."*
>
> *Sales Advisor: First pauses and looks at the sheet with confusion. "I understand how you feel about the price. Other clients who I've sold to in the past have felt the same way with regard to price, but then they found that in all cases you get what you pay for. Not only will this vehicle be more reliable thereby giving yourself peace of mind, but it will also be cheaper for you in the long run because of the decrease in maintenance and repairs."*
>
> *Client: "The payments are too high."*
>
> *Sales Advisor: First pauses and looks at the sheet with confusion. "Hmmm...I understand how you feel about the payments. I've had other clients who felt the same way, but found that when looking at the overall cost of the vehicle in reduction in insurance, maintenance, miles per gallon and an increase in peace of mind in terms of reliability and resale value, they are actually saving hundreds of dollars a year."*
>
> *Client: "I want more for my trade."*
>
> *Sales Advisor: Pauses and inspects the sheet with confusion. "I understand how you feel, I've had clients that have felt the same way as you in the past but what they found out was that there isn't a big market for vehicles with that many miles. They saved tons of time by trading in their vehicle instead of selling it and they didn't need to pay for the necessary repairs, saving them much more than money in the long run."*
>
> *Client: "I don't have the necessary down payment."*
>
> *Sales Advisor: Pauses and inspects the sheet with confusion. "I understand how you feel and I've had clients that didn't have the necessary down payment necessary to make a purchase but what they found out was that the higher the down payment the lower the monthly payment, the higher the chances of getting financed by the lenders. Also, we can give a prospective buyer time to come up with a good down payment."*

Pausing is very important. It tells the client that you're thinking about their problem, you've given undivided attention to their problem, and you're using your wealth of knowledge and experience to remedy their situation.

Once a client has told you what their pain point is in regard to the negotiation, then we can start to try to remedy it. Here are some examples:

> **Client:** "The price is too much."
>
> **Sales Advisor:** First pauses and looks at the sheet with confusion. "I understand how you _feel_ about the price. Other clients that I've sold to in the past have _felt_ the same way with regard to price, but then they _found_ that in all cases you get what you pay for. Not only will this vehicle be more reliable to you, giving you peace of mind, but will also be cheaper for you in the long run because of decrease in maintenance and repairs."

Isolating the objection:

> **Client:** "I understand what you're saying, but I've done my research and I'm not comfortable paying that much for this vehicle."
>
> **Sales Advisor:** Pauses and looks at the sheet again. "Okay, I understand. Now is price the only thing that's keeping you from buying today?"

What we need to do here is to isolate their objection to only one thing and work on that one thing.

> **Client:** "No, I don't think I can do that high of payments either."
>
> **Sales Advisor:** "Okay, so if I can get the manger to address the price and payment issue, are you ready to do business today?"
>
> **Client:** "Maybe."
>
> **Sales Advisor:** "I can't take 'maybe' into the manager's office. I need a definite answer on how we can earn your business today."

We need to go through this until we pin down what they're looking to do. We just can't go and ask the manager to lower the price and then come back and tell them to lower the payments and them come back and tell them to increase the trade-in value.

We need a solid commitment. We need to mentally get them from mentally owning the vehicle to financially owning the vehicle.

We need to discuss it.

Usually a husband and wife team will need both parties to approve before signing. You need to address both parties during the process and especially during negotiation. Again reiterate all the benefits.

If the clients tell you that they need to talk it over, tell them, "No problem, I'll give you a few minutes to discuss it." and walk away from the table and give them space. You don't want them to walk out of the dealership and talk about it or go home because once clients leave, the chances of them coming back and buying from you goes down exponentially.

Leave for about 3 to 5 minutes, but keep an eye on them. You have to keep the momentum of the sale going when you get back.

After about 3 to 5 minutes, return to the table and say, "Is everything satisfactory?" This statement opens the clients up to either saying, "Yes" or giving you an explanation of what's holding them back. Another option is to get your manager to return to the desk with you and have him say, "Hello folks, Steve here told me that you have some concerns in regard of the vehicle, I just want to come by and make sure all your questions have been answered and all your concerns have been addressed." The clients will then either say, "Yes Steve's done a great job" or explain what their concerns are.

12k. Back from the Desk Manager

You've done an excellent job in all your steps. You built trust and rapport with the client. You asked the right questions and found out what their pain points are on their current vehicle to find what their wants and needs are. Using that information, you were able to put them together with the right vehicle that they fell in love with, because you built value into it, and they also fell in love with you and the dealership.

You have 2 ways to go from here.

They absolutely love the vehicle much more than the price because you built so much value into it that they negotiated rather easily.

When coming back from the manager desk with an approval of the deal, hold out your hand for them to shake and exclaim, "Congratulations, you got the vehicle." This sends the clients over the edge from a looker to a committed financial buyer. I then proceed to ask them for driver's license, insurance and any other required documents.

They agree to your prices and term and you sent them into finance to finalize the deal and to allow finance to sell them financial and insurance products like warranty, gap insurance and other add-ons.

Add-ons are stereos, TV for the vehicles, body kits and bed liners. It's important to know that you never bring up any of these products until the negotiations are done because savvy buyers will try to have them thrown in. While waiting with your clients for finance to finalize the deal, you might want to start talking to them about these items such as warranties, insurance and vehicle add-ons like bed liners, tint, pin striping and gap insurance, since most dealerships also pay the sales advisor on any financial products the client purchases.

Get with finance to educate you about the finance products they offer and their benefits, the insurance products that they offer and their benefits and add-ons the dealership offers.

If you did everything well, then they should have bought the vehicle. If for some reason you forgot the lessons of this book or skipped some steps or didn't do a good job on some of the steps, then clients might be a little hesitant to go over the edge and buy. Here we need to turn this client over to a manager. If everything went smoothly and the client bought, then it's time to continue to delivery.

If the client did not buy the vehicle, you need to turn them over to a manager to use their wealth of experience to help you close this deal before the client leaves.

Summary of Negotiation - Presenting the Numbers, Negotiate the Offer, and Closing the Deal

The objective of the negotiation is to come to an agreement between you and the client. We're trying to change the client from mentally owning the vehicle to financially owning the vehicle. To do this we need the 3C's which are cash, credit and commitment. All are basically the same as commitment. The commitment means that the client is ready to make a decision and purchase today. You never want to present numbers to clients who aren't serious about purchasing today.

Everything else is a prelude to this step. You should have asked the right questions in fact-finding to figure out what it is that the client is searching for or what problem their trying to solve by purchasing a new vehicle and making sure all the decision makers are present. What are their limits?

The vehicle you're selling has a tremendous amount of value built into it, so much so that the price of the vehicle is considered cheap compared to the price. The vehicle is worth immensely more than the price. You've done that.

Objections with the price of the vehicle, payments, trade value and/or down payment will come up. Never take anything personally as the client is acting from a position of fear.

Isolate each objection and handle it separately.

Find ways to justify your position. Third party sources are best.

Visually show the clients any benefits.

Do your research on the price of their trade and the price of your vehicle before heading into negotiation. Fully understand that objections are part of the game and expect them. Prepare yourself for the objections of price, trade value, down payment and payment.

13.   Delivery – The last chance you get to leave a lasting impression

Purpose: To ensure the client gets a quality vehicle free of defects and damage and to ensure he is familiar with the operation of the vehicle's vital functions.

Of course you would skip this step if the client didn't buy a vehicle from you and go straight to T.O. to a manager.

So everything went well in negotiations, the clients have signed all the paperwork in finance, and now you need to deliver the vehicle to them.   This step is usually overlooked by most sales advisors that have a job mentality. We've sold them a vehicle and now begins the job of selling them, their family and their friends their next vehicle. This is the last thing that the client will remember you for.

Delivery is basically a tour of the vehicle of all its features and vital functions again. These features were explained in the product presentation and demonstration as well as their benefits. In the delivery we explain how they work. Yes, Bluetooth is great; you can hear the caller through the speakers of the vehicle which lets you keep both hands on the wheel and eyes on the road. But how do you make it work? How do you program a cell phone to work with the Bluetooth?

Satellite radio is great; you can hear stations not available on AM/FM and you can hear the same stations anywhere in the country. But how do you get to the satellite stations? How do you program the stations on the stereo?

Some really good sales advisors will even offer to take the client on another test drive as part of the delivery process so the client can really become familiar with the vehicle. This way they can build an even stronger relationship with the clients. It's a very nice touch and guarantees that the client will come back time and again to that sales advisor.

I recommend this or at least ask the client if they want to take another test drive just to get all the questions out of the way. In my experience about 5% of the people want to go on another test drive after they purchased. Most were anxious to get home and figure things on their own.

If you're lucky, the porters will have finished cleaning the vehicle before the client gets out of finance. Quickly inspect the vehicle, making sure it's presentable and that there aren't any scratches or dents. The interior is clean and smells good. The client has built trust in you and you should honor that trust by making sure they're going to be as happy as possible with their new vehicle when they drive off.

Escort them to their new vehicle and ask them to inspect the vehicle and get their approval. Any blemish or anything that they're not happy with needs to be addressed.

Most franchised dealerships have a specific routine that must be followed when delivering a vehicle. There will be a list of items that need to be covered. Each item needs to be checked off to make sure you covered it and the client needs to sign at the bottom and be given a copy. This sheet is only for new vehicles as the manufacturer wants the client to be familiar with all the new vehicle's features. This also allows the client to feel good about his purchase as well as with the manufacturer. The manufacturer will contact the client to ensure that he was treated fairly at the dealership. The manufacturer sends out a survey called the Client Satisfaction Index, or **CSI** for short, which the client fills out about his experience with the dealership he purchased from. The manufacturer keeps tab on the dealership to make sure that they're not spoiling the name or the brand. The manufacturers tie in cash and incentives to the dealership using the CSI scores. Should a dealership come in with low scores, the punishments range from light to harsh when it comes to incentives, cash and inventory.

Besides the CSI, the last thing clients will remember of you and the dealership is the delivery. This is the time to show them that even though they bought the vehicle from you, you still have their best interest at heart by giving them a detailed delivery. This will come in handy when in a few days you're going to give them a call to check up on them to see how they're doing and to see if they have any more questions.

I also required my advisors to go down a check list of items that are vitally important to every client, like where to put gas, oil, antifreeze, powers steering fluid, water and the location of the spare tire and jack. You should show them how to release the spare tire and jack if they get a flat on the road. Some vehicles had very complicated procedures to releasing the spare tire.

You should also be prepared to explain some of the complicated items, like how to set up their phone to the Bluetooth of the vehicle, how to use the GPS if the vehicle comes with it, setting the channels on the radio and how to operate keyless entry.

In my experience, nobody has really wanted any more elaborate explanations than the ones I gave. They were more excited about taking the vehicle home and showing it off rather than wanting to spend another minute at the dealership.

You should also mention to them that you'll be checking up on them from time to time in case they have any questions or concerns.

13a. Vital Areas to Cover

Go over the vehicle, explaining again how the features of the vehicle work. Start with the basics of features they'll be using every day.

- Where and how to put fuel in
- What type of gas to use
- Location and function of jack and spare tire
- Operation of emergency brakes
- Gauges and instrument panel fully explained
- Explanation of books/owner's manual
- Bluetooth setup
- Synching garage door opener with vehicle
- Function and operation of heating/air conditioning

- Navigation fully explained
- Operation of stereo system and programming of clients favorite radio stations
- Operation of major features like
  - Folding third row seats
  - Folding of second row seats
  - Installing/removing accessories
- Where major fluids go
  - Oil
  - Coolant
  - Transmission fluid
  - Power steering fluid
  - Brake fluid
  - Wiper fluid

Sales Advisor: *"You guys all finished with finance?"*

Client: *"Looks that way, all the paperwork is signed."*

Sales Advisor: *"Great, detail has finished cleaning your new vehicle and it's over here. Follow me."*

Client: *"Does this vehicle come with any books?"*

Sales Advisor: *"Yes, I have them right here. I'll explain everything. Here are the books along with a spare key. The book has details about all the features of your vehicle as well as warranty information. I'll put them here in the glove box. Make sure to take out the spare key once you get home or you can hold it if you want."*

Client: *"Okay."*

Sales Advisor: *"I just need to go over some items of the vehicle to make sure you are familiar with as well as comfortable with its uses. Everything we go over is illustrated in the books but it's a good idea to go over them before you leave the lot. Also, don't worry about remembering everything, you can contact me anytime you have a question or you can stop by and I'll be glad to show you something you aren't quite comfortable with."*

Client: *"Okay, sounds good."*

Sales Advisor: *"Let's go over the parts of the engine. This cap is where you put in engine oil, over here is where you fill the coolant, over here is where you fill the transmission fluid and over here is where you fill the power steering fluid."*

Client: *"Okay."*

Sales Advisor: *"Let's go to the trunk. You open the trunk from here as well as the switch inside the cabin. This is the spare tire and the jack is located on the side here. Let's go and sit in the vehicle so I can explain some of the gauges and features."*

Client: *"Okay."*

After you sit them down in the driver's seat, get in the passenger seat to explain the gauges and features. If there is a more than one client, have them sit in the back to watch your presentation.

Sales Advisor: *"If you turn the key but don't turn the vehicle on, you can see all the lights on the dashboard. "*

Explain what all the lights on the dashboard mean, making sure to emphasize the really important ones like low oil, temp too high, etc. You would then go into explaining how the A/C, heater, stereo, Bluetooth, navigation and garage door opener work. Set up their Bluetooth as well as their navigation and garage door opener.

Sales Advisor: *"Do you have any questions?"*
Client: *"Not at the moment."*
Sales Advisor: *"Okay, you might have questions later on. Here is my card. Give me a call anytime you need should you have any questions. Would you like to go on another test drive now that you own the vehicle?"*
Client: *"No, I think I get it."*
Sales Advisor: *"Okay, good. This dealership and I are graded by the manufacturer on every sale so you'll be getting a survey in a few weeks. It's vitally important that we get good marks on it. Please contact me if for any reason you think we don't deserve 100%."*
Client: *"You've all been great. I appreciate it a lot. Thank you."*
Sales Advisor: *"No problem, and if you or anyone else is looking for a vehicle, please have them give me a call since my business is based only on repeat and referrals. I too would greatly appreciate it. I will also be checking up on you in a few days and periodically after that just to make sure you're happy with your new vehicle."*

The last thing the client is going to remember is you taking your time explaining the major functions and features of the vehicle, so make sure he is comfortable before he drives off, if you plan on doing any more business with them. Although the CSI or survey only has to do with new vehicles, you should take care of your used car clients as they will most likely know of someone looking to purchase another vehicle.

Prior to them leaving, always ask if they're comfortable with what you've discussed and if they have any questions or need further instructions. This would be a great time to give a card to each and every person in the party in case they have friends or family looking for a vehicle in the near future.

Summary of Delivery – The last chance you get to leave a lasting impression

The delivery is the last point of contact you will most likely have with your clients so you need to make sure it's a memorable one.

Properly explain how the features of the vehicle works, especially items they will be using every day like radio, Bluetooth, light switches and safety items like seat belts and the spare tire.

Manufacturers keep tab on dealerships by sending out a report card of how the client was treated during the purchase of their new vehicle and the delivery will be your last chance to leave a good impression with them.

Make sure your clients are comfortable with you, their new vehicle and the dealership before they leave. This will allow you to contact them from time to time to check up on them and hit them up for repeat and referral business.

Rapport building or friend making doesn't end when the client leaves the lot in their new vehicle. These clients are a great source of future business in terms of repeat and referrals.

14. Turn Over (T.O.) to a Manager

Purpose: To utilize the experience and authority of a manager to help in closing a client or by increasing their options.

Turning Over (T.O.) your clients to a manager to elicit help or to use their authority to save a deal or to prevent the client from walking out or to increase options presented to a client, should be used throughout the sales process anytime you think that you might be losing the client. I hesitate in putting this in one of the sales steps because it can and should be applied to any step in the sales process. The managers have years of experience that can be used to help close the deal or prevent the client from walking out.

In any step in the process that client seems to lose interest or wants to leave, the manager needs to be notified because in essence, being a sales advisor is like owning your own business, but ultimately the client belongs to the dealership because they've put in most of the effort and cost in bringing that client to the dealership to give you an opportunity to do business.

The best way to do this is to excuse yourself to get them a business card/brochure/information while you notify the manager of the situation and if they have any ideas on the next best course of action before the client leaves. I've touched on several times in the process the importance of getting a manger involved in the transaction whether warranted or not. Clients are easily impressed when managers introduce themselves any time clients are on the lot.

As a business owner, I made it a requirement that my guys brought every client inside for me to meet. I knew that most clients didn't want to come inside, but putting that in my guys' minds kept them thinking of ways of keeping the clients from leaving. If I wasn't too busy, I'd go outside and shake their hands myself. I enjoyed it and the clients felt more important that a higher up manager is coming out to meet them.

I required my assistant sales managers to go and touch or make contact with prospective clients whenever the sales advisor would come in to get keys for a test drive or the sales advisor spent more than 10 minutes with them on the lot. It was a requirement that a manager needed to talk to every client that walked on the lot. I've fired several good sales people who let clients walk off without first notifying a manager.

Of course I didn't press too hard on this with the seasoned guys as I knew that they were professionals and wouldn't let a client go unless if there was even a small chance that they could make a sale.

The professional sales advisor does not need take this personally as it's a requirement to becoming a true professional. The dealership does in fact invest a lot of money on advertisement, sales campaigns and incentives to get clients on the lot. It's been estimated that a dealer spends on average of $300 per person in marketing. Any business that makes that much of an investment will want to make sure every client is worked to their fullest potential before leaving the car lot.

I required it of my guys and if you owned your own sales and marketing company or dealership you would also require it of your guys. It makes good business sense. Be a professional and realize that this is a business and that a sale is usually a team effort. You should not take it personally as it can only help you close deals, become more educated and make more money.

In the Meet and Greet Stage

Sales Advisor: *"Hello, welcome to ABC Motors. My name is Jeffery, how are you guys doing today?"*

Client: *"Look, Jeffery.....we just want to be left alone and look without any sales person. Is that okay with you?"*

Sales Advisor: *"I understand. Not a problem. Are you looking for new or used so I can point you to the correct direction?"*

Client: *"We don't know yet."*

Sales Advisor: *"Okay, not a problem. Our new vehicles are that way and our used vehicles are that way. Feel free to look around and I'll check back with you later. We also sell more than four hundred vehicles a month so we have a huge trade-in inventory in the back which I can also show you."*

Client: *"Okay, we'll get you if we need you."*

To the manager:

Sales Advisor: *"They don't want to deal with anyone and want to be left alone to look. They didn't even want to tell me what they were looking for."*

Manager: *"Okay...come and get me in 5 minutes and we'll take them a bottle of water and check up on them."*

You're going to get these dealer adverse individuals from time to time. You shouldn't take it personally. Remember that most clients who are shopping for a vehicle are operating out of fear. If you press them too hard, you'll lose them. It is best to treat them with respect and hold out a carrot of vehicles in the back or get contact information from them should something they're looking for comes in later on.

In the Fact-Finding Stage

Client: *"We don't have much time to look; we just stopped by to see what you have."*

Sales Advisor: *"Well, what are you looking for? Car, truck or SUV? When will be a good time to come by and really look at our inventory?"*

Client: *"We don't know, why don't you give me a card?"*

Sales Advisor: *"We also sell more than three hundred cars a month so we have a ton of trade-in cars in the back getting ready to go through the shop. When you have time, I can also show you those. I ran out of cards, hold on, I'll quickly run inside and get you one."*

On the excuse that you're getting them a card, go inside and tell the manager what's happening.

> **Sales Advisor:** *"These guys say they don't have any time to spend to really looking for a vehicle. They said they don't have much time and they don't know what they're looking for. They don't want to commit to anything. Why don't you come out and talk to them?"*
>
> **Manager:** *"They don't even know if they want a car, truck or SUV? Okay, I'll go and talk to them."*

Here, the clients seem to be very sales adverse as they won't even commit to a little time to find a vehicle. By getting the manager, you put the responsibility on them to help you retain the client.

In the Sell from Stock Stage

> **Client:** *"I don't like anything in your inventory. Why don't you give me a card?"*
>
> **Sales Advisor:** *"Okay, hold on. Let me get you a card from inside."*

To the manager:

> **Sales Advisor:** *"I showed them everything. They don't like any of our vehicles."*
>
> **Manager:** *"What are they looking for?"*
>
> **Sales Advisor:** *"Low mileage van priced around $5,000."*
>
> **Manager:** *"There is no such thing as low mileage and cheap."*
>
> **Sales Advisor:** *"I know, I showed them everything. They're about to leave. Why don't you come and talk to them?"*
>
> **Manager:** *"Okay, did you get their contact information?"*
>
> **Sales Advisor:** *"Yes."*

At the very least, try to get every client's contact information in case you come across something that they are looking for.

In the Product Demonstration Stage

> **Client:** *"I don't like the way this car drives. Seems like something is loose."*
>
> **Sales Advisor:** *"Loose? Hmmm….all of our vehicles go through the shop to make sure everything is mechanically sound as well as safe."*
>
> **Client:** *"No, I don't like this at all."*
>
> **Sales Advisor:** *"Okay, no problem. Let's see what else we can find you."*

Client: "No, I don't want to take a look at anything else. This is the only thing I liked."

Tell the manger what happened. Unfortunately this should never have happened. The mechanic should have test driven this vehicle and made sure it was safe and mechanically sound.

Sales Advisor: "The vehicle seems like there's something loose. The client hates it and doesn't want to take a look at anything else."
Manager: "We check all our vehicles. Where is the client now?"

The manager should come out and apologize and try to get them to look at something else. The dealership and you lost all credibility by having them test drive a vehicle that seems unsafe.

In the Negotiation Stage

Client: "Sorry, but the payment is still way too high. I just can't afford it. Sorry for wasting your time."
Sales Advisor: "Yeah…sorry that we couldn't make it work. Let me go and get you a card in case you change your mind."

Notify the sales manager of what's going on. Give him a chance to figure out the solution by using his wealth of knowledge and experience.

Sales Advisor: "The clients are about to leave. We can't make it work. We're $120 away from the payment they can afford to our best offer. He says he can't afford the monthly payments. You want to talk to him before he leaves?"
Manager: "Hmmm….Okay, let me try to reason with him."

The manager can also help in making a client feel important because someone with a higher authority has noticed them. Manager involvement in the negotiation phase also communicates to the client that the negotiation phase is coming to an end and there isn't any more wiggle room on the price, terms or costs. Some clients won't finalize a deal until someone with authority like a manager comes and talk to them.

In any step of the process if you feel like you're losing your client, you need to solicit help from the desk manager or the assistant sales manager. These sales warriors have been in the industry for a long time, that's why they're managers. They've seen it all and heard it all. They've been put in charge to ensure car deals get done and it's their responsibility to drive sales.

Scenario 1.

Client: "That's Okay. .It looks like you don't have what I'm looking for."

Sales Advisor: "Hold on….let me ask my manager if or when we'll be getting in something similar to what you're looking for."

Sales Advisor: "These people are looking for a V8 muscle car. We don't have anything on the lot that they want."

Sales Manager: "Our used car buyer just bought 3 of them in the auction. They'll be in tomorrow. Get their contact information and call them tomorrow when we have more information."

Sales Advisor: "We just bought 3 of the type of vehicles you're looking for and they will be here tomorrow. If you want, you can come and talk to my manager, but either way, I can let you know the details when they get here. What's your phone number?"

Scenario 2.

Client: "We're just looking; we won't be in the market for another month when we get our tax return."

Sales Advisor: "Okay….not a problem….look around and let me know if you have any questions."

Sales Manager: "What are those people looking for?"

Sales Advisor: "They won't be in the market for another month until they get their tax return."

Sales Manager: "Did you tell them about our incentives that are expiring in about a month? Did you tell them that we can give them 45 days to make their first payment so they don't have to wait a month."

Sales Advisor: "No, I completely forgot. I'll go and talk to them again."

Scenario 3.

Sales Advisor: "These guys are looking for a new minivan but in a cypress color."

Sales Manager: "Did you tell them that we can find them any color they want from one of our sister stores?"

Sales Advisor: "Yeah….but they need it today. Can we get them one today?"

Sales Manager: "Hold on, let me check the computer……..I can get them one in 3 hours. I found one 100 miles away. Let's go and talk to them."

Sales Advisor: "This is my manager, Paul."

Sales Manager: "Hello folks, I'm the sales manager and you are?"

Client: "Mary and I'm Steve."

Sales Manager: "Nice to meet you guys. The color you're looking for is very rare and there are 5 in the whole state. I managed to find one about a hundred miles away and can have it here in a few hours. Why don't you guys come inside and I can show you all the details of the van."

As a manager, the ultimate responsibility falls on their shoulder as why the sales numbers aren't higher. Managers usually enforce a zero tolerance rule to clients leaving without them knowing why.

Any good manager keeps an eye on the lot to see who's coming, who's going and who's talking to them. Any good manager also wants to know that everything was done for those clients before they leave as every client that comes into a dealership costs the dealership approximately $300 to get them there in overhead and advertising.

Any good sales manager and sales advisor knows that as sales professionals, we only have one chance to earn a client's business. The market is so competitive that once a client leaves the lot there is an extremely low chance of them ever coming back. You as a sales advisor have only one chance to make that sale and you need to utilize your sale manager's wealth of experience, talent and knowledge to close the deal.

I remember when I was green, I was working on a deal where we were selling a 3-year-old truck for $17,000, which was on sale from $19,000. The vehicle also had some really nice rims on it too. I went through the whole process beautifully. When I went in for the first pencil to present it to the manager, he informed me that the price was wrong and the price didn't include the rims. He instructed me to go and get an additional $2,500 for the rims. I was shocked because an additional $2,500 could break this deal, at the very least, it would cause me great pains for the rest of the negotiation because it would drive the payments up by another $50 at least.

It was okay I thought, because I thought to myself that if push comes to shove, we could just take the rims off and replace them with some stock wheels and tires. I went out and using my best apologizing tone and word track, I explained to them that the price didn't include the rims. The clients were a little more than angry. Luckily I had built enough trust with them that I was able to take them back out to look at the truck again and sold the aesthetics of the vehicle again. The truck in fact did look much better with the upgraded rims than with the stock rims. I also explained to them that we could replace the rims with stock ones should they want. After another 15 minutes, I convinced them to pay the extra $2,500 because the rims and tires would probably cost more somewhere else.

Again, I calmed them down and brought them back into the dealership and sat them down. I informed my manager that everything was okay. The manager prepared the first pencil and their payment came to $400 a month. The clients choked when seeing that number. They emphatically stated that they couldn't afford that in the least. It was too high. "You guys are crooks!" Is all I kept hearing, among other things. The clients did tell me that the most that they could afford was $300 a month when we were on the test drive. So we were $100 off from making the deal. "No problem, I'll see if I can make that happen." We went back and forth about the numbers. Of course, the first thing clients want is for us to reduce the price. I couldn't reduce the price because it was already discounted and I explained that to them. Also the clients were in love with the vehicle, so I knew they'd hang on a little bit more.

The only other option that I could see was to extend the terms of the loan, so instead of a 5 year loan, it would be a 6 year loan. I knew that I could sell the longer term better than I could sell to the manager a reduced price. So I went to work.

> **Sales Advisor:** *"Mr. Client, the manager won't reduce the price of the truck because it's already discounted. What if I can reduce the payments to $350 a month? I'm not promising anything but I think I can sell the manager on it. Can I earn your business If I can do that?"*

I would make sure to write all this down on paper so they could have a visual of the numbers. I wouldn't write their numbers down because what they wanted in terms of price was irrelevant and it didn't carry weight.

> **Client:** *"No, we can't afford more than $300 a month. $350 is way too much."*
> **Sales Advisor:** *"Hmmm.....what if I can reduce the payment to $335 a month? Can you live with that?"*
> **Client:** *"Absolutely not, that's even way too much. $300 is the best we can do."*

I wrote this number down too on the sheet of paper making sure to cross off the $400, then the $350 and writing $335.

At this point, I went back to my manager and told him that they won't budge from $300. At this point, he told me that he can't do it for that much based on their credit, down payment and computer calculations.

> **Sales Advisor:** *"I need a manager out here, because I don't want to lose them."*

My manager come out and introduced himself to the client, holding the paper that I was making notes on.

> **Manager:** *"Hello, Mr. Client. My name is Allen, How are you guys doing? Is my sales advisor treating you guys well? You guys drove the truck? You guys like the truck? You know that truck is on sale because we're trying to meet our sales numbers for the month. The price won't be the same in a few days."*
> **Client:** *"We like the truck but we can't afford the payment, it's too much."*
> **Manager:** *"It doesn't make mathematical sense for us to sell you that truck for $300 a month. The computer won't even allow us to sell you the truck for that amount."*

Upon looking down on the sheet I was making notes on, the manager saw the figure $335.

> **Manager:** *"Is $335 what you guys were thinking?"* Before the client could even speak, the manager said, *"Let me see if I can make that work."*

I stayed behind and chatted up the client stating that if anyone can make it work, he could. After a few minutes the manager came back out and held out his hand to the client like he was going to shake it. "Congratulations, I got it done at $335. You're all set."

I was shocked. To my surprise the clients shook the manager's hand and thanked him. I kept my mouth shut.

The clients signed all the paperwork and went through finance. While I was delivering the vehicle to them, I turned to the clients and asked them a question.

> **Sales Advisor:** "How come you didn't accept that same offer from me but you accepted the offer from the manager?"

The client, dumbfounded, shook his head and said, "I don't know".

This was not only the power of the Turn Over but also the power of the manager. He makes the client feel important, yet pressured when a manager gives them some attention.

This is a true story and the car industry is rife with stories such as this. Sometimes selling is a team effort and sometimes it is a dog and pony show and it's in the best interest of the whole dealership to sell as many vehicles as possible.

Managers will have various ways of addressing the client but it's important to give the manager as much information as possible before he comes out and talk to a client so he doesn't go out there blind.

Summary of Turn Over (T.O.) to a Manager

At any step in the sales process where the client seems like they're slipping away or about to leave, you need to get your managers involved as the next best course of action. Use your managers wealth of experience and authority to help turn the client around.

Don't consider it a weakness in asking help from a sales manager. A lot of clients feel more important if a manager acknowledges their existence. I always made it a point to talk to every client my sales force brought inside. It made the client feel important that a manager had noticed his presence and it made it a whole lot easier in case I needed to go in after my sales guy to close the deal.

Maybe the manager can relieve some of the objections or reservations they have from moving forward and a manager might be able to push them over into the next step. Turning over a client that you can't close is a rule in almost every dealership I've ever worked, including my own. You, the manager, and the dealership get paid for every sale you make, so It's vital that you work every opportunity to its fullest potential.

You, as the sales advisor, have everything to gain and nothing to lose because if you let them leave you have nothing, but if you turn them over to a manger then at least you have a fighting chance of making the deal. In most dealerships, it's the managers who decide whether the client is sellable, not the sales advisor.

At the very least you should get every client's contact information in case you come across a vehicle that they're looking for.   That's why it's important to sell your dealerships capabilities, potential and size at the meet and greet.

15. Logging in Your Efforts/Follow Up/Persist

Purpose: To record and monitor clients, past and present, to build up your sales pipeline and your repeat and referral database.

In the Keys to Success chapter, we talked about the goals you needed to set every month to achieve your target sales and income goals. If done correctly, you know what your closing ratios are, the number of people you need to talk to, the number of demos you needed to give as well as the number of write ups needed to achieve your target sales goals.

You already know by now that you will not sell to every prospect who you talk to for various reasons, like their ability to purchase, dealer inventory, timing or your sales skills. At the very least, you should be getting contact information from each and every person you talk to because even though they might not be ready to buy now, they will be ready sometime in the near future. Most clients purchase within 14 days of visiting your store.

You need to get information about the client, like names, numbers, the clients job and the spouse's name. This can help you close the deal or help to maintain a relationship with the client. They will then keep you in mind next time they or someone they know have a need to purchase a vehicle.

One of the techniques I taught my guys on getting clients' phone numbers or email were during the meet and greet or the fact-finding. I would tell them to sell the dealership's prowess and what we could do for them if we came across something they wanted or needed. They would have hope for gain and a fear of loss if they didn't give the sales advisor their contact information. The sales advisors were told to tell the clients about the volume of vehicles we got each month, various discounts, sales we ran every month as well as to give them first opportunity at our trades before anyone else. All this was true, but it needed to be properly communicated to clients.

In logging in your efforts, be as detailed as possible. Include names, occupations, needs, wants, trade-in information, time frame, price range, work and anything important that was discussed. This goes for all contacts with clients including walk ups, phone ups and internet leads. They are all opportunities to do business.

There are several good reasons to enter detailed notes into your computer system.

Professionalism

Having details on someone also conveys a sign of professionalism as well as a sign of competence. You should be entering as much information as possible about your clientele, so when a vehicle does come in that matches what they were looking for, you know for sure.

Make the Client Feel Important

I've had many instances where a client came in asking for me who I hadn't talked to for months except monthly emails or various mailers I would send them. When the reception would buzz me notifying me that Mr. Buyer was asking for me, I always made sure I looked them up in the system before meeting them to catch up on what was said or done the last time he was there. I would be at a disadvantage if I had gone to meet with the client not knowing who they were or what was discussed. I don't think the client would appreciate me asking them "Who are you again?"

You should be impressed that a client who you hadn't talked to in months comes in and asks about you, and at the same time, you need to impress the client too by appearing that you remember them with the notes you entered about them in the computer.

> **Receptionist:** *"I have a Mr. Brown here to see you."*
> **Sales Advisor:** *"Who? Does he have a first name?"*
> **Receptionist:** *"Mr. Frank Brown. He said he talked to you a few months ago."*
> **Sales Advisor:** *"Okay…make him comfortable and I'll be right down."*

This is when I would quickly look up this client. There might be many Frank Browns in the system, but most systems can be tailored in many ways and it should be easy to look up all your past clients named "Brown".

Once you look up this person, if you entered good notes in the system, find out what transpired the last time you talked to him, exactly when you last talked to him, all parties involved and anything special that happened

Then you can go and meet him. This way you don't go in blind. You'll impress him that you remember him and all his information.

> **Sales Advisor:** *"Mr. Brown…how have you been?"*
> **Mr. Brown:** *"Fine, fine….just came by to look at the new models."*
> **Sales Advisor:** *"Okay…not a problem. We haven't talked in a while, how's your wife, Stacy? Did she finally find a convertible that she was looking for?"*
> **Mr. Brown:** *"Yes…Stacy is fine. She says 'Hi.' Didn't think you'd remember us."*
> **Sales Advisor:** *"No, I remember you guys. Your wife was looking for a low mileage convertible in black I believe and we didn't have one at the time. Well, I'm glad you remembered me, thanks for asking for me."*
> **Client:** *"Not a problem, we've changed our mind and now we need a van. A new one, with leather. Do you have anything like that?"*
> **Sales Advisor:** *"We have plenty of vans. Follow me. So what changed? Why do you need a van instead of a convertible?"*

Commission Protection

Another reason you should take good notes about clients is to protect your commission. New clients are sometimes very skittish about looking at numbers and making a decision right away. New sales advisors will usually not know how to turn them to buyers until they get some experience under their belt.

Most dealers will allow you to protect your client base from anywhere from 3 to 14 days, called a grace period, since most shoppers buy within 14 days of starting their search for their next vehicle. What this means is that any client you talk to is yours for a maximum of those days. If those clients come in when you're not there and another sales advisor ends up helping them, then you will go on half of that deal because you had something to do with them returning. If you can prove that you helped the client within the grace period by entering details in your system, then you are protected. If you don't, then you're not protected. The information you entered is proof of your involvement. The computer system will automatically date the entry. Anytime you have any contact with prospective clients, make sure you enter the details in your system.

This rule also forces sales advisors to be in touch continually with any and all promising prospects or clients.

The timeline they use are the notes you enter in the computer regarding the client, including the phone number, name, address and license number.

I can't even begin to count how many times clients came in when I wasn't there. It happens all the time. Clients come and ask for you after your shift, before your shift or on your days off. For obvious reasons, the dealership can't tell them to come back because you're not there, so they pair them up with the first available sales advisor.

The first thing that the sales advisor will do is look them up in the system to see your notes and to see the last time you had any contact with them. If it was within the grace period, then you will be added on as half on that deal if the client decides to purchase.

In most reputable dealerships, if a client asks for you, then the client is automatically yours and you will be notified regardless of the protection period. If you're not there, then the client goes to the next available sales advisor but you still retain half a deal should any purchase occur.

Management Requirement

Most managers will require you to enter the details of every client in your system. From this information, managers will follow up and call these clients to ascertain their experience at your dealership.

Its best that you treat everyone with honesty, respect and professionalism.

Also, management will use these logs to put together sales reports on the number of clients, test drives, write ups and sales percentages.

Keep in mind that the clients who walk on the lot or come in to do business with the dealership are the dealership's clients. They've invested a great deal of money to get these clients into the store, so they require their sales people to add them to their database.

Maintain Relationships

You need to also do follow up with clients you could not close or sell but have gotten contact information.

If you have not sold the client, then it is a good idea is to call them before your shift ends and thank them for coming in and ask whether or not they have any questions. You're not trying to sell them anything but you are trying to stay at the forefront of their minds should they change their minds and decide to buy from your dealership. This will also communicate to them that you care about their experience and that you are providing excellent client service. What you really want is a second chance to earn their business. Having your manager make the call would also help if they have the time, but most likely the responsibility falls on the sales advisor's shoulders.

If you did sell the vehicle to a client, send them a handwritten note the same day thanking them with your contact information and call them the next day to check up on them and thank them for their business. Ask if they have any other questions or concerns on the operation of their new vehicle.

Here, we're not trying to sell them anything but trying to stay in their minds should they know anyone else looking for a vehicle.

Increase Pipeline

Having a lot of clients in your pipeline not only increases your client base of buyers, but also can increase your sales because even if the client doesn't buy from you, it doesn't mean that they won't buy from you in the future. That's because since you got their number or email, you can keep in contact with them should they or someone they know is looking for a vehicle. You should always keep in touch with each and any prospect you've come in contact with every 3 months or emailed every month using a newsletter, postcard, birthday card, anniversary card or any other excuse you can think of to keep contact with them.

Past clients who bought from you should get called every 3 months to maintain some sort of relationship while every client you talk to should be emailed every month regardless whether they did business with you or not. Send a postcard, newsletter, etc. That is why a phone number and email are so important to get before the client leaves your lot.

Making a friend after the sale or even after they say no gives you a better shot at grabbing this individual's next purchase as well as any and all referrals. By building a friendship with this client, you not only have access to him but to all his family and friends.

Monitor Performance to Become an Effective Professional

As an owner of a dealership, I knew that every client who came on the lot looking at a vehicle was there because I put out the expense of bringing them on the lot. I'd already sunk in the cost of bringing them, so I didn't want my managers or advisors to waste this opportunity for them and for me to make money.

Every dealership, including my own, has a log by the sales window that looks out onto the lot. The log is used to records each and every contact sales people have with clients. Any substantial time spent with a client is recorded as a UP. The information the managers require is their name, phone number, what type of vehicle they were looking for, if they drove anything and at what step was the sales advisor when the client left. The managers would then highlight the ones who were sold so they could see from every page the current state of the dealership.

Sample:

Date	Sales Advisor	Client	Phone	Vehicle	Demo Drive?	Last Step?
12/15/12	Mark B.	Patterson	4801234567	2010 Civic	N	Stock – Too Many Miles.
12/15/12	Jason J.	Rodriguez	6231234567	2005 Accord	Y	Delivery/Sold
12/15/12	Sam N.	Broughton	6237654321	2001 Corolla	Y	Negotiations – Bad Credit

Not only do the managers know who is taking how many UPs and their respective closing ratios, they also know what steps they were getting stuck on, as well as what the majority of the clients' interests are. Looking at a month or six months' worth of pages can give the managers a tremendous amount of information about the business. They can see trends forming to figure out what kind of vehicles clients were searching for, which sales people were working the hardest, which day seemed the busiest and at what step most of the sales people had trouble.

From this sheet, managers could also figure sales people's numbers. How many prospects were they talking to? Out of those, how many were they taking for a demo drive, and out of those, how many were they writing up, and out of those, how many were they selling?

You too can use this type of table to figure out where you are on the sale process. You can ask your managers what is expected of you in terms of percentage of people you demo, write up, sell and deliver. Most stores will want a minimum of 10 sales a month per advisor.

I generally told my sales people that they should demo 100%, write-up 100% and sell 100%. Those aren't realistic numbers, but shooting for perfection should be everyone's goal.

A better guideline would be 80% of the people you talk to should take a demo drive, out of those, 60% of them should be written up and out of those, 60% should be sold. So suppose you want to sell 20 cars a month. How many people do you have to talk to or approach to hit 20 based on the figures above?

If you talk to 70 clients a month and you are expected to get 80% of them to demo a car, then you need 56 out of those 70 to take a test drive. Out of those 56 you need to get 34 of them to come into the dealership to show them some numbers. Out of those 34 who come in to look at some numbers, you need 20 of them to buy.

So you would needs to talk to 70 clients a month or about 4 a day. The better you get at being a professional sales advisor, the easier it will be to close these clients. Also, the better you are, the less people you will need to talk to.

For example:

		Target Percentage %
UPs	70	
Demo	56	80%
Write Ups	34	60%
Sold	20	60%

For you to fully evaluate yourself, you need to keep track of all this information as well as why they did not do business with you. What step were you on before they left? After a while, you'll see trends and you will know which step you are weak in, strong in and need improving.

You need to keep track of this information on a daily basis because you need to know where you are with respect to your goals. What do you need to do to get yourself back on track? Monitoring your progress as well as knowing your strengths and weaknesses are vital to becoming a true professional.

I had all my sales advisors keep track of their progress and would have a one-on-one with them at the end of every month. It not only helped them make more money, but it helped the dealership as well.

Doing a post mortem is also a tremendous value in figuring out where you stand in terms of goals, skills, strengths and weaknesses. Constant self-evaluation and continuous learning is the sign of a true professional. What step were you still stuck in? What was the last step you got to before the client left? What could you have done better to make them stick around and move on to the next step in the process? Why did they buy from you if it got to that? Why did you fail and why did you succeed?

Summary of Logging in Your Efforts/Follow Up/Persist

At the very least when dealing with potential clients or Ups, you need to get their contact information before they leave. This will help you build your pipeline as well as establish some sort of relationship with your potential clients.

Monitoring you progress by evaluating what happened in the sales process helps you figure out which steps you do weakly and which steps you do strongly. To be a true professional, you must look at your failures and learn from them and then learn to profit from them.

Keep in constant contact with all your past clients as well as prospects. Make a phone call once every 3 months to all past clients and send a monthly email to all your contacts regardless if they did business with you or not.

You can visit **www.autosalesadvisor.com** to download follow up sheets, contact sheets and self-monitoring forms. Information that will be most relevant from your clients will be name, phone number, email, what they're looking for, time frame, decision makers and the best time to contact them.

16. Prospecting

Purpose: To increase your client pipeline as well as your sales by finding various sources of clients. The more people who know what you do, the higher your chances of a sale.

Most of the time you're not going to be able to talk to seventy people from just taking UPs. You're going to have to figure out ways of pulling in clients who aren't coming in through the door. Here are various other ways of increasing your pipeline of clients thereby increasing your sales.

Family and Friends: As soon as you get a job at the dealership of your choosing that you'll be involved with for a number of years, you need to notify everyone you know.. Advertising your new job to your family and friends is the first step in building your pipeline. Our family and friends have a wealth of contacts who can help us get established quickly. They or someone they know most likely will be in the market for a vehicle now or sometime in the near future. Let them know that it's best they come to you first.

Service: The service department at a dealership is a gold mine of opportunities. Have management give you a list and contact information of service clients who have really high mileage vehicles, vehicles that are 2 to 5 years old, as most of these people might be looking to trade into something newer or they might have signed up for really high interest rate loans that you can help lower, since in all likelihood, their credit rating has gone up if they've kept up their payments. You're going to have to look these people up in the system to find out what their current interest rates are. Ask your manager on how to go about looking up history or past deals. Make sure you don't contact people who other sales advisors have contacted recently.

Get a list from service of all their next day appointments. Look up these vehicles in the system as to their age, mileage, reason in service and time of appointment. Look for these clients when they show up for their appointment. Chat them up. Tell them that the dealership is interested in their vehicle if they are willing to sell it or trade it in. From there, find a vehicle that they can trade it in for that is better and newer.

Management: Talk to management about sending you phone leads and internet leads. You might have an internet department that handles these, but you should fight for at least the phone leads. Phone leads are a lot hotter than internet or walk-ins. Remember that the goal of an internet or phone lead is set an appointment for them to come in and from the appointment, the goal is to sell them. Appointments have a much higher closing ratio than a fresh up. Internet leads are just like UPs. Give them more information than they wanted. Present them with alternate vehicles. Always ask several questions when replying so they feel obligated in responding to your questions. The goal is to get an appointment to come in to the dealership. After the appointment, the goal is to sell them the vehicle. Sales ratios go up substantially after the client comes in to take a look at the vehicle.

Service Advisors: Service advisors talk to complaining clients all day. They are in a choice position to recommend to clients that if they're not happy with their current vehicle they should look at replacing it. That's where you come in. Make sure you're friendly with all the service advisors. Pull them aside and tell them that you'll split your commission with them if any client they send your way buys. Only the smart sales advisors do this. Even if you split the commission, you still get credit for the numbers or the volume of sales.

Networking Organizations: Join a networking organization or several of them. The more people you know who know what you do, the higher the chances of you getting a client. Most of these networking organizations are full of other business people who know a lot of people who can send you clients too. In my experience, hardly any sales advisors took advantage of networking groups. All businesses need vehicles and are looking to save money.

Past Clients: Clients who you've sold to should be called at least once every 3 months so you stay fresh in their minds in case they want to buy another vehicle or know someone who is looking for a vehicle. Send them a newsletter by email at least once a month to stay fresh in their minds. Include in your email or correspondence a little of what you know about them. Personalize the message. Be a professional. Think before you act.

Body Shops: These are gold mines as people who take their vehicles in to have them repaired will most likely want to buy another vehicle as they won't feel safe in their current one. Some are just getting it fixed so they can sell it. You can leave a poster in the waiting room of a body shop that you offer discounts to for clients of this establishment. Also remind them that trading in the vehicle before the vehicle history gets reported can save them tons of money in the trade-in. Also, let the body shop owner know that you'll pay them for every client who is referred to you who buys. Make sure you pay them. You don't want to ruin your reputation.

Gas Stations: Leave a poster or a display on the counter about the vehicles you offer that have more power, better financing or lower gas mileage. Leave some cards and pay the station owner if you sell a vehicle from a client who saw your display at the gas station. I've had tremendous success by paying busy owner-operated gas stations for allowing me to post a poster on their counter explaining my services.

People in Service: When clients come in to have their vehicles serviced, they have an hour or so to kill. Chatting it up with these clients is a great way to sell a vehicle, depending on how old of a vehicle they have, how happy they are with it, life changing events and other wants and needs. These people can be open to trading in their old vehicles for something new. Just be friendly and talk to everyone in service when you have downtime. It's a great way to pass the time while prospecting for a new sale. This is the same as service, above, except, you don't have to research everyone before talking to them. Just mingle.

Social Media: There are numerous internet services that allow sales people to keep in touch and in front of clients. Get your feet wet and try a few to get a feel for them. They're usually free and a great way to build your book of clients.

LinkedIn is a great way to prospect for clients given your tech comprehension of these programs. LinkedIn allows you to drill down to the specific income, demographics and geography of your potential clients. Keep in mind that some social media platforms do cost money. I don't have much experience with LinkedIn, but others that use it say they have decent results.

Facebook is a great way to keep in touch with past, present and future clients. Commenting on a client's page keeps in you fresh in their mind should they or someone they know is looking for a vehicle. Being friends on Facebook will allow you to get your message out to these people in real time.

Twitter is an excellent way to truly be connected to your clients. As long as you don't abuse the system by spamming them, this service is great to keep in personal contact with all your clients.

Local Businesses: You should be chatting it up with each and every local business you come in contact with. Making small chit chat will not only give you practice in making chit chat with clients, but will keep you fresh in their minds next time you do business with them. Something as simple as using the person's name and asking about them will almost always get them to want to know more about you. "Hey Phil, how are you doing today? How's business?" The first time they'll probably say, "Good and how are you?" but the second time and thereafter, they'll want to know who you are and what you do. This is most effective in the small mom and pop shops where the owners are working the counter. This way you can ask if you can leave some business cards on their counter or post a poster on their wall.

Lost Clients: Being in the car business, sooner or later you're going to come across a client that you've been working for a while who buys somewhere else. It's all part of the game and you can't sell everyone now, but a professional will be able to sell everyone sooner or later. Just because clients bought elsewhere does not mean you should drop them from your pipeline. If they bought somewhere else, congratulate them and wish them luck but ask them:

> So, how many vehicles does that make that you and your family own?
> Of all those vehicles, which one will you be replacing next?
> Why that one? What purpose does that one serve?
> When do you think that will be?

Now we know which vehicle they will be replacing, why and when. The only thing left for us to figure out is how and where because we already know what (one of their current vehicles), why (maybe it's getting too old?) and when (time frame). Keep good notes in your system and schedule a time to call them in the future to address all you've learned from this call.

Dealer Database: Most sales advisors enter all their information in a computer program called CRM (client relations/retention management). All previous and current sold, unsold, service and parts clients are recorded on this program. It's a wealth of information if you know how to mine it right. Your managers will be able to point you to the correct path but some are:

> Contacting people who purchased vehicles 3 to 4 years ago who might be in the market to trade them in.

Previous clients with very high interest rates who have been current who you can get to come in to reduce their payments and put them in another new or used vehicle.

People who have service appointments tomorrow who have vehicles that is 2 years or older who you can look up their information and then approach while they're in service to try to talk them into trading in their vehicles. You can also get the reason why they're coming in to service to figure out their pain points on their current vehicle.

Major parts purchasers like shops that you can approach to leave business cards or posters on their walls or counters for clients who want to fix their cars and then trade them in.

Past clients that purchased a new vehicle during the current month 2 to 4 years ago as most people like to shop around the same time every year.

Craigslist: If you come across a great trade or a great deal, take a picture of it and post it on Craigslist. It's free and easy. There are apps for most smart phones that can post an ad right there on the car lot. It's a great way to get clients to come in. Make sure to only leave your name and cell phone number as you don't want them to call the dealership and the lead given to another sales advisor. Check with your dealership about posting vehicles online as some might only want the internet department to do this.

Summary of Prospecting

As mentioned earlier in the book, being in auto sales is like having your own business, except you don't have to sink in any capital to start up. The sales advisor is in an excellent position to sell products that they don't own or have any responsibility for and work in an environment where they don't have to share in any of the expenses. The only investment he needs to make is in himself. Reading this book is one great way to help increase your working knowledge and years of experience.

The goal of all business owners are to increase their profits and at the same time, reduce their costs. As a professional sales advisor at the dealership, your costs are minimized to time while your profits are solely up to your hard work.

One way for business owners to increase their profits is to increase sales. In order to increase sales, the sales professional will need to prospect for those sales besides taking a UP. There are many prospecting avenues open to the professional that will need to be utilized if they are going to be successful.

Presented in this chapter are a few ways of attaining new clients, but given the fact that vehicles are a necessity of the modern world, anybody who has a license is a potential client. That is why you need to let everyone know what you do, where you do it and your level of competency. Build fear of what will happen if they don't let you help them and build hope of what they will gain if they do let you help them.

Because we don't know who is looking for a vehicle and who isn't, we need to advertise to everyone we meet no matter if it's the dry cleaner, the gas station cashier, the lady who cuts your hair or the plumber. You should be telling everyone what you do and where you do it. You never know who is in the market for a vehicle.

Check **www.salesadvisor.com** for phone scripts, internet response scripts, Ezine's and sample newsletters.

17. Sample Scenarios – Tying in all the steps

Throughout this book, we've talked about the various sales steps involved in properly selling a vehicle at a dealership as well as the underlying attributes needed to succeed in the profession of automotive sales. In this chapter, I'm going to tie together all the steps so you can see the proper way of managing and controlling the client and the sales process. Realize that there are many ways to deal with a client and their objections. In time, you'll develop your own style and skills in handling objections and the various types of clients. For now, get the big picture of selling and recognize:

- People who are willing to spend thousands of dollars on a vehicle are operating out of fear. Get in the mindset of the client. Empathize where they're coming from
- Almost everyone will have an objection or 2. It is best to address these objections that come out of fear of your specific clients
- Never take objections personally. It's part of the business
- Know where you are in the sales process to keep things from going sideways. You don't want to be in the demonstration phase when all of a sudden they decide that want to look at something else
- A professional attitude, a good product knowledge and enthusiasm are the cornerstones to a professional sales career
- Building rapport with clients build value in you, your product and your organization

The style that works best for you will emerge through experience, perseverance and your attitude

17a.   Scenario I

A potential client pulls up on your lot by the used vehicles. Spends a few minutes inside his vehicle rummaging around, grabs a few things and slowly gets out of his vehicle heading straight into the used car section toward the front line of vehicles parked by the street. Doesn't look back toward the dealership or seem to be concerned if anybody's noticed him.

He has a late model domestic sedan. There is nothing special about it, no customization; it is pretty basic but looks in good shape. It is a possible rental. There aren't any bumper stickers or vanity plates for you to comment on.

The other sales advisors look around to see if anybody's going to pick him up. You as a sales professional who has read my book and you are motivated approach the client. Nobody's going to give you anything free in this life; you must grab all you can.

Remembering the chapter on the Meet and Greet, you approach the client with a big smile, good eye contact, confident body language and demeanor and a helping attitude. You decide to go with the formal commenting greet.

Meet and Greet (Start the Rapport and Trust Building)
    Possible meets and greets:

Sales Advisor: "Hello Sir, My name is Jack. I'm one of the sales advisors here, and you are?"
Or
Sales Advisor: "Nice car out there, are you trading that in? Hello my name is Jack and I'm one of the sales advisors out here and you are?"
Or
Sales Advisor: "Hello Sir, My name is Jack. Are you here for the big sale? I'm one of the sales advisors here, and you are?"

Client: "My name is Bob, I don't want to waste your time Jack, I'm just looking."

Possible responses:

Sales Advisor: "No problem Bob, I'll help you look."
Or
Sales Advisor: "No problem Bob, most people like to look around, get some numbers and sleep on a decision before committing. Is that what you had in mind?"
Or
Sales Advisor: "No worries Bob. We sell more cars than any other dealership on the strip, in fact, more than three hundred a month. So we have a huge amount of vehicles coming through here each month and a lot of trade-ins in the back, so I'm confident we have something you might be looking for."
Or
Sales Advisor: "No problem Bob, I've been doing this for a while now, let me save you some time and energy. What is it exactly that you are looking for? Let's start with new or used?"
Or
Sales Advisor: "No problem, I can save you some time and help you look. Have you been to our dealership before?"
Client: "Yes, a while ago."
Sales Advisor: "Okay, good. So, you're a little familiar with our dealership, that we've been in business for more than thirty years; we're part of the Peabody dealer group. We have more than fifteen dealerships in the valley. This dealership has won the president's award for client service for 5 years in a row. I've been working here for more than five years and I love it. We sell more than three hundred vehicles a month so we have a huge trade-in inventory in the back waiting for pricing and shop evaluation. We get new stuff in all the time, but enough about me, let's figure out what your needs are."
Client: "You sell more than three hundred a month?"
Sales Advisor: "Yes the dealership does, not me. So what that means is that we have new inventory going through here all the time and we have access to all the other dealerships new and used car inventory as well so in total, I have access to roughly 5,000 vehicles."

In the meet and greet, we need to build up and sell ourselves and our dealership. It is here that we must start to communicate to the client all the major benefits of doing business with us. This needs to be planted in the mind of the client in the meet and greet, but touched on for the remainder of their visit.

Building a relationship or the rapport building phase starts in the meet and greet continues well after the client buys and continues for as long as you want a positive relationship with this client.

Fact-Finding/Selling Evaluation/Needs Assessment (Continue the Rapport Building, Make a Friend)

- The person asking the questions is in control
- Slow down the client to absorb your rapport building
- Always ask open ended questions
- Try to answer the W's (Who, What, Where, When and Why)
  - Who is the vehicle for? Are all the decision makers present?
  - What type of vehicle are you looking for? What will this vehicle be used for?
  - Where do you plan on using this vehicle? For what purpose?
  - When are you looking to make a purchase? Your time frame?
  - Why are you looking for another vehicle?

- Questions to ask:
  - About the client
  - About the current vehicle
  - About their needs. Questions about S.P.A.C.E.R. (Safety, Performance, Appearance, Comfort, Efficiency, Reliability)

Client: "Okay, but I don't have much time."

Sales Advisor: "Will there be a better time for you to come in, so we can do a more detailed search for what you're looking for? I just don't want you to be in a rush and make a mistake or miss something important. Bob, I've been doing this for a long time and I see people like you all the time who are in a rush who end up making a mistake."

Client: "Maybe this weekend, but let's see what you have now."

Sales Advisor: "Okay, let me ask you some questions. First of all, are you looking for new or used? Car, truck or SUV? Who will be this vehicle be for?"

Client: "I'm looking for a used car or SUV and this vehicle will be for me."

Sales Advisor: "Why used and what will this vehicle be used for?"

Client: "Used because I don't want to spend that much, I like a vehicle that's already taken the big depreciation hit. I'm a single dad and I get my kids occasionally. I have 2 kids aged around 11 and 13. So I need a vehicle that will fit them and get me around town with decent gas mileage as well as occasional road trips to see their grandparents some 1500 miles away."

Sales Advisor: "Nice. I have 4 kids of my own. I know what a big deal a car is. So safety is very important. Besides Safety, out of Performance, Appearance, Comfort, Economy and Reliability, how would you rank those as the most to least important?"

Client: "Of course, safety would be first then reliability then economy and then comfort. I'm not too hung up on performance or appearance but of course it can't look like a dog or drive like one either. Also price is very important to me. Like I said, I'm a single father of two."

Sales Advisor: "I understand Bob. My kids want me to get an Escalade but they'll have to do with a 10—year-old minivan. How much are you budgeting for in payments?"

Client: "I'm trying to stay within $350 a month max."

Sales Advisor: "Okay, sounds very good. Any money down? Sorry to be asking so many questions but I'm trying to save you time and money. I just need to find out what your needs are so I can show you the right vehicles because you said you don't have much time.

Also, I'm not here to sell you anything. I'm here to find you a vehicle that meets all your needs and hopefully make you a repeat client, so don't be afraid of telling me what's on your mind. A majority of my clients are repeat and referrals because that's how I do business."

Client: *"Yeah, I understand. I have some money down."*

Sales Advisor: *"How's your credit?"*

Client: *"It got kind of beat up in the divorce, but it's in the low 700s I think."*

Sales Advisor: *"Okay. Great....we have a lot of vehicles that would suite your needs and I'll make sure you get qualified for them and stay within budget."*

Client: *"The down is questionable but my monthly budget can't be more than that."*

Sales Advisor: *"No worries Bob...all I can do is show you vehicles and numbers and you decide if it works for your budget or not, but with what you've told me you have a lot of options at our dealership. Follow me and I'll show you a few."*

Sales Advisor: *"What are you driving now?"*

Client: *"I'm currently driving that Ford Taurus. It's a rental."*

Sales Advisor: *"Rental? What happened to your main vehicle?"*

Client: *"I got in an accident and the insurance paid me off on it, they also got me this rental."*

Sales Advisor: *"Hope you're okay. What kind of car did you have before"?*

Client: *"I had a Honda Civic."*

Sales Advisor: *"My wife has a Civic. It's great on gas but small in room. What did you like and dislike about the civic?"*

Client: *"I loved the gas mileage, it was zippy, and looked nice. I hated the ride. It was uncomfortable and too low. I also wasn't too cool with the interior size or the color. It was red."*

Sales Advisor: *"Check...no red. What do you like and hate about the Taurus?"*

Client: *"I love the room and the ride. I hate the gas mileage. I don't need a big 6 cylinder."*

Sell from Stock (Continue the Rapport Building, Make a Friend)

From what we've learned so far, safety, reliability, gas mileage, comfort and any color other than red seem to be the most important things to Bob. The more questions you ask and the more you let the client talk, the more information you can get to match his needs to the perfect vehicle on your lot or ones you have access to and to make him fall in love with that vehicle.

Even better, the more conversations you have, the better friends you become the more trust is built in you. Don't be afraid to ask personal questions that aren't too intrusive. You need to know as much as possible to find common ground. So far, the sales advisor and the client have kids, are not that wealthy and are used to driving a Civic. We need more common ground.

From what we gathered so far in asking questions, we're looking for a 4 cylinder small SUV. A large sedan will also do, but a large sedan will have a larger engine that probably won't work in terms of gas mileage unless it's a 4 cylinder.

From his monthly payment requirement, we can figure out that the price of the vehicle can't be more than $20,000 because on a 5 year loan, it's about $100 a month in payments for every $5,000 they finance. So on a $20,000 vehicle, we're looking at around $400 a month, but we don't know how much down payment he has. We can go even further to $25,000 vehicle if we think we can push his buttons and his limits in regard to down payment and monthly payments.

Remember that with good credit, it costs $20 a month for every $1,000 the client finances or borrows. So if you want to borrow $1,000, it will cost you $20 a month for 5 years or $100 for $5,000 or $200 for $10,000, etc.

Sales Advisor: *"Bob, I've been doing this a long time and I understand. We have a couple of vehicles which would fit perfectly with what you're looking for. Don't discount new vehicles. We're currently running a sale on most of our models and given the interest rates, your payments could be much lower than a used one depending on credit. Follow me and I'll show you the vehicles which would best fit your needs. What do you do Bob, if you don't mind me asking?"*

Client: *"Okay, we'll see but I don't know yet. I'm a building inspector for the county."*

Sales Advisor: *"Nice...you guys must make tons of money.   Right? Just kidding. Do you carry around a lot of tools?"*

Client: *"No we don't make much, especially in these economic times. Yeah...I do carry some tools from time to time."*

Sales Advisor: *"Okay...now I'm leaning toward a SUV but a car will also do if your tools aren't that big and heavy. You from around here Bob?"*

Client: *"Yeah...I'm from Concord."*

Sales Advisor: *"Just asking because we have an excellent service department and clients who purchase from us usually get discounts at our service department. This is one of the vehicles I was going to show you. It's a 2010 RAV4 4 cylinder. Lots of interior room, excellent gas mileage and a great ride. Also notice that it's not red. As you can see, it doesn't look like a dog either. The large tires and its high stance gives good ground clearance, but it drives like a car. Let me get the keys so we can take a look inside."*

Client: *"It's very nice, but how much is it?"*

Sales Advisor: *"It's well within your range, even with a warranty. The price is on the window, but let's make sure you like it first."*

Try not to discuss price too much on the lot. A lot of sales advisors discuss price on the lot only to scare away the client. Give vague answers like "It's within your range", "You can easily afford it", or "A lot of other things come into play about your payments like credit, interest and terms." Also, by being vague on the pricing, it intrigues them to come in and look at the numbers instead of letting themselves talk themselves out of it. Remember the process. First we have to make them fall in love with the vehicle and then get them to come in and negotiate on it. The better you get at making them fall in love with the vehicle and you, the less time you will need to spend on negotiations and the less the price will matter.

The better you match up their wants and needs from fact-finding to the demonstration and presentation, the more the client will want to take the vehicle for a test drive. The chances are higher that the client will fall in love with the vehicle if they drive it.

The better rapport you build with the client, the higher the chances are that the client will only buy from you and the less they will resist during negotiations.

Product Presentation and Demonstration

The difference between price and value is salesmanship. How do the features of the vehicle benefit the client? Personalize. Although the goal is to build up your vehicle's features and how they benefit the client, they must also like it so much that they are compelled to take a test drive.

> **Sales Advisor:** *"As you can see from the trunk, there is plenty of room, so you have plenty of space for your tools as well as luggage for when you need to take long road trips with your family. Also, there is room for any other equipment you may need to transport for you or your family. You also notice that although this is an SUV, the height for the trunk is low, so you won't need to struggle in getting items in and out of your vehicle. In terms of safety, you can see that the vehicle has airbags even in the back for your passengers. What you can't see is the frame that surrounds the rear end has special crumple zones that absorb a majority of a rear end accident, so the energy of a collision is absorbed and doesn't affect your loved ones in the car.*
>
> *"If you come to the passenger side, you'll notice that there are large sized windows, so you have better visibility, which will reduce your blind spots and your passengers in back will also enjoy better visibility. Also notice the paint which has a very thick clear coat which signifies the high quality of paint, so you can be assured of a great looking vehicle for years to come. The back seat is large and roomy which will keep your rear passengers comfortable for long journeys as well as short trips across town. Notice that the rear seats also recline, so your passengers can relax, which cuts down on a lot of back seat driving. Notice that the rear seats also fold completely down, so you can have an even larger carrying capacity as well as room to stretch out during long trips with your kids. As always, there are numerous safety features like airbags, crumple zones, 3 point seatbelts and strong door beams to protect against side impacts."*

> **Client:** *"What's the crash test rating?"*

> **Sales Advisor:** *"I'm going to have to get you the exact rating but I'm pretty sure it has a 4-star rating for the side and five stars for the front and rear. Here let me show you, if you come to the front.*

"If you look under the hood, you can see the frame on the side has even better crumple zones to absorb almost all the energy in a frontal crash, <u>so</u> the energy gets dissipated even better should you run into something, keeping the occupants safer. Also notice the engine, it's a 2.4 liter. It is an engine that they've been using forever. It's extremely reliable with about 200 horsepower. What that means for you, is because they've been using this engine design for so long, all the bugs have been worked out, <u>so</u> you get an engine with extremely good reliability and a very low cost of maintenance. Also this engine gives you 28 mph which means an even lower cost of ownership because you get to save so much in fuel as well as giving you 200 horse power. Also, the vehicle has a good ground clearance when you go to the job sites, if the job site is unpaved.

"Aside from the reliability, fuel economy, roominess lower cost of ownership, safety and horsepower, if you stand back, you notice the vehicle has a very good look to it as well as a very nice stance. Our manufacturer, through their extensive market research, has discovered that people like to hold on to their vehicles for a long time so they've styled their vehicles to look good for years to come, <u>so</u> if you decide to sell it later on or pass it on to your kids when they start driving, it'll still look good."

Client: *"Yeah...my thirteen-year-old will be driving....oh wow in 3 years."*

Sales Advisor: *"Yeah...3 years will come just like that too. By then you can give them this one and get something new for yourself. But you're going to buy from me. Right Bob?"*

Client: *"We'll see if we can get the numbers right."*

Sales Advisor: *"I'll do my best. Come and sit in the driver seat. Notice how easy it is to get in and out of the vehicle. That'll come in handy when you're driving and inspecting all the different job sites because you have to get in and out so much. You comfortable in there?"*

Client: *"Yeah...it's good."*

Sales Advisor: *"Okay. Look how much leg room, shoulder room and head room you have. It's very roomy for both the front and rear passengers. The instrument panel and controls are all within your reach and clearly marked and in a logical position, <u>so</u> you don't have to be fumbling trying to adjust a setting while driving. As one of many safety features, this vehicle has an airbag for your knees in case of a frontal crash, ABS brakes, energy absorbing headrests and 3 point seatbelts, <u>so</u> you are well protected should an accident occur. This vehicle has the latest safety features on the market today.*

"The interior fabric is very easy to clean and maintain, <u>so</u> you don't have to worry too much about cleaning it or keeping it clean.

"It has an upgraded sound system so your music or Bluetooth comes in loud and
clear.

"Let's take it for a drive, I just need your license so I can get a dealer plate."

Client: *"Okay....Here you go."*

Now that you've gotten their license you have their major contact information: address, license number, date of birth, expiration and most importantly, their full name. Follow your dealer's process on taking a vehicle for a test drive. Almost all dealers require you to get them a copy of the client's license before loaning you a dealer license plate for a test drive. The manager usually will write your name on the copy and give you a dealer plate as well as enter the name of the client on the daily log.

Sales Advisor: *"Here's your license back Bob. You ready to go?"*

Client: *"Yeah, but I can't find the way to adjust the mirrors."*

Sales Advisor: *"The switch is in the middle. Yeah, make sure you adjust all your mirrors, seats and belts."*

Client: *"Oh.....I get it."*

Go on a preplanned route to avoid rough roads, other dealers, traffic jams and depressed or rough neighborhoods. Stay quiet for the first half of the test drive so the client can get a feel for the vehicle.

Test Drive

Sales Advisor: *"Okay....go out here and take a right. At the light, take a left. At the next light, go left to get on the freeway or take a right to go on the side streets."*

Keep quiet for a while so the client can get a good feel for the vehicle, otherwise they'll think you're talking to cover up the shortcomings of the vehicle.

Sales Advisor: *"Do you plan on modifying this vehicle? The reason I ask is that we have a very good tinting department and our parts department can find you any type of rims or tires you may want to customize."*

Client: *"No, nothing so extraordinary. I might want to tint the back though."*

Sales Advisor: *"You plan on taking this car on any long trip anytime soon? The reason I ask is that your first oil change is on us so you can get it before or after your trip."*

Client: *"No, no trips anytime soon. Going to be busy with work for a while."*

Sales Advisor: *"Since you'll be using this vehicle for work, do you think your work will help you pay for it?"*

Client: *"No...they won't help pay for it, but they do reimburse gas and mileage."*

Sales Advisor: *"Doesn't seem fair, since you are using your vehicle for work."*
Client: *"Yeah....this has been discussed, but no they won't do it."*
Sales Advisor: *"So you like it so far?"*

Client: *"Yeah...it handles nicely. Has good power. I like it. It's smooth."*

Sales Advisor: *"Good, this car would be perfect for what you're looking for."*

Client: *"Seems like it."*

Sales Advisor: *"You can head back anytime you want."*

Client: *"Okay...."*

Setting the Stage

Back at the dealership, have them park near your service department or anywhere else you dealership has deemed okay to park vehicles coming back from a test drive so you can give them a small tour of your dealership should they want to come. Had they had a trade-in, then the best course of action would have been to park it next to their trade-in so they can visually see the difference between their old vehicle and the new one, if it's convenient. Parking by the service department is also a nice idea since you can start a tour there.

Sales Advisor: *"You can park over there.*
Client: *"Okay...anywhere near service?"*
Sales Advisor: *"Yeah that's where we park all the sold vehicles."*
Client: *"Sold?"*
Sales Advisor: *"It's just to let other sales advisors know that someone is interested in this vehicle and that it is temporarily unavailable."*
Client: *"Okay...I see."*
Sales Advisor: *"So Bob, you like this vehicle?"*
Client: *"Yeah...I really like this one, I don't see anything else on the lot that catches my eye. "*

Sales Advisor: *"Bob, you said you were in a hurry, do you have time to review the numbers?"*

Client: *"Yes, I think I can spare a few."*

Sales Advisor: *"Good because from everything you've told me, this vehicle is perfect for your needs. It also looks good and has good power which are icing on the cake to the safety, reliability, economy and comfort you want."*

Client: *"Yeah, it's a nice looking vehicle. I just hesitate on the numbers."*

Sales Advisor: *"Okay, good follow me."*

The Tour

You would take them on a service walk to start a small tour of your dealership. This not only slows them down a little to hear what you're saying, but also builds value in your dealership as a trusted and reputable business.

Ask your management about awards your dealerships has won, highlights, selling points or what benefits your dealership offers its clients so you can use it in the tour.

Sales Advisor: *"This is our service department. They've gotten multiple awards in client satisfaction for 5 years in a row. We have the lowest service prices in the valley. On the left is our parts department. They have OEM parts as well as some valuable add-ons for your vehicle at very competitive prices."*

"Straight ahead is our showroom. Our dealership has won the president's award 5 years in a row for client satisfaction and retention. Eighty-five percent of our business is based on repeat and referrals."

"The bathrooms are through that hall way should you need them. Let's find a quiet, out-of-the-way desk so I can show you some numbers."

After finding a desk and making the client comfortable, you would go and give the plate back to the manager and get the copy of the license back from the manager to enter the information into your computer system. The manager, in most cases, will want to know what's happening and remind you of some of the vehicle's qualities to mention, like the vehicle might have one owner, clean car fax or it is priced below market.

Start Your Write Up/Approach the Desk

Once you go to the desk to get the copy of the license and give them back the dealer plate, you can have a little discussion with your manager about what transpired on the demo drive. Most likely he'll tell you to get him the 3 C's: Cash, Credit, Commitment. You would bring back a credit application to the table to try to run credit.

Sales Advisor: "Bob would you like some refreshments or snacks? Would you like water or some popcorn?"

Client: "I'll take a water."

Sales Advisor: "Okay...I'll get you a bottle. You sure on the popcorn?"

Client: "No, I'm good."

After bringing back water for both of you:

Sales Advisor: "Okay...give me a second so I can enter the information in the computer. Bob, is this address on the license your current address?"

Client: "No, I've moved since then. It's 12345 St. Philips Ct, Concord, CA, 94532."

Sales Advisor: "You have a phone number Bob?"

Client: "Why do you need that?"

Sales Advisor: "I just need to enter everything we've discussed, to take some notes. We use the phone number as a way to look you up."

Client: "Yeah...It's 123-4567."

Sales Advisor: "Bob, for me to get you accurate numbers, I'm going to need to know your credit. I don't want to give your payments, interest and terms to find out that they were wrong. I'll give you your credit score and even if you don't buy here, at least you have your credit score. I just don't want you to have any surprises."

Client: "No, I don't want credit run right now but just assume that it's in the low 700s."

Sales Advisor: "Do you know that for sure or are you guessing?"

Client: "I kind of know."

Sales Advisor: "Okay, not a problem, but I'll leave a credit application here for you to look over. I will only need the top 5 lines filled out if you decide to allow me to run your credit."

Client: "Let's just hold off on it for now. I really like the car but the payments are what I'm concerned with."

Sales Advisor: "Okay...not a problem, just let me enter all the information into the computer: name, address, phone and driver license. How much did you want to put down?"

Client: "I don't know yet."

Sales Advisor: "Okay, but it will affect your payment and it'll be in the contract."

Client: "I just don't know yet."

Sales Advisor: "Okay...sounds good. Let me send this to management and they'll prepare an offer for you. Just hang back; it'll be a few minutes."

After entering the necessary information, you would go to the tower or desk manager's office to discuss your various options as well as costs, profit margins and vehicle details.

Manager: "So what's the story here?"

Sales Advisor: *"We have Bob here. He's really interested in the 2010 RAV4. Has some money down but doesn't know how much. Doesn't want his credit run but says it's around the low 700s. Wants the payments to be no more than $350 a month. There isn't a trade."*

Management: *"What's he do?"*

Sales Advisor: *"He's a building inspector for the county."*

Management: *"Did you make him fall in love with the vehicle?"*

Sales Advisor: *"He's getting numbers isn't he?"*

Management: *"Yeah, but he's not running credit or giving you a down, so you don't have any of the C's. You have nothing right now. All you have is a looker."*

Sales Advisor: *"Don't worry, I'm working on it."*

Management: *"Did you show him any other vehicles?"*

Sales Advisor: *"I was going to but he really liked this one and he said there isn't any other car out there that catches his eye."*

Management: *"What's he looking for?"*

Sales Advisor: *"Gas efficient, 4 cylinder, used for work and the occasional long trip with his 2 kids."*

Management: *"Here's the offer, go get me a commitment."*

Before going out there, make sure to get the vehicle's profit margins from a 3rd party source like www.Edmunds.com, www.craigslist.org or www.autotrader.com on the pricing of your vehicle to justify the price and your commission threshold.

Terms	Down Payments			Retail Price of Vehicle	
Rate of 8%	$0	$2,000	$5,000	Retail Price	$19,995
36 Months	$738 a month	$675 a month	$581 a month	Discount	0
48 Months	$575 a month	$526 a month	$453 a month	Selling Price	$19,995
60 Months	$477 a month	$437 a month	$376 a month	Options: Tint, Pin Striping, Paint Protection	$649
				Subtotal	$20,644
				License Fees	$336
				Doc Fee	$500
				Sales Tax (10%)	$2,064.40
				Trade in Allowance	0
				Net Sale Price/Amount Financed	$23,544.40

Sales Advisor: *"Okay, Bob...here are the numbers. The retail price of the 2010 RAV4 is $19,995. Adding in options of tint, pin striping and paint protection of $649, we would come to a price of $20,664. There is a license fee of approximately $336, a doc fee of $500 and a sales tax of $2,064.40. With no additional money down, your payment for 60 months would be $477, with an additional $2,000 money down your payment would be $437 and with an additional $5000 down your payment would be $376. Circle which payment would best fit your budget and sign at the bottom and I'll get the car cleaned up for you."*

You would then put your pen down in front of the client and let him absorb the numbers. Keep in mind that when anyone is shopping for a vehicle or large ticket item they have limits and budgets in mind. Anything that deviates from these numbers will be met with strong resistance. Keep this in mind, because that is exactly what this guy is thinking right now.

Your job is to figure out ways to justify you numbers because your numbers directly conflict with the client's expectations.

_____

Negotiation – getting the client from mentally owning a vehicle to financially committing to owning the vehicle.

> **Client:** "Wow…8% is the best rate you can give me?"
>
> **Sales Advisor:** "Well, given what you told me about your credit score, that is the best rate we have on used vehicles. Now if you want me to check your credit to give you a more accurate number, I could do that. Maybe your score is higher than a 700 so you can get a better rate."
>
> **Client:** "It could also be worse."
>
> **Sales Advisor:** "Yeah it could be, but were going to have to run it eventually so why don't I check so you have more accurate information to work with? I just need you to fill out the first five lines of the credit application and sign at the bottom giving me permission to run the credit. We can do the rest later."
>
> **Client:** "What if I don't want the option of tint, pin striping or paint protection?"

Sales advisors get paid on any and all extras that clients purchase. The percentages aren't that great but can add up. On these options, the sales advisor could get paid anywhere from $25 to $50.

> **Sales Advisor:** "These are options. I just presented them to you in case you wanted them. Tint comes in handy and is guaranteed for life. Paint protection helps maintain that new paint look for years to come. Pin striping looks really good on these vehicles but like I said, they're options. Your payment will only go down by about $8 a month, not much but it will be rolled into the financing."
>
> **Client:** "Okay…I want the paint protection and pin stripping taken off. Also what would my payments look like if I were to put down $10,000?"
>
> **Sales Advisor:** "Okay…I'll have the manager take out the pin stripping and paint protection. Off the top of my head, for every $1,000 change in financing, the amount the payments change is $20, so for a $10,000 difference, you're looking at about $200. So your payments would go down by $200 a month or to $277 a month for 60 months. It's to your benefit to put down as much as you can because it'll save you money in the long run in interest and fees."
>
> **Client:** "Okay….run the credit. Here's the credit app filled out."
>
> **Sales Advisor:** "What else do you have concerns with? I'll take out the pin stripping and the paint protection. Is $10,000 the amount of the down payment? It will be on the contract."
>
> **Client:** "I don't know yet, I just want to see the numbers."
>
> **Sales Advisor:** "Okay…I'll be right back."
>
> **Manager:** "Done?"
>
> **Sales Advisor:** "Not yet. Here's the credit app. He wants some changes to the proposal. Take out the pin stripping and paint protection. Take out the zero down payment completely and enter $2,000, $5,000, and $10,000 down in the down

payment section. He wants to know what his payments would be if he puts down $10,000."

Manager: "Did you tell him that for every $1,000 change in the amount financed, his payments would be affected by $20?"

Sales Advisor: "Yes I did, but he wants to see it on paper."

Manager: "Well his credit is worse than 700. He's a 650."

Sales Advisor: "Great, what does that bump his interest rate to?"

Manager: "Let me check the other credit bureaus. No, 650 is his best credit score. You do know that with his credit score, if he doesn't have a good down payment, we can't even do this deal."

Sales Advisor: "Okay...well, it is what it is. No use sugar coating it."

Manager: "Really talk up the RAV4 he's interested in. This is why I like to see credit run at the beginning so there are no surprises like this. Now he's seen the numbers at an 8% interest rate, now we have to show him payments in the 650 score. Let's see what happened on his credit.......Looks like he has a bunch of medical bills he hasn't paid off. Ask him about those to justify his score. Also looks like he had a bankruptcy 5 years ago. Ask him about that too before you show him numbers, just to get him ready for the increase."

Sales Advisor: "Okay....I think I can make it work. We've got good rapport. What are we into this vehicle? How much room do I have to maneuver?"

Manager: "We're into this RAV4 for around $18,000 including pack, so you have $2,000 to play with. Do you want me to come out there and talk to him? If I come out there I'm going to discount the vehicle to make the deal and won't care about your commission. I will most likely will turn this into a mini for you."

Sales Advisor: "No, I'll handle it."

Sales Advisor: "Bob....Here's your credit report. It appears that you have some unpaid medical bills that are affecting your credit."

Client: "Yeah.....those are still in dispute. I'm in contact with that hospital to fix all that. That shouldn't be on my credit."

Sales Advisor: "Okay...but they are on your credit. You also had a bankruptcy a few years ago."

Client: "Yeah...I was going through a divorce and my ex-wife ran up a bunch of credit cards I couldn't pay for, but that was a few years ago."

Sales Advisor: "We'll, they affected your credit tremendously. I'm surprised your credit isn't lower than it is. The best credit score we could come up with is a 650 FICO."

Client: "How does that affect my payments?"

Once we have the all the pieces of the puzzle, we can then start the negotiation to get a commitment from the client. I'll use a couple of different scenarios from here based on the different types of objections the client will come up with along with how to handle those objections.

These scenarios aren't meant to cover everything but meant to get you acquainted with the whole process of objection handling as well as going through negotiations.

Keep in mind that not all clients will be as difficult as I'm portraying, but I'll try to keep the scenario fairly difficult for the sales advisor, as an easy deal or a flop will be counterproductive for our learning purposes.

Run through these scenarios a couple of times then imagine yourself sitting across the client and discussing these objections.

The main point of the negotiation is to get a commitment from the client, no matter how ridiculous their demands are. The commitment tells management that this client is serious about purchasing today as well as mentally gets the client into a purchasing mindset.

Should the client lay down and sign by the X and then we ran credit to find out that he only qualifies for 15%, then we would come back with brand new figures. It's much easier to get the client to change once they commit and signs at the X. That is why it's very important for them to sign or commit.

A commitment is moving the client from a looker to a buyer. Once that happens, then we can either bring in the manager, a closer or give them our best shot at closing this deal by justifying as best as we can our position.

Terms	Down Payments			Retail Price of Vehicle	
Rate of 15%	$2,000	$5,000	$10,000	Retail Price	$19,995
36 Months	$738 a month	$633 a month	$460 a month	Discount	0
48 Months	$592 a month	$508 a month	$369 a month	Selling Price	$19,995
60 Months	$506 a month	$435 a month	$315 a month	Options: Tint	$399
				Subtotal	$20,394
				License Fees	$336
				Doc Fee	$500
				Sales Tax (10%)	$2,039.40
				Trade in Allowance	
				Net Sale Price/Amount Financed	$23,269.40

Sales Consultant: "Bob, Because of your credit score and other derogatory items on your credit report, your interest rate went up substantially, which affects your payments substantially. For you to purchase a decent vehicle, you're going to need to put down a good amount because the banks will want to see some more participation in the game on your part, due to the derogatory items on your credit report. Here are the various down payment options: $2,000, $5,000, or $10,000. With $5,000 down payment at 60 months, your monthly payments are $435 and with $10,000 down, payment your monthly payments are $315 a month for five years. These are well within your budget. These are more accurate numbers now that we know your actual credit score. Circle the one that best fits your budget, sign by the X at the bottom and I'll get the vehicle cleaned up for you."

 X _____

Objection – Payment and Down Payment

Client: *"I don't know.....I've been sitting here while you were talking to your manager and thinking that I really do need to keep my payments around $350, but I can't really put more than $5,000 down and now my interest rate has gone up and my payments have gone up. I don't know if this is such a good idea anymore."*

Sales Advisor: *"Hmmm......oh really? Why $350?"*

Client: *"That's all I can afford currently and $5,000 is the max I currently have for a down payment."*

To get to Bob's monthly price target of $350 a month, we either have to increase his down payment of more than $5,000, increase the term of his loan, reduce his interest rate or reduce the price of the vehicle.

The manager has already told us that we have $2,000 to negotiate with on the price of the vehicle, so at 25% commission rate that's $250 in commission we lose every time we reduce the price of this vehicle by $1,000. So that is the last piece of the puzzle we want to touch to make this deal work.

We need to go to work to increase his down payment, his payments or his terms. At $5,000 we're at $435 and we're trying to get to $350, a difference of $85. We know that for every $1,000 we get Bob to increase his down payment, we can reduce his payments by $20 and to hit $350, we're going to need him to increase his down payment by about $4,000.

Sales Advisor: *"Hmmm.......Okay let's see if we can make this work.*

Current Payment $435

Target Payment <u>$350</u>

Difference $85

"Okay, it looks like were $85 off. I think we can make this work."

As a sales advisor, the best way to respond to a payment or down payment objection is to assist the client in increasing the down payment. The arguments or objections are the same as increasing the down payment discussed previously.

You should illustrate when possible and you can use this illustration showing how increasing the down payment can help in reducing their payments.

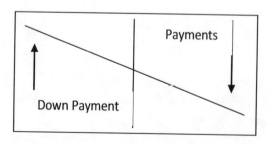

Sales Advisor: "I understand Bob, but it's to your benefit to put more money down. The more money you put down, the less the vehicle will cost you over the life of the loan due to the extra interest savings. You'll have instant equity in case you want to trade in the vehicle for another one in a few years; your payments will be smaller. It'll also be easier to get you financing with a larger down payment. As you can see, if you put down $5,000, your payments for 60 months would be $435 a month. If you put down $10,000, then your payments would be $315 a month."

Client: "I have some bills coming up for my kids and I need that extra money. The most I can put down is $5,000."

Sales Advisor: "Hmmm...can you meet me half way and put down $7,000? This will reduce your monthly payments to $395. This will also reduce the amount of interest you pay over the life of the loan as well as grant you extra instant equity should you want to trade in your vehicle. This will also help getting financing easier for you to help build your credit. The positives are enormous for the more money you put down. You see, the more money you put down the less you finance thereby reducing your monthly payments."

It's important to write these down in a 4 square format or 2 square so the client can visually see the changes.

$5,000 Down Payments
$7,000 Down Payments

$435 Monthly Payments
$395 A Month

Notice in the 4 square that I did not include the price of the vehicle or the trade-in. In this case there is no trade-in but I didn't include the price of the vehicle either because I don't want that figure to enter into the client's psyche or subconscious at the moment. I just want to concentrate on the payment and down payment, 2 things that won't affect our commission.

Client: "No....I don't have that extra $2,000 right now. Like I said I need those funds for upcoming bills."

Sales Advisor: "What If I can give you a month to come up with the extra $2,000? This way you can have time to come up with it by either selling something, saving for it or borrowing it. $40 a month can save you a lot over the life of the loan."

Client: "A month.....I guess I might be able to save some of that from my paychecks."

Sales Advisor: "Yeah....even if you have to borrow it, you won't have to pay 15% interest on it and you save almost $500 a year at $40 a month."

Client: "On second thought, I just remembered some other bills I have to catch up on. I don't think I can make it in a month."

Sales Advisor: "Okay...how about $1,500?"

Client: "No, I don't think so."

Sales Advisor: "Bob, you have to help me out here...I'm trying to make this work. We found the perfect car for you. It's got safety, style, comfort, roominess and reliability, so you're going to be saving tons of money on maintenance. All you will have to do is change the oil and fill it up on gas. The rest, the car takes care of. Now isn't that worth something?"

Client: "Yes...but you have to understand I have constraints in my life too. I'm not a rich man by any means but I need a car and I need to stick to my budget. Please understand."

Sales Advisor: "Yeah...I understand Bob. I'm not trying to pressure you. It's just that neither me nor my manager is in control of this whole deal. The real boss is the computer. If the numbers don't make sense then the computer will reject it. Can you at least give me another $1,000? So can you increase your down payment to $6,000? This will help get you financed with the banks as they want to see some vested interest. This will help reduce the total cost of ownership in terms of interest as well as fees, it will also help you rebuild your credit. Help me out here. Can you borrow the extra cash so you can keep your payments low and have a vehicle that works for you and your family?"

	~~$5,000~~ Down Payments
	~~$7,000~~ Down Payments
	$6,000 Down Payments
	~~$435~~ Monthly Payments
	~~$395~~ Month Payments
	$415 Monthly Payments

Client: "Okay....I guess you're right. I do like that vehicle and you've been very helpful. I guess I can do another $1,000. But we're still not at $350 a month."

Sales Advisor: "This is just a rough estimate but probably a little lower."

Sales advisor: "Now, why do you need to stay at exactly $350 a month in payments?"

Client: "Because after all my bills, $350 is the most I can budget for."

Sales Advisor: "There is one other thing we can do. We can increase the term of the loan from 5 years to 6 years."

Client: "What will my payments look like?"

Sales Advisor: "Let me ask my manager to run the numbers."

Manager: "You're still not done?"

Sales Advisor: "This guy won't budge off of $5,000. He had second thoughts and can't do $10,000 down but I got him to come up to a $6,000 down payment. He's still stuck that he can only do $350 a month in payments for five5 years. What does it look like if we do a 6 year loan?"

Manager: "Does he know that he's at 15% interest and if he goes to a 6 year loan, his rate will go to 18%?"

Sales Advisor: "Yeah....He might go with a 6 yr loan. What would his payments be for 6 years instead of 5 years?"

Manager: "Hold on let me run it.........$386 a month. You should be able to sell that. With his credit, I don't even know if the banks will go to 6 years either."

Sales Advisor: "Bob....Congratulations. Your payments would be $386 a month with only $6,000 down. Now remember you can pay it off as soon as you want. Some months you can pay more and others just pay $386. Just sign by the X and I'll get the vehicle cleaned up for you. You'll also be building your credit up and in about a year or so, you can refinance this at a much lower rate."

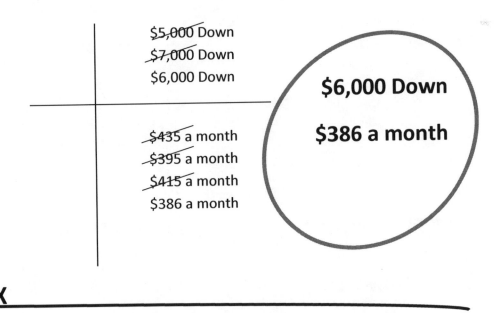

Client: "6 years...I don't know...that's a long time."

Sales advisor: *"Like I said, you can pay it off anytime you want and you're building your credit in the meantime. You can also refinance in a year at a substantially lower rate once you get a solid payment history on this loan."*

Client: *"No….that's too long…6-year loan will look like an eternity."*

Sales Advisor: *"I understand, but you have to understand the finance company's point of view. They're trying to reduce their risk by wanting more down payment as well as your ability to make the payments. A lot of people in your position do this and refinance a year from now just to build their credit, drive a decent quality vehicle and keep their payments manageable."*

So far, we're doing great because on any objection we want to stay away from changing the selling price. The first thing is talking them into accepting the payments as they are: justifying the payments! The second thing we want to respond to is increasing the down payment, maybe adjusting the term of the loan and if possible reducing the interest rate. The third item is the trade, maybe increasing the value of the trade-in. There is no trade-in in this scenario, but the pecking order still remains. The last thing is adjusting the selling price. We don't want to touch this at all or at most minimize the adjustments done to it.

The order of adjusting the price after trying to justify current prices:
1. Accepting Current Payment
2. Increase Down Payment
3. Increase Term of the Loan
4. Decrease Interest Rate
5. Increase Price of Trade
6. Decrease Price of Vehicle

Options to reduce payments:

Trade-in Value

↑

Increase

Price of the Vehicle

↓

Decrease

Term of his Loan

↑

Increase

Down Payment

↑

Increase

A majority of clients are payment buyers. What goes through their heads is whether they can afford to keep making the payments month after month. Is this vehicle worth it, to keep making payments? Payments will be the driving factor in the client's mind. The first thing that we need to reduce payments are to increase their down payment.

There are several things we can do to increase the down payment. It needs to be communicated to the client that it's to their benefit to come up with as much down payment as possible to help them get financed and to save them in the long run.

1. Give them some time to come up with the remaining portion that will make this deal work. Most dealers will give them up to a month to come up with the remaining amounts provided that they are able to
2. Somehow borrow the extra portion. Borrowing will help them as they won't have to pay the extra interest rate as they would on the loan
3. They can also sell something of value that they no longer use to come up with the extra down payment
4. Increasing their down payment also allows them to quickly build equity

There are also some things we can suggest to get them to accept the monthly payments as they currently are. Suppose the client wants payments of $200 and the best payment we can get them is $250 based on their credit, down payment and terms.

Forego some discretionary luxury monthly expense. For example, most people drink a bottle of soda a day at $1.25. At 30 days a month, that adds up to around $38 a month, so that's about $40 savings a month that they can use to pay their payments and it's good for them. At $1.50 a day, that's $45 a month savings. Reducing their dining out is another option.

Client: "Sorry Jack. I really do understand what you're saying. It's that I just can't go that long and this is all I have. If it's not meant to be, it's not meant to be. Now, all I have is $6,000 down and I can only do around $350 a month in payments. If you can do that, we can do business."

Sales Advisor: "Hmmm….Okay Bob. I don't see how that's going to work but let me get my manager to look at this. Maybe he can figure something out. Sign this at the bottom that you're willing to buy with a $6,000 down payment with $350 in monthly payments and I'll see what my manager will say."

X _____

We've done all we can to get the client to see the benefit of increasing their down payment and increasing their monthly payments, because after all, this vehicle is worth it. Sometimes the client won't give us enough information or won't budge from a number that they have set their sights on. We still get their signature and we still want to get a commitment from them. When we get that signature, what they're really signing is that they are willing to buy. It doesn't mean that we're going to give them the vehicle at that price, it just means that we'll see, and that they just moved from a looker to a buyer.

From here, we get the manager involved because it will be his call to first come out and talk to this client and then try to move numbers around to make this deal work. This will depend on the manager, business condition and the time the vehicle has been on the lot. The manager might just take a loss on this vehicle and approve $6,000 down and $350 payment even if it means reducing the price of the vehicle. Another option the manager would use is to approve the $350 a month payment provided that the client put down $6,000 and only if he'll take the 6-year loan. This way, we're only $36 away from his target instead of $85 with the 5-year loan and $5,000 down. This way, we need to discount the vehicle by a smaller amount to get to the $350 target.

The point is, the sales advisor did their job and got the commitment and now it is up to the manager to decide.

We should have done a better fact-finding to see what this client's down payment was as well as his bottom line payment requirement or his limits. We should have also known how flexible he seemed before finding him a vehicle that would meet his needs and wants.

Objection: Price

Terms	Down Payments			Retail Price of Vehicle	
Rate of 15%	$2,000	$5,000	$10,000	Retail Price	$19,995
36 Months	$738 a month	$633 a month	$460 a month	Discount	0
48 Months	$592 a month	$508 a month	$369 a month	Selling Price	$19,995
60 Months	$506 a month	$435 a month	$315 a month	Options: Tint	$399
				Subtotal	$20,394
				License Fees	$336
				Doc Fee	$500
				Sales Tax (10%)	$2,039.40
				Trade in Allowance	0.00
				Net Sale Price/Amount Financed	$23,269.40

Sales Consultant: *"Bob, because of your credit score and other derogatory items on your credit report, your interest rate went up substantially, which affects your payments substantially. For you to purchase a decent vehicle, you're going to need to put down a good amount because the banks will want to see some more participation in the game on your part. Here are the various down payment options:$2,000, $5,000, or $10,000. With a $5,000 down payment at 60 months, your monthly payments are $435 and with a $10,000 down payment, your monthly payments are $315 a month for five years. This is well within your budget. These are more accurate numbers now that we know your actual credit score. Circle the one that Best fits your budget, sign by the X at the bottom and I'll get the vehicle cleaned up for you."*

X _____

Client: "I don't know.....I've been sitting here while you were talking to your manager and I think that the price of the vehicle is too high. I don't want to pay $19,995 for it."

Sales Advisor: "Hmmm.....you think the price is high? Bob, you saw what condition this vehicle is in and you saw what kind of options it has including safety, reliability, economy and comfort. This is everything you're looking for. Right?"

Client: "Yeah but still the price is too high. I think a better price would be around $18,000."

Draw a 4 square or 1 square so the client can visually see the numbers.

Trade-in	Down Payment
$0	$5,000
Selling Price of New Vehicle	**Monthly Payment**
$19,995	$435

Sales Advisor: "$18,000? Where you getting that number?"

Client: "I've been doing some research and most are priced around that price."

Sales Advisor: The same vehicle with the same condition, mileage and color?"

Client: "Not exactly, but similar."

You need to always be prepared to justify you're asking price before you start to discount. This way, in the mind of the client, they're winning undeservedly. If you just start discounting, the client will see that the vehicle indeed is overpriced and will push for more.

Sales Advisor: "I'll see what I can do. But this vehicle is perfect for you. It matches everything you're looking for. It's in great condition and has an even better drive. It is safe and reliable for your family. I just want to save you time and headaches purchasing a lesser vehicle. What if I can get management to take off $500, do we have a deal? This will also reduce you payment a bit too."

Trade-in	Down Payment
$0	$5,000
Selling Price of New Vehicle	**Monthly Payment**
~~$19,995~~	~~$435~~
$19,495	$425

Client: *"No…… that's not enough."*

Anytime price or the trade-in is being negotiated, you can use either the book sheet or a website or a 3rd party source or the condition of the vehicle to justify your price. Any 3rd party source will help justify your price. This little bit of research should have been done in the "Approaching the Desk" step in the process. If done right, you'll also know how much commission you will lose for every $500 you discount a vehicle.

Sales Advisor: *"Bob, look at this website. This is one of the sources we use to price our vehicles. This vehicle is in excellent condition and is listed for $1,000 more than what we're listing it for. So if I take off another $500, you're actually getting a $1,500 discount. Bob, I like you and I have enjoyed our time together. I feel your pain in being a family man. I know how difficult it is but you have to help me out here. Now do we have a deal if I can get management to reduce the price to say $19,295? That's $1,750 less than the comparable market price."*

Of course you would illustrate it.

Trade-in	Down Payment
$0	$5,000
Selling Price of New Vehicle	**Monthly Payment**
~~$19,995~~	$435
~~$19,495~~	
$19,295	

-$1,750 off Market Price.

Client: *"No, that's still too much. The dealer down the street is selling one for around $17,000."*

Sales Advisor: *"$17,000? That can't be right! There's no way that it's in good condition or has low mileage like this one. It's a fact of life that you get what you pay for. I don't know about the other vehicle, all I know is about this vehicle. We're going to sell this vehicle for full retail probably sooner than later. Most likely sooner because it's in such a good condition, especially since it has good service records and one previous owner. Now there is no way I can go to $18,000, but if I can talk management to reduce the price to say $19,200, do we have a deal? That's a total savings of $1,800 off the market price."*

Trade-in	Down Payment
$0	$5,000

Selling Price of New Vehicle	
~~$19,995~~	
~~$19,495~~	
~~$19,295~~	
$19,200	-$1,800 off Market Price!

Notice that I first gave a $500 discount, then $250 and then $100. This signifies that the discount price is coming to an end and we don't have any more room to wiggle.

Client: *"No it's still not enough; I want it at $18,000. If it's not meant to be it's not meant to be."*

Sales Advisor: *"I don't know where I missed you. You liked the car, you liked the drive, and the vehicle is in excellent condition. I'm saving you over $1,800 off the market price for a comparable vehicle. Okay sign down here that you'll purchase it at $18,000 and I'll see what I can do with management."*

X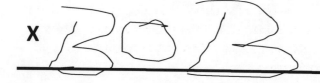

At this point, we know that if we're in this vehicle for $17,995 and management might sell it for $18,000 because at least they'll make their overhead on it. But being successful in business requires more than overhead, it requires profit. It all depends on how long the vehicle's been on the lot, condition, market and mileage. At this point, you would notify management of what's going on and let them talk to this client. Depending on many criteria, the management might sell this vehicle or may not but you've done all you can.

We also know what our mini amounts are and what our mini threshold was on this deal. If our minis are $250 and our commission rate is 20% of profit, then our mini threshold was at a discount of $1,250. For example, if we sold this vehicle for $19,995 and our cost was $17,995, then our profit would be $2,000 and at a 20% commission rate we would have made $400 commission on this vehicle. If the minimum we earn per sale is $250, then any discount given more than $1,250 has no effect on our commission. So we would need to sell this vehicle for more than ($17,995+$1,250) $19,245 to make a commission higher than our mini of $250. Selling this vehicle for anything less than $19,245 would not affect our commission because we earn a minimum of $250 per sale. If we were only paid commission, then selling by this vehicle for $19,200, we would earn $241 ($19,200-$17,995 = $1,205 x 20% = $241) and selling this vehicle for $18,000 we would get nothing.

Minis aren't the goal of the sales process because we can't be a successful sales advisor making minis. The margins aren't always this tight and minis aren't always high, but you need to recognize your thresholds when going into negotiations. On this deal, we could have made $400 or we could have made $250 for only a few hours of work. Being a professional sales advisor means knowing all the ingredients in putting together a successful deal.

17b.   Scenario II

The last scenario didn't have a trade-in involved. I wanted to keep it simple so you can get a feel for one with the objections of down payment, payment and price. Well do one here with an objection of trade. I will also keep the client fairly difficult so you can get a better feel of the negotiation process. You're not going to learn anything if the client's a lay down.

It's been a slow day, traffic has been very low. It's a Monday after all. Your shift ends at 4 and you can't wait to get off in 3 hours. It's a hot day too so your monitoring the lot from an air conditioned show room. A car drives in but heads toward the service side of the dealership. You don't think too much of it. Cars have been pulling in to service all day. You notice that the occupants of the vehicle have bypassed the service department and are heading in to the show room. Most of the other sales advisors don't notice and think they are just there walking around from service.

They seem like a typical family from the area: a middle aged, heavy set women wearing denim shorts, sandals and a blue tank top. She has a large purse slung around her shoulder gripped tight. With her is a man in his late forties to early fifties. He looks to be six feet, three inches, maybe three hundred and fifty pounds. He doesn't look like he's missed many meals. Has on gym shorts, a T shirt and a baseball hat. He seems like the jolly type as he's smiling a lot. A young girls is also with them and seems to be in her early teens, maybe thirteen. She is wearing shorts, a tank top, full makeup and flip flops. They seem ordinary, nothing out of place or special.

They wander around the showroom a little bit. As a professional, you know that everyone has potential to be a client of yours. Even if they're not in the market, you can make yourself productive by talking and prospecting with as many people as possible.

> **Sales Advisor:** "Hello, My name is Jacob. I'm a sales advisor here at Left Coast Toyota. Can I help you guys find anything, answer any questions on our big sale, help you look around?"

> **Women:** "No thank you, we're just looking around."

> **Sales Advisor:** "Okay...no problem. Anything particular you're looking for? I've been here for a while and I can save you a lot of time and answer any questions you may have."

> **Women:** "No thank you, we'll be fine."

> **Sales Advisor:** "Okay.....feel free to look around. You guys look hot, would you guys like some water?"

> **Man:** "Yeah...I guess we'll take a water."

> **Sales Advisor:** "Okay...Look around and I'll be right back."

> **Women:** "Where are your restrooms?"

> **Sales Advisor:** "Right around the corner there behind that wall."

> **Women:** "Okay, thanks."

It's been a slow day. Nothing makes the day go by faster than working a deal or interacting with people. On slow days, you won't have much interactions so love the one your with. It's an opportunity to do business. Take advantage of it. You don't get paid until you sell something.

> **Sales Advisor:** "You guys find the bathrooms?"

> **Women:** "Yes, thank you."

> **Sales Advisor:** "Here's the water....What do you guys have in service?"

> **Women:** "Oh we have an old sedan."

> **Sales Advisor:** "Oh, are you guys looking to trade it in? Oh, I forgot my name is Jacob and you are?"

Helen: "My name is Helen, this is my husband Charlie and our daughter Stacey. We're thinking about trading it in. We don't know yet."

Sales Advisor: "Hello Charlie, Stacy. It's nice to meet all of you. Okay, no problem. I can value it out for you once we find you something you like. Have you guys been at our dealership before?"

Charlie: "Yeah...we get our car serviced here once in a while."

Sales Advisor: "That's nice.... our service department has the lowest prices in the valley and we have won the service award 5 years in a row in our region which is the west coast. Also our dealership won the president's award for client satisfaction 2 years in a row. We sell more than three hundred vehicles a month so I'm confident we can find you anything you want or need. As a result, we don't do any advertising. All our business is based on repeat and referrals. We aren't the biggest dealership out there but we are the best in how we treat our clients."

Helen: "That's a nice sale speech. How much of it is true?"

Sales Advisor: Laughing, "It's not a speech. It's true. Look it up. Helen, I bet you already looked it up just like I think you looked up the exact vehicle you're looking for. You seem like the smart one who does the homework. Am I right?"

Helen: "No, like I said we're just looking."

Sales Advisor: "Okay...well let me know what you're looking for so I can save you some time. I've been doing this for a while now and I'm very familiar with our inventory. You don't want to be walking around on the lot in this hot sun by yourself do you?"

Charlie: "No I don't. I'm good here in the air conditioned showroom. We're looking to drive a new Camry."

Sales Advisor: "Okay...not a problem...let's have a seat at one of these computers and I can show you what we have in stock as well as find you any type of Camry you may be looking for. With our computer system I have access to all the area dealers' inventory and I can get you anything you may be looking for."
Fact-Finding

Sales Advisor: "Okay...give me a second to start this computer. So where you guys from?"

Helen: *"We're from San Ramon. We were driving by and decided to stop by to take a look at your new Camry's."*

Sales Advisor: *"San Ramon. Nice. My uncle lives there. San Ramon Blvd I think. So why the new Camry? Who is this vehicle going to be for? What's this vehicle going to be used for?"*

Helen: *"We've always had a Camry and it's treated us nicely. I really like the new styling of it. It's going to be an everyday vehicle for us but mainly my vehicle. "*

So far we know who the decision makers are and they are both present. We also know that in (Safety, Performance, Appearance, Comfort, Economy, Reliability (S.P.A.C.E.R.)), reliability and appearance seem to the most important. Because of their age and daughter, safety and comfort will also play into it. Safety will also be an issue but with more and more manufacturers standardizing safety, it will be included in every and all vehicles. You still should know the details of it so you can sell it in the presentation stage.

Sales Advisor: *"Nice, I own an older Camry myself. Never had any problems with it. Runs like a champ. We also have other vehicles that would probably work for you like the Corolla or the Avalon. Are you open to looking at those also?"*

Helen: *"Too small and too expensive. We have a budget: we're trying to stay at the $400 a month range.*

Sales Advisor: *"Hmmm...sounds doable. We currently have incentives of 2.9% financing on the new Camry. On approved credit of course."*

Helen: *"We both have very good credit so it's not going to be a problem."*

Sales Advisor: *"I take it the vehicle you drove in with is going to be your trade?"*

Helen: *"Yes, it's a 2005 Camry."*

Sales Advisor: *"Oh...so why are you looking to trade-in your current Camry besides the looks? In a nutshell, what do you like and dislike about your current car?"*

Helen: *"I love the reliability and the gas mileage. It has about 120,000 miles on it and I don't really like the age or the dated design. It doesn't ride as smooth as it used to. I guess it needs some shocks or something."*

Sales Advisor: *"Yeah, the new design on the Camry is nice. We have a ton of people coming in just to look at it. It's won several prestigious awards. Do you owe anything on your current Camry?"*

Helen: *"Yes, I think we owe about $3,000 on it."*

Sales Advisor: *"What is your current payment on it?"*

Helen: *"We pay around $350 a month or so."*

Sales Advisor: *"Good to know. Helen, I'm sure you've done your research. Here's a brochure of the new Camry. As you can see it comes in several different trims. There is the LE, the SE, the XLE and the Hybrid. Also, it comes in different colors, packages right here and in different engine sizes."*

Helen: *"I really like the look of the SE. In black if you have it, 4 cylinders because of the gas mileage. I also prefer leather."*

Sales Advisor: *"Let me check the computer. Looks like we do have a black 4 cylinder leather in stock. Here's what it comes with."*

If you did not have this particular one in stock you would then get them to test drive another one of equal trim so they can get a feel for it and once they've fallen in love with it, then you would find them one of their liking at another dealership where you could send out someone to pick it up.

Sales Advisor: *"Let me go and get it so you guys can see it and take it on a test drive. Hang back here and I'll park it in front."*

Charlie: *"Okay....we'll be here."*

Drive the vehicle to a comfortable area for them to look at the vehicle, preferably in front of the dealership next to the door and window.

At the vehicle, you should know five selling points to demonstrate every position.

This is where your individual presenting style will come into play. You need to custom tailor your presentation balancing your attitude of a professional with product knowledge and enthusiasm.

Position 1: The Vehicle Overall

Sales Advisor: *"The new Camry has been completely redesigned. It's lighter and more gas efficient. The new style is really sharp and crisp and unlike anything else on the road. The Camry's been the work horse for Toyota for more than thirty years. It's been the most reliable, safe and economical vehicle in its class. It has an extremely high resale value and a very low maintenance cost over its life. It has gone through some redesign to meet the changing needs of today's family like the trunk, but Helen, you already know this."*

Position 2: The Trunk

Sales Advisor: *"You can see that the trunk is bigger than its predecessor with fold down rear seats to give you even more carrying capacity. The spare is located underneath the carpet here and these new Camrys come with special frames that crumple on high impact, absorbing most of the rear crash energy, <u>so</u> to keep the occupants from feeling any of the impact. Also, notice that the lip is lower to get items in and out easier, <u>so</u> you don't have to struggle with moving cargo in and out. You also notice the rear has been redesigned to give it that sharp crisp look themed throughout the vehicle."*

Position 3: Passenger Side

Sales Advisor: *"If you come to the passenger side, you can see how different the styling is from the older models. See how nice the aerodynamics are, there are large windows, <u>so</u> you have better visibility. The doors have special side impact beams that absorb side impact much better, <u>so</u> they keep the rear passengers safer in the event of an accident. The rear seats are a lot roomier than before with high grade leather and extra leg space, <u>so</u> your occupants will be more comfortable on long drives. Also notice that the vehicle has rear airbags in the seats as well as in the pillars. The front passenger will be very comfortable and safe with increased leg room, airbags all the way around and their own climate zone."*

Position 4: The Front

Sales Advisor: *"If you come and look at the front, they've completely redesigned it to make it more aerodynamic and to give it a better stance for fuel efficiency and stability. Also, it looks much better than anything else on the road. Under the hood you can see the same engine that Camry has been using for the last 8 years. It is very reliable, durable and gas efficient. This Camry gets better gas mileage than most vehicles of the same class. It features electric steering to increase both power and gas efficiency <u>so</u> you're getting more power from using less fuel, <u>so</u> you are also saving in fuel costs. The frame surrounding the engine also has a special crumple zone to absorb a frontal impact better than any other vehicle on the road. Also, the hood is designed to fold in on itself to shield the windshield from flying debris, <u>so</u> the frame and windshield will keep the vehicles occupants safer from a frontal impact. The new Camry also comes with heavy duty shocks and springs and a redesigned suspension that absorbs most of the road vibrations and noise, <u>so</u> the occupants are more comfortable."*

Position 5: Driver Side

> **Sales Advisor:** *"Helen; come and sit in the driver's seat. Notice the different interior. The gauges are a specially designed to help reduce eye fatigue. Notice the shoulder room, head room and leg room. The interior has been completely redesigned <u>so</u> the driver and the passenger are more alert as well as more comfortable. Charlie, try it out. Even a big guy like yourself will be comfortable. Notice the airbags all the way around. It comes standard with Bluetooth, audio controls and an upgraded sound system. All new Camry's come with 2 yrs of maintenance as well as road side assistance so you won't have to worry about a thing for 2 years. That's 2 years of oil changes <u>so</u> it'll save you approximately $350 to $400 for those 2 years in maintenance fees."*

> **Sales Advisor:** *"Helen, I just need your driver's license so we can go on a quick or long test drive."*

After you make a copy of the driver's license and give it to your manager, you would then grab a dealer plate. The driver's license has valuable information, so make sure you keep it safe and secure. You can lose a great deal of trust if you misplace the client's license or a copy of it.

> **Manager:** *"What are they looking for?"*

> **Sales Advisor:** *"They're in service. I'm trying to get them to trade-in their old Camry for a new one. They just want to test drive it."*

> **Manager:** *"Just test drive it? How about buying it?"*

> **Sales Advisor:** *"Yeah test drive it, that's what they said. I'm working on them buying it."*

> **Manager:** *"Just get me a commitment."*

> **Sales Advisor:** *"You guys ready to go? Helen, you're driving first?"*

> **Helen:** *"Yes...I'll drive."*

> **Helen:** *"Okay...we're ready."*

> **Sales Advisor:** *"Okay adjust your seats, mirrors, belts. We're going to go straight then left at the stop sign. From there you can go either left to go on the freeway or right to go on the side streets."*

Test Drive/Trial Close (Mental Ownership)

> **Helen:** *"How do I turn down the A/C?"*

256

Sales Advisor: "The knob on the dash and the controls on the steering wheel. Notice that the knob is large so it makes it easier for you to find while driving and the controls are also on the wheel so you don't have to take your eyes off the road. Charlie also notice that you have your own climate control so the passenger is always comfortable, especially on long drives. You can come back some more Charlie, you have plenty of room to adjust your seat. Helen, also notice that they've reengineered the whole drive of the Camry. It's smooth, comfortable as well as sporty. They've added special sport shocks and struts as well as cushier seats for comfort and control."

"Helen, will this be your primary vehicle?"

Helen: "Yes..."

Sales Advisor: "We'll that's good because you get around 35 mpg in this car. With that much savings in gas, you guys can take it on long trips no problem."

Helen: "It does drive nice."

Sales Advisor: "Is this Camry equipped like you want it?"

Helen: "Yeah....we don't need all the bells and whistles though."

Sales Advisor: "You like it so far Helen?"

Helen: "Yeah...It's nice and drives nice."

Sales Advisor: "Charlie, would you like to drive it or is this vehicle only for Helen?"

Charlie: "No, I'm good. I trust her instincts."

Sales Advisor: "Are you guys planning a long road trip in this car? Is that why you're looking for another vehicle?"

Charlie: "Maybe...don't know yet. Depends on what you'll give us for our trade."

Sales Advisor: "Oh yeah...your Camry. How much are you looking to get for it?"

Charlie: "Well, we don't know but we know how much it's worth."

Sales Advisor: "Okay...but just to remind you, we can only give you wholesale price for it. We can only pay you what we can buy it for at the auction. I've been doing *this for a long time and most people want retail price on their trades. The good news is that our used car manager is currently giving very good money for trades as our used car inventory is very low. So depending on the condition, we may be able to give you more than wholesale. Who knows?"*

Some people want full price for their trade and need to be educated. Obviously, a dealership can't make money by paying retail for a vehicle and selling it for retail. It's a business like any other. You buy your commodities low and sell them at a markup for profit.

Helen: *"We've done our research."*

So, the information we have so far is that they like the new car. They have a vehicle which they owe $3,000 on, it has 120,000 miles on it, no down payment and they are looking for a $400 a month payment, give or take. Most people, including me, will tell you it doesn't matter what they owe on their current vehicle in regard to the value of it when they're trading it in. Just because you owe $5,000 on a vehicle that is worth $3,000 doesn't mean the dealership will pay you $5,000 for it so you can break even. If the dealership can get the same vehicle for $3,000 at an auction, then why would they pay more for it?

So given our 4 square model in the negotiation step:

Trade-in	Down Payment
Selling Price of New Vehicle	**Monthly Payment**

Mentally insert that information into the 4 square.

Trade-in -$3,000	Down Payment $0.00
Selling Price of New Vehicle $24,995	**Monthly Payment** $400

The first and only thing that we currently have to work on is getting them to love the vehicle they are driving by building as much value in it as possible.

We don't know how much they want for their current vehicle, but we do know that they are $3,000 upside down, meaning since they don't own the vehicle, they owe money on it. No matter how much we offer for the vehicle, we have to subtract $3,000 from it because we have to include this $3,000 into the financing of their new vehicle. Suppose their vehicle is worth $5,000 to the dealership, then subtracting $3,000 we have to pay the finance company, their total trade-in value is worth only $2,000.

Since they do not have a down payment, it's something that needs to be addressed or at least a seed planted in their minds.

Monthly payments seem doable at first, but if we want to sell them warranty, accessories, gap and other financial items, we might need to bump up this amount or at least plant a seed. The selling price is the last thing we want to adjust as our commission is based on it.

> **Sales Advisor:** *"Very smart of you Helen. You might think about bringing some money down as it'll dramatically affect your monthly payment. We have the cheapest extended warranties in the valley so a down payment will allow you guys to take advantage of that."*

> **Charlie:** *"We don't need extended warranties. I've been working on cars since I was 18. I know what I'm doing."*

> **Sales Advisor:** *"Yeah...but why should you when it's so cheap? Also, these new cars need computers and special equipment. You can end up doing more damage. Finance will be able to explain to you everything they cover. None of that matters though if you don't like the vehicle."*

> **Helen:** *"Yeah, I like it. It's beautiful."*

> **Sales Advisor:** *"Okay, you can head back whenever you want or you can keep test driving."*

> **Stacey:** *"I need to use the bathroom."*

> **Helen:** *"Okay, I'll head back."*

> **Sales Advisor:** *"You can park next to service, next to your vehicle if you want, but anywhere is fine."*

> **Helen:** *"Here are the keys."*

> **Sales Advisor:** *"Stacey, the bathrooms are by the parts department. So Helen you like it?"*

Helen: "Yeah…it's nice. Charlie, you like it?"

Charlie: "Depends."
Sales Advisor: "I mean, do you like it enough to own it?"

Helen: "Maybe, if you can give us a good price for our trade."

Sales Advisor: "Okay…not a problem. Come inside and let me run some numbers for you and you guys can decide if it'll work for you."

Charlie: "Okay, you want to look at some numbers honey?"

Helen: "Yeah, I guess it won't hurt."

Sales Advisor: "Okay, great, come on in. Let me show you around a little bit. This is our award winning service department. We've won the top service award for 5 years in a row. Our parts department is over there. If you notice, most of the prices are cheaper than what parts houses and they also sell accessories for all our vehicles like your new Camry. There are some refreshments here. The bathrooms are over there."

Sales Advisor: "Let's find a nice quiet desk to sit. So, what's going to happen is I'm going to enter some of your information into the computer so I can keep track of what we talked about and then do an appraisal of your vehicle so the used car manager can give you an accurate number for your trade. I will also need to run credit so my manager can give you accurate information as to the finance rate you qualify for as well as your payments. First, I need to enter some information in the system."

Charlie: "I don't want our credit run at the moment. We have very good credit and we qualify, I'm sure, for your incentives. I'm just not that comfortable with running credit until we agree with numbers."

Sales Advisor: "Okay, not a problem. I'll assume you qualify and give you numbers based on that score. Let me enter all your info in the computer for my manager. Let me get the keys to your vehicle. You can come with me when we're looking at your vehicle or you can stay here."

Charlie: "We'll stay here."

Manager: "Well, what happened?"

Sales Advisor: *"No down, they have an 05 Camry they owe $3,000 on that they are paying $350 a month on, loved the new Camry, looking for $400 a month in payments. Don't want their credit run yet."*

Manager: *"What do they do for work?"*
Sales Advisor: *"Don't know yet, been trying to sell the car."*

Manager: *"Rapport building. Make a friend. Where do they work? How long they've lived where they live? What school does the kid go to? What grade is she in? How deep is their pool? Where did they buy their last car? Who are they financed through? What makes them tick? You got to become their friend and ask questions like that and be interested in them, more than being interested in selling them a vehicle."*

Sales Advisor: *"I know, but when you're with a client you tend to get tunnel vision and concentrate on what the client's needs are, on selling and some of the steps. Give me the copy of the license and a trade-in sheet."*

Enter all the pertinent info in the computer: name, address, phone, email, driver license number, trade-in and notes.

Trade Evaluation

Manager: *"Grab a trade evaluation form and let's go see their trade."*

When at the vehicle, make sure you write down the VIN, start the vehicle and write down the mileage and run the A/C. Also make a note of the condition of the interior, noting anything that might need repair. Check all the windows to make sure they go up and down in a smooth manner. Open all the doors, trunk and hood and check for any damage or missing VIN tags in the door jams. Listen for any noises or unusual things about the vehicle. Feel every tire to gauge the depth of every tire. Run your hands along the edges to check for sharp edges indicating that the vehicle has been painted. Note any differences in the gaps between body panels.

Fill out the trade-in sheet completely.

If the clients are out there, if you see any imperfections, just make sure they notice you noticing the imperfection by gently touching or rubbing it, but don't say anything. They'll feel like they have to explain it. It doesn't matter if the client is there or not, the vehicle should speak for itself.

Note everything and anything negative about the vehicle to use in the negotiation, because it makes no sense to make their vehicle look better than it is.

You will use the VIN and other options the vehicle comes with to get the book value of what the vehicle is selling for at the auction. You'll also need this information to look up similar vehicles for sale online.

While the manager is working up the numbers, you need to quickly look up their vehicle in Kelly Blue Book, Craigslist, and on www.Edmunds.com. Most people look at Kelly Blue Book when appraising their trade. You need to check there to see what the client has been looking at. Make sure you note the trade-in, private party, auction and retail prices.

Next, check Craigslist, as this website will give a very good idea of how much these vehicle are being sold for by private parties and dealers. Only check private parties as the dealer prices will be inflated with profit.

Next check www.Edmunds.com on the trade-in value. This website is very current to market conditions and uses information from dealer auctions to price out their trades. This is a good third party source you could use to justify your prices.

No matter which websites you use, make sure you educate yourself as to the client's vehicle. Put yourself in the client's mindset. Don't forget to compare apples to apples. Don't compare an XLE with an LE or vice versa.

> On this vehicle as of the writing of this book:
> KBB Trade in value is $9,200 and private party sale is $11,200
> www.Edmunds.com trade-in value is $7,700, private party is $8,700 and retail is $9,931
> Craigslist prices are all over the place but a good ballpark would be around $9,500

Most clients' first instincts are to refer to the website with the highest value and that's probably why Kelly Blue Book always has their values high. Does it make sense to pay $11,200 for a 7-year-old vehicle with 120,000 miles on it? On this model, you can get a used certified 2009 vehicle for around $13,500 with much fewer miles.

This is why www.Edmunds.com is a little bit more realistic in that the retail is $10,000 and we need to get the vehicle for much cheaper than that, so out of these 3 websites, we would use www.Edmunds.com and Craigslist to justify our price on their trade, should they object to the value of their trade, which most likely they will since they've done their homework and are very price conscious.

If you were selling a used vehicle, then you would also do research on your vehicle to justify the selling price. Anticipating objections and concerns are part of the professional sales advisors job. Doing your homework on why someone would tell you "No" and how to handle that "No" is what sales is all about.

While the manager is putting together the deal, go out and sit with the client to chit chat about the trade or anything else or enter some information into the computer system.

> **Sales advisor:** *"It'll be just a few more minutes longer. My used car manager is calling around a few wholesalers to get a price on your trade."*

Charlie: *"Okay."*

Sales Advisor: *"Charlie, how much are your monthly payments again and when is your next payment due?"*

Charlie: *"I believe our monthly payments are $350 a month, and our next payment is due in 2 weeks."*

Sales Advisor: *"What happened with the dent on the right front fender?"*

Helen: *"I don't know. It happened in a parking lot."*

Sales Advisor: *"What about the burning smell from the engine? Have you checked that out?"*

Charlie: *"I think it's got a leak somewhere. I don't think it's that big of a deal."*

Sales Advisor: *"Are you guys going to get those fixed?"*

Helen: *"No, that's why we want to trade it in."*

Sales Advisor: *"Okay, not a problem. We'll see what we can do. Let me check to see if they got a price for your trade."*

This would be a good time to ask your manager how much wiggle room you have on this vehicle, especially if it was a used one. You need to know what your profit margin is so you know where your commission threshold is and you can fight to keep above that. Most new car deals will be minis anyway, because there isn't much mark up. The dealer makes most of its money on holdbacks and volume bonuses which the sales advisor doesn't get paid on.

Manager: *"Their Camry is worth around $7,700 but I'll offer $6,700 because we don't know how much it will be to repair some of the issues it has. How much do they want for it?"*

Sales Advisor: *"They don't want to say, but most likely they checked KBB for the value, so worst case scenario they want around $9,000 for it."*

Manager: *"So you don't have the Cash, Credit or the Commitment?"*

Sales Advisor: *"Not yet...they are interested but want to get numbers first. Don't worry, I'll present it. Just give me something I can work with."*

Manager: *"Here are the numbers...get me a commitment."*

So far, what we know is:

> The client wants to be around $400 a month payments
>
> They owe $3,000 on their vehicle
>
> Their trade has some issues that need to be fixed. It's in average condition
>
> They have no other down payment
>
> Their next payment is due in 2 weeks
>
> Our commission threshold is not that great so most likely we're looking at a mini
>
> Their vehicle is 7 years old. It has 120,000 miles on it. It is in average condition

Presenting the Numbers

Sales Consultant: *"I apologize for taking so long but here are the numbers. The price of the 2013 Camry is $24,995, there is an option of tint, pin striping, and paint protection for $699. The license fee is $432, and the documentation fee is $500. Our used car manager said the fair market value for your vehicle is $6,700 with a payoff of $3,000 that you said. With sales tax of $2,569.40, the total financed amount will be $25,495.40. At 2.9% with no money down, your payments will be $740 a month for 36 months, $563 a month for 48 months and $457 a month for 60 months. Should you want to increase your down to $2,000 or $5,000, those are the respective monthly payments along with the terms on the left side. Please circle the one that best fits with your budget and sign by the X below and I'll get the car detailed."*

> **Charlie:** *"Hold on, give us a minute to look this over."*

Here, the sales advisor should just look calm and collected and silent.

> **Helen:** *"We looked up our vehicle in Kelly Blue Book and it said that our trade-in was worth at least $9,200 and with a private party, it is worth at least $11,200. You guys are trying to rob us."*

Look at the numbers again and look them over for about 5 to 10 seconds and keep quiet. Just pause like you're trying to make sense of their objection and that it's the first time you've even thought of $9,000 for their trade.

> **Sales Advisor:** *"Helen, I understand what you're saying, but Kelly Blue Book is overpriced. Think about it Helen, if a private party is $11,200, then retail has to be around $13,000. Would you pay $13,000 for a 7-year-old vehicle with 120,000 miles on it? In actuality, the retail price on this vehicle is more like $9,000. Here, look at Craigslist and you can see what people are selling it for on the street. The numbers are all over the place but the consensus is around $9,500. People have a lot of options for $9,500. I don't think anyone would pay that much for a vehicle with as many miles as yours with the condition it is in. You have to understand that we can get the same vehicle at the auction for $6,700. I'm not trying to put down your vehicle. In fact, those Camry's are great vehicles but with the age and mileage,*

264

it's going to be a tough sale for around $9,000 or even $8,000. If I can get you $7,000 for your vehicle will that be acceptable?"

Terms	Down Payments			Retail Price of Vehicle	
Rate of 2.9%	$0	$2,000	$5,000	Retail Price	$24,995
36 Months	$740 a month	$682 a month	$595 a month	Options: Tint, Pin Striping, Paint Protection	$699
48 Months	$563 a month	$519 a month	$453 a month	Subtotal	$25,694
60 Months	$457 a month	$421 a month	$368 a month	License Fees	$432
				Doc Fee	$500
				Trade in Allowance	$6,700
				Payoff	$3,000
				Subtotal	$22,926
				Sales Tax (10%)	$2,569.40
				Net Sale Price/Amount Financed	$25,495.40

X

_____

Trade-in	Down Payment
~~$6,700~~	$0.00
$7,000	
	Monthly Payment
	$457

Charlie: *"No way...the trade-in is $9,200, that's what we want."*

Sales Advisor: *"Charlie, look at this website. This is the most realistic website when it comes to prices. You've heard of Edmunds haven't you? Here, if I plug stuff in about your vehicle, the trade-in comes in at $7,700. The reason this website is good is because they gather their information from the dealer auctions. We also have to take into consideration the condition of the vehicle. It's going to take some considerable money to get your vehicle in selling condition."*

Charlie: *"Yeah...but that car is perfect."*

Sales Advisor: *"Charlie, it's 7 years old with 120,000 miles on it. Honestly, if you had $11,000 or $12,000 would you buy a 7 yr old vehicle with 120,000 miles on it? It looks like you took care of it but just think of the next buyer. I know that you want $9,200, but we have to bring it up to specs and invest another $1,500 in it. It needs tires, that's a good $600 and other things add up."*

Helen: *"Maybe we should sell it on our own."*

Sales Advisor: *"You saw on Craigslist that their selling for around $9,500. Why would you waste all that time and effort. Selling a 7 yr-old vehicle with 120,000 miles for $9,500 is going to be tough. Plus you owe $3,000 on it which means that the buyer has to go to the bank and pay it off and then pay you. It's a hassle that most people don't want to deal with. Besides, we're willing to take it with all its problems. I want to help you guys out here but you have to help me out here too. What if I can get you $7,200, will that be acceptable? Now I'm not promising anything. All I can do is present it to my manager and recommend it."*

Trade-in	Down Payment
$6,700~~	$0.00
$7,000~~	
$7,200	
	Monthly Payment
	$457

Charlie: *"Hmmm....no. Nothing less than $8,000 will do and we're pretty firm on that."*

Sales Advisor: *"$8,000? Be reasonable...the trade-in is worth $6,700. Okay...do we have a deal if I can get you $7,300? That's $600 more than the trade-in value. Also remember that the amount of your trade also affects your taxes so $7,300 for your trade-in reduces your taxes by the tax rate of 10% so you're getting an additional $730 in tax savings."*

Trade-in	Down Payment
$6,700~~	$0.00
$7,000~~	
$7,200~~	
$7,300	
	Monthly Payment
	$457

Helen: "No...$8,000 or we walk out."

Trade-in	Down Payment
$6,700~~	$0.00
$7,000~~	
$7,200~~	
$7,300~~	
$8,000	
	Monthly Payment
	$457

Sales Advisor: "Okay...so if I can get you $8,000 for your trade we have a deal? Like I said earlier, I'm not promising you anything. All I can do is present this to my manager."

Helen: "No...we can't do anything for $457 a month. That's way too much."

Now we know that for every $1,000 change in the finance amount, payment gets affected by $20: in this case if we increased the trade value from $6,700 to $8,000, which is an increase of $1,300. So the payment has to be reduced by at least $20. So we know that if management does give them $8,000 for their trade, their payment should go down to at least $437. The next thing we want to sell them on is on increasing their down payment to reduce monthly payments, and after that, the next thing that we'll touch on is increasing their term and if need be, getting rid of the accessories like tint, paint protection and pin striping.

Sales Advisor: "One way to reduce your payments is to put some money down because as you know the more money you put down, the lower your monthly payments."

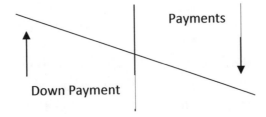

Helen: "We don't have any more money to put down."

Sales Advisor: *"What if I can give you a month to come up with additional down payment? What can you come up with in about a month?"*

Charlie: *"I don't know, maybe $500."*

Sales Advisor: *"Well, we have to know for certain because it's going to be in the contract."*

Helen: *"No, we don't have any more money to put down."*

Sales Advisor: *"Your next payment isn't due 2 weeks right? Can't you put that money down and I can give you a month to come up with even more. If you guys can put down at least $1,000, your payments will be reduced by $20. That's $20 a month."*

Trade-in	Down Payment
$6,700	$0.00
$7,000	$1,000
$7,200	
$7,300	
$8,000	

	Monthly Payment
	$457
	$417

Charlie: *"We're at a tough time right now...we can't put anything else down. I'm sorry."*

Sales Advisor: *"Not even if I give you a month?"*

Helen: *"No, I'm afraid not. Money is a little tough."*

Sales Advisor: *"Okay, not a problem. Forget about a down payment. What's the best you can do in a monthly payment? You guys have to work with me a little. I can't make this work without a little participation from you guys. One thing I can do is increase the term of the loan from five years to six years. Will that be* *acceptable? I can have it below $400 a month, but your interest rate will have to go up a little."*

Charlie: *"No...That's too long of a loan to have. Look, the most we can do for a monthly payment is $420 a month. Can you do that?"*

Sales Advisor: *"I know, but there isn't a penalty for early payments. You can pay off sooner than the seventy-two months."*

Helen: *"No, that's too long."*

Trade-in	**Down Payment**
$6,700	$0.00
$7,000	
$7,200	
$7,300	
$8,000	
	Monthly Payment
	$457
	$420

Sales Advisor: *"Okay, if I can get you $8,000 for your trade, no money down and $420 a month: do we have a deal? I need a solid commitment from you. I'm not promising anything, but all I can do is sell it to the manager. It's his call to approve it or not. Even then it's not his call. He's got to answer to the computer."*

Helen: *"Yes, that's acceptable."*

Sales Advisor: *"Okay...sign by the X at the bottom and I'll present it to the manager."*

x **Bob & Helen**

This seems like a complete loss for the dealership because their losing $1,300 on the trade if they give them $8,000 for their trade as well as discounting the price of their vehicle to get to $420 or $400 a month. Depending on the business conditions, the manager, or the length of time the vehicle's been on the lot, the manager might take this deal. The loss will be offset from the profit of the new vehicle and new vehicles usually don't have much profit in them but you did your best and got them to commit to a sale.

> **Manager:** "Let me guess, they want more for the trade?"

> **Sales Advisor:** "This is what I got. They want $8,000 for their trade, no additional money down, and they want $420 a month on a 5 yr loan only."

> **Manager:** "If I give them $8,000 for their trade, I'm down to $434 a month where am I going to get the other $14 to discount to get to $420 a month?"

> **Sales Advisor:** "Get rid of the accessories, that should give us another $10 to $15. Leaves some room for finance to sell them something."

> **Manager:** "Okay...you're down to $420. Have them fill out a credit app."

> **Sales Advisor:** "Helen, Charlie I can get your payments down to $434 a month. Any lower and I'm going to have to take out the tint, paint protection and pin striping. Can you live with $434 a month? That's only around $70 a year, but our tint has a life time warranty and you choose how dark you want it. Our pin striping is guaranteed for life and you need paint protection to keep the sun from fading your paint."

> **Helen:** "No take those off...we don't need it."

> **Sales Advisor:** "Helen, Charles, congratulations! I got $8,000 for your trade and I got your payments down to $420 a month. I need you guys to fill this credit application out so I can send your new car to detail."

From here, you would get their license and insurance of all the parties who will be on the title as well as the credit application to continue on to finance and then to delivery.

Notice that I kept the price of the vehicle out of this whole equation since that is what we get paid on. I would have preferred to keep the tint, pin striping and paint protection in the deal as well because the sales advisor also gets paid on those too. All in all, the extra money paid for their trade will come out of the price profit of the new vehicle, but this is a mini anyway as is most new vehicle purchases.

17c.   Scenario III

In this scenario, we're going to negotiate the price of the vehicle. Although I've been trying to stay away from negotiating on the price of the vehicle as your commission is based on it, some of the time you can't help it. It's the biggest part of the equation and some people will want to negotiate it down.

The higher the amount of gross profit, you, as a sales advisor, can keep in the deal, the higher your commission. This also includes the trade-in value. If your manager offers the wholesale value of $10,000 for their trade and they want $12,000 or the deal will fall apart, the extra $2,000 has to come from somewhere.

Where it's going to come from is the profit of the new vehicle their looking at. If the new or used vehicle profit is $4,000, then after giving them an extra $2,000 for their trade, the gross profit of the new or used vehicle will only be $2,000.

You, as a negotiator and as a sales advisor, need to look at the whole deal rather than only one aspect of it.

Example:

2011 Cadillac SRX Retail Price	$40,000
Dealer Cost	$35,000
Total Profit	$5,000
Trade-in: 2003 Nissan Altima	
Wholesale Price	$4,000
Client Asking Price	$6,000
Total Profit/Loss on Trade	-$2,000
Total Gross Profit	$3,000

As you can see, the dealer total cost on the selling vehicle, which is a Cadillac SRX, is $35,000, which retails for $40,000. So the total profit will be $5,000. Now suppose someone interested in the Cadillac wants to purchase it and has a trade. If the trade's book value, meaning that's what it's worth in the wholesale market, is $4,000 but the client insists that that it's worth $6,000 and he will not take anything less, then the dealer will be losing $2,000 on the trade and will offset this loss by applying to the profit of the new vehicle. So now the profit on the Cadillac will be $5,000, less the $2,000, which is $3,000. You, as a sales advisor, would get paid on the $3,000.

As a sales advisor, will take deals like this all day. At 20% commission on $3,000 is $600. The problem is that some clients are more savvy than that and will want to also negotiate the price of the vehicle down. They'll want to drop the price of the Cadillac from $40,000 to $37,000. In this case, there is no profit left for the sales advisor since there will only be $2,000 profit on the Cadillac and a $2,000 loss on the trade to net out to zero, which means that this will be a mini for the sales advisor.

This is a call that your manager will need to make, but in most cases they will take it because the vehicle has already been padded with dealer profit, called pack, like we discussed earlier. All vehicles get padded about $1,500 for sunk costs, overhead and management fees. Most dealers will say that they don't pack their vehicles, but I haven't seen any dealer that doesn't pack their vehicles.

So keep in mind during negotiations that when negotiating down the price of the vehicle and negotiating up the value of their trade, that you need to be aware of the whole deal and not only one aspect of it.

In this scenario we're going to assume that you did a great meet and greet, fact-finding, needs assessment, product presentation, demonstration and they love the vehicle. Also, they don't like any other vehicle on the lot. It's either this one or nothing. They don't have a trade, they are looking for $400 a month in payments maximum, the price of the vehicle their interested in is $19,995 and they don't have a down payment. You've already run credit and they qualify for 2.9% financing.

In this scenario if we can't meet their monthly payment requirement, the first thing we need to is justify the monthly payment as a necessity, next is to increase their down payment, next we need increase their terms, after that, we need to take out the accessories, leaving the price of the vehicle we're selling last. Throughout the whole process, we'll be up selling the vehicle.

We know that for every $1,000 change in amount financed, the payments get affected by $20. So for every $500 difference, payments should get affected by $10. Since the accessories amount to $699, if we take those out, we should be able to reduce the payment by a minimum of $10 or $12.

The numbers you want to present to them are below.

Trade-in	Down Payment
$0	$0.00
Selling Price of New Vehicle	**Monthly Payment**
$19,995	$400

Terms	Down Payments			Retail Price of Vehicle	
Rate of 2.9%	$0	$2,000	$5,000	Retail Price	$19,995
36 Months	$686 a month	$628 a month	$541 a month	Options: Tint, Pin Striping, Paint Protection	$699
48 Months	$522 a month	$478 a month	$411 a month	Subtotal	$20,694
60 Months	$423 a month	$388 a month	$334 a month	License Fees	$336
				Doc Fee	$500
				Trade in Allowance	$0
				Payoff	$0
				Subtotal	$21,530.00
				Sales Tax (10%)	$2,069.40
				Net Sale Price/Amount Financed	$23,599.40

Sales Consultant: *"The price of the vehicle is $19,995 and there is an option of tint, pin striping and paint protection for $699. There is a license fee of $336 and a documentation fee of $500. With sales tax of $2,069.40, the total financed amount will be $23,599.4. At 2.9% with no money down, your payments will be $686 a month for 36 months, $522 a month for 48 months, and $423 a month for 60 months. Should you want to increase your down to $2,000 or $5,000, those are the respective monthly payments along with the terms on the left side. Please circle the one that best fits with your budget and sign by the X below and I'll get the car all cleaned up."*

X

Client: *"Look, we don't want to play any games. We can't afford more than $400 a month."*

Sales Advisor: *"Hmmm.....why only $400 a month?"*

Client: *"After doing our budget, that's all we can afford."*

Sales Advisor: *"I know what you said, but the math doesn't make sense. To finance $23,599 for 60 months at 2.9% ,you're looking at $423 a month in payments. Now, you do have some options but I'm going to need you guys to keep an open mind because I can't bring down the payment by myself. I'm going to need some participation on your part."*

Client: *"Okay...what kind of options?"*

Sales Advisor: *"One is put some money down."*

Client: *"Stop right there...we don't have anything we can spare at the moment."*

Sales Advisor: *"Look at this."*

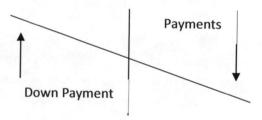

"The more money you put down, the less your payments. You should put down something because you don't want to roll the tax and license into the financing. That means you'll be paying interest on the tax and license. Does that make sense to you?"

Client: *"We understand what you're saying, but honestly we don't have anything to put down right now. If we have to, we'll wait."*

Sales Advisor: *"You don't want to wait because the special finance rate is only for this month. I don't think it'll be available next month. What if I gave you guys a month to come up with the down payment? Maybe $500 in 2 weeks and another $500 2 weeks after that? With $1,000 down I can get your payments down to about $400 easily."*

Client: *"No....we don't want to waste your time. Will you be able to do this or not?"*

Sales Advisor: "Maybe....I just need to run by all your options. Is that okay?"

Client: "Okay, I guess. We're not trying to be rude but we're in need of a vehicle but don't have that much discretionary income."

Sales Advisor: "Okay, not a problem. Another option would be to increase your term from 60 months to 72 months. I know I can get your payments down by a lot, a lot lower than $400 a month. This is probably the best option because your minimum monthly payment will be very low and you can pay more when are able and pay the minimum when you aren't."

Client: "How much lower?"

Sales Advisor: "Hold on, let me ask my manager."

Manager: "The 2.9% financing incentive is for 60 months max. For them to go to 72 months, we need to increase their interest rate to 4.5%. Their payments go down to $375. Can you get me a commitment at that or would you like me to come out and talk to them?"

Sales Advisor: "Let me present it."

Client: "Look, we've been discussing it and we don't want to 72 months. That's too long for a car loan. I know your trying to help but we can't go that long. Sorry."

Sales Advisor: "For 72 months your payments would go from $423 to $375. That's a savings of $48 a month. That's like $600 a year. Most people trade-in their vehicles every 3 yrs so you don't have to go the full term of the loan and your minimum payment will be $375 so you can pay $400 when you are able and $375 when you aren't able."

Client: "As appealing as it sounds, we can't do it. We keep our cars till the wheels fall off. 6 years is way too long for a car loan."

Sales Advisor: "Yes, but you can pay $400 a month if you wish. Not only will this reduce the amount of interest you pay over time, but also hits your $400 a month target."

Client: "No...it's too long."

Sales Advisor: "Is there any way you can meet me half way on the $400 limit? Right now you're at $423. Can you do at least $413? You like the car, right? It's *got everything you're looking for? Come on folks, I need some participation from you guys."*

Client: *"The best we can do is $400. We're on a limited budget and we want to pay the vehicle off in a maximum of five years. Please understand, we don't want to waste your time, but we have our own limits."*

Sales Advisor: *"I still don't understand why you won't do 72 months. There are so many benefits to you guys."*

Client: *"We had a 72 month loan before. Never again. That's one of the things we discussed before coming here, that we would not get into another 6 yr loan."*

	Down Payment
	$0.00
	Monthly Payment
	~~$400~~
	~~$413~~
	$410

Sales Advisor: *"Wow, can you at least do $410 a month? Just $10 a month more? That's just one meal out a month I'm asking you to skip eating out."*

Client: *"No, like we said, we're on a limited budget. If it can't be done, it can't be done. We can wait till we get some money down."*

Sales Advisor: *"The 2.9% incentives won't be here when you do decide to come back so It's imperative that we do something before the incentives go away."*

Client: *"Maybe we just can't afford right now."*

Sales Advisor: *"Okay...hold on let me see if my manager has any ideas."*

Client: *"Okay."*
Manager: *"What is going on out there?"*

Sales Advisor: "I can't get them to budge. They want a $400 a month payment for 5 years only. No more. We're $23 away."

Manager: "Okay...here are the new numbers. Get me a commitment."

Terms	Down Payments			Retail Price of Vehicle	
Rate of 2.9%	$0	$2,000	$5,000	Retail Price	$19,545
36 Months	$649 a month	$590 a month	$503 a month	Options: Tint	0
48 Months	$493 a month	$449 a month	$383 a month	Subtotal	$19,545
60 Months	$400 a month	$365 a month	$311 a month	License Fees	$336
				Doc Fee	$500
				Trade-in Allowance	$0
				Payoff	$0
				Subtotal	$20,381
				Sales Tax (10%)	$1,955
				Net Sale Price/Amount Financed	$22,336

Sales Consultant: "To get to your payment of $400, my manager decided to take a loss on this vehicle and give you a discount and he also took out the tint, pin striping and paint protection. Sign at the bottom and I'll get the vehicle ready for you."

X

Trade-in		Down Payment
$0		$0.00

Selling Price of New Vehicle		Monthly Payment
$19,545		$400

Your ultimate goal is to transfer the client from a looker to a buyer by getting a commitment.

You try to justify your price, down payment requirement, monthly payment, term and trade-in value all the while you're working to get that commitment. You can keep discounting the price, down payment requirement and payment or increase the trade-in value, but your ultimate goal will be to get that commitment.

Even if what the client wants is completely ridiculous, you write it down and get them to sign.

This scenario doesn't have anything to do with the scenario above:

Sales Advisor: "Okay, Mr. Buyer, we've been negotiating for 2 hours now. I don't want to keep you here all day so you tell me exactly what you want to do."

Trade-in	Down Payment
~~$6,000~~	~~$2,000~~
~~$6500~~	~~$1,500~~
~~$6750~~	~~$1,000~~
~~$6900~~	~~$500~~
~~$7000~~	

Selling Price of New Vehicle	Monthly Payment
~~$19,995~~	~~$400~~
~~$18,499~~	~~$375~~
$18,000	~~$350~~
~~$17,999~~	~~$300~~
	~~$250~~

Client: *"This is what I want: $8,000 for my trade, I want the vehicle discounted to $16,000, with payments of no more than $200 and I don't want to put any money down. I also want a 60 month loan or I'm walking out of here."*

Trade-in	Down Payment
~~$6,000~~	~~$2,000~~
$8,000	$0.00

Selling Price of New Vehicle	Monthly Payment
~~$19,995~~	~~$400~~
$16,000	$200

Sales Advisor: *"That doesn't make mathematical sense because we'll be taking such a big loss on this deal but okay, sign by the X and I'll present it to my manager."*

X: Client

Manager: *"You've been with this guy for 2 hours now negotiating. Is there a deal here or not?"*

Sales Advisor: *"You tell me. This is what I've got."*

Trade-in	Down Payment
$6,000	$2,000
$8,000	$0.00

Selling Price of New Vehicle	Monthly Payment
$19,995	$400
$16,000	$200

Manager: *"Is this guy serious? He actually wants us to give him $2,000 more for his trade than wholesale, and discount our vehicle by $4,000, and he wants to make $200 payments on $16,000?"*

Sales Advisor: *"Yeah...this guy is a piece of work. You're going to have to come out and talk some sense into him because I don't see a deal here."*

In this case, the client is being completely illogical thinking that any dealer would give them more for their trade and discount the price of their vehicle. Overall, the dealer would probably lose $2,000 to $3,000 on this deal. The sales advisor has done their job by selling the vehicle and getting a commitment from them. Now the manager would have to come out and talk some sense into them.

17d.   Scenario IV

This is the next step in the process where you would T.O. to a manager. Anytime you get stuck or there is a sense that the client is going to leave or he is slipping away from you, you're going have to turn it over to a manager.

A truck pulls up and a man and young girl get out. They stand by their vehicle for a second to get their bearings straight and start to walk over to the used car section. The man seems to be in his late 40's and the girl in her teens. A father and daughter perhaps.

The vehicle they drove up in is an older model truck. The body seems dinged up and there is a lot of rubbish in the back of the bed. Everything about the truck seems like it's a work truck.

As you approach the two, they seem hesitant or even bothered that they can't look without a sales advisor talking to them.

Sales Advisor: *"Hello my name is Max, I'm a sales advisor here at Big Deal Nissan. You guys just looking around?"*

Man: *"Yes, we're just looking."*

Sales Advisor: *"Okay, well, let me save you some time and energy and I'll help you look. What's your names by the way?"*

Man: *"I don't want to take up your time, we're just looking for an affordable car for my daughter here."*

Sales Advisor: *"Okay, not a problem. Look, I've been doing this for over 5 years. I'm not here to sell you anything. I'm here to help you find a vehicle that matches you needs. What are your names?"*

Man: *"Oh, sorry. My name is Matt and this is my daughter, Kelly."*

Sales Advisor: *"Nice to meet both of you. Have you guys been to our dealership before? Are you familiar with the way we do business?"*

Matt: *"No, I've driven by here many times but never came in to take a look."*

Sales Advisor: *"Okay, we'll we've been in business for over 30 years here in this community. We've sold multiple vehicles to almost everyone in this community. We've won tons of client service awards and the way we do business is that we try to build relationships for the long run because we don't do any advertising at all."*

Fact-Finding

Matt: *"Okay, good to know."*

Sales Advisor: *"This is the used car section. Is that what you're looking for? We'll the first question I should be asking is, what is affordable?"*

Matt: *"Somewhere in the area of $5,000."*

Sales Advisor: *"$5,000? Why $5,000? Is there a payment target you're trying to hit?"*

In my experience, a decent $5,000 vehicle doesn't exist. People have very big expectations about vehicles at dealerships and think they can find a low mileage, newer vehicle for around $5,000. Any vehicle that a respectable dealer has for $5,000 is usually a high mileage, older vehicle that has been kept up enough to look good, pass safety, and smog but doesn't have much life left in it. Basically it is presentable.

Matt: *"It's going to be her first car and I don't want to spend that much."*

If you do have a good $5,000 vehicle which you think these people will like, then more power to you, but first show them the inexpensive vehicles close to that price on the front lot first. If you know your inventory and know there is no vehicle close to that range, then the next best thing is for you to get their contact information just in case something does come up.

Sales Advisor: *"Matt, we sell more than three hundred vehicles a month so we get more than two hundred and fifty vehicles a month in trade-in, so I can find you guys whatever you're looking for. What kind of time frame are you looking at in purchasing a vehicle?"*

Matt: *"Maybe a month or so. Not really in a hurry. Looking for a good deal."*

Sales Advisor: *"Okay, Matt...let's look at some of the vehicles here and see if any catch your or Kelly's eyes. You guys from the area?"*

Kelly: *"Yeah, I go to Concord High but we live in Clayton. Pretty close to here."*

Sales Advisor: *"Nice. My sister lives in Clayton. So Kelly, what would this vehicle be used for?*

Kelly: *"Just to go to school and a job."*

Sales Advisor: *"Oh really, where do you work?"*

Kelly: *"In the mall."*

Sales Advisor: *"Nice. What do you do Matt?"*

Matt: *"I teach martial arts at the junior college."*

Sales Advisor: *"Really, I've been wanting to take a martial arts course. How much is that?"*

Matt: *"I think it'll be $34 a unit. It's a 3 unit class, so around $100."*

Sales Advisor: *"Give me your card. I might take you up on it."*

Kelly: *"I like this car. Looks nice."*

Matt: *"That's priced at 10,000. Way out of our price range, honey."*

Sales Advisor: *"A $10,000 vehicle will be a lot better in terms of reliability and value than a $5,000 vehicle. You guys should keep an open mind. You can even finance it for about $200 a month. You make more than $200 a month at your job Kelly, don't you?"*

Kelly: *"Yeah. I can probably afford it."*

Sales Advisor: *"Yeah, and your dad here can help you out too, maybe pay half or pay for your insurance while you pay for your car."*

Matt: *"No, It's her first car and I want her to practice on something cheap. I'll get her a nice car when she goes to college."*

Sales Advisor: *"That's too bad Kelly, anything else that catches your eye?"*

Kelly: *"Yes, but not in our price range."*

Sales Advisor: *"We have a lot of trade-ins in the back, let's go and check those out. Is that your work truck Matt?"*

Matt: *"Yeah...I also do some maintenance at our apartment building and for various other clients."*

Sales Advisor: *"How's business?"*

Matt: *"Good, been very good lately."*

Sales Advisor: *"So you can get Kelly a $10,000 vehicle?"*

Matt: *"No, it's a lot of seasonal as well as cyclical work."*

If you do find something in the back that the client likes, then all the more power to you. Follow the steps in the process and do a great presentation and demonstration. If you don't find something that the client likes then the next best thing to do other than selling them a vehicle is to get their contact information to keep an eye out in case you do get a trade-in that fits the criteria.

Sales Advisor: *"Just kidding...but really consider what I've told you. Financing a better vehicle is much better than buying something that'll leave you stranded. So Kelly, anything in the back here that catches your eye?"*

Kelly: *"No, these vehicles all have too many miles and are too old."*

Matt: *"Yeah...for $5,000 I was expecting something a little newer and less mileage."*

Sales Advisor: *"This is what we currently have but we get stuff in here all the time. We get more than two hundred and fifty trade-ins a month. So what is it exactly that you're looking for so I can keep an eye out?"*

This is where you would take out a sheet of paper and start taking notes in front of the client.

Kelly: *"I don't know something lower miles, newer, within $5,000."*

Sales Advisor: *"Okay, so a car? What range in miles? $5,000 max not including tax and license? Light or dark colors? How old can it be? Will a manual work? Any particular make or model? 2 or 4 door?"*

Matt: *"Yeah a car. It can't be more than 80,000 in miles. $5,000 max not including tax and license. No light colors. Not more than 5 years old. Has to be automatic. Preferable Japanese. Preferable 4 door."*

Kelly: *"A VW will also do."*

Sales Advisor: *"Okay, so your time range is about a month?"*

Matt: *"Yeah, but we're looking for a deal."*

Sales Advisor: *"Okay, not a problem. Like I said, we sell more than two hundred and fifty vehicles a month so we get lots of trade-ins. What's a good number to reach you when I do run across a car like this?"*

Matt: "You can reach me at 123-4567."

Sales Advisor: "You have a good email so I can send you photos? Also, can you receive texts on this number?"

Matt: "Yeah, you can send me texts on that number and my email is matt@carpenter123.com."

Sales Advisor: "Okay, hold on a second, let me ask my manager if he knows of any vehicles coming in that would fit your needs and I'll grab you guys a card too."

Manager: "What's going on?"

Sales Advisor: "Their looking for a $5,000 vehicle with less than 80,000 miles on it and less than 4 yrs old. Have any ideas?"

Manager: "You show them vehicles in the back?"

Sales Advisor: "Yeah, but nothing that they liked."

Manager: "Did you get their contact information?"

Sales Advisor: "Yeah."

Manager: "No, nothing coming in that fits that range. What's their name and number so I can log them in?"

Sales Advisor: "Matt and Kelly."

Back with the clients:

Sales Advisor: "Here's a card. Call me for any reason should you have any questions. My manager said there's nothing else coming in that meets those criteria, but like I said, we get a lot of vehicles going through here every month so I can keep an eye out. Thanks for stopping in and I'll be in touch. Matt, consider what we discussed about financing. You can get a much better vehicle for not much more money. I'd be more than happy to sit down with you to give you all your options."

Matt: "Okay, I appreciate it. I'll let you know."

During your career as a sales advisor, you're going to run into these types of clients from time to time. Even though we can't do anything for them at the moment, they're still considered an opportunity to do business (OTDB) because they are potential clients for the right vehicle. The least you can do is to talk them into giving you their contact information in case we find a vehicle for them in the future.

Also, any respectable or responsible manager will want to know what happened with the client you were talking to and whether or not you got their contact information. Remember, it's your opportunity to sell them a vehicle but it's the dealerships client.

17e. Scenario VI – Straight Dialogue

In this scenario, we'll take the deal straight through to the delivery without any explanation of why I'm doing what I'm doing. By now you should know the reasons for various actions and expected outcomes. Keep the big picture in mind and that is to sell them a vehicle. Keeping as much profit in the deal is icing on the cake.

Saturday is the busiest at a dealership and all the sales people are working. You think it is incredible that there are so many people here on a Saturday afternoon. The showroom looks pretty busy but most are from service that are killing time looking at the new models while their vehicles are getting worked on. This is the last Saturday of the month. There are 5 more days left until the end of the month and you need at least 3 more sales to hit your volume bonus. You've already had 3 ups that went nowhere. Many sales people are with clients and even more are outside waiting for clients to walk up. You know that if you go out on the lot, you're going to be 8th in line for the next client. You decide to start to talk to some service clients. You know that if someone is looking they can be buying. You know that your job is to turn these people from a looker to a buyer.

You notice an older couple looking at the new luxury sedan on the showroom. You know from this book that older people have better credit and money to spend. They just need to get excellent service. The man seems to be in his fifties and his wife seems to be around the same age. They are dressed fairly conservative with little skin showing and appear to be very clean cut.

> **Sales Advisor:** *"Hello, you guys finding everything okay? Have any questions?"*
> **Women:** *"Yes, thank you. No we don't have any questions. We're just killing some time."*
> **Sales Advisor:** *"Okay, great. That's the new sedan that just came out."*
> **Man:** *"It's nice."*
> **Sales Advisor:** *"Are you guys here from service?"*
> **Man:** *"Yeah, we have a minivan in getting an oil change."*
> **Sales Advisor:** *"Nice, how's that treating you?"*
> **Women:** *"Excellent. Can't complain."*
> **Sales Advisor:** *"My name is Marcus by the way, what are your names?"*
> **Man:** *"I'm Chuck and this is my wife Sheryl."*
> **Sales Advisor:** *"Nice to meet both of you. Where you guys from?"*
> **Chuck:** *"We're from San Jose. We're just up here visiting family and decided to stop in to get an oil change since we had a coupon."*

Sales Advisor: *"Nice. I used to live in San Jose. Right off of Santa Clara St. Did you know that San Jose is the safest largest city in the U.S.?"*

Sheryl: *"I've heard that somewhere."*

Sales Advisor: *"Yeah and it's pretty cheap in some areas too and it's got great weather. Anyway, I don't want to bore you with stuff you already know. So you guys like the new sedan?"*

Chuck: *"Yeah, it's nice isn't it?"*

Sales Advisor: *"Yeah, you think it looks nice? The ride's even more incredible. They've engineered special rubber sealers to keep the outside noise down to nothing and special mounts to keep the road vibrations completely silent. It's much more comfortable and quiet than your van because I test drive both all day. What year is your van?"*

Sheryl: *"It's a 2008 XLE."*

Sales Advisor: *"Oh an XLE? That's nice. Yeah, on those vans, it doesn't make sense to get anything less than an XLE. It's the perfect balance for a minivan. What do you like about it? What do you use it for?"*

Sheryl: *"It's nice and roomy and reliable. We hauled our kids around but they've all gone to college now.*

Sales Advisor: *"Congratulations. I guess you've done it then. Finished your parental duties?"*

Sheryl: *"No, we still worry about them all the time."*

Sales Advisor: *"Yeah, I have two small kids. I always think about them and they're safety. I guess you never lose that. Oh my, I guess my parents are thinking about me right now."*

Chuck: *"Probably."*

Sales Advisor: *"We'll that's life, change is always coming and you have to move on and adapt. So you won't need such a big vehicle anymore. Maybe it's time to pass it on to someone who can make better use of it. Have you thought about selling it? My used car manager is really looking for vans and he's willing to pay good money for it. How many miles you got on it? What condition is it in?"*

Chuck: *"It's got around 75,000 miles on it, excellent condition."*

Sales Advisor: *"Are you the first owners? Any accidents?"*

Sheryl: *"Yes, we're the first owners. No accidents."*

Sales Advisor: *"Excellent, my manager would be very excited to know that. We have several clients with large families looking for a good used van. We're even looking to buy used vans out of state and bring them here to certify because so many people are looking for certified vans from us."*

Sheryl: *"Really?"*

Sales Advisor: *"Yeah, certified vehicles go through a 200 point inspection and everything gets brought up to factory specification so whoever buys it is guaranteed a perfect vehicle. Certified vehicles also come at no charge with a huge warranty."*

Chuck: *"That's nice to know."*

Sales Advisor: *"If you're interested, I can price it out for you on what we would pay you if you want to sell it outright or trade it in. It'll just take a second and if you decide to trade it in, you don't have to pay for the service. You have to wait anyway, might as well get some info."*

Chuck: *"No, we're not in the market. We're just killing time right now. That van has been very good to us."*

Sales Advisor: *"Okay, just a suggestion since you have time to kill and you can go on a test drive in this new sedan."*

Chuck: *"Yeah...I would like to drive this. Go ahead and get me a price on the van. It's the silver 08 XLE in service."*

Sales Advisor: *"Okay. I need some information really quickly. What is your last name so I can look it up at service?"*

Chuck: *"Our last name is Stevens."*

Sales Advisor: *"Okay, do you owe any money on it or you own it outright?"*

Sheryl: *"We own it outright."*

Sales Advisor: *"Okay, great. Let me get some information from your vehicle and give it to my manager. I'll also get the keys to this vehicle so you can take a look at it."*

After a few minutes:

Sales Advisor: *"Here are the keys to the sedan you're looking at. Play with the options. I'm going to check out your van. I'll be right back."*

Manager: *"What have you got?"*

Sales Advisor: *"I have Chuck and Sheryl. They have a 2008 XLE minivan in service with around 75,000 miles on it and they own it outright. Here is the trade-in evaluation sheet. Can you price it out for me? The vehicle is in service if you want to look at it."*

Manager: *"Well, what are they interested in? I don't want to price it out if they aren't going to buy anything."*

Sales Advisor: *"They're looking at the sedan out there. They may be interested in that."*

Manager: *"Okay, I'll see what I can do but I'm not giving any numbers unless they're interested in buying something. Why go through all the hassles if they aren't going to buy anything?"*

Sales Advisor: *"Okay, I'll go and see if they like the sedan."*

Sales Advisor: *"Hey Chuck. My manager is looking for a price. How do you guys like the sedan?"*

Chuck: *"It's nice. It has a very nice interior."*

Sales Advisor: *"Yeah, this new sedan has won a lot of awards for style and comfort and innovation and safety. It has airbags everywhere as well as the latest navigation and Bluetooth. Look at the trunk. It's huge right? They've incorporated* several unique safety features in the back where the frame will actually crumple in on itself if hit from behind at speeds of over 25 mph, _so_ the occupants don't feel any of the energy. It's trunk space is 50 cubic inches bigger than the previous models, but you can't tell from the outside. The back seats fold down to give you even more carrying capacity."

"On the passenger side, you can see that it has huge windows, _so_ the driver doesn't have any blind spots. The rear seats recline, _so_ the rear passengers can recline and get really comfortable. The doors have special side energy absorbing beams as well as curtain airbags and side airbags, _so_ the passengers are fully protected in the event of a side impact. Also, look at the leg room. The passengers have a lot of space _so_ their nice and comfortable. The front passenger also have their own climate control as well as power seat controls with memory, _so_ the passenger can be very comfortable and pampered, especially on long drives.   Do you guys take any long trips?"

Sheryl: "Maybe, if we decide to go and see our kids in college."

Sales Advisor: "Great, this sedan will be perfect since it's so comfortable. This sedan is also very gas efficient yet has plenty of power. Look at the engine. That's the same engine design that they've been using for more than twenty years. Its gas efficient as well as powerful, but more importantly it's very durable. All you have to do basically is change the oil. It has more than two hundred horsepower yet it gets over 30 mpg, _so_ you'll be assured of having the power you need as well the savings in maintenance and fuel. You can't go wrong with that. Like the rear end, the frame is designed to crumple in on itself in case of a frontal collision to absorb all that energy. The hood also is designed to fold to protect the windshield from flying debris, _so_ the safety features are built into it to keep you guys and your occupants safe in case of an accident. The transmission is a very low maintenance, highly reliable system designed to monitor the wheels to keep them from slipping, _so_ the car is always gripping the road and going where it's being pointed to.

"Look at the brakes. Notice how big they are. They've designed the brakes to be large and to stop you faster, but more importantly with their patented brake system, they've designed them to give you as much control as possible without locking up the wheels. Also notice the large shocks. The suspension, along with specially designed motor mounts, are there to absorb as much road vibrations as possible, _so_ the occupants don't feel much of the road noise, engine noise or vibration, _so_ what you get is a much smoother and quieter vehicle that lets the occupants feel like they're floating. This vehicle will be much more comfortable than your van.

"Here Chuck, come and sit in the driver's seat. I know you already looked at the dash, but let me show you some things. The vehicle itself has specially designed rubber seals all the way around to eliminate 99% of the exterior noise, <u>so</u> once you close the door you don't hear anything but your own breath. Did you notice the backup camera? You can change the view so you can see more or less of the rear, <u>so</u> you don't back up over anything. This vehicle has special dash lighting to eliminate eye fatigue, <u>so</u> the driver is much more alert and awake driving at night. This vehicle comes with standard Bluetooth, <u>so</u> you can answer you calls without fumbling for your phone or driving with one hand. Also, do you notice the large windshield? That's designed to give you as much view as possible, <u>so</u> you have a better view of the outside world. The windshield also has a special patented film embedded inside it designed to reflect any harmful UV sunlight, <u>so</u> the occupants are not exposed to harmful sun rays. The dash has been designed to be intuitive, <u>so</u> the driver isn't fumbling for the controls and keeps their eyes on the road.

"The best part of this vehicle is the comfort. It's quiet and smooth. You really feel like your floating.

"Let's go for a test drive. I just need a license from one of you. You've got time right?"

Chuck: *"Nice sales pitch Marcus, but we're not interested in buying today. We're just killing time."*

Sales Advisor: *"That's funny. It's not a sales pitch. This is an awesome vehicle. I test drove it when I first started here and loved it. It's my favorite model of this dealership. Unfortunately, I currently don't have the money to buy one, but someday. That's fine. I have nothing else to do and you have to wait for your van. Take it for a test drive and think it over, no pressure. Don't worry, I'm not going to charge you."*

Sheryl: *"I'd like to drive it."*

Sales Advisor: *"Sure, I mean you're killing time aren't you? What better way than test driving a new vehicle?"*

Sheryl: *"Here's my license."*

Sales Advisor: *"Okay, I'll go and get a dealer plate and I'll be right back to take this vehicle out of the showroom."*

Manager: *"We'll what's going on?"*

Sales Advisor: *"They say they're not interested in trading in or purchasing but we're going on a test drive."*

Manager: *"What, why?"*

Sales Advisor: *"Because there's nothing else to do. Traffic has died down. There are fifteen guys outside and I've finished making my calls for the day, and the more* *people you test drive the higher your sales. Besides if they won't buy today, they'll buy eventually. Hopefully from me."*

Once the vehicle has been taken out of the showroom or a comparable one has been pulled from the lot:

Sales Advisor: *"You guys ready? Who's driving first?"*
Sheryl: *"I'll drive first."*
Sales Advisor: *"Okay, make sure your seats are adjusted, your seatbelt is on, you mirrors are adjusted and know where the turn signals are."*
Sheryl: *"Okay, I'm ready."*
Sales Advisor: *"You ready Chuck?"*
Chuck: *"Yup."*
Sales Advisor: *"Sheryl, go straight out of the drive way and take a left. When you come to the light, you can go left again to get on the freeway or go right to go on city streets."*
Sheryl: *"I want to go on the freeway."*
Sales Advisor: *"Go where you like. Really test drive it. I've got nothing better to do."*
Sheryl: *"This is nice. Much smoother and comfortable than the van."*

Stay quiet for a while and let the clients sell themselves on the vehicle.

Sales Advisor: *"So what do you guys do out there in San Jose?"*
Chuck: *"I work in San Francisco for the parks department and Sheryl is a financial planner for the city."*
Sales Advisor: *"Oh, okay...I love the city. Don't get out there much. How long have you guys lived out in San Jose?"*
Sheryl: *"About 2 years. Bought a house when they were very cheap."*
Sales Advisor: *"Yeah, my cousin just bought a house in the hills. I don't think it was that cheap though. I guess prices have gone up."*
Chuck: *"Yeah, they really have. Lucky for us."*
Sales Advisor: *"Chuck, would you like to drive?"*
Chuck: *"No, I'm good for now. I'll trust her."*
Sales Advisor: *"Are you guys going to take this vehicle for any long trips?"*
Chuck: *"We're not really into the market right now for a new vehicle."*
Sales Advisor: *"Oh, I see. See how quiet and smooth it is. It would be nice to go on a long trip in this vehicle."*
Sheryl: *"Yeah...it drives like a dream. It's quiet and smooth."*
Sales Advisor: *"Glad you like it. You can head back whenever you want Sheryl. Maybe we can get you a good deal on your van so you can take this car home."*
Sheryl: *"Sounds tempting."*

Sales Advisor: "Yeah, and you're at a point in the van's life when it's worth the most before a steep decline in price because once a vehicle is 5 years old or over 100,000 miles, then it isn't worth that much because most people perceive it to be too old or have too many miles. We also can't certify vehicles over 80,000 miles, so dealers won't pay that much for them because the warranty companies won't issue warranties."

Sheryl: "Really?"

Chuck: "It's a clean van. It's got a life left in it."

Sales Advisor: "Probably true as most of our vehicles are all very reliable but I'm talking about depreciation, price, trade-in and value."

Sheryl: "How much does a 2008 XLE van sell for?"

Sales Advisor: "I don't know, but we'll find out. What something sells for and what we buy it for are 2 different things. We buy wholesale at auctions."

Chuck: "You guys can pick that van up for cheap?"

Sales Advisor: "I don't know for exactly what but remember that when you buy a vehicle at a franchise dealer like ours, we have to spend a considerable amount to get the vehicles certified and brought up to specifications."

Sheryl: "Okay, where do I go from here?"

Sales Advisor: "So you like it Sheryl?"

Sheryl: "Yeah...It's very nice."

Sales Advisor: Turn left here and you can park it near service."

After getting out, look at the vehicle.

Sales Advisor: "Did you like it Sheryl?"

Sheryl: "Very nice. It was smooth and comfortable."

Sales Advisor: "Yeah, and it's an extremely safe vehicle. It has airbags all the way around and special crumple zones all the way around. It has the latest technology like Bluetooth, navigation and controls on the steering wheel. There are extra-large brakes and shocks for comfort and control and duel climate zones. There is an extremely reliable power train that'll save you tons of money on maintenance and upkeep that has tons of power and high MPG. It's also a beautiful vehicle, totally redesigned."

Sheryl: "Yeah. I like the design too."

Sales Advisor: "You like it enough to drive it home? I know Chuck said you guys aren't really in the market, but if the numbers are agreeable will you guys at least entertain the idea?"

Chuck: "No."

Sheryl: "At least let's look at the numbers. It doesn't hurt."

Chuck: "I like that van. It's treated us well. It's got a lot of life in it."

Sales Advisor: "Yeah, but the value of it is going down every day because of its mileage and year. Also there is currently a very high demand for those vans and *there probably won't be later, when we get all those out-of-state vans in. So they won't give you that much for your van later on, should you want to trade it in."*

Sheryl: *"Okay, let's look at the numbers."*

Sales Advisor: *"Okay, come on in and I can run some numbers by you. At least you have something solid to think over, besides you still have to wait for your van to get finished."*

Chuck: *"Okay but just to look at the numbers."*

Sales Advisor: *"There are some refreshments here and the bathrooms are over there. You've been here before, so I'm sure you're familiar with our dealership and our award winning service department. You know that we won the top client service award for the region, 5 years in a row?"*

Chuck: *"Yes we know."*

Sales Advisor: *"Okay, let's find a nice quiet spot so we can look at some numbers. I just need to enter some information to keep track of what we've talked about."*

Go to the manager to get the copy of the license you made earlier.

Manager: *"Any progress?"*

Sales Advisor: *"A little. The husband is dead against buying a new car but the wife wants to look at some numbers."*

Manager: *"So do you think you have a deal or not?"*

Sales Advisor: *"Not sure but I've got to work it all the way through. Maybe not today but soon. I don't know yet. I got to work over the husband. She's at least open minded."*

Manager: *"So what you're saying is that you wasted all this time and you have no deal?"*

Sales Advisor: *"I'm saying I don't know yet. I work everyone to their fullest potential. The more time I spend with them, the more loyalty they will have with me. The more rapport I will build with them."*

Manager: *"Okay, that's fine. Enter their information into the computer and I've already looked at their trade and got information on it."*

Sales Advisor: *"Okay, I'll be right back."*

Back at the desk with the client:

Sales Advisor: *"So this information on the license is your current address?"*

Chuck: *"Yes."*

Sales Advisor: *"What is your current phone number? We won't be calling you, but we sort our clients based on phone numbers because there might be over 5 Chuck Stevens in our system.*

Chuck: *"It's 123-4567."*

Sales Advisor: "Okay, let me put in some notes. You have a 2008 XLE minivan and you are interested in the sedan. Did you want to put any extra money down to help reduce you payments or would you like to pay cash?"

Chuck: "No more money down. We just want to look at numbers."

Sales Advisor: "Okay, I understand. It's just that I need to get all this information for my manager. So are you looking to finance? Can I run your credit?"

Sheryl: "No, we don't want our credit run. Just assume it's enough to qualify for the incentive rates. Our van is our down payment."

Sales Advisor: "Okay. What finance terms are you comfortable with?"

Chuck: "Ah, around 5 years or less."

Sales Advisor: "Okay. Let me tell my manager that all the information he requires is in the computers. Feel free to get some refreshments and I'll be right back."

Back at the desk manager:

Sales Advisor: "All their information is in the system. The van is their down payment. They want around 5 years of financing. They say they have very good credit and I believe them."

Manager: "What kind of payment are they looking for?"

Sales Advisor: "I never asked what payment they want. Whatever they want will be too low. Instead I asked about what kind of terms they're looking for."

Manager: "Okay, here is the offer. Get me a commitment."

Sales Advisor: "Hold on, I have to get pricing on their van. Wow, this type of van is selling on Craigslist for around $14,000. Cars.com has some around $17,000 but that's because they're dealers and Edmunds.com has this van's trade-in value at $12,000 and it retails for around $14,000."

Manager: "Remember that this model is an old model. They've redesigned them since 08 so it's almost 5 years old. It's gone through some changes already."

Sales Advisor: "How much profit do I have on this sedan?"

Manager: "Marcus, it's a new car and most likely you'll make more on the mini than on the commission. The selling price is $35,000 and we've discounted it $2,000 so I think there's $1,500 profit on it, so if you get all of it then at your commission rate you'll make $300, that is if they don't want the price of the van discounted or any increase in their trade-in value."

Sales Advisor: "That's what I'm shooting for. What room do I have for the trade?"

Manager: "I'm giving them all the money at $12,000. We can pick this van up at the auction for around $11,800 so I'm giving you $12,000 to make the deal."

Sales Advisor: "Okay, I'll see what I can do."

Sales Advisor: "Hey, Sheryl, Chuck. You guys comfortable?"

Chuck: "Let's have the bad news."

Sales Advisor: *"You mean good news. Your van is worth a lot more than I thought."*

Sheryl: *"Really?"*

Sales Advisor: *"Yes, here are the numbers. The price of the sedan is $35,000. Because of our sale we've given you a $2,000 discount to get to a price of $33,000. With the option of tint, pin striping and paint protection of $649, the price of the sedan is $33,649. With the license fee of $750, doc Fee of $500 and our used car manager's fair market value for your van of $12,000, it comes to $22,899. With sales tax on the new sedan less your trade-in, it comes to $3,364.90 for a total financed price of $26, 263.90. With a $5,000 down payment, your payments for 60 months is $381, $470 for 48 months, and $617 a month for 36 months with 2.9% financing. Please circle whichever payment fits your budget and sign at the bottom and I'll get the car ready for you."*

Terms	Down Payments			Retail Price of Vehicle	
Rate of 2.9%	$0	$2,000	$5,000	Retail Price	$35,000
36 Months	$763 a month	$705 a month	$617 a month	Discount	-$2,000
48 Months	$580 a month	$536 a month	$470 a month	Options: Tint, Pin Striping, Paint Protection	$649.00
60 Months	$471 a month	$435 a month	$381 a month	Subtotal	$33,649
				License Fees	$750
				Doc Fee	$500
				Trade in Allowance	- $12,0000
				Payoff	$0.00
				Subtotal	$22,899
				Sales Tax (10%) Cost of vehicle less trade.	$3,364.90
				Net Sale Price/Amount Financed	$26,263.90

Chuck: "Hold on, let me take a look at this."

Sales Advisor: "Take your time."

Sheryl: "The tint, pin striping and paint protection are options?"

Sales Advisor: "Yes, but the tint is done here, you choose how dark you want it and it has a lifetime warranty. The pin striping also has a lifetime warranty. The paint protection helps the paint from fading. These are add-ons that help maintain the value of your vehicle and keep it looking good. The tint and pin striping can be transferred to the new owner should you decide to sell it in a few years."

Chuck: "Hold on, $12,000 is way too cheap for the van. I've seen them selling for over $17,000 and ours is in excellent condition."

Sales Advisor: "I believe you're looking at retail prices at dealerships. My used car manager checked to see how much this van is going for at the auction and it's a little less than $12,000 but in the interest of client service he offered $12,000."

Sheryl: "Okay, I understand the whole business thing but it's selling on the street for around $15,500. Why would we sell it for $12,000?"

Sales Advisor: "This van is selling on Craigslist for around $14,000. Here take a look at this computer. On Edmunds.com when you enter all the details of your van, its trade-in value is exactly $12,000 and It retails for $14,000. This website is the most accurate on vehicle values as it also takes into effect the dealer auctions. It'll cost us another $1,400 to certify it not to mention all the other details and other costs like smog and safety involved in getting a vehicle ready for the front line."

Chuck: "No, $12,000 is too low. Like I said, I like that van. It's got a lot of life left in it. You have to do better than that."

Sales Advisor: "Okay, well what number are you thinking of and I can ask my manager?"

Chuck: "I was thinking of around $13,500."

Sales Advisor: "$13,500. Chuck, the van retails for $14,000. Remember that every vehicle we get, we have to spend at least $1,000 to $1,500 to refurbish it and certify it. Look, what if I can get you a better price for your trade, say $12,500? Can we do business then?"

Trade-in

~~$12,000~~

$12,500

Chuck: "No. Like I said, we don't want to put any more money down but we also can't have more than $400 a month in payments."

Sales Advisor: "Okay, well, let's work on one problem at a time. Your van is 5 years old and a model back since it's gone through a redesign. Now I don't think I can get the manager to get you $13,500 since he told me that he's all in at $12,000. Can you at least meet me half

297

way at $12,750? This will also save you in taxes because we deduct the price of the trade before we assess taxes. Can you guys at least get to $12,750?"

Chuck: "No way, I'll take $13,000 and no less."

Sheryl: "It's a steal for you guys at $13,000."

Sales Advisor: "It's not. Like the website showed you. The trade-in value is $12,000 so after $1,500 in reconditioning the cost of the van, it will be $13,500 and it retails for $14,000. Okay, I'm not promising but if I can get you $13,000 will you be happy with the whole deal?"

Trade-in

~~$12,000~~

~~$12,500~~

~~$12,750~~

$13,000

Sheryl: "Yes, except the monthly payment is undoable."

Sales Advisor: "Okay but that's mathematically unsound. Why must you be at $400?"

Chuck: "That's all we can afford at this time. Like I said, we don't need this vehicle. We're just looking at the numbers."

Sales Advisor: "One way to reduce your payment amount is to put some money down. Can you guys at least put down $3,000? Not only will this reduce your taxes but it will also reduce the amount of interest and fees you'll pay over time."

Trade-in	Down Payment
~~$12,000~~	$3,000
~~$12,500~~	
~~$12,750~~	
$13,000	
	Monthly Payment
	~~$471~~
	$400

"As you can see, this will reduce your payment to $400 easily with some change left over."

Chuck: "No, $13,000 is enough for a down payment."

Sales Advisor: "I'm not promising you $13,000. I just said I'll present it to management. The deal has to make sense for both of us. The computer won't accept one-way deals for the client and the finance companies won't accept one-way deals for the dealership. So it has to make sense for all involved. That's why I need your help here. Can you at least come up to $420 a month? That means you need to forgo a movie a month or lunch at a restaurant once a month. It means giving up your can of soda for ten days a month. That's why I'm asking you for at least $1,000 extra for a down payment. It's a win-win situation."

Sheryl: "Marcus, with college tuition and expenses, we can't do it. Sorry. We're not in a position to spend that much money."

Sales Advisor: "Okay, I understand. I'm not trying to push you. It's just that it has to make sense for all involved. Another way we can help reduce your monthly payments is to take the financing from 5 to 6 years. We can definitely get there if I can get your approval. We'll be way under $400 and this way, your commitment will be under $400, but you can pay more when you want to and less when you don't and there isn't an early payment penalty."

Chuck: "No way...we had a 6 year loan before. Never again."

Sales Advisor: "Okay, I understand. What's the best you can do in terms of payment above $400? I mean, you like the sedan, right? It's superior to all other vehicles out there in terms of safety, reliability and comfort."

Sheryl: "Marcus, look. We can't do anything above $400. We're just looking at numbers. We like the sedan but we don't have to buy."

Sales Advisor: "Sheryl, the van you have there is only going to depreciate. This is your chance to get as much money for it as possible. Like I said before, we have a high demand for those vans once they are certified and only a dealership can certify them. As dealers, we can get them at $12,000 at the auction so, on the street they're not worth as much. I don't know where I missed you guys. I came up $1,000 on your trade from $12,000 to $13,000 and now we're trying to get to $400 in payments."

Chuck: "We can reduce the price of the sedan."

Sales Advisor: "There isn't enough profit in the sedan for me to discount it to get to $400. I don't think the management will go for increasing the price on your trade by $1,000 and reducing the price on our vehicle too. That won't make sense. Besides, we already discounted $2,000 from the MSRP. Is there any way we can increase the term of the loan to 6 years? This will give you an enormous amount of space for your minimum of $400."

Chuck: "No way. Cant' do it."

Sales Advisor: "Okay, hold on. Let me ask my manager if he has any ideas. I'll be right back but please give the 6 year loan a chance or discuss if you can increase your monthly payment to $430 or $425. Okay, hold on. We'll figure this out."

Manager: "Do you want me to come out there and close them?"

Sales Advisor: "Probably, but here's where we are."

Trade-in	Down Payment
$12,000	$3,000
$12,500	$0.00
$12,750	
$13,000	

	Monthly Payment
	$471
	$400

Manager: "They want $13,000 for their trade and $400 payments with no additional down? Will they go to 6 years?"

Sales Advisor: "No. Absolutely not. I brought it up a couple of times."

Manager: "What about the sales price of the sedan."

Sales Advisor: "Yeah, well, they mentioned that but I didn't even want to go there. I thought I'd come in here first before we go there."

Manager: "Even if we give them $13,000 for their trade and take out the optional tint, pin striping and paint protection, we're at $441 a month. At $20 for every $1,000 reduction in price of the sedan, we would need to discount this sedan by $2,000. I just don't have that much in the vehicle to give it to them."

Sales Advisor: "I know, that's why I steered clear away from the price. I told them earlier, I came in here to really think about increasing their monthly payment requirement because we can't make this work. So can we make this work somehow?"

Manager: "No, this is a big loss for us to do it. I'm willing to take a loss sometimes to meet our numbers but we don't need to take this loss right now. We sold good today."

Sales Advisor: "Okay, come out and talk to them."

Manager: "Hello Folks, my name is Jerry and I'm the sales manager. How are you guys doing?"

Sheryl: "Fine and you?"

Manager: "Good, thanks. Is Marcus treating you alright?"

Sheryl: "He's been great but we can't seem to agree on the numbers."

Manager: "You're looking at the sedan there? You guys like it?"

Chuck: "Like we told Marcus. We like the sedan. We were in here in service killing time in the showroom. We're really not in the market to purchase a vehicle today. We still like our van. It's has a lot of life left in it. We'd take the sedan home if we can work a deal but if we can't, then we can't."

Manager: *"Okay, I understand. I've been looking at what you've been discussing with Marcus. Your van is selling at the wholesalers for around $12,000 and I called a number of them. Their consensus was around $12,000 and that's what I gave you. Now even if I can give you $13,000 for your trade which I would be willing to do in the spirit of doing business and we get rid of the tint option, we're still $40 away from your target of $400. Have you guys discussed increasing the term of your financing or increasing the monthly payments? The term would probably be the best for everyone."*

Chuck: *"We'll what about reducing the price of the sedan?"*

Manager: *"For me to get to $400, we would have to reduce the price by another $2,000. We already discounted it by $2,000 and I don't have another $2,000 in it to give to you."*

Sheryl: *"Well, we're willing to go to $420 a month if that would work."*

Manager: *"It won't, I'm sorry. The best I can do is $430 a month and that's because I'll discount the vehicle $500. This my maximum. If you increase your term to 6 years, we can get the loan down way lower than $400 and we can keep your tint and paint protection. I'd love to do business with you guys but ultimately the computer is in charge. I wouldn't even be able to get something like that passed it. Okay? Let me know, guys. Those are the best options we have. We'll give you $13,000 for your trade with no additional money down and $430 a month or you can increase your finance term to 6 years. We're not making any money on this deal. I don't know if you're familiar with new car pricing, but we usually have very slim margins on them. Okay, you guys think about it. Thanks for coming in."*

Chuck: *"Thanks, we'll think about it."*

Manager: *"The 6 year term is the best because you get everything you need on this deal."*

Sheryl: *"I don't know, I think we need to think about it."*

Sales Advisor: *"I understand. The new vehicle can help save you more than the $20 in gas and maintenance a month alone. It's also a lot more comfortable than your van, isn't it? Your van won't be worth that much to us in a month when we'll get the new inventory in. I'll give you guys a few minutes alone to think about it."*

After a few minutes:

Sales Advisor: *"Well, have you guys finished discussing it?"*

Chuck: *"Sheryl? What do you think?"*

Sheryl: *"I guess we can live with $430."*

Sales Advisor: *"Chuck, can you also live with it?"*

Chuck: *"I guess I can."*

Sales Advisor: *"Great, so this is what the deal looks like. Sign at the bottom and I'll send your new vehicle to get washed and get the paperwork started."*

Trade-in	Down Payment
~~$12,000~~	~~$3,000~~
~~$12,500~~	$0.00
~~$12,750~~	
$13,000	

Vehicle Price	Monthly Payment
$34,500	~~$471~~
	$430

x Chuck & Sheryl

Chuck: "We found the same sedan last night for $36,500 at another dealership and thought that was a steal."

Sales Advisor: "So, this whole time you really were in the market to purchase a new sedan and you were just acting so you could get a better deal."

Sheryl: "Yeah. We still did great. Got an extra $1,000 for the trade and an extra $500 reduction on the sedan."

Sales Advisor: "Wow, you guys fooled me. You guys were a grind. I was ready to let you go."

Chuck: "No, you did well. We went over our routine this morning. We practiced several times."

Sales Advisor: "Man, so we should add the tint, pin striping and the paint protection back in since you got such a good deal. I guess it worked out for everyone."

Chuck: "No, we don't want tint or pin striping or paint protection."

This scenario was meant to show you the games that some clients play. Most clients are operating out of fear but some clients, like the know it alls, know what they're doing. Present the numbers with confidence and project yourself with confidence. You're an advisor and not a sales man. Sometimes it is what it is. The deal has to make sense for everyone. Your job is to help the client see things your way, get them a good deal and make them a client for life.

17f.   Scenario VII – Straight Dialogue

A car pulls up in front of the dealership and the passenger, a woman, gets out and asks where the bathroom is. Another sales advisor directs her to the bathroom but then loses interest. After you ask the sales advisor what the client is looking for, he just says, "The bathroom."

Sales Advisor: *"Are they looking for a bathroom or a car?"*

Salesman: *"They're just looking for the bathroom."*

Sales Advisor: *"Aren't you going to follow up with them?"*

Salesman: *"No, you can pick them up of you want."*

After a few minutes, you approach the driver, which is a man in his late 20's. Their vehicle is an older sedan that seems to be in really good condition. It looks to have new tires and the definitely looks garage-kept. It's not a popular sedan but it seems to be well kept.

Sales Advisor: *"Hello, how are you doing today?"*

Driver: *"I'm just waiting for my wife. She went in to use the bathroom."*

Sales Advisor: *"No, worries. I like your car. I just sold one like it last week but it wasn't in this good condition."*

Driver: *"This was my dad's. He kept it up pretty well."*

Sales Advisor: *"Nice of him to give it to you. The one I sold was a 1995 I think."*

Driver: *"No, this is a 98 and has over 180,000 miles on it."*

Sales Advisor: *"Wow, that's a lot. My name is Peter by the way."*

Driver: *"Daniel. Nice to meet you Pete."*

Sales Advisor: *"Yeah, same here. Let me know if you need anything."*

Daniel: *"I have to wait for my wife but we'll come and get you should we need anything."*

Sales Advisor: *"No problem, I'll be happy to help you guys out if you're looking for another vehicle."*

Daniel: *"Good to know."*

After a few minutes:

Receptionist: *"Hey, Peter? That couple over there is looking for you."*

Sales Advisor: *"Okay, thanks."*

Daniel: *"Hey Peter, I'm glad we found you. This is my wife, Ginger."*

Sales Advisor: *"Nice to meet both of you. What can I do for you guys today?"*

Ginger: *"We'll Pete, the car we have outside used to be Daniels dad's vehicle but he passed away. It's kind of old and it seems to have some problems starting in the mornings so we'd like to find another vehicle."*

Sales Advisor: *"Okay, no problem. Follow me to one of the desks here and let me get some information from you."*

Ginger: *"Okay."*

Sales Advisor: *"Okay, let me ask you some questions so we can see what your options are. Is that okay?"*

Daniel: *"Sure."*

Sales Advisor: *"Don't worry, it won't take long. I've doing this for over 4 years and this dealership sells more than three hundred cars a month so I'm confident we can find something you both will like."*

303

Ginger: "Okay."

Sales Advisor: "Okay. Who is this vehicle for?"

Daniel: "Mainly for her."

Sales Advisor: "Ginger, what will you be using this vehicle for?"

Ginger: "Mainly for daily commute and running around town."

Sales Advisor: "In terms of **Safety, Performance, Appearance, Comfort, Efficiency and Reliability,** what are the most important attributes of your next vehicle?"

Daniel: "Affordability."

Sales Advisor: "Good one but we're just looking to find a vehicle that meets your needs at the moment."

Ginger: "I guess reliability would be first, and then safety, then efficiency as gas prices are becoming ridiculous, and then comfort. I'm not too much into performance but it should have a decent look to it. It doesn't have to look like a Bentley but it can't look like a dog either."

Sales Advisor: "Okay, so I guess a four cylinder sedan or small SUV would do? They're pretty safe as well as reliable and with a 4 cylinder, it is efficient."

Daniel: "Look, we don't want to waste your time. We're looking for something affordable and all we have for a down payment is my dad's old sedan."

Sales Advisor: "We'll what's affordable?"

Ginger: "Peter, we don't have much disposable income at the moment. We can't pay more than $250 a month in payments."

Sales Advisor: "Why $250?"

Daniel: "We don't make that much money at the moment. That's all we can do."

Sales Advisor: "Is there a way you can bump up those payments to $300 a month? I can find you much better cars at that payment level because in finance terms for every $5000 you finance, you pay around $100 a month, so at the $300 a month payment level, you'll be able to purchase a much better vehicle. It just leaves a lot of options open for you, a more reliable, less mileage, and comfortable vehicle."

Ginger: "I'm not sure. That's stretching it a bit."

Sales Advisor: "Think about it and keep your options open. It's easy to find an extra $50 a month. Just cut out your daily soda or eat out 2 times less a month. It's not that much to invest in your next vehicle. Also on your trade-in. Do you own it or are you making payments?"

Daniel: "No, we own it."

Sales Advisor: "Okay, not a problem. That'll definitely help with you payments. I'll get the manager to give you guys a good deal on it as well as keep your payments low. Don't worry. This dealership has won the top client service award 5 years in a row. They'll bend over backwards to make you a client for life. Also, a majority of my clients are repeat or referrals so I help a lot of people out whenever I can."

Ginger: "That would be great if you can get us a good vehicle close to our target."

Sales Advisor: "Well, that's what you're paying us for: our expertise in knowing and selling the good vehicles, knowing what to look for and what to avoid. Our used car *buyers have a combined experience of more than one hundred years. They know a good vehicle just by the look and drive of it. They know all the major problems with certain makes and models and they know which ones to stay away from. That's why we have a 1 month exchange program. We're so confident in our vehicles that we can afford to let the client exchange their vehicles if they're not happy with them."*

Daniel: *"Is that so?"*

Sales Advisor: *"Yeah, all you have to worry about is finding a vehicle that fits your needs, leave the rest to us. From what you told me, I think I have some really good vehicles for you to look at. One more thing. How's your credit, since you'll be financing?"*

Ginger: *"Mine is great but Pete's is pretty beat up."*

Sales Advisor: *"Do you know your score?"*

Ginger: *"Yeah, I checked it online last week. It's about 710."*

Sales Advisor: *"That's a good score. Under 680 will be tough to finance. What about job history?"*

Ginger: *"I have a gross income of about $3000 a month and I've been working there for about 2 years."*

Sales Advisor: *"Great, then you can afford more than $250 a month. You have paystubs that can back that up?"*

Ginger: *"No, we can't afford much more than that. Yes, I have paystubs that I can get online."*

Sales Advisor: *"Okay, great. I can show you some vehicles on the computer here that I think would be perfect for you or we can go walk the lot."*

Daniel: *"Let's walk the lot and see what catches our eye."*

Ginger: *"Wait, let's see on the computer first. This way we can grab the keys to something we like."*

Sales Advisor: *"Okay, let me log on and we can get started on finding you a vehicle that's reliable, safe, efficient and comfortable."*

17g.   Scenario VIII – Phone Pop "What's Your Best Price?"

The phone rings at your desk.

Caller: *"Hello."*

Sales Advisor: *"Thanks for calling ABC Motors, my name is Marcus. What can I help you with today?"*

Caller: *"Hello Marcus, my name is Bill Roland. I'm calling on the used 2008 White Camry that you have on your website. Is that still available?"*

Sales Advisor: *"Oh, that is a great vehicle. Very clean. We've had a lot of activity regarding that vehicle. Let me check to see if that vehicle is still here because we sell around 10 cars a day and I don't want you to drive over here if the vehicle's* *been sold. It should take me 5 minutes or less to get the status. What is the best number to reach you?"*

Bill: *"Okay. My number is 123-456-7890."*

Sales Advisor: *"Okay, Mr. Roland. Are you only looking for this specific Camry or a similar sedan? We have more than five hundred vehicles available."*

Bill: *"Marcus, I'm only looking for that white Camry."*

Sales Advisor: *"Okay, Mr. Roland, I'll call you right back to give you the status."*

After a few minutes:

Sales Advisor: *"Hello, I'm trying to reach Bill Roland."*

Bill: *"This is Bill."*

Sales Advisor: *"Mr. Roland, this is Marcus from ABC Motors calling you back on the 2008 Camry you called about. Is this a good time?"*

Bill: *"Yes."*

Sales Advisor: *"Mr. Roland, That Camry is still available. It was almost sold this morning but they couldn't get the financing done because the clients didn't get approved. I'm at the vehicle right now. The Camry is in pristine condition. It is fully loaded, with leather, Bluetooth, clean car fax and has about 55,000 miles. It is still under warranty and it's certified. When is a good time for you to come by and take a look at the Camry yourself?"*

Bill: *"Marcus, I don't need to look at it. I've driven them before."*

Sales Advisor: *"Mr. Roland, not all used vehicles are the same. You might not like the drive. You might not like the interior. This vehicle might be different than what you have in mind. It's always best to come and look and feel for yourself."*

Bill: *"It's okay Marcus. I know how they are. I see the pictures on the internet. True, I haven't driven that one, but I've driven enough of them. My question is: what is the best price you can give me on that vehicle?"*

Sales Advisor: *"Mr. Roland, I can't give you a price on a vehicle that you haven't even looked at or test driven or know for sure you like it. We're the number one dealership in the valley, and we didn't get that way by not being aggressive on our pricing. We don't do any advertising. Most of our clients are from repeat and referrals. I know for a fact that my manager always gives the best deals to people who are on the showroom floor. Don't worry Mr. Roland. We don't bite."*

Bill: *"Marcus, the listed price is $18,999. Now what is the best price you can quote me?"*

Sales Advisor: *"Mr. Roland, this Camry has low miles, has a 3 year bumper-to-bumper warranty and a clean car fax. You really need to see it to appreciate it. Like I said, the manager will give you the best deal he can, if you sit face-to-face with him. Also, even if you don't buy from us, you'll be more educated at the next dealership you go to. When's a good time to come in and personally look at it?"*

Bill: *"Marcus, I just need your best price."*

Sales Advisor: *"Mr. Roland. The best thing to do is come and take a look at it. If you like it, I won't let price get in the way of us to do business. My name is Marcus at ABC Motors by interstate 17 and the 101. When can you come by? I'll make sure the vehicle is ready for you to drive so you won't waste any time."*

Bill: *"I don't know yet, I guess I can come by in an hour."*

Sales Advisor: *"No problem, Mr. Roland. I'll make sure the vehicle is ready for you. Ask for Marcus. Call me if anything changes so I can make myself available to other clients and thanks for calling."*

In no way do these scenarios represent all the different interactions that you're going to have with clients. They are written to get you into the environment of making a sale and so you can get a feel for what is important in the interaction you will have with clients.

1. To build trust in yourself, dealership and your product
2. To find exactly what the client is searching for
3. To match your products to the clients' needs and wants
4. To sell the features of the product by showing how they benefit the client
5. To prepare yourself for any objections at any given step in the sales process and how to handle those objections
6. To build up your repeat and referral business

These are the basic elements or ingredients to being a successful and professional sales advisor, sales consultant or agent. The client must first trust you and your organization for them to open up to as to their wants and needs.

It will be your job to match those needs to what your product can offer to the client. You have to show and explain to the client that the product you're selling will make their life better. That is called building value.

As a professional, you must be conscious of the fear the client is operating out of that culminates in objections. Once you become versed and seasoned in your line of work, you will hear the same objections time and time again. If you're a professional, you'll address these objections early in the sales process and handle them so they don't come up again.

In order to be successful in any sales position, you need to base your whole career on repeat and referrals. Without those clients bringing you new business and buying from you again and again, you won't reach your maximum potential. Sales is sometimes a numbers game when it comes to the number of people you talk to, to the number of people you test drive, to the number of people you present numbers to.

The repeat and referrals clients do one thing that a new client can never do, and that is to sell themselves and be pre-sold. The client who does business with you again or was referred to you by someone, has already been sold by someone who they trust much more than you and that's their friend or themselves.

Treat every person you come across in life and career with respect, even if you don't know them. You don't know the road they've traveled or the journey they have taken to stand before you. Some say respect is earned. I say respect should be given, regardless of status. You'll see in time that even if they're not your clients, treating people with respect enables people to elevate you as a friend, instead of just an acquaintance or a business contact.

The big picture is that this is a business and nothing should be taken personally because you want make the sale and maximize your commission and the client is looking to retain as much of their money and to reduce as much future risk as possible.

The true test of a professional sales advisor is to keep up their motivation in the face adversity, naysayers and sometimes a hostile environment. As a professional, you need to learn that this is your career, and having a career means continuous learning, continuous advancement and being paid extremely well. Always keep yourself open to new ideas and techniques to increase the amount of tools in your toolbox. This alone will set you apart from the mediocre.

Check www.salesadvisor.com to help your career, help you make more than you ever thought possible and for tools you can add to your toolbox to set you apart from the mediocre.

18. Afterword

In this book, I've illustrated as best as I could what you can expect entering the field of automotive sales. Like any profession, a little bit of knowledge goes a long way. That has been my goal throughout this book. I've tried to incorporate as much information as possible written in a repetitive style so you can easily absorb the main concepts needed to succeed, but there's always more to learn. Most of it you can only get through experience, but with this book, you're at least three years ahead of any green pea, freshy or newbie.

The Profession

The profession of an Automotive Sales Advisor can be extremely lucrative and a rewarding career and at times extremely frustrating and stressful like any profession or career. A big hurdle that you, as a sales advisor, will need to overcome when dealing with clients is the fact that car salesmen have an extremely bad reputation.

At one point, people didn't have a choice, they had to deal with their local dealerships and the only way to find what they were looking for, was to go from one dealership to another or find ads in the paper, relying only on what the salesmen told them. Since sales people had no formal training, they would tell the client anything they wanted to hear as long as the sales transaction was consummated. People weren't savvy in terms of finance rates, terms or their options which resulted in some dealership taking advantage of these unsuspecting clients.

That's all changed with the advent of the internet. Prospective clients have access to not just their local dealerships inventory, but inventory nationwide and in some cases worldwide. They have access to all the costs, markups, add-ons, rates, terms, reports, reviews, other people's experience's with your product, dealership and options. In most cases, the client is even more versed in the options of the vehicle and your competition than you, the sales advisor.

This needs to be communicated to your clients at the initial meeting as well as throughout the sales process. The clients need to be aware that all the information you possess is on the internet and they can double check anything they want anytime they want. Prices, invoice, rebates, costs and profit are all on the internet if any one wishes to search for them.

It can be as simple as communicating to the client, "Look, I know what people think of car salesmen or of dealerships. We're not like that. We really mainly rely on repeat and referrals for our business. I'm not here to sell you anything. I'm here to find a vehicle that fits your needs and wants. So just let me know what you concerns are and I'll be better able to find something that can work for you." Or something similar. You'll be able to come up with your own disarming statement to overcome the negative reputation of the car salesman. Just the fact that you're addressing this issue speaks volumes.

Professional Reassurance

So if people do have access to so much information, why do they even need to speak to a sales advisor and why does a dealership need sales advisors? Why doesn't the client just walk up to the dealership and say I want model X with package Y in black? Why doesn't the client shop for a vehicle like they do with toilet paper, soda, peanut butter or potato chips? All the ingredients are on the website as well as other marketing material. They've seen what it looks like and whether it appeals to them or not. They know the reliability ratings. They don't need a sales advisor to test drive the vehicle.

So why does a client and a dealership need a sales advisor?

The simple answer is because the client needs to be reassured that they're doing the right thing and the dealership needs the sales advisor to assure the clients that they are making the right decision. Like I've stated earlier, most clients who walk onto a lot are operating out of fear and hope. If left to their own thinking, they'll talk themselves out of a decision as big as purchasing a vehicle that by its very nature, requires a lot of capital and even more commitment. Buying a car is a serious commitment that they will have to live with for at least 3 years or more.

In any purchase with a significant cost, the client needs to be reassured that the decision they're making is the right one. Even at big box retailers, people seek out sales associates when shopping for T.V.s, computers, furniture or tablets to assure themselves that what they're about to do is the right thing, even though they've done their research online. Even if the sales associate has no knowledge of the product, with just a little bit of reassurance the client will go from a looker to a buyer. With as little as saying, "We've never had any returns of that model." or "We've never had anyone complain about this brand." or "We've sold a lot of these computers." is enough reassurance for the client to purchase.

Could you imagine if there were not any sales associates or advisors to push the client over from a looker to a purchaser and to drive sales? You'd have a bunch of shoppers standing around poking, peeling and scratching their heads as what to do next. They'd be stuck in the looker mode for a long time.

In a nutshell, that's the name of the game in sales. You're assuring the clients that they're making the right decision. The only way you can do this is by being a professional which is made up of your attitude, product knowledge and enthusiasm.

So how does one go about being a professional in reassurance?

Like I wrote about earlier, you have to build trust with the client. To build trust in auto sales you need 3 key ingredients.

Professional Attitude – An attitude that you can get things done. You're working for the client. You're looking out for the client. Competence. Confidence.
Product Knowledge – Not just knowledge on the vehicles, but also knowledge in the sales process. Knowledge about the client and how to tie the vehicle's features to the benefits of the client.
Enthusiasm – This alone will get you to 8 cars a month. Enthusiasm for yourself, dealership and your product. This is the amount of energy you exude when your interacting with the client in regard to them, yourself, your product, your dealership and the benefits they will derive by buying from you.

In reality, people don't trust themselves. Whenever you think back, the bad decisions stick out a lot higher than the good decisions. This is the same with all people, including yourself. This gives people the most angst when making a decision that will have such a huge impact on their life for years to come.

A sales advisor with a professional attitude, product knowledge and enthusiasm gives off trust to everyone they come in contact with. These 3 attributes are the foundation for any successful career or life.

Sales is for Friendship Building

Sales in general has a bad reputation, yet it covers every aspect of our daily social interactions with other people. Anytime you're dealing with another person, you're selling something: either an idea, yourself or a product. Sometimes all three, but you are always selling yourself.

You sell yourself by becoming someone's friend and by not trying to sell them something. You build trust by holding the other person's interest above yours. People always build long time relationships with trustful people. In the end when all is said and done, life, success, prosperity or ambition has a foundation of people and the strength of those relationships.

Sales is one of the last lucrative occupations left that doesn't require an advanced degree. Some are born with this gift of gab where they're personality is attuned to the needs, wants and fears of others, thereby allowing themselves to be more endearing and influential to others. This craft or gift used to be called speech craft. We know it today as charisma defined as, "compelling attractiveness or charm that can inspire devotion in others".

This character or trait is extremely important in being successful in sales and can be mastered over time using specific sales techniques, like asking the right questions, finding common ground and addressing fears and building on hope. Key elements to do this successfully are the right attitude, product knowledge and enthusiasm.

Even if you're not in sales, you still subconsciously use sales techniques. A dentist sells their experience and qualifications to make recommendations on procedures that not only benefit the patient but also the dentist. They build a sense of urgency by using fear and a sense of wellbeing by utilizing the hope for gain.

Men and women interact in a bar setting by selling themselves to each other. They first make themselves presentable. Then comes the meet and greet followed by qualifying by asking questions of one another to find out about their wants and needs. They then tailor their presentation to match what they can offer to the wants, needs and benefits of the other. They then go on a few dates continuing the fact-finding which may result in negotiations to close the deal. The prospects talk all this over with their friends and get their advice which is the same as turning it over to a manager. Definitely some follow up is required to close. You might be so good at the fact-finding and negotiation that they might be a flop and get closed the first night.

Although the profession of an Automotive Sales Professional will not be for everyone, at its core the steps learned in this book can be applied to everyday life situations. Learn and make the steps your own and assess where you are in the process with relation to someone you know, decisions you have to make or the outcome you wish to see. Have you done your proper fact-finding? Have you done a proper presentation and demonstration based on your findings? What is the ultimate goal of your negotiation?

After all, that is what sales is all about regardless of the product you're selling.

- Find the proper decision maker or makers
- Build trust with them with proper attitude, product knowledge and enthusiasm
- Get them to open up about their pain points. What are their needs and wants?
- Present yourself and your product that meets or exceeds the clients wants and needs. Show how the feature of your product benefits the client
- Recognize what objections may come up and isolate and address them based on what you found out in the fact-finding

It's important to keep in mind the big picture in sales and that is to build relationships. It's very shortsighted to think that a sale is a onetime event. The sale is just the beginning of your relationship. Your reputation or relationships will help propel your wallet, career and especially your quality of life.

The Future

The future of the business is moving online. More and more people are using the internet to search for their next vehicle as the internet has made car shopping a lot more transparent. The available information and your skill on using that information to your advantage can only help your career. Already people can get any piece of information they want with just a click of the mouse so it's to your advantage to figure out the behavior of your potential clients. The only thing that this does is to increase the sales process with a few more objections.

I believe that the future of car sales will go to a one-price policy, where negotiating is going to go away. Negotiations are the main pain point to many car buyers. I've worked for dealerships where they followed a one-price policy. The clients were extremely happy with their decision and came back time and time again because they had such a good experience purchasing. A sale lasted an hour after they picked out their vehicle as opposed to 4 or more hours in a negotiation-style dealership.

The dealership also made a good profit because they did not negotiate on the prices. Already some manufacturers are testing the waters for going to a one-price policy. All it will take is one of the big 4 makers to change policy and the rest will follow suit. Sales advisors in the future will be more of a vehicle presenter and a true advisor than a sales negotiator. Sales advisors in the future will not need to spend much time showing the numbers or negotiating but instead concentrate on fact-finding, making a friend and matching the client's needs to the their vehicles.

One might incorrectly think that price is the driving factor in increasing sales, but studies have shown that the people who paid the least were the least happy with their purchase. People who paid an average amount were the happiest because they thought they were treated fairly and with professionalism. Negotiation really takes a lot out of the sales advisor and the client, leaving both with feelings of resentment, rivalry and dissatisfaction. Buyers aren't necessarily looking for the best price, but the best service.

Just imagine being a client at a dealership where a $20,000 vehicle is slowly negotiated down to $19,000. Most likely, when the clients leave that dealership, they will have feelings of regret of not negotiating the price down further, leaving money on the table and a feeling of being taken advantage of thereby completely poisoning their enjoyment of their new vehicle. Paying more than one should purchasing anything always leaves clients bitter and resentful.

Give Yourself Commitment

In your career and your life, you need to commit yourself to becoming the best at whatever you do. It doesn't matter the job, task or role you play. You need to shoot for stellar instead of "good enough". Success demands your best because the world is filled with mediocrity. There are only a handful of stars and out of those, there are only a handful of superstars. The difference between them is the hard work, preparation and most importantly, the commitment to becoming the best that they can be. Just think about movie stars in Hollywood. Each year millions of people attempt to become stars but only a handful succeed and most of those fizzle out a year or 2 after reaching the top. Only the ones who continue their commitment to becoming the best stay at the top.

I ask you to do the same. Give yourself the commitment to succeed. It won't be an easy road to follow but a worthwhile journey that will reward you, far more than you've ever imagined. The world is full of average to below-average people. Separate yourself from them by shooting for being the best you can be at whatever you do. You'll see in time that opportunities will seek you out instead of you seeking out opportunities.

By following what I've outlined in this book and studying it over and over again until the information becomes yours, you're guaranteeing yourself distance from mediocrity or from the average in the field of automotive sales.

Nothing worthwhile in life, is easy.

For you to get to the six-figure mark, you're going to first learn the basics and then master the advanced techniques. The rest will be easy.

Treat everyone with respect, know your product, and make it a joy to know you, to do business with you and you'll have a career and life with no regrets. I thank you for purchasing this book and allowing me to impart some of the wisdom I've attained over my career and life.

I too am working to set myself apart from the crowd and will continue to write on the subject of business, sales and life. Please look for my upcoming books and help me build my book of friends.

I wish you all great rewards in your career, your life and the decisions you make.

To learn more, visit **www.autosalesadvisor.com** and sign up. I'll have information for you that will be relevant to business, your career and your path in life. Professionals need the right tools for the job and being a member will help you get those tools to succeed and stay ahead of the curve.

M.I. Seka

28214290R00191

Made in the USA
Lexington, KY
10 December 2013